ARABIC VERBS

JOHN MACE

الأفعال العربية

فَعَلَ
فَعَّلَ
فَاعَلَ
أَفْعَلَ
تَفَعَّلَ
تَفَاعَلَ
اِنْفَعَلَ
اِفْتَعَلَ
اِفْعَلَّ
اِسْتَفْعَلَ

HIPPOCRENE BOOKS, INC.
NEW YORK

Other titles by John Mace:
Basic Arabic Workbook
Intermediate Arabic Workbook
Arabic For Today: A Student, Business and Professional Course in Spoken and Written Arabic
Arabic Grammar: A Revision and Reference Guide (3rd edition)
Teach Yourself Arabic Script (2nd edition)
Persian Grammar: For Revision and Reference

Typeset by John Mace

ISBN-13: 978-0-7818-1229-0
ISBN-10: 0-7818-1229-1

For information, address:
HIPPOCRENE BOOKS, INC.
171 Madison Avenue
New York, NY 10016
www.hippocrenebooks.com

Printed in the United States of America

Contents

Introduction

This book aims to help you to form and use the Arabic verb correctly.

Part I explains the verb's structure and working.

Part II is a set of 155 numbered tables showing all common verb patterns, arranged first by class or sub-class and then by Form, I to X.

Part III is a list of common verbs, entered alphabetically by the 3rd person masculine singular (هو) active form of the past tense. It shows:

- the 155 verbs appearing in full in Part II,
- 1094 further verbs, with a table number showing where to find the identical pattern in Part II.

The Roman transcription reflects pronunciation rather than spelling.

The **Index to Part I** lists alphabetically the themes studied in Part I.

The **Index to Part II** lists numerically the verb tables of Part II.

Page 6 shows the layout of the information given in each table; the explanations are superimposed in frames on a typical table (no. **23**).

The abbreviations and symbols used in this book are:

acc.	accusative	m.	masculine	I-X	Form (I to X)
adj.	adjective	neg.	negative	اُ	predicated verb
an.	animate	nom.	nominative	أنْ	أنْ + subjunctive verb
conj.	conjunction	o.s.	oneself, itself	ج	plural
def.	definite	pers.	person(al)	ه	direct person-object
e.o.	each other	pl.	plural	هـ	direct thing-object
f.	feminine	prep.	preposition(al)	π	with present tense
gen.	genitive	Q	quadriliteral	°	impersonal
impv.	imperative	s.	singular	§	paragraph in Part I
inan.	inanimate	s.o	someone	†	rare word or form
indef.	indefinite	subjunc.	subjunctive	+	and
fig.	figurative(ly)	vb.	verb(al)	/, \	or

The specialised terms in this list are explained in Part I.

Layout of typical table in Part II

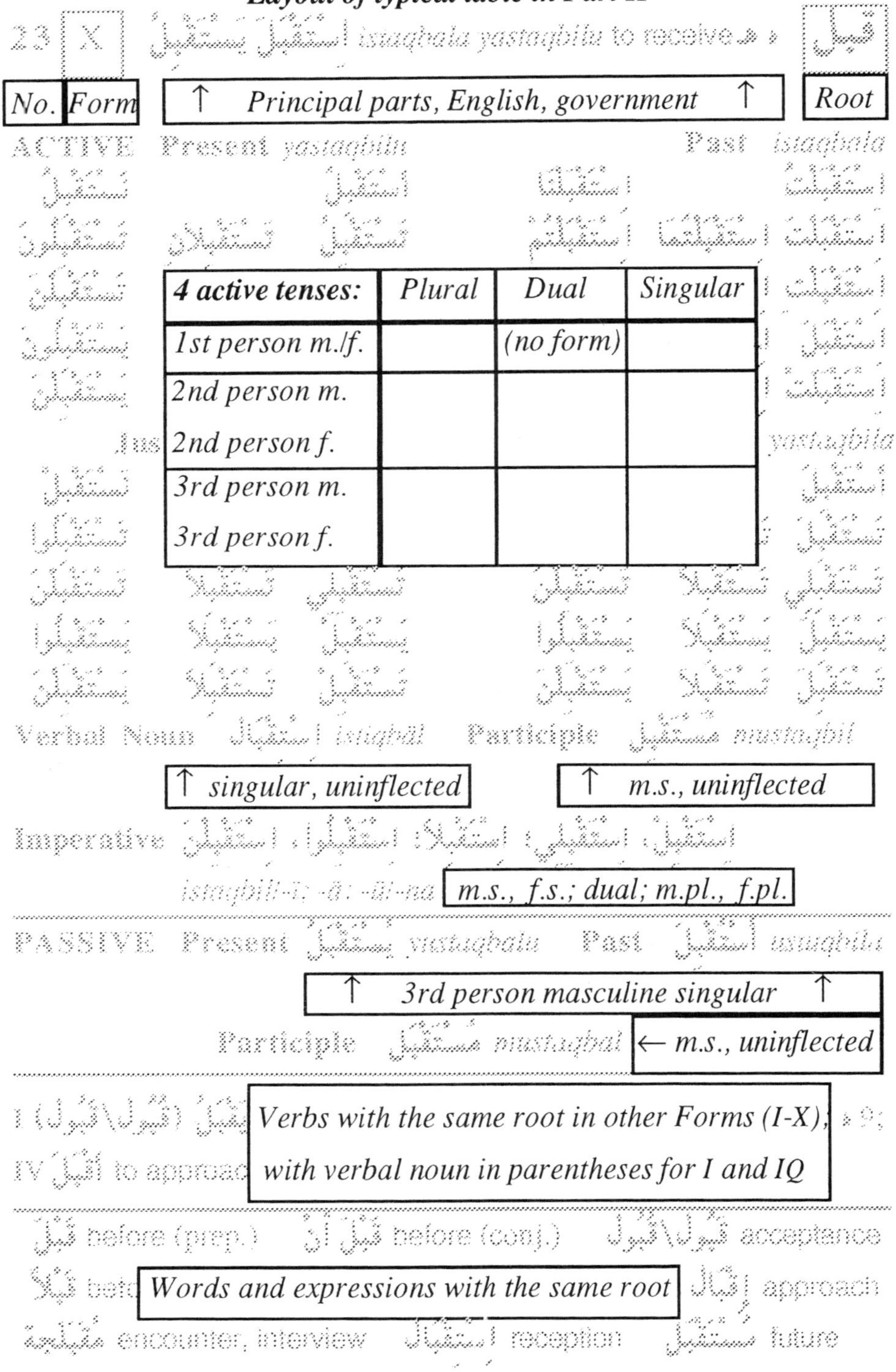

Part I – Form and use of the verb

1 . General

In Arabic as in other languages, the verb is that word or expression in a sentence which indicates the action or the situation:

كتبت الرسالة. *katabat ar-risāla*. She wrote the letter.

ماذا حدث؟ *mādha ḥadath?* What happened?

اذكر اسمك. *udhkur ismaka*. Mention your name.

ليس صعبًا. *laysa sa'ban*. It is not difficult.

In this book we study only those parts of Arabic grammar relating to the form and use of the verb.

2 . Equations

The simplest Arabic sentences have no verb at all:

أنا مريض\مريضة. *'ana marīḍ(a)*. I am ill.

أنت مهندس طيّب. *'anta muhandis ṭayyib*. You are a good engineer.

هل مكتبك في البلد؟ *hal maktabuka fi l-balad?* Is your office in town?

مكتبي هنا\هناك. *maktabī huna/hunāka*. My office is here/there.

We can call such a sentence an *equation*, since it consists of two equivalent parts, like an algebraic equation such as x = 2.

Note:

- The sentence starts with a *subject* (I, you, your office, my office) which is then described (ill), or identified (a good engineer) or located (in town, here, there) by a *predicate*.
- There is no verb; juxtaposing subject + predicate gives a meaning equivalent to the English present tense of 'to be' (am, is, are).
- All equations must be present in time. If we change the time to

past or future, we need a verb. We explore such verbs in § 13. In the sentences given above, the subject is *definite* and the predicate is *indefinite* in form and/or meaning. Equations with a definite predicate also exist. They are rarer. Most of them have a *pronoun* subject:

أنا المندوب المصري. *'ana l-mandūb al-miṣrī.*

I am the Egyptian delegate.

When such an equation starts with a noun subject, we reiterate the subject with a pronoun:

المندوب المصري هو الرئيس. *al-mandūb al-miṣrī huwa r-ra'īs.*

The Eqyptian delegate ('he') is the chairman.

Equations of the two types shown above must also be *affirmative.* For the corresponding negative a verb (see § 13) is used.

If the equation has a meaning equivalent to English 'There is/are ...', the equation is reversed and begins with its predicate. The other rules still apply:

في المدينة جامعة. *fī l-madīna jāmi'a.*

('In the city a university') There is a university in the city.

في التقرير أغلاط كثيرة. *fī t-taqrīr 'aghlāṭ kathīra.*

There are many errors in the report.

This is the traditional formula. We also find the predicates هناك *hunāka* ('there') used for 'There is/are ...' and هنا *huna* ('here') used for 'Here is/are ...' :

هناك جامعة في المدينة. *hunāka jāmi'a fī l-madīna.*

There is a university in the city.

هنا المتحف. *huna l-matḥaf.* Here is the museum.

In questions, أين *'ayna* 'where' is also put first:

أين مكتبه؟ *'ayna maktabuhu?* Where is his office?

'There is no/not ...' can also be expressed with an equation. This is the only type of negative equation possible. The device used is called *categorical negation*, and it consists of the particle لا *lā* followed by the *accusative* of the subject, without the indefinite *tanwīn*:

لا أمرَ أهمّ من هذا. *lā 'amr**a** 'ahamm min hādha,*

There is no matter more important than this.

لا بدّ من هذا الشرح. *lā budd**a** min hādha sh-sharḥ.*

There is no escaping/avoiding this explanation.

Note that the accusative ending *-a* is always pronounced in this construction.

See also the end of § 26 for an alternative expression for 'there is/are'.

3 . Triliteral root; principal parts

All Arabic verbs have a *root*, from which all the verb parts are derived. The root consists of letters which in principle remain, in the same order, throughout the verb. Most verbs have a *triliteral* root, i.e. one with three root letters. An example is the root كتب ***k t b*** conveying the basic idea 'write'. This root gives us derivatives such as:

كتبنا ***k**a**t**a**b**na* we wrote   كاتب ***k**ā**t**i**b*** clerk, writer

كتابة ***k**i**t**ā**b**a* writing   مكتوب *ma**kt**ū**b*** written, letter

مكتب *ma**kt**a**b*** office   مكتبة *ma**kt**a**b**a* library, bookshop

يكاتب *yu**k**ā**t**i**b**u* he corresponds with (etc.)

The root letters are usually identified as first, second and third; or initial, middle/medial and final.

In European languages it is common to designate a verb by its *infinitive*: '(to) write, escribir, écrire, schreiben, писать'. This is the form listed in a dictionary. Arabic has no infinitive; instead the verb is identified by one or both of its *principal parts*:

- The *first principal part* is the 3rd person masculine singular (هو) form of the past tense, e.g. كتب *kataba*.
- The *second principal part* is the same person of the present tense, e.g. يكتب *yaktubu*.

This verb is therefore referred to as *kataba* or (more fully) *kataba yaktubu.* In a sentence, these words mean respectively 'he wrote' and 'he writes'; but as a reference form they are translated into English with our infinitive: '*kataba yaktubu* to write'. This is the identification used throughout this book. (NB the particle 'to' is omitted from the English in Part III, for brevity).

A few verbs, some of them important, have a *quadriliteral* root, i.e. one with four root letters. An example of a quadriliteral verb is ترجم يترجم *tarjama yutarjimu* 'to translate'. All reference to roots, verbs etc. throughout this book is to triliteral roots, verbs etc., unless quadriliteral roots or verbs are specified.

4. Class of verb

Arabic verbs fall into four main classes, the last of which has four sub-classes, giving us in total seven types varying in the composition of their roots:

- *Sound.* Sound verbs have roots of three consonants, i.e. letters other than ا *'alif,* و *wāw* or ي *yā'*. ء *hamza* is also excluded. In the sound class the root letters are in principle always all present, and do not change. Example of a sound verb:

  كتب يكتب *kataba yaktubu* to write
- *Hamzated.* Hamzated roots have a root letter *hamza* and two sound root letters, the *hamza* root letter occuring in any of the three positions depending on the root. In Part II the tables for initial-, middle- and final-root letter *hamza* are given separately. Examples of hamzated verbs:
  - Initial *hamza:* أكل يأكل *'akala ya'kulu* to eat
  - Middle *hamza:* سأل يسأل *sa'ala yas'alu* to ask, enquire
  - Final *hamza:* قرأ يقرأ *qara'a yaqra'u* to read

  In practice the hamzated verbs follow the sound pattern; but they are usually studied separately because of the occasional difficulty in writing *hamza*.

- *Doubled.* Doubled roots have identical sound (i.e. consonantal) middle and final root letters. The initial root letter is also mostly sound. In some forms of the doubled verb, the identical root letters come together, pronounced as a doubled consonant (i.e. held for longer) and written as a single consonant (to which the sign ـّ shadda may be added); in other forms the identical root letters are separated by a vowel. A typical doubled verb:

  ظلّ يظلّ *ẓalla yaẓallu* to remain

- *Weak.* The weak class falls into four sub-classes:
  - *Assimilated*, with (mostly) initial-root letter و and two sound root letters. Some assimilated verbs, less numerous and less common, have initial-root letter ي . Examples:

    initial و : وجد يجد *wajada yajidu* to find

    initial ي : يقن ييقن *yaqina yayqanu* to be sure

  - *Hollow*, with a weak letter و or ي as middle root letter, and sound initial and final root letters. The weak middle root letter can become another letter, or even disappear, in different forms. Examples:

    middle و : قال يقول *qāla yaqūlu* to say

    middle ي : زاد يزيد *zāda yazīdu* to increase

  - *Final-weak* (also called *Defective*), with sound initial and middle root letters, and a weak letter و or ي as final root letter. Examples:

    final و : عفا يعفو *'afa ya'fū* to forgive

    final ي : رمى يرمي *rama yarmī* to throw

  - *Doubly weak*, with one sound root letter and two weak root letters, و , ي or (NB) *hamza*, which for this sub-class also counts as weak. Examples of doubly weak verbs:

    نوى ينوي *nawa yanwī* to intend

حيّ يحيا *ḥayya yaḥya* to live

جاء يجيء *jā'a yajī'u* to come

Some roots with root letters of different types can be deemed to belong to more than one class or sub-class. The preamble to each set of tables in Part II explores each class or sub-class more fully.

5 . Subject; person, gender, number, agreement

Subject. The *subject* of a verb is that person, creature, thing, place or idea which performs the action or undergoes the situation of the verb. The subject is expressed by a noun or pronoun. In the examples given below, the subject is underlined. The first three have a noun subject:

كتب الكاتب الرسالة. *katab al-kātib ar-risāla.*
The clerk wrote the letter.

يتغيّر الوضع تمامًا. *yataghayyar al-waḍ' tamāman.*
The situation is changing completely.

ترفض القاهرة الاقتراح. *tarfiḍ al-qāhira al-iqtirāḥ.*
Cairo rejects the proposal.

In most sentences with a verb having a pronoun subject, the subject is shown by the personal ending and/or personal prefix of the verb itself:

يتعلّمون الأفعال العربية. *yata'allamūna l-'af'āl al-'arabīya.*
They are learning ('the') Arabic verbs.

The pronoun subject in such a sentence may additionally be explicitly stated, e.g. for emphasis:

من يكذب؟ هو يكذب. *man yakdhib? huwa yakdhib.*
Who is lying? He is lying.

For an equation, the subject is that person, creature, thing, place or idea about whom or which the equation is written.

البرنامج مفيد. *al-barnāmaj mufīd.*
The programme is useful.

في التقرير جداول كثيرة. *fī t-taqrīr jadāwil kathīra.*
There are many tables in the report.

In an equation, any pronoun subject must be explicit, since there is no verb to show it otherwise. Here it is not necessarily emphatic in tone:

أين المكتبة؟ هي بعيدة. *'ayna l-maktaba? hiya ba'īda.*
Where is the library? It is far.

Person, gender, number. Pronoun subjects exist in three *persons* (1st, 2nd, 3rd); two *genders* (masculine, feminine) and three *numbers* (singular, dual, plural). Note that in this chapter the singular, dual and animate-plural columns run from right to left, as in the tables in Part II:

pers., m./f.	animate plural	dual	singular
1st m./f.	نحن *naḥnu* we	–	أنا *'ana* I
2nd m.	أنتم *'antum* you	أنتما *'antuma* you both	أنت *'anta* you
" f.	أنتن *'antunna* you		أنت *'anti* you
3rd m.	هم *hum* they	هما *huma* they both	هو *huwa* he/it
" f.	هن *hunna* they		هي *hiya* she/it/ they

Note:

- The *1st person* is the person(s) speaking, the *2nd* the person(s) or creature(s) spoken to, the *3rd* the person(s), thing(s), creature(s), place(s) or idea(s) spoken about.
- In the 3rd person, *masculine* and *feminine* singular forms are used respectively to refer to or to replace masculine and feminine singular nouns. But see below for the *plural.*
- The *dual* is used for a subject of two persons, creatures etc.
- The *animate plural* is used only for a group of more than two people. The masculine plural forms are used for a group of male persons and for a group of mixed company; the feminine plurals are used only for an exclusively female group. For plurals of subjects other than people, the *inanimate* plural is used; this is identical to the *feminine singular* form. This distinction runs right through the language, affecting not only plural pronouns and

verbs but plural nouns and adjectives also. Thus English 'they' is expressed with هم or هنّ only for people; 'they' for animals, things etc. is هي . The animate/inanimate distinction applies only to the 3rd persons plural, not to the 1st or 2nd persons and not to the singular or dual.

- The 1st person has one form for both genders, and its plural is used for the missing dual form. In the 2nd and 3rd persons the dual has one form for both genders.

Agreement. The person, gender and number of each verb form correspond exactly to the distribution of the subject pronouns as shown in the table and notes given above. Noun subjects take the verb in the 3rd person. (Minor exception: a few noun expressions used as deferential titles, e.g. سيادة *siyādat* 'excellency', may be treated as 2nd or 3rd person according to context.)

6 . Pronunciation

In reading aloud or otherwise enunciating a formal text there are today three forms of pronunciation, *full, pause* and *short*:

- *Full pronunciation.* In full pronunciation, every word is fully pronounced with all its grammatical endings:

  دخل وجلس. *dakhala wa-jalasa.*

  He entered and sat down.

  Principal parts of verbs (§ 3) are usually quoted in full pronunciation, e.g. كتب يكتب *kataba yaktubu.* A few set expressions (e.g. لا بدّ *lā budda*, see § 2) are also usually pronounced full. But otherwise full pronunciation is heard only in the most formal reading, e.g. religious or ceremonial.

- *Pause pronunciation.* Pause pronunciation is like full pronunciation except that the last word before a logical pause is (with few exceptions) pronounced only so far as its last alphabetical letter:

دخل وجلس. *dakhala wa-jalas.*

Final ة... before a pause is pronounced *-a*:

هي معلّمة. *hiya mu'allima.* She is a teacher.

Pause pronunciation is still very common in e.g news broadcasts.

- *Short pronunciation.* In short pronunciation we pronounce (with a few important exceptions) only as far as the last alphabetical letter (or ة *tā' marbūṭa* or ء *hamza*) of each word:

  دخل وجلس. *dakhal wa-jalas.*

  ملاقاة الأصدقاء السنوية *mulāqāt al-'aṣdiqā' as-sanawīya*
  the friends' annual reunion

  Short pronunciation is becoming more common in all but very formal situations. Of the three forms of pronunciation shown, it is the nearest to unscripted educated spoken Arabic.

The transcription used in this book is in short pronunciation except where stated otherwise.

7. Past tense

The Arabic past tense (also known as the perfect tense) denotes an action which took place or a situation which occurred some time before being reported in the sentence. This tense corresponds approximately to the English past and perfect tenses ('he wrote, he has written'):

كتبت التقرير أمس. *katabt at-taqrīr 'ams.*
I wrote the report yesterday.

درست اللجنة الميزانية. *darasat al-lajna l-mīzānīya.*
The committee has studied the budget.

ذهبنا إلى المحطة. *dhahabna 'ila l-maḥaṭṭa.*
We went to the station.

أين جلستم؟ *'ayna jalastum?* Where did you sit?

The completion of the action may be emphasised by putting the particle

قد *qad* ('already', but usually left untranslated in English) before the verb:

قد قرأت الوثيقة. *qad qara't al-wathīqa.*

I have read/finished reading the document.

Forming the past tense. The example given below is of the sound verb كتب يكتب *kataba yaktubu* 'to write'. The tense is formed from the first principle part (§ 3). The principle part itself, with nothing added, gives us the 3rd pers. m. s. (هو) form. For the other persons, the final *-a* is dropped from the principle part, giving us كتب.. *katab-*. To this a personal ending is added for the subject:

	animate plural	dual	singular
1 m./f.	كتبنا *katabna*	–	كتبت *katabtu*
2 m. 2 f.	كتبتم *katabtum* كتبتنّ *katabtunna*	كتبتما *katabtuma* كتبتما *katabtuma*	كتبت *katabta* كتبت *katabti*
3 m. 3 f.	كتبوا *katabū* كتبن *katabna*	كتبا *katabā* كتبتا *katabatā*	كتب *kataba* كتبت *katabat*

Note:

- See § 5 for the distribution and use of the persons, genders and numbers. The notes given there also apply here.
- The model verb كتب has vowelling *-a-a-* in its first principle part. Other verbs may be vowelled *-a-i-* or *-a-u-* in this part; allowing for this difference, they also follow the table.
- The short-vowel endings *-a* and *-u* shown in small type are dropped in short pronunciation (§ 6) when no pronoun-object suffix is added to the verb (you will note that this happens to the هو form itself in this circumstance). The other vowel endings shown are retained in short pronunciation.
- The dual forms are identical for both genders in the 2nd person, as in the pronouns. But, unlike the pronouns, the 3rd person dual

verb varies for gender.

- The final ا *'alif* of the هم form is silent. It is dropped in writing also when a pronoun-object suffix is added to the verb.
- It is a rule that when a final long vowel is followed by *hamzat al-waṣl* (= a weak vowel) in the same phrase, the long vowel is shortened and the weak vowel is dropped:

  كتبوا رسالةً. *katabū risāla.* They wrote a letter.

  but: كتبوا الرسالة. *katabu r-risāla.* They wrote the letter.

  (The *a*- of ..ال is weak, and is silent after any vowel.)
- This table is valid as it stands for all verb roots of the following classes or sub-classes (§ 4):
  - sound (three different consonantal root letters), e.g. كتب, درس *darasa* 'to study'
  - hamzated, e.g. أكل , سأل , قرأ (subject to the rules for writing *hamza*, see the preamble to Tables 24-57)
  - assimilated, initial و or ي , e.g. وجد , يقن

  For the remaining classes and sub-classes (doubled, hollow, final-weak, doubly weak) the table applies but with some variants. These are explained in the preamble to each set of tables in Part II.

Negative. The past tense can be made negative by putting the particle ما *mā* before the verb:

ما كتبت الرسالة. *mā katabat ar-risāla.*

She did not write the letter.

This is a correct negative, but an alternative construction, considered better style, is made with a different device. This is studied in § 22.

8. Present tense

The Arabic present tense (also known as the imperfect tense or, more correctly, the imperfect indicative tense) is used for an action or situation which occurs as it is being reported, or which is expected to occur imminently. It corresponds approximately to the two English tenses 'I write' and 'I am writing' (now or in the immediate future):

تذهب إلى المدرسة كل يوم. *tadhhab 'ila l-madrasa kull yawm.*
She goes to school every day.

أكتب الجواب الآن. *'aktub al-jawāb al-'ān.*
I am writing the answer now.

نبحث التفاصيل في الاجتماع. *nabḥath at-tafāṣīl fī l-ijtimā'.*
We are discussing/shall discuss the details in the meeting.

Forming the present tense. The example given below is of the sound verb كتب يكتب *kataba yaktubu* 'to write'. The tense is formed from the second principle part (§ 3). The principle part itself, with nothing added, gives us the 3rd pers. m. s. (هو) form. For the other persons, the personal prefix ..يـ *ya-* and the final *-u* are dropped from this principle part, giving us ...كتب... *ktub-* (note that the initial and middle root letters fall together). To this a personal prefix and personal ending are added for the subject:

	animate plural	dual	singular
1 m./f.	نكتب *naktubu*	–	أكتب *'aktubu*
2 m. 2 f.	تكتبون *taktubūna* تكتبن *taktubna*	تكتبان *taktubāni* تكتبان *taktubāni*	تكتب *taktubu* تكتبين *taktubīna*
3 m. 3 f.	يكتبون *yaktubūna* يكتبن *yaktubna*	يكتبان *yaktubāni* تكتبان *taktubāni*	يكتب *yaktubu* تكتب *taktubu*

Note:

- See § 5 for the distribution and use of the persons, genders and numbers. The notes given there also apply here.
- The model verb كتب has vowelling *-u-* in its second principle part. Other verbs may be vowelled *-a-* or *-i-*; allowing for this difference, they also follow the table.

- The short-vowel endings *-a* and *-i* shown in small type are dropped in short pronunciation (§ 6) when no pronoun-object suffix is added to the verb (you will note that this happens to the هو form itself in this circumstance). All other vowel endings shown in the table are retained in short pronunciation.
- The dual forms are identical for both genders in the 2nd person, but the 3rd person dual verb varies for gender.
- This table is valid as it stands for all verb roots in Form I (i.e. the basic form) of the following classes or sub-classes (§ 4):
  - sound (three different consonantal root letters), e.g. كتب, درس
  - hamzated, e.g. أكل , سأل , قرأ (the rules for writing *hamza* in different forms may entail spelling changes; these are explained in the preamble to Tables 24 to 57)
  - assimilated with initial ي and two different consonants, e.g. يقن (initial-و verbs have an irregular present tense)

  For the remaining classes and sub-classes (doubled, assimilated with initial و, hollow, final-weak, doubly weak) the table applies but with some variants. These are explained in the preamble to each set of tables in Part II.

Negative. The present tense is negated by putting the particle لا *lā* before the verb:

لا يدرسون الأفعال العربية. *lā yadrusūna l-'af'āl al-'arabīya.*
They are not studying Arabic verbs.

9 . Future particle

The present tense (§ 8) is commonly used for the imminent future. A future action or situation can also be expressed using a particle; this form is used for the more distant future, or for emphasis, or when intention is implied.

The future particle is the word سوف *sawfa*, or its variant which is the prefix ..سـ *sa-* attached to the present-tense verb form itself. Both particle and prefix are invariable for person, gender and number:

سوف أدرس الأرقام اليوم. *sawfa 'adrus al-'arqām al-yawm.*
I shall examine the figures today.

ماذا سيحدث؟ *mādha sa-yaḥduth?*
What will happen?

سوف *sawfa* is usually given its full pronunciation, even when the rest of the sentence is pronounced 'short'.

Negative. The future verb can be negated with سوف لا *sawfa lā*:

سوف لا نكتب الرسالة. *sawfa lā naktub ar-risāla.*
We shall not write the letter.

But it is more common, and considered better style, to use another device, which we study in § 21.

10. Continuous past tense

Arabic makes a *continuous past tense* to express past actions or situations which were continuous, habitual or repeated. Examine:

كنت أسكن في دمشق عندما وصل. *kunt 'askun fī dimashq 'indamā waṣal.* I was living in Damascus when he arrived.

كانوا دائمًا يجلسون جنبي. *kānū dā'iman yajlisūna jambī.*
They used always to sit next to me.

The tense is formed with the appropriate person of the *past* tense of the hollow verb كان يكون *kāna yakūnu* followed by the appropriate person of the *present* tense of the operative verb. The first example given above shows the tense expressing a long action interrupted by a short one; the second example shows the two verbs separated by an adverb showing how the action occurred.

Negative. The continuous past tense is usually negated with ما *mā* before the form of كان *kāna*:

ما كانوا يسكنون في دمشق. *mā kānū yaskunūna fī dimashq.*
They were not living in Damascus.

See the end of § 7, negation of the past tense. كان يكون *kāna yakūnu* is one of the few verbs where ما *mā* is in fact the preferred particle for forming the negative.

All the examples shown here have pronoun subjects. § 20 shows how to use this and other compound tenses with a noun subject.

11. Pluperfect tense

When we have two actions or situations occurring at different times in the past, we can use the *pluperfect* tense for the earlier event:

كنّا قد قرأنا الوثيقة قبل وصوله. *kunna qad qara'na l-wathīqa qabl wuṣūlihi.* We had read the document before his arrival.

This tense is formed with the appropriate person of the *past* tense of the hollow verb كان يكون *kāna yakūnu* followed by the particle قد *qad* (§ 7), then the appropriate person of the *past* tense of the operative verb.

قد may be omitted but is usually retained. The example given above could have read ... كنّا قرأنا الوثيقة .

The Arabic pluperfect tense is not consistently used; often the past tense is preferred, possibly with قد to emphasise the earlier timing:

(قد) قرأنا الوثيقة قبل وصوله. *(qad) qara'na l-wathīqa qabl wuṣūlihi.*

Negative. The pluperfect tense is usually negated with ما *mā* before the form of كان *kāna*:

ما كان (قد) كتب الرسالة. *mā kān (qad) katab ar-risāla.*
He had not written the letter.

See the end of § 10, negation of the continuous past tense, for the common use of ما *mā* with كان يكون *kāna yakūnu.*

All the examples shown here have pronoun subjects. § 20 shows how to use this and other compound tenses with a noun subject.

12. Government; direct and prepositional object

All verbs have a *subject*, for which see § 5. Some verbs have in addition an *object*, explained below, or a *predicate*, examined in § 2. The relation of a verb to its object or predicate (if any) is called its *government*.

Direct object. The object of a verb is that person, creature, thing, place or idea which is affected by the action of the verb. In this example:

كتب الرالة. *katab ar-risāla.* He wrote the letter.

the object of the verb كتب *katab* is الرسالة *ar-risāla* 'the letter'. It is a *direct object*, i.e. one directly suffering the action.

The noun expressing the direct object stands in the *accusative case*, but this fact is evident in unpointed writing and with short pronunciation only when the noun has one of the indefinite endings ...اً\...ىً *-an,* or a possessive suffix, or the dual ending ...ين *-ayn* or the masculine sound plural ending ...ين *-īn*:

كتب تقريراً فنّيًا. *katab taqrīran fannīyan.*
He wrote a technical report.

كتب تقريره السنوي. *katab taqrirahu s-sanawī.*
He wrote his annual report.

سألنا المهندسين. *sa'alna l-muhandisayn/l-muhandisīn.*
We asked the (two) engineers.

The object can also be governed not directly but through a preposition, giving us a *prepositional object*. Most verbs with a prepositional object have also a direct object, with one object relating to a thing, the other to a person:

دفع النقود إلى المحاسب. *dafa' an-nuqūd 'ila l-muḥāsib.*
He paid the money to the accountant.

إلى المحاسب *'ila l-muḥāsib* is here a prepositional object.

(NB: In English we can often omit the prepositions 'to' and 'for' ('He paid the accountant the money.'); no preposition can correctly be omitted in Arabic.)

The noun expressing the prepositional object stands in the *genitive case*, but this fact is evident in unpointed writing and with short pronunciation only when the noun has a possessive suffix, or the dual ending ...ين *-ayn* or the masculine sound plural ending ...ين *-īn*:

دفع النقود إلى سوّاقه. *dafa' an-nuqūd 'ila sawwāqihi.*
He paid the money to his driver.

دفع النقود إلى السوّاقين. *dafa' an-nuqūd 'ila s-sawwāqayn/ as-sawwāqīn.* He paid the money to the (two) drivers.

An Arabic verb will not necessarily have the same government as its nearest English equivalent:

طلب الأجرة من الراكب. *ṭalab al-'ujra min ar-rākib.*
('They asked the fare from the passenger.')
They asked the passenger for the fare.

(In Arabic, طلب has a direct thing-object الأجرة 'the fare' and a prepositional person-object من الراكب 'from the passenger'. The government of the English verb 'ask' is the opposite of this.)

A few Arabic verbs have two direct objects:

منحوا الموظّفين إضافةً. *manaḥu l-muwaẓẓafīn 'iḍāfatan.*
They granted the employees a (pay) rise.

سألت الكاتب التفاصيل. *sa'alt al-kātib at-tafāṣīl.*
I asked the clerk the details.

Direct pronoun object. In the examples given above the object is a noun. The object can also be a pronoun ('me, him, them' etc.). The Arabic object pronoun is a suffix; when the object is direct it is attached to its verb, taking the following form:

	animate plural	dual	singular
1 m./f.	...نا *-na* us		...ني *-nī* me
2 m. 2 f.	...كم *-kum* you ...كنّ *-kunna* you	...كما *-kuma* you both	...ك *-ka* you ...ك *-ki* you
3 m. 3 f.	...هم *-hum* them ...هنّ *-hunna* them	...هما *huma* them both	...ه *-hu* he/it ...ها *-ha* her/it/them

See § 5 for the distribution and use of the persons, genders and numbers. As in the subject pronouns, the dual forms are identical for both genders.

Before the pronoun suffix is added to the verb:

- any short vowel ending the verb and *dropped* for short pronunciation must be restored:

  كتب الرسالة. *katab ar-risāla.* He wrote the letter.

  but: كتبها. *katabaha.* He wrote it.

  أعرف المندوبين. *'a'rif al-mandūbīn.* I know the delegates.

  but: أعرفهم. *'a'rifuhum.* I know them.

- in the past tense, three plural endings change in pronunciation or spelling, or both:
  - the 1st person plural ...نا *-na* is pronounced *-nā́-* (the vowel is lengthened and stressed; the spelling is unchanged),
  - ...تم *-tum* becomes ...تمو... *-tumū́-* (additional stressed long vowel),
  - ...وا is written ...و... pronounced *-ū́-* (long and stressed).

  قد قرأناها. *qad qara'nā́ha.* We have read it.

  ماذا سألتموني؟ *mādha sa'altumū́nī?* What did you ask me?

  عرفوك. *'arafū́ka/'arafū́ki.* They knew you.

It is a general rule that when any of the 3rd-person pronoun suffixes other than ...ها is attached to a word ending in *-i*, ...ي *-ī* or ...ي *-ay*, that suffix changes its vowel *-u-* also to *-i-*. In other words, ...ه, ...هما, ...هم and ...هنّ are pronounced respectively *-hi, -hima, -him* and *-hinna* in this circumstance:

يطلبانه. *yaṭlubānihi*. They are both requesting it.

Prepositional pronoun object. For a pronoun object which is prepositional, the pronoun is suffixed to its preposition in the same way as the direct object is suffixed to its verb, allowing for the following modifications.

The form equivalent to English 'me' after a preposition is ...ي *-ī*. When it is added to a preposition:

- if the preposition has a final vowel heard only in full pronunciation, that vowel is *dropped*:

  مع *ma'a* with → معي *ma'ī* with me

- من *min* 'from' and عن *'an* 'from, about' + ...ي become respectively منّي *minnī* and عنّي *'annī*.
- ب *bi* 'in, with' and ل *li* 'to, for' lose their vowel:

  بي *bī* in/with me　　لي *lī* to/for me

- final ...ي *-ī* or ...ى *-a* of a preposition + pronoun ...ي become respectively ...يّ *-īyya* and ...يّ *-ayya*:

  في *fī* in → فيّ *fīyya* in me
  إلى *'ila* to → إليّ *'ilayya* to me

When a pronoun suffix other than ...ي is added:

- if the preposition has a final vowel which is heard only in full pronunciation, that vowel is *restored*:

  مع *ma'a* with → معه *ma'ahu* with him/it

- the preposition ل is pronounced *la-*: له *lahu* to/for him
- final ...ى *-a* of a preposition becomes ...يـ... *-ay-*:

  إلى *'ila* in → إلينا *'ilayna* to us
  على *'ala* on → عليكم *'alaykum* to you

The rule under which ...ه (etc.) are pronounced *-hi* (etc.) after *-i*/*-ī*/*-ay* (see above) applies also after a preposition:

به *bihi* in/with him عليهم *'alayhim* on them

The term 'government' relates also to the *predicate* (if any) of a verb. Verbs with predicates are studied in § 13 below.

The Introduction lists the symbols used in Parts II and III to indicate the government of each verb.

13. Predicated verbs

In § 2 we encountered the predicate of an equation (a sentence with no verb). Predicates also occur after certain verbs denoting *being* or *becoming*, the most important of which is كان يكون *kāna yakūnu* 'to be', used for expressing the past and future equivalents of an equation, which you recall is always present in time. The predicate of كان يكون, when a noun or adjective, is always in the *accusative case*:

كان مريضاً. *kān marīḍan.* He was ill.

كانوا موظّفين طيّبين. *kānū muwaẓẓafīn ṭayyibīn.*
They were good employees.

Do not confuse the predicate of a verb with a direct object (§ 12). Both stand in the accusative; but, unlike an object, the predicate is not someone or something affected by the verb; it identifies or describes the subject exactly as does the predicate of an equation.

As in an equation, the predicate of كان may be another word or expression which e.g. locates the subject:

كانت مظاهرة في الميدان. *kānat muẓāhara fi l-maydān.*
There was a demonstration in the square.

The present tense of كان , i.e. يكون , often itself denotes the future, without the future particle (§ 9) which for this verb is not essential:

(سـ)يكون صعباً عليك. *(sa-)yakūn ṣa'ban 'alayka/'alayki.*
It will be difficult for you.

Other predicated verbs are:

ليس *laysa* not to be
ظلّ يظلّ *ẓalla yaẓallu* to remain
بقي يبقى *báqiya yabqa* to remain
صار يصير *ṣāra yaṣīru* to become
دام يدوم *dāma yadūmu* to last
عاد يعود *'āda ya'ūdu* to go/come back
زال يزال *zāla yazālu* to cease to be/do

Note:

- ليس 'not to be' exists only in the past tense, which for this verb has (NB) *present meaning*. It gives us the negative of an equation:

  ليسوا مسؤولين. *laysū mas'ūlīn.*
  They are not responsible.

- ظلّ , بقي and صار present no special difficulty:

  ظلّ\بقي صديقًا مخلصًا. *zall/baqi ṣadīqan mukhliṣan.*
  He remained a sincere friend.

  صار الوضع معقّداً. *ṣār al-waḍ' mu'aqqadan.*
  The situation became complicated.

- دام يدوم 'to last' is most commonly found as a past-tense expression ما دام *mā dām* (etc.) used as the English equivalent of 'while', 'for as long as':

  سنبقى ما دام الوضع خطيراً. *sa-nabqa mā dām al-waḍ' khaṭīran.* We shall stay as long as the situation is dangerous.

  ما دمت معك أنا مستعدّ. *mā dumt ma'aka 'ana musta'idd.*
  While/As long as I am with you I am ready.

- عاد يعود literally means 'to go/come back'. It can be predicated in this meaning: عاد فقيراً. *'ād faqīran.* 'He returned poor'. But its commonest use is in the negative of the past tense ما عاد *mā 'ād*, conveying the meaning of English 'to be no longer':

  ما عادت غنيةً. *mā 'adat ghanīya.*

She was no longer rich.

ما عدنا موظّفين صغاراً. *mā 'udna muwaẓẓafīn sighāran.*

We were no longer junior ('small') employees.

- زال يزال is most commonly found in the negative of either the past tense ما زال *mā zāl* or of the present tense لا يزال *lā yazāl*, with the meaning of the English 'still to be':

ما زالوا معلّمين هامّين. *mā zālū mu'allimīn hāmmīn.*

They are still important teachers.

لا يزال في دمشق. *lā yazāl fī dimashq.*

He is still in Damascus.

In Parts II and III, predicated verbs are indicated by the symbol اً.

Negative. You can see from the examples given here that, as for كان, so for the other predicated verbs the commonest way to form the negative in the past is with ما *mā*.

14. Verbs used with the present tense

The predicated verbs (the commonest ones are listed in § 13 above) can be used with a following present tense, some with special meaning.

كان 'to be' gives us the continuous past tense (§ 10):

كنّا نسكن هنا. *kunna naskun huna.* We used to live here.

ظلّ 'to continue': ظللت أدرس في القاهرة. *ẓalalt 'adrus fī l-qāhira.*

I continued studying/to study in Cairo.

بقي 'to keep ...ing': يبقى يسأل نفس السؤال. *yabqa yas'al nafs as-su'āl.* He keeps asking the same question.

صار 'to begin': صرنا نجد مشاكل أخرى. *ṣirna najid mashākil 'ukhra.* We began to find other difficulties.

ما دام 'as long as': ما دمت تسكن هنا بيتي بيتك. *mā dumt taskun huna baytī baytuka.* As long as you live here, my house is yours.

عاد 'again': عادت تشكو منه. *'ādat tashkū minhu.*

She complained again about it/him.

ما عاد 'no longer': بعد ذلك ما عدت أكتب مقالات سياسيةً.

ba'd dhālika mā 'udt 'aktub maqālāt sīyāsīya.

After that I no longer wrote political articles.

زال 'to stop ...ing': يزالون يحفرون. *yazālūna yaḥfirūna*

They are stopping drilling.

ما زال\لا يزال 'still': حتّى بعد القضية ما زال\لا يزال يشكو.

ḥatta ba'd al-qaḍīya ma zāl/lā yazāl yashkū.

Even after the case he still complained/complains.

A few other important verbs can also be used in this way:

بدأ يبدأ *bada'a yabda'u* to begin

كاد يكاد *kāda yakādu* almost to ...

بدأنا نشكّ في النتائج. *bada'na nashukk fi n-natā'ij*

We began to doubt ('in') the results.

كادوا ينسون أهمّ تفصيل. *kādū yansawna 'ahamm tafṣīl.*

They almost forgot the most important detail.

It is important to remember that whereas the first verb can often be either in the past or present tense, the second verb must be in the present tense to give the meanings shown here.

Verbs (both predicated and others) which can be used as first verb in this construction are marked 'π' in Parts II and III.

15. Increased forms

All the verbs studied so far have been in the so-called *Form I* which is the basic form. There are also *increased forms* in which a prefix or a middle part is added to the root, often to give a variant of the basic meaning. We identify each Form with a Roman number, I to X. Of the increased forms we need to know only Forms II to VIII and X; Form IX, very rare, is included in this book for reference.

No root has all Forms; some are even not found in Form I. Use only those Forms you know; you may not invent your own.

Unlike Form I, each increased form has the same vowelling for all roots. We examine below each increased form with an appropriate model verb.

<table>
<tr><th>Form, root</th><th>Model verb, principal parts</th><th>to …</th></tr>
<tr><td>II علم 'lm</td><td>علّم يعلّم 'allama yu'allimu</td><td>teach</td></tr>
<tr><td colspan="3">Middle root letter is doubled. Verb is often causative, i.e. causes its direct object to do the action implicit in the root (here, علم know).</td></tr>
<tr><td>III نسب nsb</td><td>ناسب يناسب nāsaba yunāsibu</td><td>suit</td></tr>
<tr><td colspan="3">'alif after first root letter. Often has direct object.</td></tr>
<tr><td>IV رسل rsl</td><td>أرسل يرسل 'arsala yursilu</td><td>send</td></tr>
<tr><td colspan="3">Past tense prefixed with ...أ 'a-. First two root letters fall together throughout. Takes direct object. Verb is often causative.</td></tr>
<tr><td>V علم 'lm</td><td>تعلّم يتعلّم ta'allama yuta'allamu</td><td>leam</td></tr>
<tr><td colspan="3">Prefix ta-, middle root letter doubled. Both tenses have -a- before final root letter. Complementary meaning of Form II. Rarely has direct object.</td></tr>
<tr><td>VI ظهر ẓhr</td><td>تظاهر يتظاهر taẓāhara yataẓāharu</td><td>demonstrate (politically)</td></tr>
<tr><td colspan="3">As Form V, except 'alif after first root letter instead of doubled middle root letter. Complementary meaning of Form III. Rarely has direct object.</td></tr>
<tr><td>VII سحب sḥb</td><td>انسحب ينسحب insáḥaba yansáḥibu</td><td>withdraw</td></tr>
<tr><td colspan="3">Past tense prefixed with weak i-. -n- before initial root letter in both tenses. Verb is often passive in meaning (i.e. subject does not perform the action, but undergoes it). Always stressed as shown. No object.</td></tr>
</table>

VIII قرح *qrḥ*	اقترح يقترح *iqtáraḥa yaqtáriḥu*	propose
As Form VII, except *-t-* after initial root letter instead of *-n-* before it, in both tenses. Always stressed as shown. See also indent below. No easily identifiable special meaning added to root. Often has direct object.		

IX حمر *ḥmr*	احمرّ يحمرّ *iḥmarra yaḥmarru*	turn red
NB Shown for reference only; rare Form with few verbs. Past tense prefixed with weak *i-*. Last two root letters fall together in most persons. All verbs relate to colour or physical defect. No object.		

X قبل *qbl*	استقبل يستقبل *istaqbala yastaqbilu*	receive
Past tense prefixed with *ist-* (weak *i-*), present has *-st-* after personal prefix. First two root letters fall together. Often adds to basic verb a meaning of 'trying to make ...' or 'considering to be...'. Often has direct object.		

The models given are all sound. The patterns shown above apply to all roots of the sound and hamzated classes. Doubled and weak verbs follow the same patterns as sound roots, but with modifications to accommodate respectively the identical or weak root letters. The preambles in Part II show examples and explain the alternative forms and variants. Note further:

- The personal endings for the past and present tenses are the same as for Form I, shown in §§ 7 and 8 above. The present-tense personal prefixes of Forms V-X have the vowel *-a-* (*'a-, ta-, ya-, na-*); those of Forms II-IV have the vowel *-u-* (*'u-, tu-, yu-, nu-*).
- The past tense mostly has *-a-* and the present tense has *-i-* before the final root letter, but Forms V and VI have *-a-* before the final root letter in both tenses.
- Since the vowelling is regular, we can identify each increased

form by quoting only the first principal part, unlike Form I where we need both parts because of the variable vowelling. Thus we quote e.g. علّم II with one part but كتب يكتب I with both.

- Examine Form VIII. The ..ـتـ... -*t*- of Form VIII is replaced in the following way in certain roots:
  - after initial root letter ص or ض it is replaced by ...ط... :

    اصطنع يصطنع *iṣṭána'a yaṣṭáni'u* to manufacture

    اضطرب يضطرب *iḍṭáraba yaḍṭáribu* to clash
  - after initial root letter ز it is replaced by ...د... :

    ازدحم يزدحم *izdáḥama yazdáḥimu* to swarm
  - initial root letter ط is doubled instead of adding ..ـتـ...:

    اطّلع يطّلع *iṭṭála'a yaṭṭáli'u* to be informed
  - initial root letter د or ذ becomes ...دّ... instead of adding ..ـتـ...:

    (root دحر) ادّحر يدّحر *iddáḥara yaddáḥiru* to be repelled

    (root ذخر) ادّخر يدّخر *iddákhara yaddákhiru* to keep

    (This last example is an extremely rare case of a sound root letter itself undergoing a change. This verb has also the regular form †اذّخر يذّخر *idhdhákhara yadhdhákhiru*†, less common.)

The notation I to X is western. Arabs refer to the Forms by quoting the appropriate first principal part of the root فعل *f'l* in each Form, thus:

I	فعل	*fa'ala*	II	فعّل	*fa''ala*
III	فاعل	*fā'ala*	IV	أفعل	*'af'ala*
V	تفعّل	*tafa''ala*	VI	تفاعل	*tafā'ala*
VII	انفعل	*infá'ala*	VIII	افتعل	*iftá'ala*
IX	افعلّ	*if'alla*	X	استفعل	*istaf'ala*

Many of these words are of course theoretical, since no root has all ten Forms. The Form I verb فعل يفعل *fa'ala yaf'alu* is 'to do'.

16. Using a dictionary

In most dictionaries published since the 1980's the Arabic entries are listed alphabetically by the word, as with most other languages. The Arabic-English/English-Arabic dictionary of N. Awde and K. Smith (pub. Bennett and Bloom 2004) is a leading example of this type. Part III of this verb book is also word-based.

Most older Arabic-English dictionaries list Arabic entries based on roots not by the word but by the root itself; thus you find e.g. تعلّم V not under ت but under its root علم. Words not based on a recognised root appear alphabetically among the roots. Hans Wehr's *Dictionary of Modern Written Arabic* (originally pub. Otto Harrassowitz, Wiesbaden 1966, with many reprints) is the fullest and most prestigious root-based dictionary for English-speakers.

You need to be able to use both types of dictionary.

17. Participle

One important derivative of the verb, in Arabic as in English, is the *participle*. Arabic has an *active* participle and a *passive* participle. The participle is an adjective or noun (Arabic makes no grammatical distinction, and, where the meaning permits, one can be used for the other). Many common adjectives and nouns are in fact participles.

The active participle identifies or describes who or what performs the action or experiences the situation. From كتب يكتب *kataba yaktubu* I the active participle is كاتب *kātib* 'writing, writer'. The passive participle identifies or describes who or what undergoes the action; the passive participle of كتب يكتب is مكتوب *maktūb* 'written'.

Not all theoretically possible participles are in common use.

Participles are regularly formed, as follows:

- Form I. Use model verb كتب يكتب:
  Active: كاتب *kātib* writing, writer; *Passive*: مكتوب *maktūb* written

- Forms II-IV and VII-X. *Active*: Take the second principal part, remove the personal ending, substitute prefix مـ... *mu-* for the personal prefix يـ... . *Passive*: Take first principal part, remove personal ending, add prefix مـ... *mu-*.

  Examples with model verbs (§ 15):

  II علّم: معلّم *mu'allim* teaching, teacher; *mu'allam* taught

  III ناسب : مناسب *munāsib* suitable, *munāsab* suited

  IV أرسل : مرسل *mursil* sender, *mursal* sent

  VII انسحب: منسحب *munsáḥib* withdrawing, *munsáḥab* †*

  VIII اقترح: مقترح *muqtáriḥ* proposer, *muqtáraḥ* proposed

  X استقبل: مستقبل *mustaqbil* receiver, *mustaqbal* front, future

  * theoretical form, very rare (not used at all for this verb)

- Forms V and VI. *Active*: as for Forms II-IV etc, but with one extra step; change the vowel after the middle root letter of the second principal part from *-a-* to *-i-*. *Passive*: as for Forms II-IV etc. Examples:

  V تعلّم: متعلّم *muta'allim* scholar, apprentice, *muta'allam* learnt

  VI تظاهر: متظاهر *mutaẓāhir* demonstrator, *mutaẓāhar*† (see note * in the previous indent)

These forms are valid as they stand for sound and hamzated verbs, and valid with some modification for verbs of other classes (doubled and weak). The preambles in Part II give details for each class or sub-class.

Because there is often no difference in alphabetical spelling between active and passive participle in the increased forms, we may need to seek help from the context to read the participle correctly.

The formulæ and examples shown in the indents above give us the indefinite masculine singular participle. A participle has also definite, feminine or plural forms where the meaning permits it:

(الـ)معلّمة *(al-)mu'allima* the/a (woman) teacher

الإجراءات المقترحة *al-'ijrā'āt al-muqtáraḥa* (inan. pl.)

the proposed measures

Most participles of increased forms make an animate plural on the sound pattern:

معلّمون\معلّمات *mu'allimūn/-āt* teachers (m./f.)

المتظاهرون *al-mutaẓāhirūn* the demonstrators

Some Form I masculine participles have a broken plural, especially when the participle is used as a noun:

كاتب ج كتّاب *kātib kuttāb* writer(s), clerk(s)

عامل ج عمّال *'āmil 'ummāl* workman/men

عامل ج أعوامل *'āmil 'a'wāmil* factor(s)

طالب ج طلاّب *ṭālib ṭullāb* student(s)

مكتوب ج مكاتيب *maktūb makātīb* letter(s)

but: (الـ)قارئ ج (الـ)قارئون *(al-)qāri' (al-)qāri'ūn* (the) reader(s)

راجع ج راجعون *rāji' rāji'ūn* returning

كاتبة ج كاتبات *kātiba kātibāt* writer(s)/clerk(s) (f.)

طالبة ج طالبات *ṭāliba ṭālibāt* student(s) (f.)

The active participle agrees fully with the subject which it identifies or qualifies:

إجراءات مناسبة *'ijrā'āt munāsiba* suitable measures

من الراجعين *min ar-rāji'īn* from those returning

The passive participle of a verb taking a direct object (§ 12), and used to qualify or identify that object, agrees fully with it:

الإجراءات المبحوثة اليوم *al-'ijrā'āt al-mabḥūtha l-yawm*
the measures discussed today

A passive participle also agrees fully with a predicate (§§ 2, 13) which it qualifies or identifies:

صار حساباً معقّداً. *ṣār ḥisāban mu'aqqadan.*
It became a complicated calculation.

But the passive participle of a verb taking a *prepositional* object becomes impersonal and always stands in the masculine singular form.

The full gender and number of the object are then shown in a pronoun suffix attached to the preposition:

موظّفون معتمد عليهم *muwaẓẓafūn muʻtámad ʻalayhim*
reliable employees ('employees [it is] relied on them')

الأرقام المشكوك فيها *al-'arqām al-mashkūk fīha*
the doubtful ('doubted in them') figures

Impersonal passives are marked ° in Part II.

Negative. A participle, like any adjective, can be negated by putting before it the word غير *ghayr* 'other than':

طلاّب غير حاضرين *ṭullāb ghayr ḥāḍirīn*
students not present

أموال غير مستعملة *'amwāl ghayr mustaʻmala*
unused funds

The compound is made definite by defining the participle, not غير:

الطلاّب غير الحاضرين *aṭ-ṭullāb ghayr al-ḥāḍirīn*
the students not present

الأموال غير المستعملة *al-'amwāl ghayr al-mustaʻmala*
the unused funds

Participle for verb. Being an adjective-cum-noun, a participle can often be used as predicate of an equation; we have seen examples.

In addition, a predicated *active* participle can sometimes have the force of its corresponding verb. These two sentences mean the same thing:

participle: زملاؤنا مسافرون اليوم. *zumalā'una **musāfirūn** al-yawm.*
verb: زملاؤنا يسافرون اليوم. *zumalā'una **yusāfirūna** l-yawm.*
Our colleagues travel/are travelling today.

18. Verbal noun

The verbal noun, derived from the verb, denotes the activity of the verb:

كتابة *kitāba* (the act of) writing

The verbal noun of Form I is irregular and must be learned with each verb. Some examples (a few verbs have more than one verbal noun, sometimes with different meanings):

Form I verb, to ...	Verbal noun
كتب يكتب *kataba yaktubu* write	كتابة *kitāba* writing
قرأ يقرأ *qara’a yaqra’u* read	قراءة *qirā’a* reading
عرف يعرف *‘arafa ya‘rifu* know	معرفة ج معارف *ma‘rifa ma‘ārif*, عرفان *‘irfān* knowledge
عمل يعمل *‘amila ya‘malu* do, work	عمل ج أعمال *‘amal ’a‘māl* action, work
سأل يسأل *sa’ala yas’alu* ask	سؤال ج أسئلة *su’āl ’as’ila* question مسألة ج مسائل *mas’ala masā’il* matter
طلب يطلب *ṭalaba yaṭlubu* request	طلب *ṭalab* request, also مطلبة ج مطالب *maṭlaba maṭālib*

The plurals, where used, of these verbal nouns are sound (ات... *-āt*) unless shown otherwise.

Verbal nouns of the increased forms are regularly formed. The patterns are best learned from model verbs:

Form, verb, to ...	Verbal noun
II عُلّم *‘allama* teach	تعليم *ta‘līm* tuition
III نوسب *nāsaba* suit	مناسبة *munāsaba* suitability, occasion
III* قاتل *qātala* fight against	مقاتلة *muqātala* } fight against قتال *qitāl* }
IV أرسل *’arsala* send	إرسال *’irsāl* despatch
V تعلّم *ta‘allama* learn	تعلّم *ta‘allum* learning
VI تظوهر *taẓāhara* demonstrate	تظاهر *taẓāhur* pretence, demonstration**

VII	انسحب *insáḥaba* withdraw	انسحاب *insiḥāb* withdrawal	
VIII	اقترح *iqtáraḥa* propose	اقتراح *iqtirāḥ* proposal	
IX	احمرّ *iḥmarra* go red	احمرار *iḥmirār* reddening	
X	استقبل *istaqbala* receive	استقبال *istiqbāl* reception	
* A few Form III verbs have alternative verbal nouns, as shown. ** Technically correct; but the commoner word for 'demonstration' is مظاهرة *muẓāhara* (verbal noun of ظاهر *ẓāhara* III 'to support').			

These forms are valid as they stand for sound and hamzated verbs, and valid with some modification for verbs of other classes (doubled and weak). The preambles in Part II give details for each class or sub-class. Note that the verbal noun of Form IV begins with *hamza*, while those of Forms VII-X begin with a weak vowel which is dropped after a preceding vowel in the same phrase.

Not all theoretically possible verbal nouns are in common use.

The plural of most verbal nouns of increased forms is sound (...ات *-āt*):

مناسبات ، اقتراحات *munāsabāt, iqtirāḥāt*
occasions, proposals

Use of the verbal noun. Like any noun, a verbal noun can take a possessive suffix, or an adjectival ending ...ي *-ī*, where appropriate:

اقتراحي *iqtirāḥī* my proposal

تعليمي *ta'līmī* tutorial, educational

The direct object of a verbal noun is expressed with a possessive construction or an expression with ل *li-*:

تعليم اللغات شيء صعب. *ta'līm al-lughāt shay' ṣa'b.* Teaching languages ('The teaching of languages') is something difficult.

تعليمهم للغة العربية ممتاز. *ta'līmhum li-l-lugha l-'arabīya mumtāz.* Their teaching of Arabic ('the Arabic language') is excellent.

In these examples the verbal noun is subject of the verb. It may also be the direct or prepositional object of a verb:

تدرس اللجنة اقتراحنا. *tadrus al-lajna qtirāḥana.*

The committee is studying our proposal.

نشكركم على اقتراحكم. *nashkurukum 'ala qtirāḥikum.*

We thank you for your proposal.

Other important uses of the verbal noun are examined in § 27.

Negative. The verbal noun can be negated by putting it in definite form after the noun عدم *'adam* 'lack (of)':

عدم الاستعمال *'adam al-isti'māl* disuse

لعدم التعاون *li-'adam at-ta'āwun*

through ('for') non-cooperation

19. Quadriliteral root

A few verbs, some of them important, have not three but four letters in their root. They are called *quadriliteral* roots and verbs. We show them in this book with the letter Q. All quadriliteral verbs either belong to the sound class or they follow the sound pattern.

Form IQ. Except for the verbal noun, Form IQ follows exactly the pattern of triliteral Form II (§ 15), if we allow that the second and third root letters behave like the doubled middle root letter of the triliteral pattern. Our model for IQ is ترجم يترجم *tarjama yutarjimu* 'to translate', root ترجم *t r j m*. Compare II and IQ:

II علّم يعلّم *'a**ll**ama yu'a**ll**imu* to teach

IQ ترجم يترجم *ta**rj**ama yuta**rj**imu* to translate

Participles: *Active* مترجم *mutarjim* 'translator', *Passive* مترجم *mutarjam* 'translated'.

The IQ verbal noun is irregular. For this verb it is ترجمة ج تراجم *tarjama tarājim* 'translation'. Other IQ verbs, with verbal nouns, are:

برهن على *barhana 'ala* to prove: برهان ج براهن *burhān barāhin* proof

زلزل *zalzala* to rock, shake: زلزال *zilzāl* rocking, shaking

تلفز *talfaza* to televise: تلفزة *talfaza* television

تلفن *talfana* to telephone: (verbal noun not used)

Form IIQ. Form IIQ is the only common quadriliteral increased form. It follows in all respects (including the verbal noun) the pattern of triliteral Form V (§ 15), if we equate the quadriliteral second and third root letters to the triliteral doubled middle root letter, and allow that IIQ has no passive participle. A good IIQ model is تزلزل يتزلزل *tazalzala yatazalzalu* 'to quake', root زلزل *z l z l*. Compare Forms V and IIQ:

V تعلّم يتعلّم *ta'a**ll**ama yata'a**ll**amu* to learn

IIQ تزلزل يتزلزل *taza**lz**ala yataza**lz**alu* to quake

Active participle: متزلزل *mutazalzil* quaking

Verbal noun: تزلزل *tazalzul* quaking

Other IIQ verbs:

تسلسل *tasalsala* to be in sequence

توشوش *tawashwasha* to whisper

20. Verbal sentence, nominal sentence

Arabic sentences fall into two types, the *verbal* sentence and the *nominal* sentence.

Verbal sentence. The verbal sentence is the commoner of the two patterns. In a verbal sentence the verb occurs earlier than its subject, often appearing as first word in the sentence.

One type of verbal sentence is that with a pronoun subject which is implicit, i.e. built into the verb as a personal ending and/or personal prefix. In this type the verb agrees fully with the subject in person, gender and number (respecting the different uses of the masculine and feminine animate plurals, and the inanimate plural, see § 5):

كتبوا\يكتبون تقريراً. *katabū/yaktubūna taqrīran.*

They wrote/are writing a report.

كانا شخصين بسيطين. *kānā shakhṣayn basīṭayn.*

They were both simple people.

The other common and important type of verbal sentence is one which has a stated noun as subject. In such a sentence, the verb agrees in gender with the noun subject; but its number (NB) is always singular for an animate subject (even when that subject is dual or plural). The verb is inanimate plural for an inanimate plural subject:

كتب\يكتب المهندسون التقرير. *katab/yaktub al-muhandisūn* (m. pl.) *at-taqrīr*. The engineers wrote/are writing the report.

كان أصدقائي فقراء. *kān 'aṣdiqā'ī* (m. pl.) *fuqarā'*. My friends were poor.

نجحت\تنجح المظاهرات. *najaḥat/tanjaḥ al-muẓāharāt*. (inan. pl..). The demonstrations succeeded/are succeeding.

A word or expression other than the subject may precede the verb; the sentence is still a verbal sentence provided that the verb occurs earlier than the subject:

اليوم سيرسل السفراء الخبر. *al-yawm sa-yursil as-sufarā' al-khabar*. Today the ambassadors will send the message.

قد كتب المهندس التقرير. *qad katab al-muhandis at-taqrīr*. The engineer has written the report.

Only one verb or verb component may occur earlier than the subject. If there is a second verb with the same subject, or if the verb itself is compound (e.g. as in §§ 10, 11), every verb or verbal component other than the first one follows the subject and agrees fully with it:

دخل المندوبون وجلسوا. *dakhal al-mandūbūn wa-jalasū*. The delegates entered and sat down.

كان المحاسبون يدرسون الميزانية. *kān al-muḥasibūn yadrusūna l-mīzānīya*. The accountants were studying the budget.

Remember that قد *qad* stays with the operative verb:

كان الكاتب قد كتب النمرة. *kān al-kātib qad katab an-numra*. The clerk had written the number.

Nominal sentence. In this type of sentence the subject occurs earlier than its verb. In such a sentence, the verb agrees fully (person, gender, number) with the subject.

A sentence with an explicit (i.e. stated) pronoun subject and a verb is a nominal sentence. So is any equation (§ 2), whatever its subject:

نحن كتبنا التقرير. *naḥnu katabna t-taqrīr.*
We wrote the report. (or, emphatically:) *We* wrote the report.

أنا بقيت يومين فقط. *'ana baqīt yawmayn faqaṭ.*
I stayed only two days ('two days only').

هي\المعلّمة مريضة. *hiya/al-mu'allima marīḍa.*
She/The teacher is ill.

Most nominal sentences other than equations have a noun subject, with a 3rd-person verb agreeing fully with it:

المحاسبون درسوا\يدرسون الميزانية. *al-muḥāsibūn darasu/ yadrusūna l-mīzānīya.* The accountants studied/are studying the budget.

المهندسون بقوا يومين فقط. *al-muhandisūn báqū yawmayn faqaṭ.*
The engineers stayed only two days.

These nominal sentences are correct as they stand; however, for those having a verb, it is considered better style to introduce them with the all-purpose conjunction إنّ *'inna.* This word adds no meaning to the sentence; it merely announces that a nominal sentence follows.

When إنّ *'inna* is used with a pronoun subject, the pronoun is suffixed to إنّ. The suffix is the same as that used with prepositions (§ 12):

إنّنا كتبنا التقرير. *'innana katabna t-taqrīr.*
We wrote the report.

إنّهم بقوا يومين فقط. *'innahum báqū yawmayn faqaṭ.*
They stayed two days only.

NB: There are two forms for إنّ + the first-person suffixes:

إنّي\إنّني *'innī, 'innanī* I ... إنّا\إنّنا *'inna, 'innana* we ...

When إنّ *'inna* is used with a noun subject, the noun goes into the *accusative* case, but this fact is evident in unpointed writing and with short pronunciation only when the noun has a possessive suffix, or the dual ending ...ين *-ayn* or the masculine sound plural ending ...ين *-īn*:

إنّ محاسبنا درس\يدرس الميزانية. *'inna muḥāsibana daras/yadrus al-mīzānīya.* Our accountant studied/is studying the budget.

إنّ المحاسبين درسوا\يدرسون الميزانية. *'inna l-muḥāsibīn darasu/ yadrusūna l-mīzānīya.* The accountants studied/are studying the budget.

We can introduce an equation with إنّ (applying the rules shown above), but this is not so much a preferred option as it is with a sentence containing a verb. Equations without إنّ are very common:

كاتبنا مريض. *kātibuna marīḍ.*
إنّ كاتبنا مريض. *'inna kātibana marīḍ.*
} Our clerk is ill.

In a nominal sentence, with or without إنّ, no special problem of word-order or of agreement arises when we have two verbs with the same subject, or a compound verb:

المندوبون دخلوا وجلسوا. *al-mandūbūn dakhalū wa-jalasū.* The delegates entered and sat down.

إنّ الكاتب كان (قد) كتب الجواب. *'inna l-kātib kān (qad) katab al-jawāb.* The clerk had written the reply.

21. Subjunctive

The subjunctive tense (more correctly the subjunctive mood of the present tense) is used to denote actions or situations which are not real but possible.

Forming the subjunctive. The subjunctive is derived from the present tense (§ 8) as shown in this chart (with the subjunctive of كتب يكتب *kataba yaktubu* I as a model):

	animate plural	dual	singular
1 m./f.	نكتب *naktuba*	–	أكتب *'aktuba*
2 m. 2 f.	تكتبوا *taktubū* تكتبن *taktubna*	تكتبا *taktubā* تكتبا *taktubā*	تكتب *taktuba* تكتبي *taktubī*
3 m. 3 f.	يكتبوا *yaktubū* يكتبن *yaktubna*	يكتبا *yaktubā* تكتبا *taktubā*	يكتب *yaktuba* تكتب *taktuba*

Present-tense prefixes, and the feminine plural forms, are unchanged. The other present-tense endings change as follows for the subjunctive:

- The full-pronunciation ending *-u* becomes *-a* (also dropped in short pronunciation when no suffix follows).
- The 2nd person f. s. ending ين... *-īna* shortens to ي... *-ī*.
- The dual ending ان... *-āni* shortens to ا... *-ā*.
- The masculine plural ending ون... *-ūna* shortens to وا... *-ū* (the *'alif* being silent, and dropped in writing when a suffix is added).

These endings are valid for Forms I to X of all classes of verb with a sound final root letter (sound, hamzated, doubled, assimilated and hollow). They are also valid, with some modification, for final-weak and doubly weak roots. The preambles in Part II explain these variants.

Negative future. See § 9. The more common negative future of the verb is formed with the particle لن *lan* + subjunctive:

لن أكتبها. *lan 'aktubaha.* I shall/will not write it.

Purpose, ability, probability, will. The most important use of the subjunctive is to express ideas such as purpose, ability, probability and will. For this the subjunctive verb follows a conjunction such as:

أنْ *'an* that, to
ألاّ *'allā* (NB stress) that ... not, not to ...
ل ، لأنْ، كي، لكي *li-, li-'an, kay, li-kay* in order that, so as to
لئلاّ *li-'allā* (NB stress) in order that ... not, so as not to
حتّى *ḥatta* in order that, in order to

Note:

- The verb preceding the conjunction can be in any tense; the verb following the conjunction is always subjunctive.
- The clause* introduced by one of these conjunctions has the form of a verbal sentence (§ 20).
- The subject of the verbs on either side of the conjunction need not be the same.
- English often uses an infinitive with 'to' instead of the second (subjunctive) verb.

(* A *clause* is a group of words centred on a subject + verb, and making at least limited sense. In the examples given below, the clause starts with the conjunction.)

أنْ is frequently used after verbs such as the following:

أراد *'arāda* IV to want
فضّل *faḍḍala* II to prefer
استطاع *istaṭā'a* X can, to be able
حاول *ḥāwala* III to try

(used impersonally):
يمكن *yumkinu* IV it is possible
يجب (على) *yajibu* I *('ala)* it is necessary
يجوز (ل) *yajūzu* I *(li-)* it is likely/permitted

Typical sentences:

أريد أنْ أكتب رسالةً. *'urīd 'an 'aktub risāla.*
I want to write ('that I write') a letter.

فضّلت أنْ يكتبها المحاسب. *faḍḍalt 'an yaktubaha l-muḥāsib.*
I preferred that the accountant (should) write it.

يستطيع زملاؤنا أنْ يدفعوا الحساب. *yastaṭī' zumalā'una 'an yadfa'u l-ḥisāb.* Our colleagues can/are able to pay the bill.

ماذا حاولتم أنْ تعملوا؟ *mādha ḥāwaltum 'an ta'malū?*
What were you trying to do ('that you do')?

The past tense of أراد *'arāda* IV is little used; for past time, the continuous past tense is preferred:

كنت أريد أنْ أكتبها. *kunt 'urīd 'an 'aktubaha.*
I wanted ('was wanting') to write it.

The three verbs used impersonally stand in the هو form when followed by أنْ . Their personal connotation can be shown with an object; for يمكن *yumkin* this object is direct, for يجب *yajib* the object is prepositional after على , and for يجوز *yajūz* the object is prepositional after ل . Further, the continuous past tense with كان *kāna* is used instead of the simple past of these three verbs:

يمكن أنْ يسافر زملاؤنا إلى دمشق. *yumkin 'an yusāfir zumalā'una 'ila dimashq.* Our colleagues may ('It is possible that our colleagues') travel to Damascus.

كان يمكن\يمكننا أنْ نجاوب. *kān yumkin(una) 'an nujāwib.*
We could have replied ('It was possible that we reply').

يجب (عليهم) أنْ يساعدونا. *yajib ('alayhim) 'an yusā'idūna.*
They must ('It is necessary on them that they') help us.

كان يجب أنْ يعمل زملاؤه كذلك. *kan yajib 'an ya'mal zumalā'uhu ka-dhālika.* His colleagues had to do so ('like that').

يجوز (لها) أنْ ترجع. *yajuz (laha) 'an tarji'.* She may return.

ألاّ *'allā* 'that ... not, not to' is the negative of أنْ:

أريد ألاّ تتداخل في هذا الأمر. *'urīd 'allā tatadākhal fī hādha l-'amr.* I want you not to interfere in this matter.

This last example expresses an indirect command, which we explore further in § 24.

The remaining conjunctions express purpose, and may be preceded by any verb which makes sense:

بقينا لكي يساعدنا زملاؤنا. *baqīna li-kay yusā'idana zumalā'una.* We stayed so that our colleagues might help us.

بقينا لنساعدهم. *baqīna li-nusā'idahum.*
We stayed so as to ('in order that we might') help them.

أسكت لئلاّ أتداخل. *'askut li-'allā 'atadākhal.*

I remain silent, so as not to ('so that I may not) interfere.

NB: حتّى *ḥatta* is also used with the past tense, in the meaning 'until':

بقيت\أبقى حتّى وصلوا. *baqīt/'abqa ḥatta waṣalū.*

I am staying until they have arrived./ I stayed until they arrived.

22. Jussive

The jussive tense (more correctly, the jussive mood of the present tense) expresses various forms of wish; it also has other uses.

Forming the jussive. The jussive is derived from the subjunctive; the only change from subjunctive to jussive is that the full-pronunciation subjunctive ending *-a* is dropped (i.e. *'aktuba*, *taktuba*, *yaktuba* and *naktuba* become *'aktub*, *taktub*, *yaktub* and *naktub*). Personal prefixes, and all other subjunctive endings, are unchanged. This formula is valid for sound and hamzated roots. The preambles to each set of tables in Part II explain the variants for other classes and sub-classes.

Wishes. In expressing wishes the jussive follows the conjunction

ل *li-* let (me, him etc.) ...

or one of its variants فل\ول *fa-l-, wa-l-* so let (me, him etc.) ...

All these are written with the jussive verb as one word:

لنذهب. *li-nadhhab.* Let us go.

تفضل أنْ يدخل فليدخل. *tufaḍḍil 'an yadkhul fa-l-yadkhul.*

You prefer that he come in, so have him come in.

A negative wish is expressed with لا *lā* + jussive:

لا نتداخل. *lā natadākhal.* Let us not interfere.

See also § 25 for another way of expressing wishes.

Negative in past time. See § 7. Except for كان and the other predicated verbs (§ 13), ما + past tense is a less preferred option to express the negative in past time. The preferred formula (which in a few cases is obligatory) is the particle لم *lam* + jussive. Examine:

لم أكتب الرسالة. لم أكتبها. *lam 'aktub ar-risāla. lam 'aktubha.*
I did not write the letter. I did not write it.

لم يحاول أنْ يساعدنا. *lam yuḥāwil 'an yusā'idana.*
He did not try to help us.

23. Imperative

The imperative or direct-command form ('do!', 'do not!') exists only in the 2nd persons. It is derived from the jussive (§ 22) as shown below.

Affirmative. To derive the affirmative imperative of a verb, take the appropriate 2nd-person form of the jussive. This form has the personal prefix ...تـ\...تو *ta-* , *tu-* or *tū-*. Then:

If the prefix is ...تو *tū-*, replace this with ...أو *'aw-*:

توقف *tūqif* IV you stop → أوقف *'awqif* stop

If the prefix is ...تـ *ta-* or *tu-*, remove this prefix. Then:

- if the resulting form begins with a single consonant + vowel, this is the imperative:

  تظلّ *taẓall* I you stay → ظلّ *ẓall* stay
  تعلّم *tu'allim* II you teach → علّم *'allim* teach
  تتذكّر *tatadhakkar* V you remember → تذكّر *tadhakkar* remember
  تترجم *tutarjim* IQ you translate → ترجم *tarjim* translate

- if the resulting form begins with two consonants or a doubled consonant, then add a prefix to make the imperative:
  - for Form IV, the prefix is ...أ *'a-*:

    ترسل *tursil* IV you send → أرسل *'arsil* send
  - for other than Form IV, look at the vowel following the middle root letter. Then:

    if this vowel is *-u-*, prefix a weak vowel ...ا *u-*:

    تكتب *taktub* I you write → اكتب *uktub* write

    if this vowel is other than *-u-*, prefix a weak vowel ...ا *i-*:

تقرأ *taqra'* I you read → اقرأ *iqra'* read

تتّخذ *tattákhidh* VIII you take → اتّخذ *ittákhidh* take

Negative. The negative imperative is simply لا *lā* + jussive form (with its personal prefix):

لا تعلّم\لا ترسل *lā tu'allim, lā tursil* do not teach/send

The forms shown are all masculine singular. The feminines, duals and plurals are all made similarly from the corresponding jussive form.

These rules apply to verbs with a consonant as final root letter. See the preambles in Part II for their use with final- and doubly weak verbs.

The written imperative as it stands above is found mainly in advertisements, instructions and invitations, or in correspondence, and then only with a limited number of verbs. Common examples:

اشرب اللبن. *ishrab al-laban.* Drink milk.

تفضّل\تفضّلي\تفضّلوا *tafaḍḍal/-ī/-ū* Please, be so kind

تفضّلوا بالحضور *tafaḍḍalū bi-l-ḥuḍūr*

Please attend ('Be so kind with the attendance').

افتح هنا. *iftaḥ huna.* Open here.

اذكر اسم الوالد. *udhkur ism al-wālid.*

Give ('Mention') (your) father's name.

It is often politer to use an indirect command (§ 21), with a subjunctive:

نرجو منكم ألاّ تدخّنوا. *narjū minkum 'allā tudakhkhinū.*

We request ('from') you not to smoke.

§ 22 examines wishes, which are a quasi-imperative form for the 1st and 3rd persons.

24. Indirect speech; statement, question, command

When the statement of another speaker is quoted verbatim, this is termed *direct speech*:

يقول "يرسل كاتبي الرسالة". *yaqūl "yursil kātibi r-risāla".*

He says "My clerk is sending the letter".

يقول "محاسبنا غائب". *yaqūl "muḥāsibuna ghā'ib".*

He says "Our accountant is absent".

It is commoner, however, in Arabic as in English, to paraphrase the speaker's words; this is *indirect speech*, also known as *reported speech*. In Arabic as in English, indirect speech falls into three types: indirect statement, indirect question and indirect command or request.

Indirect statement. English introduces an indirect statement with the conjunction 'that'; the Arabic conjunction is إنّ *'inna* after the verb قال يقول *qāla yaqūlu* I 'to say', and أنّ *'anna* after any other verb of reporting. We met إنّ in § 20 (nominal sentences); in the context of indirect statement both Arabic conjunctions translate into English as 'that'. In English we may often omit 'that'; we do not omit إنّ or أنّ . Both إنّ *'inna* and أنّ *'anna* 'that' are followed either by a noun subject in the accusative, or a pronoun subject in the form of a suffix. The clause beginning with either of them has the form of a nominal sentence. Examine first

يقول إنّ كاتبه يرسل الرسالة. *yaqūl 'inna kātibahu yursil ar-risāla.*

He says (that) his clerk is sending the letter.

يؤكّد أنّ محاسبهم غائب. *yu'akkid 'anna muḥāsibahum ghā'ib.*

He confirms that their accountant is absent.

Examine now

قال إنّ كاتبه يرسل الرسالة. *qāl 'inna kātibahu yursil ar-risāla.*

He said that his clerk was sending ('is sending') the letter.

أكّد أنّ محاسبهم غائب. *'akkad 'anna muḥāsibahum ghā'ib.*

He confirmed that their accountant was ('is') absent.

قال إنّ محاسبهم سيكون غائبًا. *qāl 'inna muḥāsibahum sa-yakūn ghā'iban.* He said their accountant would ('will') be absent.

In these the verb of speech is in the past, but the paraphrase remains in the tense or time-context used by the original speaker; Arabic does not have the English so-called 'sequence of tenses'. The sentence

أكّد أنّه أرسل الرسالة. *'akkad 'annahu 'arsal ar-risāla.*
would mean 'He confirmed that his clerk had (previously) sent ...'

قالت إنّها مريضة. *qālat 'innaha marīḍa.*
She said she was ill.

أعلنوا أنّهم (قد) أرسلوا الرسالة. *'a'lanū 'annahum (qad) 'arsalu r-risāla.* They announced that they had (already) sent the letter.

Indirect question. For indirect questions soliciting the answer 'yes' or 'no', the conjunction is إذا *'idha* or ما إذا *mā 'idha* 'whether'. The timing of the original direct question is again respected:

سأل (ما) إذا ندرس التقرير. *sa'al (mā) 'idha nadrus at-taqrīr.*
He asked whether we were studying the report.

سأل (ما) إذا درسنا التقرير. *sa'al (mā) 'idha darasna t-taqrīr.*
He asked whether we had studied the report.

'or not' in questions is أم لا *'am lā:*

سأل (ما) إذا سندرس التقرير أم لا. *sa'al (mā) 'idha sa-nadrus at-taqrīr 'am lā.* He asked whether we would study the report or not.

English often uses 'if' in the meaning 'whether' ('He asked if we were studying ...'); avoid confusing it with 'if' in a *condition* ('If it rains ...'), studied in § 25, which also uses إذا but with different tenses.

For other than 'yes/no' answers, the indirect question begins with the appropriate interrogative word or expression:

سألتهم أين يسكنون. *sa'altuhum 'ayna yaskunūna.*
I asked them where they lived.

قل لنا ما هو عنوانك. *qul la-na mā huwa 'unwānuka.*
Tell ('to') us what your adress is.

The rules of indirect statement and indirect question apply not only after a verb of expression, but also after a verb of perception:

اعتقدت أنّها غائبة. *a'taqadt 'annaha ghā'iba.*
I believed she was absent.

لم أعرف إذا هي غائبة. *lam 'a'rif 'idha hiya ghā'iba.*

I did not know whether she was absent.

Indirect command. See § 21. The conjunction أنْ 'that, to' or its negative ألاّ *'allā*, is used to introduce an indirect command or indirect request. The verb after أنْ goes into the subjunctive, irrespective of the time-sequence:

طلبنا من الكاتب أنْ يكتبها. *ṭalabna min al-kātib 'an yaktubaha.* We asked the clerk to write it. ('We asked from the clerk that he write it.')

سنرجو منهم ألاّ يحضروا. *sa-narjū minhum 'allā yaḥḍurū.* We shall ask them not to attend.

Direct command is the imperative, for which see § 23.

When the verb of speech takes a prepositional thing-object (§ 12), the preposition is usually retained, and immediately precedes the conjunction introducing the clause of indirect speech:

أخبرنا بأنّه سيكون غائبًا. *'akhbarna bi-'annahu sa-yakūn ghā'iban.* He informed us that he would be absent.

25. Condition and concession

A conditional sentence is one which states in what circumstances the statement will be true. A concessional sentence states the opposite, i.e. *despite* what circumstances the statement will be true. In Arabic, both types follow a similar structure which determines the form of the verb to be used. Both types of sentence consist of two parts: the *condition* or *concession*, and the main statement, which we can call the *response.* The condition or concession mostly precedes the response.

Conditions. We distinguish between *real* conditions, which are likely or at least possible ('if it rains ...') and *unreal* conditions which are impossible or at least unlikely ('if we had known ...').

Real conditions. In real conditions, the condition is introduced by إذا *'idha* 'if' and has verbal-sentence structure. The verb of the condition stands in a past tense (past, continuous past or pluperfect), whatever the time-sequence:

إذا كان ممكنًا ... *'idha kān mumkinan ...*

If it is possible ...

إذا عرفه زملاؤنا ... *'idha 'arafahu zumalā'una ...*

If our colleagues know (it) ...

When the response follows the condition, strict grammar demands that it, too, has its verb in a past tense or the imperative; but in modern practice the choice is free. If the response does however begin with anything other than a past- or present-tense verb, it is introduced by ف *fa-* for a verbal sentence, or by فإنّ *fa-'inna* for a nominal sentence (including an equation). Both particles are best translated (if at all) with 'then':

إذا كان ممكنًا ساعدتك. *'idha kān mumkinan sā'adtuka.*

إذا كان ممكنًا أساعدك. *'idha kān mumkinan 'usā'iduka.*

If it is possible, I will help you.

إذا عرفه زملاؤنا فليخبرونا. *'idha 'arafahu zumalā'una fa-l-yukhbirūna.* If our colleagues know ('it'), let them tell us.

إذا عرفتموه فأخبرونا. *'idha 'araftumūhu fa-'akhbirūna.*

If you know ('it'), tell us.

إذا وافقت أنت فإنّي مستعدّ أيضًا. *'idha wāfaqt 'anta fa-'innī musta'idd 'ayḍan.* If you agree, I am ready too.

Although the verb ليس *laysa* 'not to be' (§ 13) is past-tense in form, it is introduced by ف *fa-*:

إذا رفضه فليس الوضع سهلاً. *'idha rafaḍahu fa-laysa l-waḍ' sahlan.* Ih he refuses ('it') the situation is not easy.

Negative. To negate a real condition, only the formula لم *lam* + jussive is used in the condition. For the verb in the response the choice is free, except that ما + past is avoided, and we must begin with ف:

إذا لم يعرفه فلا يستطيع أنْ يخبرنا. *'idha lam ya'rifhu fa-lā yastaṭī' 'an yukhbirana.* If he does not know he cannot tell us.

Unreal condition. Unreal conditions are introduced by لو *law* 'if' and most often have verbal-sentence structure, or (far less commonly) لو أنّ *law 'anna* with nominal-sentence structure. With either structure, its verb stands in a past tense (past, continuous past or pluperfect), whatever the time-sequence:

لو كان ممكنًا ... *law kān mumkinan ...*
If it were possible ...

لو عرفوه ... *law ʿarafūhu ...* If they knew (it) ...

لو كانوا (قد) عرفوه ... *law kānū (qad) ʿarafūhu ...*
If they had known (it) ...

When the response follows the condition, it is introduced by the particle ل *la-*, which is translated (or not) as is ف *fa-*. The response has the structure of a verbal sentence, and its verb also stands in a past tense:

لو كان ممكنًا لساعدتك. *law kān mumkinan la-sāʿadtuka.*
If it were possible I would help you.

لو عرفه زملاؤنا لأخبرونا. *law ʿarafahu zumalā'una la-'akhbarūna.* If our colleagues knew, they would tell us.

لو كان زملاؤنا قد عرفوه لأخبرونا\لكانوا أخبرونا. *law kān zumalā'una qad ʿarafūhu la-'akhbarūna/la-kānū 'akhbarūna.*
If our colleagues had known, they would have told us.

If the response precedes the condition (real or unreal), only the rules concerning the condition apply. Everything else is free, and ف\ل are dropped:

سأساعدك إذا كان ممكنًا. *sa-'usāʿiduka 'idha kān mumkinan.*
I will help you if it is possible.

أخبرونا إذا عرفتموه. *'akhbirūna 'idha ʿaraftumūhu.*
Tell us, if you know.

إنّي\أنا مستعدّ أيضًا إذا وافقت أنت. *'innī/'ana mustaʿidd 'ayḍan 'idha wāfaqt 'anta.* I am ready too, if you agree.

ساعدتك لو كان ممكنًا. *sāʿadtuka law kān mumkinan.*

I would help you if it were possible.

أخبرنا زملاؤنا لو عرفوه. *'akhbarana zumalā'una law arafūhu.*

Our colleagues would tell us if they knew.

كان زملاؤنا أخبرونا لو كانوا قد عرفوه.

kān zumalā'una 'akhbarūna law kānū qad arafūhu.

Our colleagues would have told us if they had known.

Negative. A negative unreal condition has لم + jussive; any negative response has ما + past:

لو لم يعرفه لما استطاع أنْ يخبرنا. *law lam ya'rifhu la-mā staṭā' 'an yukhbirana.* If he did not know he could not tell us.

إنْ *'in*. Another introductory conjunction for conditions is إنْ *'in* 'if'. It is now seldom used except in set expressions like

إنْ شاء الله *'in shā 'allāh* (commonly pronounced *'inshalla*) ('if God wills') hopefully, I/we hope

إنْ وجد(ت) *'in wujid(at)*

if (there is/are/were) any

This last expression has a passive verb (see § 26) meaning 'it was/they were found'; وجد *wujid* is used for a masculine subject, وجدت *wujidat* for a feminine singular or inanimate plural subject.

Such set expressions are now hardly seen as conditionals, and the conditional rules are not necessarily applied to the rest of the sentence.

إنْ شاء الله ينجح مؤتمركم. *'inshalla yanjaḥ mu'támarukum.*

I hope your conference is successful.

اذكر أمثالاً إنْ وجدت. *udhkur 'amthālan 'in wujidat.*

Give ('mention') examples, if any.

Wishes. In § 22 we studied one form of wish. A wish can also be expressed with an unreal condition without its response:

لو كنّا أغنياء! *law kunna 'aghniyā'!*

If (only) we were rich!

لو لم يعملوا هكذا. *law lam ya'malū hākadha.*

If (only)/ I wish they wouldn't do that.

Concession. Concessive sentences follow the conditional rules. The concessive clause is introduced by

حتّى ولو *ḥatta wa-law* even if	من *man* whoever
مهما *mahmā* whatever	أينما *'aynamā* wherever
كيفما *kayfamā* however	متى ما *mata mā* whenever
مع أنّ *ma' 'anna* although	

حتّى ولو *ḥatta wa-law* follows the rules of unreal conditions. Concessions following the '-ever' conjunctions are usually real. مع أنّ *ma' 'anna* is real, with a nominal sentence (which may be an equation):

حتّى ولو عرفه لما أخبرنا. *hatta wa-law 'arafahu la-mā 'akhbarana.* Even if he knew he would not tell us.

كيفما عملت فلن ينجح. *kayfamā 'amilt fa-lan yanjaḥ.* Whatever ('However') you do, it will not succeed.

مع أنّها صغيرة فهي شاطرة. *ma' 'annaha ṣaghīra fa-hiya shāṭira.* Although (she is) young she is clever.

26. Passive voice

The verbs shown so far (other than وجد(ت) *wujid(at)* in § 25) are in the *active voice*, in which the subject of the verb performs the action or experiences the situation. We have also the *passive voice*, in which the subject of the verb *undergoes* the action. An example of a passive verb in English is 'The letter *was written* yesterday.'

We have already encountered the passive participle in § 17. The passive verb exists theoretically in all persons and all tenses, but in practice only the 3rd persons singular of the past and present tenses are commonly met and need to be learned. Further, passive forms differ from the active only in the vowels of the root and of the personal prefixes; the personal endings and the consonants of the personal prefixes remain. Since the vowelling is regular, even for Form I, the passive is most easily learned from the passive principal parts of the model verbs:

Form, Verb	Passive principal parts	he/it is/was ...
I كتب	كُتب يُكتب *kutiba yuktabu*	written
II علّم	عُلّم يعلّم *'ullima yu'allamu*	taught
III ناسب	نوسب يناسب *nūsiba yunāsabu*	suited
IV أرسل	أُرسل يُرسل *'ursila yursalu*	sent
V تدخّل	تُعلّم يُتعلّم *tu'ullima yuta'allamu*	learnt
VI تظاهر	تُظوهر يُتظاهر *tuẓūhira yutaẓāharu°*	(see fifth
VII انسحب	أُنسحب يُنسحب *unsúḥiba yunsáḥabu°*	indent below)
VIII اقترح	أُقترح يُقترح *uqtúriha yuqtárahu*	proposed
IX	(no passive voice)	
X استقبل	أُستقبل يُستقبل *ustuqbila yustaqbalu*	received

Note:

- The typical vowel pattern is *u-i* for the first principal part and *u-a* for the second principal part in Forms I and IV, with variants for Forms with more syllables. Forms III and VI have ...و... *-ū-* in the first principal part (where the corresponding active form has ...ا... *-ā-*). This pattern is valid as it stands for sound and hamzated roots, and valid with some modification for other classes (doubled and weak). Details are given in each preamble in Part II.
- Where a final short vowel is dropped in short pronunciation in the active verb, so it is in the corresponding passive:

  كُتب التقرير أمس. *kutib at-taqrīr 'ams.*

  The report was written yesterday.

- All the persons can be derived from these parts, but in practice the only ones commonly found apart from هو are the هي and هم forms, with personal ending ...ت *-at* and ...وا *-ū* respectively in the past tense, and prefix-plus-ending تُـ.. *tu...u* and يُـ..ون *yu...ūna* respectively in the present tense (the ending being added to the final root letter in all examples). The tables in Part II give only the principal parts.

- Often the alphabetical spelling of a verb does not make clear whether it is active or passive. At best, the context tells us; but even newsreaders make mistakes, despite the fact that news bulletins and articles often have a passive. Examine:

أكّد أمس أنّ ...

As it stands, this could be read *'akkad 'ams 'anna ...* 'He confirmed yesterday that ...' but could equally well be *'ukkid 'ams 'anna ...* 'It was confirmed yesterday that ...'. Sometimes in text the first syllable is pointed ُ... where this identifies a passive. We have used this device in some examples in this paragraph.

- The passive verb takes the personal form shown below:
  - For a verb whose active voice has a direct object, that object becomes the subject of the passive verb, which agrees with it following the normal rules:

    كُتبت\تُكتب الرسالات اليوم. *kutibat/tuktab ar-risālāt al-yawm.* The letters were/are being written today.

  - For a verb whose active voice has a prepositional object, the passive verb is always in the هو form, and the preposition appears with it. There is no explicit subject:

    يُشكّ في أرقامنا. *yushakk fī 'arqāmina.* ('It is doubted in our figures.') Our figures are doubted/in doubt./There is doubt about our figures.

  - For a verb whose active form has no object (typically, many in Forms V and VI, and all those in Form VII), the passive, where used at all, is *impersonal* in meaning, and is found only in the هو form. There is no explicit subject:

    تُظوهر *tuẓūhir* VI ('it was demonstrated') there was a demonstration

يُتظاهر *yutaẓāhar* VI there is a demonstration

أُنسحب\يُنسحب *unsúḥib/yunsáḥab* VII

there was/is a withdrawal, someone was/is withdrawing

Impersonal passives are marked ° in Part II.

- Verbs taking a predicate (§ 13) are not used in the passive.
- The passive participle is explained in § 17. The passive voice has no verbal noun (§ 18) and no imperative (§ 23).

Instrument and Agent. An Arabic sentence with a passive form may state the *instrument* (i.e. the thing) by which the action of the verb is effected:

كُتب التقرير بواسطة برنامج آخر. *kutib at-taqrīr bi-wāsiṭat barnāmaj 'ākhar*. The report was written with ('by means of') another program.

But Arabic avoids stating the *agent* (= the person) responsible. If the agent is to be stated, it is better to use an active verb. The English sentence 'The report was written by the accountant.' is better cast as 'The accountant wrote the report.':

كتب المحاسب التقرير. *katab al-muḥāsib at-taqrīr.*

This is standard Arabic grammar. In the press, however, we may find a passive with an agent in imitation of Western practice, using the compound preposition من قبل *mij qibali* 'on the part of' to express the concept 'by'. You need to know this construction, but you are recommended to use it only sparingly, if at all:

كُتب التقرير من قبل المحاسب. *kutib at-taqrīr min qibal al-muḥāsib.*

There is, there are. In § 2 we studied the reversed equation as a means of expressing English 'There is/are ...'. We can alternatively express this idea with a verbal sentence beginning with the passive verb form يوجد *yūjad* 'there is' (masculine singular, literally 'it is found') or its feminine + inanimate plural form توجد *tūjad* 'there is/are':

يوجد كمبيوتر في المكتب. *yūjad kambyūtir fi-l-maktab.*

There is a computer in the office.

توجد مكتبة في الجامعة. *tūjad maktaba fi-l-jāmi'a.*
There is a library in the university.

لا يوجد مطعم في المصنع. *lā yūjad maṭ'am fi-l-maṣna'.*
There is no restaurant in the factory.

The negative لا يوجد *lā yūjad* is also used for 'nil' in statistical tables.

27. Further expressions with the verbal noun

The verbal noun, explained in § 18, is a versatile derivative. Here are further important uses of it.

Replacing a clause. A verbal noun is often used (and sometimes preferred) instead of a clause containing أنْ + subjunctive verb (§ 21). Examine these pairs:

يستطيع أنْ يترجم الرسالة. *yastaṭī' 'an yutarjim ar-risāla.*
He can translate the letter.

يستطيع ترجمة الرسالة. *yastaṭī' tarjamat ar-risāla.* ('He is capable of the translation of the letter') He can translate the letter.

أريد أنْ يرسلوها اليوم. *'urīd 'an yursilūha l-yawm.*
I want them to send it today.

أريد إرسالها اليوم. *'urīd 'irsālaha l-yawm.*
I want it sent ('I want its despatch') today.

إنّنا نحاول أنْ نساعدكم. *'innana nuḥāwil 'an nusā'idakum.*
We are trying to help you.

إنّنا نحاول مساعدتكم. *'innana nuḥāwil musā'adatakum.*
('We are attempting your assistance') We are trying to help you.

يجب أنْ يقرأ الوثيقة. *yajib 'an yaqra' al-wathīqa.*
He must read the document.

يجب عليه قراءة الوثيقة. *yajib 'alayhi qirā'at al-wathīqa.*
('Reading the document is necessary for him') He must read the document.

Compound verbal expressions. It is common, especially in journalists' Arabic, to use an all-purpose verb + a definite verbal noun instead of a simple 'operative' verb. Useful examples are:

- قام يقوم ب *qāma yaqūmu* I *bi-* 'to undertake' + definite verbal noun, with active meaning. Compare:

  أرسل\يرسل\سيرسل الوثيقة. *'arsal/yursil/sa-yursil al-wathīqa.* He has sent/is sending/will send the document.

  with: قام بإرسال الوثيقة. *qām bi-'irsāl al-wathīqa.* He has sent ('undertaken the sending of') the document.

  يقوم بإرسال الوثيقة. *yaqūm bi-'irsāl al-wathīqa.* He is sending ('undertaking the sending of') the document.

  سيقوم بإرسال الوثيقة. *sa-yaqūm bi-'irsāl al-wathīqa.* He will send ('undertake the sending of') the document.

- جرى يجري *jara yajrī* I 'to flow, to proceed' + definite verbal noun, to show a continuous passive action. Compare:

  دُرست\تُدرس الويثقة يومين. *durisat/tudras al-wathīqa yawmayn.* The document was/is being studied for two days.

  جرت\تجري دراسة الوثيقة يومين. *jarat/tajrī dirāsat al-wathīqa yawmayn.* The document was/is being studied ('the study of the document was/is proceeding') for two days.

  This construction can also be used with general meaning, i.e. non-passive and impersonal, when there is no object. Compare:

  يحفرون الآن. *yaḥfirūna l-'ān.* They are drilling now.

  يجري الحفر الآن. *yajri l-ḥafr al-'ān.* 'The drilling is proceeding now.' They are/There is drilling now.

- تمّ يتمّ *tamma yatimmu* I 'to be concluded' + definite verbal noun, to denote a completed past passive action. The past tense of تمّ is commonest in this construction. Examine these pairs:

  دُرس الاقتراح خلال الاجتماع. *duris al-iqtirāḥ khilāl*

al-ijtimāʿ. The proposal was studied during the meeting.

تمّت دراسة الاقتراح خلال الاجتماع. *tammat dirāsat al-iqtirāḥ khilāl al-ijtimāʿ*. The proposal was studied during the meeting.

حُفِرت البئر هذه السنة. *ḥufirat al-biʾr hādhihi s-sana.*

تمّ حفر البئر هذه السنة. *tamm ḥafr al-biʾr hādhihi s-sana.*

The well was drilled this year.

The last two constructions shown are common and effective ways of avoiding the use of a passive verb. Do not interpret them too literally.

Absolute object. Examine:

بحثوا الموضوع بحثًا طويلاً. *baḥathu l-mawḍūʿ baḥthan ṭawīlan*. They discussed the subject at length ('a long discussion').

درست الوثيقة دراسةً عميقةً. *darast al-wathīqa dirāsatan ʿamīqatan*. I studied the document in depth ('a deep study').

This construction is called the *absolute object*. In it we have a verb followed by an expression consisting of the corresponding verbal noun + adjective, the expression modifying the verb in the manner of an adverb. The verbal noun and its adjective are in the indefinite accusative case, given full pronunciation in this usage.

The verbal noun may instead be part of a possessive expression (where we do not of course find the endings *-an, -atan*):

اهتمّت به اهتمام أمّ. *ihtammat bihi htimām ʾumm.*

She cared for him like a mother ('cared for him a mother's care').

The verbal noun is more common in Arabic than is its equivalent expression in English. Correct and effective use of the verbal noun gives style to your Arabic.

Part II – Verb Tables

Sound

The sound class is the most regular class. It is the only class in which all the root letters are always of the same kind. The root letters of a sound verb are also different from each other, and are consonants, i.e. not ا, و or ي. ء *hamza* is also excluded. Hamzated verbs follow the sound pattern, but we study them separately because of the occasional spelling difficulty.

All quadriliteral verbs either belong to the sound class or follow the sound pattern.

The information given in §§ 7, 8, 17, 18, 21-23 and 26 relates to sound verbs, which can be seen as the basis of the verbal system. Verbs in other classes follow the sound patterns except where noted otherwise.

Within the sound class, the doubled final root letter of the rare Form IX (no. **22**) follows the pattern of the doubled verbs. See page 123.

1 | **I** | كَتَبَ يَكْتُبُ *kataba yaktubu* to write هـ | **كتب**

ACTIVE	**Present**	*yaktubu*			**Past** *kataba*
نَكْتُبُ		أَكْتُبُ	كَتَبْنَا		كَتَبْتُ
تَكْتُبُونَ	تَكْتُبَانِ	تَكْتُبُ	كَتَبْتُمْ	كَتَبْتُمَا	كَتَبْتَ
تَكْتُبْنَ	تَكْتُبَانِ	تَكْتُبِينَ	كَتَبْتُنَّ	كَتَبْتُمَا	كَتَبْتِ
يَكْتُبُونَ	يَكْتُبَانِ	يَكْتُبُ	كَتَبُوا	كَتَبَا	كَتَبَ
يَكْتُبْنَ	تَكْتُبَانِ	تَكْتُبُ	كَتَبْنَ	كَتَبَتَا	كَتَبَتْ

	Jussive	*yaktub*			**Subjunctive** *yaktuba*
نَكْتُبْ		أَكْتُبْ	نَكْتُبَ		أَكْتُبَ
تَكْتُبُوا	تَكْتُبَا	تَكْتُبْ	تَكْتُبُوا	تَكْتُبَا	تَكْتُبَ
تَكْتُبْنَ	تَكْتُبَا	تَكْتُبِي	تَكْتُبْنَ	تَكْتُبَا	تَكْتُبِي
يَكْتُبُوا	يَكْتُبَا	يَكْتُبْ	يَكْتُبُوا	يَكْتُبَا	يَكْتُبَ
يَكْتُبْنَ	تَكْتُبَا	تَكْتُبْ	يَكْتُبْنَ	تَكْتُبَا	تَكْتُبَ

Verbal Noun كِتَابَة *kitāba* **Participle** كَاتِب *kātib*

Imperative أُكْتُبْ، أُكْتُبِي؛ أُكْتُبَا؛ أُكْتُبُوا، أُكْتُبْنَ *uktub, -ī; -ā; -ū, -na*

PASSIVE **Present** يُكْتَبُ *yuktabu* **Past** كُتِبَ *kutiba*

Participle مَكْتُوب *maktūb*

II كَتَّبَ to make (s.o) write ه 7; III كَاتَبَ to correspond with ه 9;

IV/X أَكْتَبَ\اِسْتَكْتَبَ to dictate to ه، هـ 10/23;

VI تَكَاتَبَ to correspond with e.o. 12; VII اِنْكَتَبَ to subscribe 13;

VIII اِكْتَتَبَ to copy, to subscribe (money) هـ 14

كِتَابَة writing كِتَاب ج كُتُب book مَكْتُوب ج مَكَاتِيب letter

كِتَابَةً in writing كِتَابِي written, textual مَكْتَب ج مَكَاتِب office, desk

كَاتِبَة (f.)، كَاتِب ج كُتَّاب (m.) clerk مَكْتَبَة ج مَكَاتِب library, bookshop

2 | I | عَرَفَ يعْرِفُ *'arafa ya'rifu* to know ه هـ | عرف

ACTIVE	**Present**	*ya'rifu*		**Past**	*'arafa*
نَعْرِفُ		أعْرِفُ	عَرَفْنَا		عَرَفْتُ
تَعْرِفُونَ	تَعْرِفَانِ	تَعْرِفُ	عَرَفْتُمْ	عَرَفْتُمَا	عَرَفْتَ
تَعْرِفْنَ	تَعْرِفَانِ	تَعْرِفِينَ	عَرَفْتُنَّ	عَرَفْتُمَا	عَرَفْتِ
يَعْرِفُونَ	يَعْرِفَانِ	يَعْرِفُ	عَرَفُوا	عَرَفَا	عَرَفَ
يَعْرِفْنَ	تَعْرِفَانِ	تَعْرِفُ	عَرَفْنَ	عَرَفَتَا	عَرَفَتْ
	Jussive	*ya'rif*		**Subjunctive**	*ya'rifa*
نَعْرِفْ		أعْرِفْ	نَعْرِفَ		أعْرِفَ
تَعْرِفُوا	تَعْرِفَا	تَعْرِفْ	تَعْرِفُوا	تَعْرِفَا	تَعْرِفَ
تَعْرِفْنَ	تَعْرِفَا	تَعْرِفِي	تَعْرِفْنَ	تَعْرِفَا	تَعْرِفِي
يَعْرِفُوا	يَعْرِفَا	يَعْرِفْ	يَعْرِفُوا	يَعْرِفَا	يَعْرِفَ
يَعْرِفْنَ	تَعْرِفَا	تَعْرِفْ	يَعْرِفْنَ	تَعْرِفَا	تَعْرِفَ

Vb. Noun مَعْرِفَة ج مَعَارِف *ma'rifa ma'ārif* **Participle** عَارِف *'ārif*

Imperative اِعْرِفْ، اِعْرِفِي؛ اِعْرِفَا؛ اِعْرِفُوا، اِعْرِفْنَ *i'rif, -ī; -ā; -ū, -na*

PASSIVE **Present** يُعْرَفُ *yu'rafu* **Past** عُرِفَ *'urifa*

Participle مَعْرُوف *ma'rūf*

II عَرَّفَ to acquaint with ه هـ 7; V تَعَرَّفَ to become acquainted with ب\إلى 11; VI تَعَارَفَ to get to know e.o. ب 12; VIII اِعْتَرَفَ to acknowledge هـ , to recognise ب 14; X اِسْتَعْرَفَ to perceive هـ 23

تَعْرِيف announcement تَعْرِيف ج تَعَارِيف tariff عَارِف ب familiar with

اِعْتِرَاف confession مَعْرُوف well-known; kindness

مُعْتَرَف به approved تَعَرُّف ب\إلى acquaintance with

عِرْفَان الفَضْل gratitude اِعْمَل مَعْرُوفًا be so kind as to

اِعْتِرَافًا ب in recognition of من المَعْرُوف أنّ it is well known that

3 | **I** | جَمَعَ يَجْمَعُ *jama'a yajma'u* to collect هـ | **جمع**

ACTIVE Present *yajma'u*			**Past** *jama'a*		
نَجْمَعُ		أَجْمَعُ	جَمَعْنَا		جَمَعْتُ
تَجْمَعُونَ	تَجْمَعَانِ	تَجْمَعُ	جَمَعْتُمْ	جَمَعْتُمَا	جَمَعْتَ
تَجْمَعْنَ	تَجْمَعَانِ	تَجْمَعِينَ	جَمَعْتُنَّ	جَمَعْتُمَا	جَمَعْتِ
يَجْمَعُونَ	يَجْمَعَانِ	يَجْمَعُ	جَمَعُوا	جَمَعَا	جَمَعَ
يَجْمَعْنَ	تَجْمَعَانِ	تَجْمَعُ	جَمَعْنَ	جَمَعَتَا	جَمَعَتْ

Jussive *yajma'*			**Subjunctive** *yajma'a*		
نَجْمَعْ		أَجْمَعْ	نَجْمَعَ		أَجْمَعَ
تَجْمَعُوا	تَجْمَعَا	تَجْمَعْ	تَجْمَعُوا	تَجْمَعَا	تَجْمَعَ
تَجْمَعْنَ	تَجْمَعَا	تَجْمَعِي	تَجْمَعْنَ	تَجْمَعَا	تَجْمَعِي
يَجْمَعُوا	يَجْمَعَا	يَجْمَعْ	يَجْمَعُوا	يَجْمَعَا	يَجْمَعَ
يَجْمَعْنَ	تَجْمَعَا	تَجْمَعْ	يَجْمَعْنَ	تَجْمَعَا	تَجْمَعَ

Verbal Noun جَمْع *jam'* **Participle** جَامِع *jāmi'*

Impv. اِجْمَعْ، اِجْمَعِي؛ اِجْمَعَا؛ اِجْمَعُوا، اِجْمَعْنَ *ijma', -ī; -ā; -ū, -na*

PASSIVE Present يُجْمَعُ *yujma'u* **Past** جُمِعَ *jumi'a*

Participle مَجْمُوع *majmū'*

II جَمَّعَ to assemble هـ 7; IV أَجْمَعَ to agree on على 10;

V تَجَمَّعَ to congregate 11; VIII اِجْتَمَعَ to have a meeting 14;

X اِسْتَجْمَعَ to summarise هـ 23

جَمْع collection, addition, plural (يوم الـ)جُمْعَة Friday جَمَاعَة group

جَامعة university, community مَجْمُوع total اِجْتِمَاع meeting

جَمْعِية association جَمِيع all (plural) تَجْمِيع assembly (of parts)

جَمْعِيًا altogether اِجْتِمَاعِي social

اِسْتَجْمَعَ قُوتَهُ\أَفْكَارَهُ to gather one's strength/thoughts

4 | **I** | عَمِلَ يَعْمَلُ *'amila ya'malu* to do, make هـ, to work | **عمل**

ACTIVE Present *ya'malu*			**Past** *'amila*		
نَعْمَلُ		أَعْمَلُ	عَمِلْنَا		عَمِلْتُ
تَعْمَلُونَ	تَعْمَلَانِ	تَعْمَلُ	عَمِلْتُمْ	عَمِلْتُمَا	عَمِلْتَ
تَعْمَلْنَ	تَعْمَلَانِ	تَعْمَلِينَ	عَمِلْتُنَّ	عَمِلْتُمَا	عَمِلْتِ
يَعْمَلُونَ	يَعْمَلَانِ	يَعْمَلُ	عَمِلُوا	عَمِلَا	عَمِلَ
يَعْمَلْنَ	تَعْمَلَانِ	تَعْمَلُ	عَمِلْنَ	عَمِلَتَا	عَمِلَتْ

Jussive *ya'mal*			**Subjunctive** *ya'mala*		
نَعْمَلْ		أَعْمَلْ	نَعْمَلَ		أَعْمَلَ
تَعْمَلُوا	تَعْمَلَا	تَعْمَلْ	تَعْمَلُوا	تَعْمَلَا	تَعْمَلَ
تَعْمَلْنَ	تَعْمَلَا	تَعْمَلِي	تَعْمَلْنَ	تَعْمَلَا	تَعْمَلِي
يَعْمَلُوا	يَعْمَلَا	يَعْمَلْ	يَعْمَلُوا	يَعْمَلَا	يَعْمَلَ
يَعْمَلْنَ	تَعْمَلَا	تَعْمَلْ	يَعْمَلْنَ	تَعْمَلَا	تَعْمَلَ

Vb. Noun عَمَل ج أَعْمَال *'amal 'a'māl* **Participle** عَامِل *'āmil*

Imperative اِعْمَلْ، اِعْمَلِي؛ اِعْمَلَا؛ اِعْمَلُوا، اِعْمَلْنَ *i'mal, -ī; -ā; -ū, -na*

PASSIVE **Present** يُعْمَل *yu'malu* **Past** عُمِلَ *'umila*

Participle مَعْمُول *ma'mūl*

III عَامَلَ to treat ه 9; IV أَعْمَلَ to put to work هـ 10;

VI تَعَامَلَ to do business with e.o. 12; X اِسْتَعْمَلَ to use هـ 23

عَمَل ج أَعْمَال work — عَمَلِي practical — عَامِل effective

عَامِل ج عُمَّال worker — عَامِل ج أَوَامِل factor — عَمَلِيَة operation

مَعْمَل ج مَعَامِل laboratory — عُمْلَة currency — تَعَامُل transaction

عَمِيل ج عُمَلَاء client — نَقَابَة عُمَّال trade union

قُوَة عَامِلَة workforce — عَمَلاً ب in accordance with

سُوء المُعَامَلَة illtreatment — حِزْب العُمَّال Labour Party

5 | I | كَثُرَ يَكْثُرُ *kathura yakthuru* to be numerous | كثر

ACTIVE	**Present** *yakthuru*			**Past** *kathura*	
نَكْثُرُ		أَكْثُرُ	كَثُرْنَا		كَثُرْتُ
تَكْثُرُونَ	تَكْثُرَانِ	تَكْثُرُ	كَثُرْتُمْ	كَثُرْتُمَا	كَثُرْتَ
تَكْثُرْنَ	تَكْثُرَانِ	تَكْثُرِينَ	كَثُرْتُنَّ	كَثُرْتُمَا	كَثُرْتِ
يَكْثُرُونَ	يَكْثُرَانِ	يَكْثُرُ	كَثُرُوا	كَثُرَا	كَثُرَ
يَكْثُرْنَ	تَكْثُرَانِ	تَكْثُرُ	كَثُرْنَ	كَثُرَتَا	كَثُرَتْ

	Jussive *yakthur*			**Subjunctive** *yakthura*	
نَكْثُرْ		أَكْثُرْ	نَكْثُرَ		أَكْثُرَ
تَكْثُرُوا	تَكْثُرَا	تَكْثُرْ	تَكْثُرُوا	تَكْثُرَا	تَكْثُرَ
تَكْثُرْنَ	تَكْثُرَا	تَكْثُرِي	تَكْثُرْنَ	تَكْثُرَا	تَكْثُرِي
يَكْثُرُوا	يَكْثُرَا	يَكْثُرْ	يَكْثُرُوا	يَكْثُرَا	يَكْثُرَ
يَكْثُرْنَ	تَكْثُرَا	تَكْثُرْ	يَكْثُرْنَ	تَكْثُرَا	تَكْثُرَ

Verbal Noun كَثْرَة *kathra* **Participle** كَاثِر *kāthir*

Imperative أُكْثُرْ، أُكْثُرِي؛ أُكْثُرَا؛ أُكْثُرُوا، أُكْثُرْنَ *ukthur, -ī; -ā; -ū, -na*

PASSIVE not used

I/III كَثَرَ يَكْثُرُ (كَثْر) \ كَاثَرَ to outnumber هـ 1/9; II/IV كَثَّرَ \ أَكْثَرَ to increase هـ 7/10; VI تَكَاثَرَ to band together against على 12; X اِسْتَكْثَرَ to find excessive هـ 23

كَثِير ج كِثَار much (adj.), many كَثِيراً greatly كُثْر abundance

أَكْثَرِيَة majority أَكْثَر من more than الأَكْثَر (the) most

كَثِيراً مَا often أَكْثَر إِفَادَةً more useful أَحْسَن بِكَثِير much better

على الأَكْثَر at most أَكْثَر من ذلك moreover

يُكَثِّر \ كَثَّر خَيْرَكَ (God) bless you أَكْثَرِيَة مُطْلَقَة absolute majority

6 **IQ** تَرْجَمَ يُتَرْجِمُ *tarjama yutarjimu* to translate هـ **ترجم**

ACTIVE	**Present** *yutarjimu*			**Past**	*tarjama*
نُتَرْجِمُ		أُتَرْجِمُ	تَرْجَمْنَا		تَرْجَمْتُ
تُتَرْجِمُونَ	تُتَرْجِمَانِ	تُتَرْجِمُ	تَرْجَمْتُمْ	تَرْجَمْتُمَا	تَرْجَمْتَ
تُتَرْجِمْنَ	تُتَرْجِمَانِ	تُتَرْجِمِينَ	تَرْجَمْتُنَّ	تَرْجَمْتُمَا	تَرْجَمْتِ
يُتَرْجِمُونَ	يُتَرْجِمَانِ	يُتَرْجِمُ	تَرْجَمُوا	تَرْجَمَا	تَرْجَمَ
يُتَرْجِمْنَ	تُتَرْجِمَانِ	تُتَرْجِمُ	تَرْجَمْنَ	تَرْجَمَتَا	تَرْجَمَتْ
	Jussive	*yutarjim*	**Subjunctive**		*yutarjima*
نُتَرْجِمْ		أُتَرْجِمْ	نُتَرْجِمَ		أُتَرْجِمَ
تُتَرْجِمُوا	تُتَرْجِمَا	تُتَرْجِمْ	تُتَرْجِمُوا	تُتَرْجِمَا	تُتَرْجِمَ
تُتَرْجِمْنَ	تُتَرْجِمَا	تُتَرْجِمِي	تُتَرْجِمْنَ	تُتَرْجِمَا	تُتَرْجِمِي
يُتَرْجِمُوا	يُتَرْجِمَا	يُتَرْجِمْ	يُتَرْجِمُوا	يُتَرْجِمَا	يُتَرْجِمَ
يُتَرْجِمْنَ	تُتَرْجِمَا	تُتَرْجِمْ	يُتَرْجِمْنَ	تُتَرْجِمَا	تُتَرْجِمَ

Verbal Noun تَرْجَمَة ج تَرَاجِم *tarjama tarājim*

Participle مُتَرْجِم *mutarjim*

Imperative تَرْجِمْ، تَرْجِمِي؛ تَرْجِمَا؛ تَرْجِمُوا، تَرْجِمْنَ *tarjim, -ī; -ā; -ū, -na*

PASSIVE **Present** يُتَرْجَمُ *yutarjamu* **Past** تُرْجِمَ *turjima*

Participle مُتَرْجَم *mutarjam*

تَرْجَمَة ج تَرَاجِم translation, preface

مُتَرْجِم translator

تَرْجُمَان ج تَرَاجِيم\تَرَاجِمَة translator

مُتَرْجَم translated

7 II عَلَّمَ يُعَلِّمُ *'allama yu'allimu* to teach ه هـ **علم**

ACTIVE	**Present** *yu'allimu*			**Past** *'allama*	
نُعَلِّمُ		أُعَلِّمُ	عَلَّمْنَا		عَلَّمْتُ
تُعَلِّمُونَ	تُعَلِّمَانِ	تُعَلِّمُ	عَلَّمْتُمْ	عَلَّمْتُمَا	عَلَّمْتَ
تُعَلِّمْنَ	تُعَلِّمَانِ	تُعَلِّمِينَ	عَلَّمْتُنَّ	عَلَّمْتُمَا	عَلَّمْتِ
يُعَلِّمُونَ	يُعَلِّمَانِ	يُعَلِّمُ	عَلَّمُوا	عَلَّمَا	عَلَّمَ
يُعَلِّمْنَ	تُعَلِّمَانِ	تُعَلِّمُ	عَلَّمْنَ	عَلَّمَتَا	عَلَّمَتْ

	Jussive *yu'allim*			**Subjunctive** *yu'allima*	
نُعَلِّمْ		أُعَلِّمْ	نُعَلِّمَ		أُعَلِّمَ
تُعَلِّمُوا	تُعَلِّمَا	تُعَلِّمْ	تُعَلِّمُوا	تُعَلِّمَا	تُعَلِّمَ
تُعَلِّمْنَ	تُعَلِّمَا	تُعَلِّمِي	تُعَلِّمْنَ	تُعَلِّمَا	تُعَلِّمِي
يُعَلِّمُوا	يُعَلِّمَا	يُعَلِّمْ	يُعَلِّمُوا	يُعَلِّمَا	يُعَلِّمَ
يُعَلِّمْنَ	تُعَلِّمَا	تُعَلِّمْ	يُعَلِّمْنَ	تُعَلِّمَا	تُعَلِّمَ

Verbal Noun تَعْلِيم *ta'līm* **Participle** مُعَلِّم *mu'allim*

Imperative عَلِّمْ، عَلِّمِي؛ عَلِّمَا؛ عَلِّمُوا، عَلِّمْنَ *'allim, -ī; -ā; -ū, -na*

PASSIVE **Present** يُعَلَّمُ *yu'allamu* **Past** عُلِّمَ *'ullima*

Participle مُعَلَّم *mu'allam*

I عَلِمَ يَعْلَمُ (عِلْم ج عُلُوم) to know ه هـ\ب 4; IV أَعْلَمَ to notify هـ\ب 10; V تَعَلَّمَ to learn هـ 11; X اِسْتَعْلَمَ to enquire of s.o. about ه\عن هـ 23

عِلْم ج عُلُوم knowledge, science عِلْمِي scientific تَعْلِيم teaching

عَالِم ج عُلَمَاء scholar مُعَلِّم\مُعَلِّمَة teacher تَعْلِيمِي educational

مُتَعَلِّم apprentice إِعْلَام notification مَعْلُوم of course

مَعْلُومَات (pl.) information اِسْتِعْلَام inquiry عَلَامَة (تِجَارِيَّة) (trade) mark

عَالَم ج عَوَالِم world تَعْلِيمَات (pl.) instructions على عِلْم ب aware of

8 | IIQ | تَزَلْزَلَ يَتَزَلْزَلُ *tazalzala yatazalzalu* to quake (said literally of the earth, or figuratively otherwise) | زلزل

ACTIVE Present *yatazalzalu*			**Past** *tazalzala*		
نَتَزَلْزَلُ		أَتَزَلْزَلُ	تَزَلْزَلْنَا		تَزَلْزَلْتُ
تَتَزَلْزَلُونَ	تَتَزَلْزَلَانِ	تَتَزَلْزَلُ	تَزَلْزَلْتُمْ	تَزَلْزَلْتُمَا	تَزَلْزَلْتَ
تَتَزَلْزَلْنَ	تَتَزَلْزَلَانِ	تَتَزَلْزَلِينَ	تَزَلْزَلْتُنَّ	تَزَلْزَلْتُمَا	تَزَلْزَلْتِ
يَتَزَلْزَلُونَ	يَتَزَلْزَلَانِ	يَتَزَلْزَلُ	تَزَلْزَلُوا	تَزَلْزَلَا	تَزَلْزَلَ
يَتَزَلْزَلْنَ	تَتَزَلْزَلَانِ	تَتَزَلْزَلُ	تَزَلْزَلْنَ	تَزَلْزَلَتَا	تَزَلْزَلَتْ

Jussive *yatazalzal*			**Subjunctive** *yatazalzala*		
نَتَزَلْزَلْ		أَتَزَلْزَلْ	نَتَزَلْزَلَ		أَتَزَلْزَلَ
تَتَزَلْزَلُوا	تَتَزَلْزَلَا	تَتَزَلْزَلْ	تَتَزَلْزَلُوا	تَتَزَلْزَلَا	تَتَزَلْزَلَ
تَتَزَلْزَلْنَ	تَتَزَلْزَلَا	تَتَزَلْزَلِي	تَتَزَلْزَلْنَ	تَتَزَلْزَلَا	تَتَزَلْزَلِي
يَتَزَلْزَلُوا	يَتَزَلْزَلَا	يَتَزَلْزَلْ	يَتَزَلْزَلُوا	يَتَزَلْزَلَا	يَتَزَلْزَلَ
يَتَزَلْزَلْنَ	تَتَزَلْزَلَا	تَتَزَلْزَلْ	يَتَزَلْزَلْنَ	تَتَزَلْزَلَا	تَتَزَلْزَلَ

Verbal Noun تَزَلْزُلٌ *tazalzul* **Participle** مُتَزَلْزِل *mutazalzil*

Impv. تَزَلْزَلْ، تَزَلْزَلِي؛ تَزَلْزَلَا؛ تَزَلْزَلُوا، تَزَلْزَلْنَ *tazalzal, -ī; -ā; -ū, -na*

PASSIVE does not exist in Form IIQ

IQ زَلْزَلَ يُزَلْزِلُ (زِلْزَال) to shake 6 ه ه

زَلْزَلَة ج زَلَازِل earthquake

زَلْزَال\زِلْزَال convulsion, earthquake

زِلْزَالِي seismic

عِلْم الزِلْزَال seismology

اِسْتِكْشَاف\مَسْح زِلْزَالِي seismic exploration/survey

9 **III** نَاسَبَ يُنَاسِبُ *nāsaba yunāsibu* to suit ه هـ **نسب**

ACTIVE **Present** *yunāsibu* **Past** *nāsaba*

نَاسَبْتُ		نَاسَبْنَا
نَاسَبْتَ	نَاسَبْتُمَا	نَاسَبْتُمْ
نَاسَبْتِ	نَاسَبْتُمَا	نَاسَبْتُنَّ
نَاسَبَ	نَاسَبَا	نَاسَبُوا
نَاسَبَتْ	نَاسَبَتَا	نَاسَبْنَ

أُنَاسِبُ		نُنَاسِبُ
تُنَاسِبُ	تُنَاسِبَانِ	تُنَاسِبُونَ
تُنَاسِبِينَ	تُنَاسِبَانِ	تُنَاسِبْنَ
يُنَاسِبُ	يُنَاسِبَانِ	يُنَاسِبُونَ
تُنَاسِبُ	تُنَاسِبَانِ	يُنَاسِبْنَ

Subjunctive *yunāsiba*

أُنَاسِبَ		نُنَاسِبَ
تُنَاسِبَ	تُنَاسِبَا	تُنَاسِبُوا
تُنَاسِبِي	تُنَاسِبَا	تُنَاسِبْنَ
يُنَاسِبَ	يُنَاسِبَا	يُنَاسِبُوا
تُنَاسِبَ	تُنَاسِبَا	يُنَاسِبْنَ

Jussive *yunāsib*

أُنَاسِبْ		نُنَاسِبْ
تُنَاسِبْ	تُنَاسِبَا	تُنَاسِبُوا
تُنَاسِبِي	تُنَاسِبَا	تُنَاسِبْنَ
يُنَاسِبْ	يُنَاسِبَا	يُنَاسِبُوا
تُنَاسِبْ	تُنَاسِبَا	يُنَاسِبْنَ

Verbal Noun مُنَاسَبَة *munāsaba* **Participle** مُنَاسِب *munāsib*

Imperative نَاسِبْ، نَاسِبِي؛ نَاسِبَا؛ نَاسِبُوا ، نَاسِبْنَ *nāsib, -ī; -ā; -ū, -na*

PASSIVE **Present** يُنَاسَبُ *yunāsabu* **Past** نُوسِبَ *nūsiba*

Participle مُنَاسَب *munāsab*

I نَسَبَ يَنْسُبُ\يَنْسِبُ (نِسْبَة) to correlate with, relate to إلى هـ 1/ 2;

VI تَنَاسَبَ to (be) relate(d) to e.o. 12;

VIII اِنْتَسَبَ to belong to إلى 14; X اِسْتَنْسَبَ to approve of هـ 23

مُنَاسَبَة suitability, occasion, opportunity مُنَاسِب appropriate

نِسْبَة relationship, ratio نِسْبَة مِئَوِيَة percentage نِسْبِي relative (adj.)

نِسْبِيَة relativity بِالنِسْبَة إلى relative to مُتَنَاسِب proportionate

مُنْتَسِب associate(d) مَنْسُوب ألى pertaining to اِنْتِسَاب affiliation

10 **IV** أَخْبَرَ يُخْبِرُ *'akhbara yukhbiru* to inform ه ب **خبر**

ACTIVE

Past *'akhbara*

أَخْبَرْتُ		أَخْبَرْنَا
أَخْبَرْتَ	أَخْبَرْتُمَا	أَخْبَرْتُمْ
أَخْبَرْتِ	أَخْبَرْتُمَا	أَخْبَرْتُنَّ
أَخْبَرَ	أَخْبَرَا	أَخْبَرُوا
أَخْبَرَتْ	أَخْبَرَتَا	أَخْبَرْنَ

Present *yukhbiru*

أُخْبِرُ		نُخْبِرُ
تُخْبِرُ	تُخْبِرَانِ	تُخْبِرُونَ
تُخْبِرِينَ	تُخْبِرَانِ	تُخْبِرْنَ
يُخْبِرُ	يُخْبِرَانِ	يُخْبِرُونَ
تُخْبِرُ	تُخْبِرَانِ	يُخْبِرْنَ

Subjunctive *yukhbira*

أُخْبِرَ		نُخْبِرَ
تُخْبِرَ	تُخْبِرَا	تُخْبِرُوا
تُخْبِرِي	تُخْبِرَا	تُخْبِرْنَ
يُخْبِرَ	يُخْبِرَا	يُخْبِرُوا
تُخْبِرَ	تُخْبِرَا	يُخْبِرْنَ

Jussive *yukhbir*

أُخْبِرْ		نُخْبِرْ
تُخْبِرْ	تُخْبِرَا	تُخْبِرُوا
تُخْبِرِي	تُخْبِرَا	تُخْبِرْنَ
يُخْبِرْ	يُخْبِرَا	يُخْبِرُوا
تُخْبِرْ	تُخْبِرَا	يُخْبِرْنَ

Verbal Noun إِخْبَار *'ikhbār* **Participle** مُخْبِر *mukhbir*

Imperative أَخْبِرْ، أَخْبِرِي؛ أَخْبِرَا؛ أَخْبِرُوا، أَخْبِرْنَ *'akhbir, -ī; -ā; -ū, -na*

PASSIVE **Present** يُخْبَرُ *yukhbaru* **Past** أُخْبِرَ *'ukhbira*

Participle مُخْبَر *mukhbar*

I (خُبْر\خِبْرَة) خَبَرَ يَخْبُرُ to test, experience هـ 1;

II خَبَّرَ to notify ه ب 7; VIII اِخْتَبَرَ to do research into هـ 14;

X اِسْتَخْبَرَ to enquire of s.o. about ه عن 23

خَبَر ج أَخْبَار news, message خِبْرَة experience مُخْبِر reporter

اِخْتِبَار test خَبِير ج خُبَرَاء expert مُخْتَبَر laboratory

اِخْتِبَارِي experimental اِسْتِخْبَار inquiry مُخَابَرَة communication

ذو خِبْرَة experienced خِدْمَة مُخَابَرَات intelligence service

11 | V | تَدَخَّلَ يَتَدَخَّلُ *tadakhkhala yatadakhkhalu* | **دخل**

to intervene/interfere in في

ACTIVE Present *yatadakhkhalu*

أتَدَخَّلُ		نَتَدَخَّلُ
تَتَدَخَّلُ	تَتَدَخَّلانِ	تَتَدَخَّلُونَ
تَتَدَخَّلِينَ	تَتَدَخَّلانِ	تَتَدَخَّلْنَ
يَتَدَخَّلُ	يَتَدَخَّلانِ	يَتَدَخَّلُونَ
تَتَدَخَّلُ	تَتَدَخَّلانِ	يَتَدَخَّلْنَ

Past *tadakhkhala*

تَدَخَّلْتُ		تَدَخَّلْنَا
تَدَخَّلْتَ	تَدَخَّلْتُمَا	تَدَخَّلْتُمْ
تَدَخَّلْتِ	تَدَخَّلْتُمَا	تَدَخَّلْتُنَّ
تَدَخَّلَ	تَدَخَّلاَ	تَدَخَّلُوا
تَدَخَّلَتْ	تَدَخَّلَتَا	تَدَخَّلْنَ

Jussive *yatadakhkhal*

أتَدَخَّلْ		نَتَدَخَّلْ
تَتَدَخَّلْ	تَتَدَخَّلاَ	تَتَدَخَّلُوا
تَتَدَخَّلِي	تَتَدَخَّلاَ	تَتَدَخَّلْنَ
يَتَدَخَّلْ	يَتَدَخَّلاَ	يَتَدَخَّلُوا
تَتَدَخَّلْ	تَتَدَخَّلاَ	يَتَدَخَّلْنَ

Subjunctive *yatadakhkhala*

أتَدَخَّلَ		نَتَدَخَّلَ
تَتَدَخَّلَ	تَتَدَخَّلاَ	تَتَدَخَّلُوا
تَتَدَخَّلِي	تَتَدَخَّلاَ	تَتَدَخَّلْنَ
يَتَدَخَّلَ	يَتَدَخَّلاَ	يَتَدَخَّلُوا
تَتَدَخَّلَ	تَتَدَخَّلاَ	يَتَدَخَّلْنَ

Verbal Noun تَدَخُّل *tadakhkhul* **Participle** مُتَدَخِّل *mutadakhkhil*

Impv. تَدَخَّلْ، تَدَخَّلِي؛ تَدَخَّلاَ؛ تَدَخَّلُوا، تَدَخَّلْنَ *tadakhkhal, -ī; -ā; -ū, -na*

PASSIVE° **Present** يُتَدَخَّلُ *yutadakhkhalu* **Past** تُدُخِّلَ *tudukhkhila*

Participle مُتَدَخَّل *mutadakhkhal*

I دَخَلَ يَدْخُلُ (دُخُول) to enter هـ\في\إلى 1;

II دَخَّلَ to insert هـ 7; IV أدْخَلَ to admit ه هـ 10;

VI تَدَاخَلَ 12 = V تَدَخَّلَ **11**

دَخْل income — دَاخِل inside (noun, prep.) — دَاخِلِي internal

دُخُول entrance (act) — مَدْخَل ج مَدَاخِل entrance (place) — دَخِيلَة core

تَدَخُّل\تَدَاخُل intervention, interference — عَدَم التَدَخُّل non-intervention

حَرْب دَاخِلِيَّة civil war — وِزَارَة (الأُمُور) الدَاخِلِيَّة Ministry of the Interior

12 | **VI** | تَظَاهَرَ يَتَظَاهَرُ *tazāhara yatazāharu* | **ظهر**

to demonstrate against على, to feign ب

ACTIVE Present *yatazāharu*			**Past** *tazāhara*		
نَتَظَاهَرُ		أَتَظَاهَرُ	تَظَاهَرْنَا		تَظَاهَرْتُ
تَتَظَاهَرُونَ	تَتَظَاهَرَانِ	تَتَظَاهَرُ	تَظَاهَرْتُمْ	تَظَاهَرْتُمَا	تَظَاهَرْتَ
تَتَظَاهَرْنَ	تَتَظَاهَرَانِ	تَتَظَاهَرِينَ	تَظَاهَرْتُنَّ	تَظَاهَرْتُمَا	تَظَاهَرْتِ
يَتَظَاهَرُونَ	يَتَظَاهَرَانِ	يَتَظَاهَرُ	تَظَاهَرُوا	تَظَاهَرَا	تَظَاهَرَ
يَتَظَاهَرْنَ	تَتَظَاهَرَانِ	تَتَظَاهَرُ	تَظَاهَرْنَ	تَظَاهَرَتَا	تَظَاهَرَتْ
Jussive *yatazāhar*			**Subjunctive** *yatazāhara*		
نَتَظَاهَرْ		أَتَظَاهَرْ	نَتَظَاهَرَ		أَتَظَاهَرَ
تَتَظَاهَرُوا	تَتَظَاهَرَا	تَتَظَاهَرْ	تَتَظَاهَرُوا	تَتَظَاهَرَا	تَتَظَاهَرَ
تَتَظَاهَرْنَ	تَتَظَاهَرَا	تَتَظَاهَرِي	تَتَظَاهَرْنَ	تَتَظَاهَرَا	تَتَظَاهَرِي
يَتَظَاهَرُوا	يَتَظَاهَرَا	يَتَظَاهَرْ	يَتَظَاهَرُوا	يَتَظَاهَرَا	يَتَظَاهَرَ
يَتَظَاهَرْنَ	تَتَظَاهَرَا	تَتَظَاهَرْ	يَتَظَاهَرْنَ	تَتَظَاهَرَا	تَتَظَاهَرَ

Verbal Noun تَظَاهُر *tazāhur* **Participle** مُتَظَاهِر *mutazāhir*

Impv. تَظَاهَرْ، تَظَاهَرِي؛ تَظَاهَرَا؛ تَظَاهَرُوا، تَظَاهَرْنَ *tazāhar, -ī; -ā; -ū, -na*

PASSIVE° **Present** يُتَظَاهَرُ *yutazāharu* **Past** تُظُوهِرَ *tuzūhira*

Participle مُتَظَاهَر *mutazāhar*

I ظَهَرَ يَظْهَرُ (ظُهُور) to appear اً 3;

II ظَهَّرَ to endorse (e.g. a document) هـ 7;

IV/X أَظْهَرَ\اسْتَظْهَرَ to show ه هـ 10/23

ظُهْر ج أَظْهَار noon ظُهُور appearance ظَهْر ج ظُهُور\أَظْهُر back (noun)

مَظْهَر ج مَظَاهِر appearance الظَّاهِر (لي) أَنَّ it seems (to me) that

مُظَاهَرَة demonstration (political) مُتَظَاهِر demonstrator

تَظَاهُر demonstration, dissemblance ظَاهِرَة ج ظَوَاهِر phenomenon

13 | VII | انْقَلَبَ يَنْقَلِبُ *inqálaba yanqálibu* to be overturned | قلب

ACTIVE **Present** *yanqálibu*			**Past** *inqálaba*		
نَنْقَلِبُ		أَنْقَلِبُ	انْقَلَبْنَا		انْقَلَبْتُ
تَنْقَلِبُونَ	تَنْقَلِبَانِ	تَنْقَلِبُ	انْقَلَبْتُمْ	انْقَلَبْتُمَا	انْقَلَبْتَ
تَنْقَلِبْنَ	تَنْقَلِبَانِ	تَنْقَلِبِينَ	انْقَلَبْتُنَّ	انْقَلَبْتُمَا	انْقَلَبْتِ
يَنْقَلِبُونَ	يَنْقَلِبَانِ	يَنْقَلِبُ	انْقَلَبُوا	انْقَلَبَا	انْقَلَبَ
يَنْقَلِبْنَ	تَنْقَلِبَانِ	تَنْقَلِبُ	انْقَلَبْنَ	انْقَلَبَتَا	انْقَلَبَتْ

Jussive *yanqálib*			**Subjunctive** *yanqáliba*		
نَنْقَلِبْ		أَنْقَلِبْ	نَنْقَلِبَ		أَنْقَلِبَ
تَنْقَلِبُوا	تَنْقَلِبَا	تَنْقَلِبْ	تَنْقَلِبُوا	تَنْقَلِبَا	تَنْقَلِبَ
تَنْقَلِبْنَ	تَنْقَلِبَا	تَنْقَلِبِي	تَنْقَلِبْنَ	تَنْقَلِبَا	تَنْقَلِبِي
يَنْقَلِبُوا	يَنْقَلِبَا	يَنْقَلِبْ	يَنْقَلِبُوا	يَنْقَلِبَا	يَنْقَلِبَ
يَنْقَلِبْنَ	تَنْقَلِبَا	تَنْقَلِبْ	يَنْقَلِبْنَ	تَنْقَلِبَا	تَنْقَلِبَ

Verbal Noun انْقِلاَب *inqilāb* **Participle** مُنْقَلِب *munqálib*

Impv. انْقَلِبْ، انْقَلِبِي؛ انْقَلِبَا؛ انْقَلِبُوا، انْقَلِبْنَ *inqálib, -ī; -ā; -ū, -na*

PASSIVE° **Present** يُنْقَلَبُ *yunqálabu* **Past** أُنْقُلِبَ *unqúliba*

Participle مُنْقَلَب *munqálab*

I/II قَلَبَ يَقْلِبُ (قَلْب)\قَلَّبَ to invert, reverse ﻫ 2/7;

V تَقَلَّبَ to be inverted/reversed 11

قَلْب ج قُلُوب heart قَلْبِي cardiac, cordial قَلْبِيًّا cordially

قَلاَّب\مُنْقَلِب variable انْقِلاَب coup d'état تَقَلُّب inversion

قَالِب ج قَوَالِب mould, matrix ضعيف\لطيف القَلْب faint-/kindhearted

المُنْقَلَب الصَيْفِي\الشَتَوِي Tropic of Cancer/Capricorn

مَقْلُوب inverted انْقَلَبَ ظَهْرًا لِبَطْن to be turned upside down

14 **VIII** اِعْتَبَرَ يَعْتَبِرُ *i'tábara ya'tábiru* to consider هـ , to esteem ه **عبر**

ACTIVE **Present** *ya'tábiru* — **Past** *i'tábara*

Present (pl.)	Present (du.)	Present (sg.)	Past (pl.)	Past (du.)	Past (sg.)
نَعْتَبِرُ		أَعْتَبِرُ	اِعْتَبَرْنَا		اِعْتَبَرْتُ
تَعْتَبِرُونَ	تَعْتَبِرَانِ	تَعْتَبِرُ	اِعْتَبَرْتُمْ	اِعْتَبَرْتُمَا	اِعْتَبَرْتَ
تَعْتَبِرْنَ	تَعْتَبِرَانِ	تَعْتَبِرِينَ	اِعْتَبَرْتُنَّ	اِعْتَبَرْتُمَا	اِعْتَبَرْتِ
يَعْتَبِرُونَ	يَعْتَبِرَانِ	يَعْتَبِرُ	اِعْتَبَرُوا	اِعْتَبَرَا	اِعْتَبَرَ
يَعْتَبِرْنَ	تَعْتَبِرَانِ	تَعْتَبِرُ	اِعْتَبَرْنَ	اِعْتَبَرَتَا	اِعْتَبَرَتْ

Jussive *ya'tábir* — **Subjunctive** *ya'tábira*

Jussive (pl.)	Jussive (du.)	Jussive (sg.)	Subjunctive (pl.)	Subjunctive (du.)	Subjunctive (sg.)
نَعْتَبِرْ		أَعْتَبِرْ	نَعْتَبِرَ		أَعْتَبِرَ
تَعْتَبِرُوا	تَعْتَبِرَا	تَعْتَبِرْ	تَعْتَبِرُوا	تَعْتَبِرَا	تَعْتَبِرَ
تَعْتَبِرْنَ	تَعْتَبِرَا	تَعْتَبِرِي	تَعْتَبِرْنَ	تَعْتَبِرَا	تَعْتَبِرِي
يَعْتَبِرُوا	يَعْتَبِرَا	يَعْتَبِرْ	يَعْتَبِرُوا	يَعْتَبِرَا	يَعْتَبِرَ
يَعْتَبِرْنَ	تَعْتَبِرَا	تَعْتَبِرْ	يَعْتَبِرْنَ	تَعْتَبِرَا	تَعْتَبِرَ

Verbal Noun اِعْتِبَار *i'tibār* **Participle** مُعْتَبِر *mu'tábir*

Impv. اِعْتَبِرْ، اِعْتَبِرِي؛ اِعْتَبِرَا؛ اِعْتَبِرُوا، اِعْتَبِرْنَ *i'tábir, -ī; -ā; -ū, -na*

PASSIVE **Present** يُعْتَبَرُ *yu'tábaru* **Past** أُعْتُبِرَ *u'túbira*

Participle مُعْتَبَر *mu'tábar*

I (عَبْر) عَبَرَ يَعْبُرُ to cross هـ 1; II عَبَّرَ to express عن 7

عَبْرَ across, beyond — عَبْر\عُبُور crossing

عِبْرِي Hebrew — اِعْتِبَار consideration, esteem — عِبْرَة admonition, precept

عِبَارَة expression — تَعْبِير عن expression of

مُعَبِّر عن expressive of — مَعْبَر ج مَعَابِر crossing-point

في كُلِّ اِعْتِبَار in every respect — اِعْتِبَاراً من with effect from

اِعْتِبَاراً لِ in view of — أَخَذَ بِعَيْنِ الاِعْتِبَار to take into account

15 | VIII | اتَّبَعَ يَتَّبِعُ *ittába'a yattábi'u* to follow ه ه , to comply with ه | **تبع**

ACTIVE	**Present** *yattábi'u*			**Past** *ittába'a*	
نَتَّبِعُ		أَتَّبِعُ	اتَّبَعْنَا		اتَّبَعْتُ
تَتَّبِعُونَ	تَتَّبِعَانِ	تَتَّبِعُ	اتَّبَعْتُمْ	اتَّبَعْتُمَا	اتَّبَعْتَ
تَتَّبِعْنَ	تَتَّبِعَانِ	تَتَّبِعِينَ	اتَّبَعْتُنَّ	اتَّبَعْتُمَا	اتَّبَعْتِ
يَتَّبِعُونَ	يَتَّبِعَانِ	يَتَّبِعُ	اتَّبَعُوا	اتَّبَعَا	اتَّبَعَ
يَتَّبِعْنَ	تَتَّبِعَانِ	تَتَّبِعُ	اتَّبَعْنَ	اتَّبَعَتَا	اتَّبَعَتْ

	Jussive *yattábi'*			**Subjunctive** *yattábi'a*	
نَتَّبِعْ		أَتَّبِعْ	نَتَّبِعَ		أَتَّبِعَ
تَتَّبِعُوا	تَتَّبِعَا	تَتَّبِعْ	تَتَّبِعُوا	تَتَّبِعَا	تَتَّبِعَ
تَتَّبِعْنَ	تَتَّبِعَا	تَتَّبِعِي	تَتَّبِعْنَ	تَتَّبِعَا	تَتَّبِعِي
يَتَّبِعُوا	يَتَّبِعَا	يَتَّبِعْ	يَتَّبِعُوا	يَتَّبِعَا	يَتَّبِعَ
يَتَّبِعْنَ	تَتَّبِعَا	تَتَّبِعْ	يَتَّبِعْنَ	تَتَّبِعَا	تَتَّبِعَ

Verbal Noun اِتِّبَاع *ittibā'* **Participle** مُتَّبِع *muttábi'*

Imperative اِتَّبِعْ، اِتَّبِعِي؛ اِتَّبِعَا؛ اِتَّبِعُوا، اِتَّبِعْنَ *ittábi', -ī; -ā; -ū, -na*

PASSIVE **Present** يُتَّبَعُ *yuttába'u* **Past** أُتُّبِعَ *uttúbi'a*

Participle مُتَّبَع *muttába'*

I (تَبَعٌ\تَبَاعَة) تَبِعَ يَتْبَعُ = 4 اِتَّبَعَ VIII **15**; III تَابَعَ to follow up ه 9;

IV أَتْبَعَ to subordinate s.o to s.o ه ه 10;

VI تَتَابَعَ to occur successively 12; X اِسْتَتْبَعَ to entail ه 23

تَبِعَة consequence تَبِع ج تَبَعَة subsequent تَابِعِيَّة nationality

تَبَع subordinate, subordination تَتَابُع succession تِبَاعًا successively

اِتِّبَاع compliance with مُتَّبَع complied with اِتِّبَاعًا ل in compliance with

16 | **VIII** | اِدَّحَرَ يَدَّحِرُ *iddáḥara yaddáḥiru* to be repelled, to collapse | **دحر**

ACTIVE

Present *yaddáḥiru*			**Past** *iddáḥara*		
نَدَّحِرُ		أَدَّحِرُ	اِدَّحَرْنَا		اِدَّحَرْتُ
تَدَّحِرُونَ	تَدَّحِرَانِ	تَدَّحِرُ	اِدَّحَرْتُمْ	اِدَّحَرْتُمَا	اِدَّحَرْتَ
تَدَّحِرْنَ	تَدَّحِرَانِ	تَدَّحِرِينَ	اِدَّحَرْتُنَّ	اِدَّحَرْتُمَا	اِدَّحَرْتِ
يَدَّحِرُونَ	يَدَّحِرَانِ	يَدَّحِرُ	اِدَّحَرُوا	اِدَّحَرَا	اِدَّحَرَ
يَدَّحِرْنَ	تَدَّحِرَانِ	تَدَّحِرُ	اِدَّحَرْنَ	اِدَّحَرَتَا	اِدَّحَرَتْ

Jussive *yaddáḥir*			**Subjunctive** *yaddáḥira*		
نَدَّحِرْ		أَدَّحِرْ	نَدَّحِرَ		أَدَّحِرَ
تَدَّحِرُوا	تَدَّحِرَا	تَدَّحِرْ	تَدَّحِرُوا	تَدَّحِرَا	تَدَّحِرَ
تَدَّحِرْنَ	تَدَّحِرَا	تَدَّحِرِي	تَدَّحِرْنَ	تَدَّحِرَا	تَدَّحِرِي
يَدَّحِرُوا	يَدَّحِرَا	يَدَّحِرْ	يَدَّحِرُوا	يَدَّحِرَا	يَدَّحِرَ
يَدَّحِرْنَ	تَدَّحِرَا	تَدَّحِرْ	يَدَّحِرْنَ	تَدَّحِرَا	تَدَّحِرَ

Verbal Noun اِدِّحَار *iddiḥār* **Participle** مُدَّحِر *muddáḥir*

Imperative اِدَّحِرْ، اِدَّحِرِي؛ اِدَّحِرَا؛ اِدَّحِرُوا، اِدَّحِرْنَ *iddáḥir, -ī; -ā; -ū, -na*

PASSIVE none

I (دَحْر) دَحَرَ يَدْحَرُ to repel ه 3

مَدْحُور repelled, expelled

اِدِّحَار collapse

اِنْدِحَار rout, ruin

17 **VIII** اِزْدَحَمَ يَزْدَحِمُ *izdáḥama yazdáḥimu* to throng with بِ **زحم**

ACTIVE

Past *izdáḥama*

اِزْدَحَمْتُ		اِزْدَحَمْنَا
اِزْدَحَمْتَ	اِزْدَحَمْتُمَا	اِزْدَحَمْتُمْ
اِزْدَحَمْتِ	اِزْدَحَمْتُمَا	اِزْدَحَمْتُنَّ
اِزْدَحَمَ	اِزْدَحَمَا	اِزْدَحَمُوا
اِزْدَحَمَتْ	اِزْدَحَمَتَا	اِزْدَحَمْنَ

Present *yazdáḥimu*

أَزْدَحِمُ		نَزْدَحِمُ
تَزْدَحِمُ	تَزْدَحِمَانِ	تَزْدَحِمُونَ
تَزْدَحِمِينَ	تَزْدَحِمَانِ	تَزْدَحِمْنَ
يَزْدَحِمُ	يَزْدَحِمَانِ	يَزْدَحِمُونَ
تَزْدَحِمُ	تَزْدَحِمَانِ	يَزْدَحِمْنَ

Subjunctive *yazdáḥima*

أَزْدَحِمَ		نَزْدَحِمَ
تَزْدَحِمَ	تَزْدَحِمَا	تَزْدَحِمُوا
تَزْدَحِمِي	تَزْدَحِمَا	تَزْدَحِمْنَ
يَزْدَحِمَ	يَزْدَحِمَا	يَزْدَحِمُوا
تَزْدَحِمَ	تَزْدَحِمَا	يَزْدَحِمْنَ

Jussive *yazdáḥim*

أَزْدَحِمْ		نَزْدَحِمْ
تَزْدَحِمْ	تَزْدَحِمَا	تَزْدَحِمُوا
تَزْدَحِمِي	تَزْدَحِمَا	تَزْدَحِمْنَ
يَزْدَحِمْ	يَزْدَحِمَا	يَزْدَحِمُوا
تَدَّحِرْ	تَزْدَحِمَا	يَزْدَحِمْنَ

Verbal Noun اِزْدِحَام *izdiḥām* **Participle** مُزْدَحِم *muzdáḥim*

Imperative اِزْدَحِمْ، اِزْدَحِمِي؛ اِزْدَحِمَا؛ اِزْدَحِمُوا، اِزْدَحِمْنَ
izdáḥim, -ī; -ā; -ū, -na

PASSIVE none

I/III زَحَمَ يَزْحَمُ (زَحْم)\زَاحَمَ to jostle ه 3/9; VI تَزَاحَمَ to crowd together 12

زَحْم\زِحَام\مُزْدَحَم\اِزْدِحَام throng — مُزَاحَمَة\تَزَاحُم competition

مُزَاحِم rival — مُزْدَحِم crowded

18 VIII **اِصْطَنَعَ يَصْطَنِعُ** *iṣṭána'a yaṣṭáni'u* **صنع**

to manufacture هـ

ACTIVE

Past *iṣṭána'a*

اِصْطَنَعْتُ		اِصْطَنَعْنَا
اِصْطَنَعْتَ	اِصْطَنَعْتُمَا	اِصْطَنَعْتُمْ
اِصْطَنَعْتِ	اِصْطَنَعْتُمَا	اِصْطَنَعْتُنَّ
اِصْطَنَعَ	اِصْطَنَعَا	اِصْطَنَعُوا
اِصْطَنَعَتْ	اِصْطَنَعَتَا	اِصْطَنَعْنَ

Present *yaṣṭáni'u*

أَصْطَنِعُ		نَصْطَنِعُ
تَصْطَنِعُ	تَصْطَنِعَانِ	تَصْطَنِعُونَ
تَصْطَنِعِينَ	تَصْطَنِعَانِ	تَصْطَنِعْنَ
يَصْطَنِعُ	يَصْطَنِعَانِ	يَصْطَنِعُونَ
تَصْطَنِعُ	تَصْطَنِعَانِ	يَصْطَنِعْنَ

Subjunctive *yaṣṭáni'a*

أَصْطَنِعَ		نَصْطَنِعَ
تَصْطَنِعَ	تَصْطَنِعَا	تَصْطَنِعُوا
تَصْطَنِعِي	تَصْطَنِعَا	تَصْطَنِعْنَ
يَصْطَنِعَ	يَصْطَنِعَا	يَصْطَنِعُوا
تَصْطَنِعَ	تَصْطَنِعَا	يَصْطَنِعْنَ

Jussive *yaṣṭáni'*

أَصْطَنِعْ		نَصْطَنِعْ
تَصْطَنِعْ	تَصْطَنِعَا	تَصْطَنِعُوا
تَصْطَنِعِي	تَصْطَنِعَا	تَصْطَنِعْنَ
يَصْطَنِعْ	يَصْطَنِعَا	يَصْطَنِعُوا
تَصْطَنِعْ	تَصْطَنِعَا	يَصْطَنِعْنَ

Verbal Noun اِصْطِنَاع *iṣṭinā'* **Participle** مُصْطَنِع *muṣṭáni'*

Imperative اِصْطَنِعْ، اِصْطَنِعِي؛ اِصْطَنِعَا؛ اِصْطَنِعُوا، اِصْطَنِعْنَ

iṣṭáni', -ī; -ā; -ū, -na

PASSIVE **Present** يُصْطَنَعُ *yuṣṭána'u* **Past** أُصْطُنِعَ *uṣṭúni'a*

Participle مُصْطَنَع *muṣṭána'*

I صَنَعَ يَصْنَعُ (صَنْع\صُنْع) to contrive ه 3; II صَنَّعَ to industrialise هـ 7;

V تَصَنَّعَ to feign هـ 11; X اِسْتَصْنَعَ to cause to be made هـ 23

صَنْع\صُنْع production صَنْعِي synthetic صِنَاعَة craft, industry

صِنَاعِي\مُصْطَنِع artificial تَصْنِيع industrialisation اِصْطِنَاع manufacture

مَصْنَع ج مَصَانِع factory مَصْنُوع product تَصَنُّع pretence

دَوْلَة صِنَاعِيَة industrialised country

19 VIII اضْطَرَبَ يَضْطَرِبُ *iḍṭáraba yaḍṭáribu* to clash ضرب

ACTIVE Present *yaḍṭáribu*

نَضْطَرِبُ		أَضْطَرِبُ
تَضْطَرِبُونَ	تَضْطَرِبَانِ	تَضْطَرِبُ
تَضْطَرِبْنَ	تَضْطَرِبَانِ	تَضْطَرِبِينَ
يَضْطَرِبُونَ	يَضْطَرِبَانِ	يَضْطَرِبُ
يَضْطَرِبْنَ	تَضْطَرِبَانِ	تَضْطَرِبُ

Past *iḍṭáraba*

اضْطَرَبْنَا		اضْطَرَبْتُ
اضْطَرَبْتُمْ	اضْطَرَبْتُمَا	اضْطَرَبْتَ
اضْطَرَبْتُنَّ	اضْطَرَبْتُمَا	اضْطَرَبْتِ
اضْطَرَبُوا	اضْطَرَبَا	اضْطَرَبَ
اضْطَرَبْنَ	اضْطَرَبَتَا	اضْطَرَبَتْ

Jussive *yaḍṭárib*

نَضْطَرِبْ		أَضْطَرِبْ
تَضْطَرِبُوا	تَضْطَرِبَا	تَضْطَرِبْ
تَضْطَرِبْنَ	تَضْطَرِبَا	تَضْطَرِبِي
يَضْطَرِبُوا	يَضْطَرِبَا	يَضْطَرِبْ
يَضْطَرِبْنَ	تَضْطَرِبَا	تَضْطَرِبْ

Subjunctive *yaḍṭáriba*

نَضْطَرِبَ		أَضْطَرِبَ
تَضْطَرِبُوا	تَضْطَرِبَا	تَضْطَرِبَ
تَضْطَرِبْنَ	تَضْطَرِبَا	تَضْطَرِبِي
يَضْطَرِبُوا	يَضْطَرِبَا	يَضْطَرِبَ
يَضْطَرِبْنَ	تَضْطَرِبَا	تَضْطَرِبَ

Verbal Noun اضْطِرَاب *iḍṭirāb* **Participle** مُضْطَرِب *muḍṭárib*

Imperative اضْطَرِبْ، اضْطَرِبِي؛ اضْطَرِبَا؛ اضْطَرِبُوا، اضْطَرِبْنَ

iḍṭárib, -ī; -ā; -ū, -na

PASSIVE° **Present** يُضْطَرَبُ *yuḍṭárabu* **Past** أُضْطُرِبَ *uḍṭúriba*
Participle مُضْطَرَب *muḍṭárab*

I ضَرَبَ يَضْرِبُ (ضَرْب) to strike ه هـ, to multiply by هـ في 2;
III ضَارَبَ to fight with ه 9; IV أَضْرَبَ to go on strike 10;
VI تَضَارَبَ to fight e.o. 12

ضَرْبَة blow, stroke ضَرْب beating, multiplication إِضْرَاب strike
مُضْرِب striker مُتَضَارِب incompatible اضْطِرَاب commotion
ضَرِيبَة ج ضَرَائِب tax ضَرِيبَة الدَخْل income tax تَضَارُب conflict
ضَرَبَ ضَرِيبَةً على to levy a tax on

20 VIII اِطَّلَعَ يَطَّلِعُ *iṭṭála'a yaṭṭáli'u* to become aware of على **طلع**

ACTIVE

Past *iṭṭála'a*

اِطَّلَعْتُ		اِطَّلَعْنَا
اِطَّلَعْتَ	اِطَّلَعْتُمَا	اِطَّلَعْتُمْ
اِطَّلَعْتِ	اِطَّلَعْتُمَا	اِطَّلَعْتُنَّ
اِطَّلَعَ	اِطَّلَعَا	اِطَّلَعُوا
اِطَّلَعَتْ	اِطَّلَعَتَا	اِطَّلَعْنَ

Present *yaṭṭáli'u*

أَطَّلِعُ		نَطَّلِعُ
تَطَّلِعُ	تَطَّلِعَانِ	تَطَّلِعُونَ
تَطَّلِعِينَ	تَطَّلِعَانِ	تَطَّلِعْنَ
يَطَّلِعُ	يَطَّلِعَانِ	يَطَّلِعُونَ
تَطَّلِعُ	تَطَّلِعَانِ	يَطَّلِعْنَ

Subjunctive *yaṭṭáli'a*

أَطَّلِعَ		نَطَّلِعَ
تَطَّلِعَ	تَطَّلِعَا	تَطَّلِعُوا
تَطَّلِعِي	تَطَّلِعَا	تَطَّلِعْنَ
يَطَّلِعَ	يَطَّلِعَا	يَطَّلِعُوا
تَطَّلِعَ	تَطَّلِعَا	يَطَّلِعْنَ

Jussive *yaṭṭáli'*

أَطَّلِعْ		نَطَّلِعَ
تَطَّلِعْ	تَطَّلِعَا	تَطَّلِعُوا
تَطَّلِعِي	تَطَّلِعَا	تَطَّلِعْنَ
يَطَّلِعْ	يَطَّلِعَا	يَطَّلِعُوا
تَطَّلِعْ	تَطَّلِعَا	يَطَّلِعْنَ

Verbal Noun اِطِّلَاع *iṭṭilā'* **Participle** مُطَّلِع *muṭṭáli'*

Imperative اِطَّلِعْ، اِطَّلِعِي؛ اِطَّلِعَا؛ اِطَّلِعُوا، اِطَّلِعْنَ *iṭṭáli', -ī; -ā; -ū, -na*

PASSIVE° **Present** يُطَّلَعُ *yuṭṭála'u* **Past** أُطُّلِعَ *uṭṭúli'a*
Participle مُطَّلَع *muṭṭála'*

I طَلَعَ يَطْلُعُ (طُلُوع\مَطْلَع) to climb, mount هـ, to rise 1;
III طَالَعَ to examine هـ 9; IV أَطْلَعَ to notify ه على\من 10;
V تَطَلَّعَ to watch for إلى 11; X اِسْتَطْلَعَ to consult ه 23

طُلُوع rising (noun) مَطْلَع ج مَطَالِع point of departure مُطَالِع reader
مُطَالَعَة perusal طُلُوع الشَّمْس\القَمَر sun-/moonrise اِسْتِطْلَاع research
اِطِّلَاع examination, information مُطَّلِع (على) observer, aware (of)

21 | **VIII** | اظَّلَمَ يَظَّلِمُ *izzálama yazzálimu* to suffer wrong | **ظلم**

ACTIVE Present *yazzálimu* **Past** *izzálama*

Present			Past		
نَظَّلِمُ		أَظَّلِمُ	اظَّلَمْنَا		اظَّلَمْتُ
تَظَّلِمُونَ	تَظَّلِمَانِ	تَظَّلِمُ	اظَّلَمْتُمْ	اظَّلَمْتُمَا	اظَّلَمْتَ
تَظَّلِمْنَ	تَظَّلِمَانِ	تَظَّلِمِينَ	اظَّلَمْتُنَّ	اظَّلَمْتُمَا	اظَّلَمْتِ
يَظَّلِمُونَ	يَظَّلِمَانِ	يَظَّلِمُ	اظَّلَمُوا	اظَّلَمَا	اظَّلَمَ
يَظَّلِمْنَ	تَظَّلِمَانِ	تَظَّلِمُ	اظَّلَمْنَ	اظَّلَمَتَا	اظَّلَمَتْ

Jussive *yazzálim*			**Subjunctive** *yazzálima*		
نَظَّلِمْ		أَظَّلِمْ	نَظَّلِمَ		أَظَّلِمَ
تَظَّلِمُوا	تَظَّلِمَا	تَظَّلِمْ	تَظَّلِمُوا	تَظَّلِمَا	تَظَّلِمَ
تَظَّلِمْنَ	تَظَّلِمَا	تَظَّلِمِي	تَظَّلِمْنَ	تَظَّلِمَا	تَظَّلِمِي
يَظَّلِمُوا	يَظَّلِمَا	يَظَّلِمْ	يَظَّلِمُوا	يَظَّلِمَا	يَظَّلِمَ
يَظَّلِمْنَ	تَظَّلِمَا	تَظَّلِمْ	يَظَّلِمْنَ	تَظَّلِمَا	تَظَّلِمَ

Verbal Noun اظِّلاَم *izzilām* **Participle** مُظَّلِم *muzzálim*

Impv. اظَّلِمْ، اظَّلِمِي؛ اظَّلِمَا؛ اظَّلِمُوا، اظَّلِمْنَ *izzálim, -ī; -ā; -ū, -na*

PASSIVE° Present يُظَّلَمُ *yuzzálamu* **Past** أُظُّلِمَ *uzzúlima*

Participle مُظَّلَم *muzzálam*

I (ظَلْم\ظُلْم) ظَلَمَ يَظْلِمُ to oppress ه 2; IV أَظْلَمَ to be(come) dark 10;

V تَظَلَّمَ to complain about من 11; VII انْظَلَمَ 13 = VIII اظَّلَمَ **21**

ظُلْم oppression, suppression — ظَلاَمَة injustice

ظَالِم iniquitous — مَظْلُوم wronged

ظُلْماً wrongfully — مَظْلَمَة ج مَظَالِم injustice

مُظْلِم dark — ظُلْمَة\ظَلاَم\إِظْلاَم darkness

22 | IX | اِحْمَرَّ يَحْمَرُّ *iḥmarra yaḥmarru* to be/turn red, blush | حمر

ACTIVE **Present** *yaḥmarru*

نَحْمَرُّ		أَحْمَرُّ
تَحْمَرُّونَ	تَحْمَرَّانِ	تَحْمَرُّ
تَحْمَرِرْنَ	تَحْمَرَّانِ	تَحْمَرِّينَ
يَحْمَرُّونَ	يَحْمَرَّانِ	يَحْمَرُّ
يَحْمَرِرْنَ	تَحْمَرَّانِ	تَحْمَرُّ

Past *iḥmarra*

اِحْمَرَرْنَا		اِحْمَرَرْتُ
اِحْمَرَرْتُمْ	اِحْمَرَرْتُمَا	اِحْمَرَرْتَ
اِحْمَرَرْتُنَّ	اِحْمَرَرْتُمَا	اِحْمَرَرْتِ
اِحْمَرُّوا	اِحْمَرَّا	اِحْمَرَّ
اِحْمَرَرْنَ	اِحْمَرَّتَا	اِحْمَرَّتْ

Jussive (ii)† *yaḥmarir*

نَحْمَرِرْ		أَحْمَرِرْ
تَحْمَرُّوا	تَحْمَرَّا	تَحْمَرِرْ
تَحْمَرِرْنَ	تَحْمَرَّا	تَحْمَرِّي
يَحْمَرُّوا	يَحْمَرَّا	يَحْمَرِرْ
يَحْمَرِرْنَ	تَحْمَرَّا	تَحْمَرِرْ

Subjunc.+ Jussive (i) *yaḥmarra*

نَحْمَرَّ		أَحْمَرَّ
تَحْمَرُّوا	تَحْمَرَّا	تَحْمَرَّ
تَحْمَرِرْنَ	تَحْمَرَّا	تَحْمَرِّي
يَحْمَرُّوا	يَحْمَرَّا	يَحْمَرَّ
يَحْمَرِرْنَ	تَحْمَرَّا	تَحْمَرَّ

Verbal Noun اِحْمِرَار *iḥmirār* **Participle** مُحْمَرّ *muḥmarr*

Imperative اِحْمَرَّ\اِحْمَرِرْ †، اِحْمَرِّي؛ اِحْمَرَّا: اِحْمَرُّوا، اِحْمَرِرْنَ

iḥmarra/iḥmarir†, iḥmarrī; iḥmarrā; iḥmarrū, iḥmarirna

PASSIVE does not exist in Form IX

II حَمَّرَ to make red, to roast, to fry ه 7

حُمْر (an. pl.) ،حَمْرَاء (f.) ،أَحْمَر (m.) red

اِحْمَرَار reddening

مُحَمَّر roast(ed), fried

حِمَار ج حَمِير donkey

تَحْتَ الأَحْمَر infra-red

حُمْرَة redness

الهِلَال الأَحْمَر the Red Crescent

الصَّلِيب الأَحْمَر the Red Cross

البَحْر الأَحْمَر the Red Sea

أَكْثَر حُمْرَةً redder

23 | **X** | **اِسْتَقْبَلَ يَسْتَقْبِلُ** *istaqbala yastaqbilu* to receive ه هـ | **قبل**

ACTIVE

Past *istaqbala*

اِسْتَقْبَلْتُ		اِسْتَقْبَلْنَا
اِسْتَقْبَلْتَ	اِسْتَقْبَلْتُمَا	اِسْتَقْبَلْتُمْ
اِسْتَقْبَلْتِ	اِسْتَقْبَلْتُمَا	اِسْتَقْبَلْتُنَّ
اِسْتَقْبَلَ	اِسْتَقْبَلاَ	اِسْتَقْبَلُوا
اِسْتَقْبَلَتْ	اِسْتَقْبَلَتَا	اِسْتَقْبَلْنَ

Present *yastaqbilu*

أَسْتَقْبِلُ		نَسْتَقْبِلُ
تَسْتَقْبِلُ	تَسْتَقْبِلاَنِ	تَسْتَقْبِلُونَ
تَسْتَقْبِلِينَ	تَسْتَقْبِلاَنِ	تَسْتَقْبِلْنَ
يَسْتَقْبِلُ	يَسْتَقْبِلاَنِ	يَسْتَقْبِلُونَ
تَسْتَقْبِلُ	تَسْتَقْبِلاَنِ	يَسْتَقْبِلْنَ

Subjunctive *yastaqbila*

أَسْتَقْبِلَ		نَسْتَقْبِلَ
تَسْتَقْبِلَ	تَسْتَقْبِلاَ	تَسْتَقْبِلُوا
تَسْتَقْبِلِي	تَسْتَقْبِلاَ	تَسْتَقْبِلْنَ
يَسْتَقْبِلَ	يَسْتَقْبِلاَ	يَسْتَقْبِلُوا
تَسْتَقْبِلَ	تَسْتَقْبِلاَ	يَسْتَقْبِلْنَ

Jussive *yastaqbil*

أَسْتَقْبِلْ		نَسْتَقْبِلْ
تَسْتَقْبِلْ	تَسْتَقْبِلاَ	تَسْتَقْبِلُوا
تَسْتَقْبِلِي	تَسْتَقْبِلاَ	تَسْتَقْبِلْنَ
يَسْتَقْبِلْ	يَسْتَقْبِلاَ	يَسْتَقْبِلُوا
تَسْتَقْبِلْ	تَسْتَقْبِلاَ	يَسْتَقْبِلْنَ

Verbal Noun اِسْتِقْبَال *istiqbāl* **Participle** مُسْتَقْبِل *mustaqbil*

Imperative اِسْتَقْبِلْ، اِسْتَقْبِلِي؛ اِسْتَقْبِلاَ؛ اِسْتَقْبِلُوا، اِسْتَقْبِلْنَ

istaqbil, -ī; -ā; -ū, -na

PASSIVE **Present** يُسْتَقْبَلُ *yustaqbalu* **Past** أُسْتُقْبِلَ *ustuqbila*

Participle مُسْتَقْبَل *mustaqbal*

I قَبِلَ يَقْبَلُ (قُبُول\قَبُول) to accept ه هـ\ب 4; III قَابَلَ to face ه هـ 9;

IV أَقْبَلَ to approach على 10; V تَقَبَّلَ to accept هـ 11;

VI تَقَابَلَ to face e.o. 12; VIII اِقْتَبَلَ 14 = X اِسْتَقْبَلَ 23

قَبْلَ before (prep.) قَبْلَ أَنْ before (conj.) قَبُول\قُبُول acceptance

قَبْلاً beforehand مُقَابِل remuneration إِقْبَال approach

مُقَابَلَة encounter, interview اِسْتِقْبَال reception مُسْتَقْبَل future

مِن قِبَل on the part of قَابِل لِلـ... worthy of مُقْبِل next

Hamzated

Hamzated verbs have ء as one root letter. In almost all these verbs both other root letters are sound; one example (no. **29**) has a weak middle root letter (ي) but as this verb occurs only in Forms II and V the weak root letter is stable (i.e. is consonantal in form, *y*).

(Verbs with ء as middle root letter and a weak final root letter [و or ي], or vice versa, are counted as doubly weak verbs, for which see p. 205. Further, two hamzated roots (أمّ and أسّ) are shown, as is more appropriate, among the doubled verbs; see nos. **63** and **67**.)

In hamzated verbs the sound patterns shown in §§ 7, 8, 17, 18, 21-23 and 26 apply, with the exceptions shown below.

Spelling. Root-letter ء plus a neighbouring vowel or non-root-letter ء produces special forms in spelling and pronunciation:

- initial/middle/final [أأ\أأ] → آ *'ā* (see nos. **24** and **47**),
- initial [...ائـ] often → ...ايـ *ī-* (see nos. **26** and **34**),
- initial [...اؤْ] → ...او *ū-* (see no. **25**),
- initial [...أؤْ] → ...أو *'ū-* (see no. **31**).

Verbs with initial *hamza*:

- The Form I affirmative impv. of three important verbs is irregular:
  أكل يأكل *'akala ya'kulu* I 'to eat' (no. **24**), impv. كل *kul* (etc.)
  أخذ يأخذ *'akhadha ya'khudhu* I 'to take', impv. خذ *khudh* (etc.)
  أمر يأمر *'amara ya'muru* I 'to order', impv. كل *mur* (etc.)
  Their negative imperative is regular: لا تأكل\لا تأخذ\لا تأمر *lā ta'kul, lā ta'khudh, lā ta'mur* etc.
- In Form VIII of root أخذ the root letter ء plus the ت of Form VIII become ...تّـ... *-tt-* : اتّخذ *ittákhadha* VIII 'to take' (no. **35**).

Verbs with middle *hamza*: No. **37** has a less common alternative jussive and imperative pattern, not found in other verbs of this type.

Verbs with final *hamza*: Form II verbal noun is made on the model تهنئة *tahni'a* 'congratulation' (see no. **50**).

24 | **I** | **أَكَلَ يَأْكُلُ** *'akala ya'kulu* to eat هـ | **أكل**

ACTIVE

Present *ya'kulu*

نَأْكُلُ		آكُلُ
تَأْكُلُونَ	تَأْكُلَانِ	تَأْكُلُ
تَأْكُلْنَ	تَأْكُلَانِ	تَأْكُلِينَ
يَأْكُلُونَ	يَأْكُلَانِ	يَأْكُلُ
يَأْكُلْنَ	تَأْكُلَانِ	تَأْكُلُ

Past *'akala*

أَكَلْنَا		أَكَلْتُ
أَكَلْتُمْ	أَكَلْتُمَا	أَكَلْتَ
أَكَلْتُنَّ	أَكَلْتُمَا	أَكَلْتِ
أَكَلُوا	أَكَلَا	أَكَلَ
أَكَلْنَ	أَكَلَتَا	أَكَلَتْ

Jussive *ya'kul*

نَأْكُلْ		آكُلْ
تَأْكُلُوا	تَأْكُلَا	تَأْكُلْ
تَأْكُلْنَ	تَأْكُلَا	تَأْكُلِي
يَأْكُلُوا	يَأْكُلَا	يَأْكُلْ
يَأْكُلْنَ	تَأْكُلَا	تَأْكُلْ

Subjunctive *ya'kula*

نَأْكُلَ		آكُلَ
تَأْكُلُوا	تَأْكُلَا	تَأْكُلَ
تَأْكُلْنَ	تَأْكُلَا	تَأْكُلِي
يَأْكُلُوا	يَأْكُلَا	يَأْكُلَ
يَأْكُلْنَ	تَأْكُلَا	تَأْكُلَ

Verbal Noun أَكْل *'akl* **Participle** آكِل *'ākil*

Imperative كُلْ، كُلِي؛ كُلَا؛ كُلُوا، كُلْنَ *kul, -ī; -ā; -ū, -na*

PASSIVE **Present** يُؤْكَلُ *yu'kalu* **Past** أُكِلَ *'ukila*

Participle مأْكُول *ma'kūl*

II/IV أَكَّلَ\آكَلَ to feed ه هـ 28/31; III آكَلَ to dine with ه 30;

V/VI تَأَكَّلَ\تَآكَلَ to be eaten away/eroded 32/33

أَكْل food, meal	مَأْكَل مَآكِل food
آكِل eater	مأْكُول edible
غُرْفَة الأَكْل dining room	أَكَّال glutton(ous)
تَأَكُّل\تَآكُل\ائْتِكَال erosion, corrosion	أُكَال pustule
مُتَأَكِّل\مُتَآكِل eroded, corroded	آتَى أُكْلَةً to bear fruit

25 | **I** | أَمَلَ يَأْمُلُ *'amala ya'mulu* to hope for, expect ه هـ | **أمل**

ACTIVE

Present *ya'mulu*			Past *'amala*		
نَأْمُلُ		آمُلُ	أَمَلْنَا		أَمَلْتُ
تَأْمُلُونَ	تَأْمُلاَنِ	تَأْمُلُ	أَمَلْتُمْ	أَمَلْتُمَا	أَمَلْتَ
تَأْمُلْنَ	تَأْمُلاَنِ	تَأْمُلِينَ	أَمَلْتُنَّ	أَمَلْتُمَا	أَمَلْتِ
يَأْمُلُونَ	يَأْمُلاَنِ	يَأْمُلُ	أَمَلُوا	أَمَلاَ	أَمَلَ
يَأْمُلْنَ	تَأْمُلاَنِ	تَأْمُلُ	أَمَلْنَ	أَمَلَتَا	أَمَلَتْ

Jussive *ya'mul*			Subjunctive *ya'mula*		
نَأْمُلْ		آمُلْ	نَأْمُلَ		آمُلَ
تَأْمُلُوا	تَأْمُلاَ	تَأْمُلْ	تَأْمُلُوا	تَأْمُلاَ	تَأْمُلَ
تَأْمُلْنَ	تَأْمُلاَ	تَأْمُلِي	تَأْمُلْنَ	تَأْمُلاَ	تَأْمُلِي
يَأْمُلُوا	يَأْمُلاَ	يَأْمُلْ	يَأْمُلُوا	يَأْمُلاَ	يَأْمُلَ
يَأْمُلْنَ	تَأْمُلاَ	تَأْمُلْ	يَأْمُلْنَ	تَأْمُلاَ	تَأْمُلَ

Verbal Noun أَمَل ج آمَال *'amal 'āmāl* **Participle** آمِل *'āmil*

Imperative أُومُلْ، أُومُلِي؛ أُومُلاَ؛ أُومُلُوا ، أُومُلْنَ *ūmul, -ī; -ā; -ū, -na*

PASSIVE **Present** يُؤْمَلُ *yu'malu* **Past** أُمِلَ *'umila*

Participle مَأْمُول *ma'mūl*

II أَمَّلَ to expect of من هـ , to give hope to ه 28;

V تَأَمَّلَ to ponder هـ\في 32

أَمَل ج آمَال ب\في hope/expectation of — أَمَل كاذِب false hope

مأمَل ج مَآمِل hope — مَأْمُول expected

آمِل\مُؤَمِّل hopeful — مُتَأَمِّل contemplative

أَمَلَ خَيْراً to hope for the best — لا أَمَلَ في\ب there is no hope of

26 | I أَسَرَ يَأْسِرُ *'asara ya'siru* to capture ه ,
to captivate (fig.) ه هـ **أسر**

ACTIVE	**Present**	*ya'siru*		**Past**	*'asara*
نَأْسِرُ		آسِرُ	أَسَرْنَا		أَسَرْتُ
تَأْسِرُونَ	تَأْسِرَانِ	تَأْسِرُ	أَسَرْتُمْ	أَسَرْتُمَا	أَسَرْتَ
تَأْسِرْنَ	تَأْسِرَانِ	تَأْسِرِينَ	أَسَرْتُنَّ	أَسَرْتُمَا	أَسَرْتِ
يَأْسِرُونَ	يَأْسِرَانِ	يَأْسِرُ	أَسَرُوا	أَسَرَا	أَسَرَ
يَأْسِرْنَ	تَأْسِرَانِ	تَأْسِرُ	أَسَرْنَ	أَسَرَتَا	أَسَرَتْ

	Jussive	*ya'sir*		**Subjunctive**	*ya'sira*
نَأْسِرْ		آسِرْ	نَأْسِرَ		آسِرَ
تَأْسِرُوا	تَأْسِرَا	تَأْسِرْ	تَأْسِرُوا	تَأْسِرَا	تَأْسِرَ
تَأْسِرْنَ	تَأْسِرَا	تَأْسِرِي	تَأْسِرْنَ	تَأْسِرَا	تَأْسِرِي
يَأْسِرُوا	يَأْسِرَا	يَأْسِرْ	يَأْسِرُوا	يَأْسِرَا	يَأْسِرَ
يَأْسِرْنَ	تَأْسِرَا	تَأْسِرْ	يَأْسِرْنَ	تَأْسِرَا	تَأْسِرَ

Verbal Noun أَسْر *'asr* **Participle** آسِر *'āsir*

Impv. اِيسِرْ، اِيسِرِي؛ اِيسِرَا؛ اِيسِرُوا، اِيسِرْنَ *īsir, -ī; -ā; -ū, -na*

PASSIVE **Present** يُؤْسَرُ *yu'saru* **Past** أُسِرَ *usira*
Participle مَأْسُور *ma'sūr*

X اِسْتَأْسَرَ to surrender (o.s.) 36

أَسِير ج أُسَرَاء captive

أَسْر captivity

بِأَسْرِهِ in entirety

آسِر captor, captivating

اِسَار captivity, enthralment

مَأْسُور ب captivated by

وَقَعَ في اِسَار to fall into the clutches of

27 | I | أَمِنَ يَأْمَنُ *'amina ya'manu* to be safe from هـ\من | أمن

ACTIVE

Past *'amina*

أَمِنْتُ		أَمِنَّا
أَمِنْتَ	أَمِنْتُمَا	أَمِنْتُمْ
أَمِنْتِ	أَمِنْتُمَا	أَمِنْتُنَّ
أَمِنَ	أَمِنَا	أَمِنُوا
أَمِنَتْ	أَمِنَتَا	أَمِنَّ

Present *ya'manu*

آمَنُ		نَأْمَنُ
تَأْمَنُ	تَأْمَنَانِ	تَأْمَنُونَ
تَأْمَنِينَ	تَأْمَنَانِ	تَأْمَنَّ
يَأْمَنُ	يَأْمَنَانِ	يَأْمَنُونَ
تَأْمَنُ	تَأْمَنَانِ	يَأْمَنَّ

Subjunctive *ya'mana*

آمَنَ		نَأْمَنَ
تَأْمَنَ	تَأْمَنَا	تَأْمَنُوا
تَأْمَنِي	تَأْمَنَا	تَأْمَنَّ
يَأْمَنَ	يَأْمَنَا	يَأْمَنُوا
تَأْمَنَ	تَأْمَنَا	يَأْمَنَّ

Jussive *ya'man*

آمَنْ		نَأْمَنْ
تَأْمَنْ	تَأْمَنَا	تَأْمَنُوا
تَأْمَنِي	تَأْمَنَا	تَأْمَنَّ
يَأْمَنْ	يَأْمَنَا	يَأْمَنُوا
تَأْمَنْ	تَأْمَنَا	يَأْمَنَّ

Verbal Noun أَمَان *'amān* **Participle** آمِن *'āmin*

Imperative إِيمَنْ، إِيمَنِي؛ إِيمَنَا؛ إِيمَنُوا، إِيمَنَّ *īman, -ī; -ā; -ū, -na*

PASSIVE **Present** يُؤْمَنُ *yu'manu* **Past** أُمِنَ *'umina*

Participle مأْمُون *ma'mūn*

I أَمُنَ يَأْمُنُ (أَمَانَة) to be reliable 25 (but with ُ... *-u-* in past tense);

II أَمَّنَ to insure هـ , to reassure ه 28; IV آمَنَ to believe in ب 31;

VIII/X اِئْتَمَنَ، اِيتَمَنَ†\اِسْتَأْمَنَ to trust ه 34/36

أَمْن safety أَمَان security آمِن peaceful مأْمُون reliable

اِئْتِمَان\اِسْتِئْمَان trust, credit إِيمَان ب belief in مُؤْمِن faithful

مُؤْتَمَن على entrusted with تَأْمِين insurance مُؤَمَّن عليه insured

مُؤَمِّن insurer أَمِين ج أُمَنَاء reliable, trustee أَمِين عَامّ secretary gen.

28 | **II** | أَكَّدَ يُؤَكِّدُ *'akkada yu'akkidu* to confirm هـ
to assure ل هـ | **أكد**

ACTIVE

Present *yu'akkidu*			**Past** *'akkada*		
نُؤَكِّدُ		أُؤَكِّدُ	أَكَّدْنَا		أَكَّدْتُ
تُؤَكِّدُونَ	تُؤَكِّدَانِ	تُؤَكِّدُ	أَكَّدْتُمْ	أَكَّدْتُمَا	أَكَّدْتَ
تُؤَكِّدْنَ	تُؤَكِّدَانِ	تُؤَكِّدِينَ	أَكَّدْتُنَّ	أَكَّدْتُمَا	أَكَّدْتِ
يُؤَكِّدُونَ	يُؤَكِّدَانِ	يُؤَكِّدُ	أَكَّدُوا	أَكَّدَا	أَكَّدَ
يُؤَكِّدْنَ	تُؤَكِّدَانِ	تُؤَكِّدُ	أَكَّدْنَ	أَكَّدَتَا	أَكَّدَتْ

Jussive *yu'akkid*			**Subjunctive** *yu'akkida*		
نُؤَكِّدْ		أُؤَكِّدْ	نُؤَكِّدَ		أُؤَكِّدَ
تُؤَكِّدُوا	تُؤَكِّدَا	تُؤَكِّدْ	تُؤَكِّدُوا	تُؤَكِّدَا	تُؤَكِّدَ
تُؤَكِّدْنَ	تُؤَكِّدَا	تُؤَكِّدِي	تُؤَكِّدْنَ	تُؤَكِّدَا	تُؤَكِّدِي
يُؤَكِّدُوا	يُؤَكِّدَا	يُؤَكِّدْ	يُؤَكِّدُوا	يُؤَكِّدَا	يُؤَكِّدَ
يُؤَكِّدْنَ	تُؤَكِّدَا	تُؤَكِّدْ	يُؤَكِّدْنَ	تُؤَكِّدَا	تُؤَكِّدَ

Verbal Noun تأْكِيد *ta'kīd* **Participle** مُؤَكِّد *mu'akkid*

Imperative أَكِّدْ، أَكِّدِي؛ أَكِّدَا؛ أَكِّدُوا، أَكِّدْنَ *'akkid, -ī; -ā; -ū, -na*

PASSIVE **Present** يُؤَكَّدُ *yu'akkadu* **Past** أُكِّدَ *'ukkida*

Participle مُؤَكَّد *mu'akkad*

V تَأَكَّدَ to be sure of من 32

تأْكِيد confirmation, assurance

أَكِيد\مُؤَكَّد certain (of things)

أَكِيداً\بالتأْكِيد certainly

تَأَكُّد assurance

مُتَأَكِّد من sure/convinced of

29 **II** أيَّدَ يُؤَيِّدُ *'ayyada yu'ayyidu* to support ه **أيد**

ACTIVE **Present** *yu'ayyidu*			**Past** *'ayyada*		
نُؤَيِّدُ		أُؤَيِّدُ	أيَّدْنا		أيَّدْتُ
تُؤَيِّدُونَ	تُؤَيِّدانِ	تُؤَيِّدُ	أيَّدْتُمْ	أيَّدْتُما	أيَّدْتَ
تُؤَيِّدْنَ	تُؤَيِّدانِ	تُؤَيِّدِينَ	أيَّدْتُنَّ	أيَّدْتُما	أيَّدْتِ
يُؤَيِّدُونَ	يُؤَيِّدانِ	يُؤَيِّدُ	أيَّدُوا	أيَّدا	أيَّدَ
يُؤَيِّدْنَ	تُؤَيِّدانِ	تُؤَيِّدُ	أيَّدْنَ	أيَّدَتا	أيَّدَتْ

Jussive *yu'ayyid*			**Subjunctive** *yu'ayyida*		
نُؤَيِّدْ		أُؤَيِّدْ	نُؤَيِّدَ		أُؤَيِّدَ
تُؤَيِّدُوا	تُؤَيِّدا	تُؤَيِّدْ	تُؤَيِّدُوا	تُؤَيِّدا	تُؤَيِّدَ
تُؤَيِّدْنَ	تُؤَيِّدا	تُؤَيِّدِي	تُؤَيِّدْنَ	تُؤَيِّدا	تُؤَيِّدِي
يُؤَيِّدُوا	يُؤَيِّدا	يُؤَيِّدْ	يُؤَيِّدُوا	يُؤَيِّدا	يُؤَيِّدَ
يُؤَيِّدْنَ	تُؤَيِّدا	تُؤَيِّدْ	يُؤَيِّدْنَ	تُؤَيِّدا	تُؤَيِّدَ

Verbal Noun تأييد *ta'yīd* **Participle** مُؤَيِّد *mu'ayyid*

Imperative أيِّدْ، أيِّدِي؛ أيِّدا؛ أيِّدُوا، أيِّدْنَ *'ayyid, -ī; -ā; -ū, -na*

PASSIVE **Present** يُؤَيَّدُ *yu'ayyadu* **Past** أُيِّدَ *'uyyida*

Participle مُؤَيَّد *mu'ayyad*

V تأيَّدَ to be supported 32

تأييد support

مُؤَيِّد supporter

تأييداً ل in support of

مُؤَيَّد\متأيِّد supported

30 | **III** | آخَذَ يُؤَاخِذُ *'ākhadha yu'ākhidhu* | **أخذ**

to blame for ه على\ب

ACTIVE Present *yu'ākhidhu* — **Past** *'ākhadha*

نُؤَاخِذُ		أُؤَاخِذُ	آخَذْنَا		آخَذْتُ
تُؤَاخِذُونَ	تُؤَاخِذَانِ	تُؤَاخِذُ	آخَذْتُمْ	آخَذْتُمَا	آخَذْتَ
تُؤَاخِذْنَ	تُؤَاخِذَانِ	تُؤَاخِذِينَ	آخَذْتُنَّ	آخَذْتُمَا	آخَذْتِ
يُؤَاخِذُونَ	يُؤَاخِذَانِ	يُؤَاخِذُ	آخَذُوا	آخَذَا	آخَذَ
يُؤَاخِذْنَ	تُؤَاخِذَانِ	تُؤَاخِذُ	آخَذْنَ	آخَذَتَا	آخَذَتْ

Jussive *yu'ākhidh* — **Subjunctive** *yu'ākhidha*

نُؤَاخِذْ		أُؤَاخِذْ	نُؤَاخِذَ		أُؤَاخِذَ
تُؤَاخِذُوا	تُؤَاخِذَا	تُؤَاخِذْ	تُؤَاخِذُوا	تُؤَاخِذَا	تُؤَاخِذَ
تُؤَاخِذْنَ	تُؤَاخِذَا	تُؤَاخِذِي	تُؤَاخِذْنَ	تُؤَاخِذَا	تُؤَاخِذِي
يُؤَاخِذُوا	يُؤَاخِذَا	يُؤَاخِذْ	يُؤَاخِذُوا	يُؤَاخِذَا	يُؤَاخِذَ
يُؤَاخِذْنَ	تُؤَاخِذَا	تُؤَاخِذْ	يُؤَاخِذْنَ	تُؤَاخِذَا	تُؤَاخِذَ

Verbal Noun مُؤَاخَذَة *mu'ākhadha* **Participle** مُؤَاخِذ *mu'ākhidh*

Imperative آخِذْ، آخِذِي؛ آخِذَا؛ آخِذُوا، آخِذْنَ *'ākhidh, -ī; -ā; -ū, -na*

PASSIVE Present يُؤَاخَذُ *yu'ākhadhu* **Past** أُوخِذَ *'ūkhidha*

Participle مُؤَاخَذ *mu'ākhadh*

I أَخَذَ يَأْخُذُ (أَخْذ) to take هـ , to begin ب\في\π 24;

VIII اِتَّخَذَ to take هـ **35**

مُؤَاخَذَة objection, blame — أَخْذ\اتِّخَاذ taking, acceptance

لا تُؤَاخِذْنِي pardon me — أَخَذَ فِكْرَةً عن to get an idea of

مأْخُوذَات (pl.) takings — أَخَذَ بِعَيْنِ الاعْتِبَار to take into account

أَخَذَ رَأْي to take the opinion of — اِتَّخَذَ شَكْل to take the form of

اِتَّخَذَ إِجْرَاءَات to take measures/steps — اِتَّخَذَ قَرَاراً to adopt a resolution

31 | IV | آجَرَ يُؤْجِرُ *'ājara yu'jiru* to hire out ه هـ | **أجر**

ACTIVE	**Present** *yu'jiru*			**Past** *'ājara*	
نُؤْجِرُ		أُوجِرُ	آجَرْنَا		آجَرْتُ
تُؤْجِرُونَ	تُؤْجِرَانِ	تُؤْجِرُ	آجَرْتُمْ	آجَرْتُمَا	آجَرْتَ
تُؤْجِرْنَ	تُؤْجِرَانِ	تُؤْجِرِينَ	آجَرْتُنَّ	آجَرْتُمَا	آجَرْتِ
يُؤْجِرُونَ	يُؤْجِرَانِ	يُؤْجِرُ	آجَرُوا	آجَرَا	آجَرَ
يُؤْجِرْنَ	تُؤْجِرَانِ	تُؤْجِرُ	آجَرْنَ	آجَرَتَا	آجَرَتْ

	Jussive *yu'jir*			**Subjunctive** *yu'jira*	
نُؤْجِرْ		أُوجِرْ	نُؤْجِرَ		أُوجِرَ
تُؤْجِرُوا	تُؤْجِرَا	تُؤْجِرْ	تُؤْجِرُوا	تُؤْجِرَا	تُؤْجِرَ
تُؤْجِرْنَ	تُؤْجِرَا	تُؤْجِرِي	تُؤْجِرْنَ	تُؤْجِرَا	تُؤْجِرِي
يُؤْجِرُوا	يُؤْجِرَا	يُؤْجِرْ	يُؤْجِرُوا	يُؤْجِرَا	يُؤْجِرَ
يُؤْجِرْنَ	تُؤْجِرَا	تُؤْجِرْ	يُؤْجِرْنَ	تُؤْجِرَا	تُؤْجِرَ

Verbal Noun إِجَار *'ījār* **Participle** مُؤْجِر *mu'jir*

Impv. آجِرْ، آجِرِي؛ آجِرَا؛ آجِرُوا، آجِرْنَ *'ājir, -ī; -ā; -ū, -na*

PASSIVE **Present** يُؤْجَرُ *yu'jaru* **Past** أُوجِرَ *'ūjira*

Participle مُؤْجَر *mu'jar*

I أَجَرَ يَأْجُرُ (أَجْر) to remunerate ه 25; II أَجَّرَ 28 = IV آجَرَ **31**;

X اِسْتَأْجَرَ to take on hire ه هـ 36

إِيجَار\إِيجَارَة rent, lease — أَجْر ج أُجُور remuneration

تَأْجِير leasing — أُجْرَة rate, fee, fare

مَأْجُور salaried — مُؤَجِّر landlord, lessor

مُسْتَأْجِر tenant, lessee — بَيْت لِلإِيجَار house to let

أَجِير ج أُجَرَاء، (m.) أَجِيرَة (f.) day labourer

32 **V** | **أخر**

تَأَخَّرَ يَتَأَخَّرُ *ta'akhkhara yata'akhkharu*

to be delayed, to fall behind **عن**

ACTIVE Present *yata'akhkharu*

أَتَأَخَّرُ		نَتَأَخَّرُ
تَتَأَخَّرُ	تَتَأَخَّرَانِ	تَتَأَخَّرُونَ
تَتَأَخَّرِينَ	تَتَأَخَّرَانِ	تَتَأَخَّرْنَ
يَتَأَخَّرُ	يَتَأَخَّرَانِ	يَتَأَخَّرُونَ
تَتَأَخَّرُ	تَتَأَخَّرَانِ	يَتَأَخَّرْنَ

Past *ta'akhkhara*

تَأَخَّرْتُ		تَأَخَّرْنَا
تَأَخَّرْتَ	تَأَخَّرْتُمَا	تَأَخَّرْتُمْ
تَأَخَّرْتِ	تَأَخَّرْتُمَا	تَأَخَّرْتُنَّ
تَأَخَّرَ	تَأَخَّرَا	تَأَخَّرُوا
تَأَخَّرَتْ	تَأَخَّرَتَا	تَأَخَّرْنَ

Jussive *yata'akhkhar*

أَتَأَخَّرْ		نَتَأَخَّرْ
تَتَأَخَّرْ	تَتَأَخَّرَا	تَتَأَخَّرُوا
تَتَأَخَّرِي	تَتَأَخَّرَا	تَتَأَخَّرْنَ
يَتَأَخَّرْ	يَتَأَخَّرَا	يَتَأَخَّرُوا
تَتَأَخَّرْ	تَتَأَخَّرَا	يَتَأَخَّرْنَ

Subjunctive *yata'akhkhara*

أَتَأَخَّرَ		نَتَأَخَّرَ
تَتَأَخَّرَ	تَتَأَخَّرَا	تَتَأَخَّرُوا
تَتَأَخَّرِي	تَتَأَخَّرَا	تَتَأَخَّرْنَ
يَتَأَخَّرَ	يَتَأَخَّرَا	يَتَأَخَّرُوا
تَتَأَخَّرَ	تَتَأَخَّرَا	يَتَأَخَّرْنَ

Vb. Noun **تَأَخُّر** *ta'akhkhur* **Participle** **مُتَأَخِّر** *muta'akhkhir*

Impv. **تَأَخَّرْ، تَأَخَّرِي؛ تَأَخَّرَا؛ تَأَخَّرُوا، تَأَخَّرْنَ** *ta'akhkhar, -ī; -ā; -ū, -na*

PASSIVE° **Present** **يُتَأَخَّرُ** *yuta'akhkharu* **Past** **تُؤُخِّرَ** *tu'ukhkhira*

II **أَخَّرَ** to delay **هـ** , to suspend **ه** 28

تَأَخُّر\تَأْخِير delay

آخَر ج أُخَر، (f.) أُخْرَى (m.) other

آخِر ج أَوَاخِر last

مُتَأَخِّر delayed, retarded

مُؤَخَّر rear (noun)

أَخِير last, most recent

أَخِيراً recently, finally

الأَخِير the latter

مُتَأَخِّرَات (pl.) arrears

إِلَى آخِرِه et cetera

مَرَّةً أُخْرَى once more

من وَقْتٍ إلى آخَر from time to time

آخِر\أَوَاخِر الشَّهْر\السَّنَة the end/the last part of the month/year

33 VI تَآلَفَ يَتَآلَفُ *ta'ālafa yata'ālafu* **ألف**

to be in harmony with مع

ACTIVE

Past *ta'ālafa*

تَآلَفْتُ		تَآلَفْنَا
تَآلَفْتَ	تَآلَفْتُمَا	تَآلَفْتُمْ
تَآلَفْتِ	تَآلَفْتُمَا	تَآلَفْتُنَّ
تَآلَفَ	تَآلَفَا	تَآلَفُوا
تَآلَفَتْ	تَآلَفَتَا	تَآلَفْنَ

Present *yata'ālafu*

أَتَآلَفُ		نَتَآلَفُ
تَتَآلَفُ	تَتَآلَفَانِ	تَتَآلَفُونَ
تَتَآلَفِينَ	تَتَآلَفَانِ	تَتَآلَفْنَ
يَتَآلَفُ	يَتَآلَفَانِ	يَتَآلَفُونَ
تَتَآلَفُ	تَتَآلَفَانِ	يَتَآلَفْنَ

Subjunctive *yata'ālafa*

أَتَآلَفَ		نَتَآلَفَ
تَتَآلَفَ	تَتَآلَفَا	تَتَآلَفُوا
تَتَآلَفِي	تَتَآلَفَا	تَتَآلَفْنَ
يَتَآلَفَ	يَتَآلَفَا	يَتَآلَفُوا
تَتَآلَفَ	تَتَآلَفَا	يَتَآلَفْنَ

Jussive *yata'ālaf*

أَتَآلَفْ		نَتَآلَفْ
تَتَآلَفْ	تَتَآلَفَا	تَتَآلَفُوا
تَتَآلَفِي	تَتَآلَفَا	تَتَآلَفْنَ
يَتَآلَفْ	يَتَآلَفَا	يَتَآلَفُوا
تَتَآلَفْ	تَتَآلَفَا	يَتَآلَفْنَ

Verbal Noun تَآلُف *ta'āluf* **Participle** مُتَآلِف *muta'ālif*

Imperative تَآلَفْ، تَآلَفِي؛ تَآلَفَا؛ تَآلَفُوا، تَآلَفْنَ *ta'ālaf, -ī; -ā; -ū, -na*

PASSIVE° **Present** يُتَآلَفُ *yuta'ālafu* **Past** تُؤُولِفَ *tu'ūlifa*

Participle مُتَآلَف *muta'ālaf*

I أَلِفَ يأْلَفُ (أَلْف) to be familiar with ه هـ 27; II أَلَّفَ to form (a committee etc.), compose هـ 28; V تَأَلَّفَ to consist of من 32; VIII †اِئْتَلَفَ\اِيتَلَفَ to unite/form a coalition with ب 34, = VI تَآلَفَ 33

تَآلُف harmony مُتَآلِف harmonious أُلْفَة familiarity

تَأْلِيف ج تَآلِيف\تَوَالِيف composition مُؤَلِّف composer, author

تَأْلِيف formation (committee etc.) مُؤَلَّف من composed of

مَأْلُوف familiar, custom(ary) †اِئْتِلاَف\اِيتِلاَف coalition

34 **VIII** اِئْتَمَرَ\اِيتَمَرَ† يَأْتَمِرُ *i'támara/ītámara*† *ya'támiru* **أمر**

to deliberate about, conspire against بـ

ACTIVE **Present** *ya'támiru* | **Past** *i'támara/ītámara*†

Present

نَأْتَمِرُ		آتَمِرُ
تَأْتَمِرُونَ	تَأْتَمِرَانِ	تَأْتَمِرُ
تَأْتَمِرْنَ	تَأْتَمِرَانِ	تَأْتَمِرِينَ
يَأْتَمِرُونَ	يَأْتَمِرَانِ	يَأْتَمِرُ
يَأْتَمِرْنَ	تَأْتَمِرَانِ	تَأْتَمِرُ

Past

اِئْتَمَرْنَا		اِئْتَمَرْتُ\اِيتَمَرْتُ†
اِئْتَمَرْتُمْ	اِئْتَمَرْتُمَا	اِئْتَمَرْتَ
اِئْتَمَرْتُنَّ	اِئْتَمَرْتُمَا	اِئْتَمَرْتِ
اِئْتَمَرُوا	اِئْتَمَرَا	اِئْتَمَرَ
اِئْتَمَرْنَ	اِئْتَمَرَتَا	اِئْتَمَرَتْ

Jussive *ya'támir*

نَأْتَمِرْ		آتَمِرْ
تَأْتَمِرُوا	تَأْتَمِرَا	تَأْتَمِرْ
تَأْتَمِرْنَ	تَأْتَمِرَا	تَأْتَمِرِي
يَأْتَمِرُوا	يَأْتَمِرَا	يَأْتَمِرُ
يَأْتَمِرْنَ	تَأْتَمِرَا	تَأْتَمِرْ

Subjunctive *ya'támira*

نَأْتَمِرَ		آتَمِرَ
تَأْتَمِرُوا	تَأْتَمِرَا	تَأْتَمِرَ
تَأْتَمِرْنَ	تَأْتَمِرَا	تَأْتَمِرِي
يَأْتَمِرُوا	يَأْتَمِرَا	يَأْتَمِرَ
يَأْتَمِرْنَ	تَأْتَمِرَا	تَأْتَمِرَ

Vb. Noun اِئْتِمَار\اِيتِـ...† *i'timār/īt-*† **Participle** مُؤْتَمِر *mu'támir*

Imperative اِئْتَمِرْ\اِيتَمِرْ†، اِئْتَمِرِي؛ اِئْتَمِرَا؛ اِئْتَمِرُوا؛ اِئْتَمِرْنَ

i'támir/ītámir†, *-ī; -ā; -ū, -na*

PASSIVE° **Present** يُؤْتَمَرُ *yu'támaru* **Past** أُوتُمِرَ *ūtúmira*

Participle مُؤْتَمَر *mu'támar*

I أَمَرَ يَأْمُرُ (أَمْر ج أَوَامِر) to order ه ب\أَنْ 24; III آمَرَ to consult ه 30;

VI تَآمَرَ to conspire against على, to confer 33

اِئْتِمَار\مُؤَامَرَة counsel, conspiracy مُؤْتَمَر conference آمِر commander

أَمْر ج أُمُور matter أَمْر ج أَوَامِر command أَمِير ج أُمَرَاء prince, emir

إِمَارَة principality, emirate إِمْرَة authority مَأْمُور official (noun)

لأَمْرٍ مَا for some reason تَحْتَ أَمْرِكَ at your command/service

35 VIII اتَّخَذَ يَتَّخِذُ *ittákhadha yattákhidhu* to take هـ أخذ

ACTIVE

Past *ittákhadha*

اتَّخَذْتُ		اتَّخَذْنَا
اتَّخَذْتَ	اتَّخَذْتُمَا	اتَّخَذْتُمْ
اتَّخَذْتِ	اتَّخَذْتُمَا	اتَّخَذْتُنَّ
اتَّخَذَ	اتَّخَذَا	اتَّخَذُوا
اتَّخَذَتْ	اتَّخَذَتَا	اتَّخَذْنَ

Present *yattákhidhu*

أَتَّخِذُ		نَتَّخِذُ
تَتَّخِذُ	تَتَّخِذَانِ	تَتَّخِذُونَ
تَتَّخِذِينَ	تَتَّخِذَانِ	تَتَّخِذْنَ
يَتَّخِذُ	يَتَّخِذَانِ	يَتَّخِذُونَ
تَتَّخِذُ	تَتَّخِذَانِ	يَتَّخِذْنَ

Subjunctive *yattákhidha*

أَتَّخِذَ		نَتَّخِذَ
تَتَّخِذَ	تَتَّخِذَا	تَتَّخِذُوا
تَتَّخِذِي	تَتَّخِذَا	تَتَّخِذْنَ
يَتَّخِذَ	يَتَّخِذَا	يَتَّخِذُوا
تَتَّخِذَ	تَتَّخِذَا	يَتَّخِذْنَ

Jussive *yattákhidh*

أَتَّخِذْ		نَتَّخِذْ
تَتَّخِذْ	تَتَّخِذَا	تَتَّخِذُوا
تَتَّخِذِي	تَتَّخِذَا	تَتَّخِذْنَ
يَتَّخِذْ	يَتَّخِذَا	يَتَّخِذُوا
تَتَّخِذْ	تَتَّخِذَا	يَتَّخِذْنَ

Verbal Noun اتِّخَاذ *ittikhādh* **Participle** مُتَّخِذ *muttákhidh*

Impv. اتَّخِذْ، اتَّخِذِي؛ اتَّخِذَا؛ اتَّخِذُوا، اتَّخِذْنَ *ittákhidh, -ī; -ā; -ū, -na*

PASSIVE **Present** يُتَّخَذُ *yuttákhadhu* **Past** أُتُّخِذَ *uttúkhidha*

Participle مُتَّخَذ *muttákhadh*

See **30**

36 X اسْتأْنَفَ يَسْتأْنِفُ *ista'nafa yasta'nifu* to resume هـ — أنف

ACTIVE

Past *ista'nafa*

اسْتأْنفْتُ		اسْتأْنفْنا
اسْتأْنفْتَ	اسْتأْنفْتُما	اسْتأْنفْتُمْ
اسْتأْنفْتِ	اسْتأْنفْتُما	اسْتأْنفْتُنَّ
اسْتأْنفَ	اسْتأْنفا	اسْتأْنفُوا
اسْتأْنفَتْ	اسْتأْنفَتا	اسْتأْنفْنَ

Present *yasta'nifu*

أسْتأْنِفُ		نَسْتأْنِفُ
تَسْتأْنِفُ	تَسْتأْنِفانِ	تَسْتأْنِفُونَ
تَسْتأْنِفِينَ	تَسْتأْنِفانِ	تَسْتأْنِفْنَ
يَسْتأْنِفُ	يَسْتأْنِفانِ	يَسْتأْنِفُونَ
تَسْتأْنِفُ	تَسْتأْنِفانِ	يَسْتأْنِفْنَ

Subjunctive *yasta'nifa*

أسْتأْنِفَ		نَسْتأْنِفَ
تَسْتأْنِفَ	تَسْتأْنِفا	تَسْتأْنِفُوا
تَسْتأْنِفِي	تَسْتأْنِفا	تَسْتأْنِفْنَ
يَسْتأْنِفَ	يَسْتأْنِفا	يَسْتأْنِفُوا
تَسْتأْنِفَ	تَسْتأْنِفا	يَسْتأْنِفْنَ

Jussive *yasta'nif*

أسْتأْنِفْ		نَسْتأْنِفْ
تَسْتأْنِفْ	تَسْتأْنِفا	تَسْتأْنِفُوا
تَسْتأْنِفِي	تَسْتأْنِفا	تَسْتأْنِفْنَ
يَسْتأْنِفْ	يَسْتأْنِفا	يَسْتأْنِفُوا
تَسْتأْنِفْ	تَسْتأْنِفا	يَسْتأْنِفْنَ

Verbal Noun اسْتِئْناف *isti'nāf* **Participle** مُسْتأْنِف *musta'nif*

Imperative اِسْتأْنِفْ، اِسْتأْنِفِي؛ اِسْتأْنِفا؛ اِسْتأْنِفُوا، اِسْتأْنِفْنَ
ista'nif, -ī; -ā; -ū, -na

PASSIVE **Present** يُسْتأْنَفُ *yusta'nafu* **Past** أُسْتُؤْنِفَ *ustu'nifa*
Participle مُسْتأْنَف *musta'naf*

I (أنَف) أنِفَ يأْنَفُ to scorn مِن\أنْ 27

اسْتِئْناف	resumption, appeal (in law)	آنِف	preceding
أنْف ج أُنُوف	nose	آنِف الذِكْر	aforementioned
قَدَّمَ اسْتِئْنافًا	to make an appeal (in law)	آنِفًا	previously
اسْتِئْنافِي	appellate (court)		

37 | **I** | سَأَلَ يَسْأَلُ *sa'ala yas'alu* to ask ه هـ | **سأل**

(NB: The rarer alternative jussive + imperative without the middle root letter is found only in this verb, not in other verbs of this type.)

ACTIVE **Present** *yas'alu* **Past** *sa'ala*

نَسْأَلُ		أَسْأَلُ	سَأَلْنَا		سَأَلْتُ
تَسْأَلُونَ	تَسْأَلَانِ	تَسْأَلُ	سَأَلْتُمْ	سَأَلْتُمَا	سَأَلْتَ
تَسْأَلْنَ	تَسْأَلَانِ	تَسْأَلِينَ	سَأَلْتُنَّ	سَأَلْتُمَا	سَأَلْتِ
يَسْأَلُونَ	يَسْأَلَانِ	يَسْأَلُ	سَأَلُوا	سَأَلَا	سَأَلَ
يَسْأَلْنَ	تَسْأَلَانِ	تَسْأَلُ	سَأَلْنَ	سَأَلَتَا	سَأَلَتْ

Jussive *yas'al/yasal†* **Subjunctive** *yas'ala*

نَسْأَلْ		أَسْأَلْ\أَسَلْ†	نَسْأَلَ		أَسْأَلَ
تَسْأَلُوا	تَسْأَلَا	تَسْأَلْ	تَسْأَلُوا	تَسْأَلَا	تَسْأَلَ
تَسْأَلْنَ	تَسْأَلَا	تَسْأَلِي	تَسْأَلْنَ	تَسْأَلَا	تَسْأَلِي
يَسْأَلُوا	يَسْأَلَا	يَسْأَلْ	يَسْأَلُوا	يَسْأَلَا	يَسْأَلَ
يَسْأَلْنَ	تَسْأَلَا	تَسْأَلْ	يَسْأَلْنَ	تَسْأَلَا	تَسْأَلَ

Vb. Noun سُؤَال ج أَسْئِلَة ؛ مَسْأَلَة ج مَسَائِل **Participle** سَائِل *sā'il*

su'āl 'as'ila; mas'ala masā'il

Imperative اِسْأَلْ\سَلْ† ، اِسْأَلِي؛ اِسْأَلَا؛ اِسْأَلُوا ، اِسْأَلْنَ

is'al/sal†, -ī; -ā; -ū, -na

PASSIVE **Present** يُسْأَلُ *yus'alu* **Past** سُئِلَ *su'ila*

Participle مَسْؤُول\مَسْئُول *mas'ūl*

III سَاءَلَ to question ه **41**; V تَسَأَّلَ\تَسَوَّلَ to beg 43/102;

VI تَسَاءَلَ to wonder about عن , to ask e.o. 44

سُؤَال ج أَسْئِلَة question مَسْأَلَة ج مَسَائِل matter سَائِل petitioner

مَسْؤُول\مَسْئُول عن responsible for مَسْؤُولِيَة\مَسْئُولِيَة responsibility

38 **I** بَؤُسَ يَبْؤُسُ *ba'usa yab'usu* to be brave **بأس**

ACTIVE

Present *yab'usu*

نَبْؤُسُ		أَبْؤُسُ
تَبْؤُسُونَ	تَبْؤُسَانِ	تَبْؤُسُ
تَبْؤُسْنَ	تَبْؤُسَانِ	تَبْؤُسِينَ
يَبْؤُسُونَ	يَبْؤُسَانِ	يَبْؤُسُ
يَبْؤُسْنَ	تَبْؤُسَانِ	تَبْؤُسُ

Past *ba'usa*

بَؤُسْنَا		بَؤُسْتُ
بَؤُسْتُمْ	بَؤُسْتُمَا	بَؤُسْتَ
بَؤُسْتُنَّ	بَؤُسْتُمَا	بَؤُسْتِ
بَؤُسُوا	بَؤُسَا	بَؤُسَ
بَؤُسْنَ	بَؤُسَتَا	بَؤُسَتْ

Jussive *yab'us*

نَبْؤُسْ		أَبْؤُسْ
تَبْؤُسُوا	تَبْؤُسَا	تَبْؤُسْ
تَبْؤُسْنَ	تَبْؤُسَا	تَبْؤُسِي
يَبْؤُسُوا	يَبْؤُسَا	يَبْؤُسْ
يَبْؤُسْنَ	تَبْؤُسَا	تَبْؤُسْ

Subjunctive *yab'usa*

نَبْؤُسَ		أَبْؤُسَ
تَبْؤُسُوا	تَبْؤُسَا	تَبْؤُسَ
تَبْؤُسْنَ	تَبْؤُسَا	تَبْؤُسِي
يَبْؤُسُوا	يَبْؤُسَا	يَبْؤُسَ
يَبْؤُسْنَ	تَبْؤُسَا	تَبْؤُسَ

Verbal Noun بَأْس *ba's* **Participle** not used

Imperative أُبْؤُسْ، أُبْؤُسِي؛ أُبْؤُسَا؛ أُبْؤُسُوا، أُبْؤُسْنَ *ub'us, -ī; -ā; -ū, -na*

PASSIVE None

I بَئِسَ يَبْأَسُ (بُؤْس) to be wretched **39**

بَأْس courage

بُؤْس misery

بَائِس\بَئِيس ج بُؤَسَاء wretched

لا بَأْسَ never mind

أَيْ بَأْس؟ what does it matter?

39 I بَئِسَ يَبْأَسُ *ba'isa yab'asu* to be wretched بأس

ACTIVE	**Present**	*yab'asu*		**Past**	*ba'isa*
نَبْأَسُ		أَبْأَسُ	بَئِسْنَا		بَئِسْتُ
تَبْأَسُونَ	تَبْأَسَانِ	تَبْأَسُ	بَئِسْتُمْ	بَئِسْتُمَا	بَئِسْتَ
تَبْأَسْنَ	تَبْأَسَانِ	تَبْأَسِينَ	بَئِسْتُنَّ	بَئِسْتُمَا	بَئِسْتِ
يَبْأَسُونَ	يَبْأَسَانِ	يَبْأَسُ	بَئِسُوا	بَئِسَا	بَئِسَ
يَبْأَسْنَ	تَبْأَسَانِ	تَبْأَسُ	بَئِسْنَ	بَئِسَتَا	بَئِسَتْ

	Jussive	*yab'as*		**Subjunctive**	*yab'asa*
نَبْأَسْ		أَبْأَسْ	نَبْأَسَ		أَبْأَسَ
تَبْأَسُوا	تَبْأَسَا	تَبْأَسْ	تَبْأَسُوا	تَبْأَسَا	تَبْأَسَ
تَبْأَسْنَ	تَبْأَسَا	تَبْأَسِي	تَبْأَسْنَ	تَبْأَسَا	تَبْأَسِي
يَبْأَسُوا	يَبْأَسَا	يَبْأَسْ	يَبْأَسُوا	يَبْأَسَا	يَبْأَسَ
يَبْأَسْنَ	تَبْأَسَا	تَبْأَسْ	يَبْأَسْنَ	تَبْأَسَا	تَبْأَسَ

Verbal Noun بُؤْس *bu's* **Participle** بَائِس *bā'is*

Imperative اِبْأَسْ، اِبْأَسِي؛ اِبْأَسَا؛ اِبْأَسُوا، اِبْأَسْنَ *ib'as, -ī; -ā; -ū, -na*

PASSIVE none

See **38**

40 | **II** | رَأَّسَ يُرَئِّسُ *ra''asa yura''isu* to appoint as head | **رأس**

ACTIVE	**Present** *yura''isu*			**Past** *ra''asa*	
نُرَئِّسُ		أُرَئِّسُ	رَأَّسْنَا		رَأَّسْتُ
تُرَئِّسُونَ	تُرَئِّسَانِ	تُرَئِّسُ	رَأَّسْتُمْ	رَأَّسْتُمَا	رَأَّسْتَ
تُرَئِّسْنَ	تَزْدَحِمَانِ	تُرَئِّسِينَ	رَأَّسْتُنَّ	رَأَّسْتُمَا	رَأَّسْتِ
يُرَئِّسُونَ	يُرَئِّسَانِ	يُرَئِّسُ	رَأَّسُوا	رَأَّسَا	رَأَّسَ
يُرَئِّسْنَ	تُرَئِّسَانِ	تُرَئِّسُ	رَأَّسْنَ	رَأَّسَتَا	رَأَّسَتْ

	Jussive *yura''is*			**Subjunctive** *yura''isa*	
نُرَئِّسْ		أُرَئِّسْ	نُرَئِّسَ		أُرَئِّسَ
تُرَئِّسُوا	تُرَئِّسَا	تُرَئِّسْ	تُرَئِّسُوا	تُرَئِّسَا	تُرَئِّسَ
تُرَئِّسْنَ	تُرَئِّسَا	تُرَئِّسِي	تُرَئِّسْنَ	تُرَئِّسَا	تُرَئِّسِي
يُرَئِّسُوا	يُرَئِّسَا	يُرَئِّسْ	يُرَئِّسُوا	يُرَئِّسَا	يُرَئِّسَ
يُرَئِّسْنَ	تُرَئِّسَا	تُرَئِّسْ	يُرَئِّسْنَ	تُرَئِّسَا	تُرَئِّسَ

Verbal Noun تَرْئِيس *tar'īs* **Participle** مُرَئِّس *mura''īs*

Imperative رَئِّسْ، رَئِّسِي؛ رَئِّسَا؛ رَئِّسُوا، رَئِّسْنَ *ra''is, -ī; -ā; -ū, -na*

PASSIVE **Present** يُرَأَّسُ *yura''asu* **Past** رُئِّسَ *ru''isa*

Participle مُرَأَّس *mura''as*

I رَأَسَ يَرْأَسُ (رِئَاسَة\رِيَاسَة) to head هـ 37 (no alternative subjunctive/jussive); V تَرَأَّسَ to be appointed head/chairman, to take the chair **43**

رَأْس ج رُءُوس head رَئِيس ج رُؤَسَاء chief, chairman, president

رَئِيسِي main رِئَاسَة\رِيَاسَة leadership, chairmanship, presidency

رَأْسًا directly رَأْس مَال\رَأْسْمَال capital (finance) رَأْسْمَالِي capitalist

رَأْسْمَالِيَة capitalism رَئِيس وُزَرَاء prime minister رَأْس السَنَة New Year

41 | III سَاءَلَ يُسَائِلُ *sā'ala yusā'ilu* to question ه | سأل

ACTIVE	**Present**	*yusā'ilu*		**Past**	*sā'ala*
نُسَائِلُ		أُسَائِلُ	سَاءَلْنَا		سَاءَلْتُ
تُسَائِلُونَ	تُسَائِلَانِ	تُسَائِلُ	سَاءَلْتُمْ	سَاءَلْتُمَا	سَاءَلْتَ
تُسَائِلْنَ	تُسَائِلَانِ	تُسَائِلِينَ	سَاءَلْتُنَّ	سَاءَلْتُمَا	سَاءَلْتِ
يُسَائِلُونَ	يُسَائِلَانِ	يُسَائِلُ	سَاءَلُوا	سَاءَلَا	سَاءَلَ
يُسَائِلْنَ	تُسَائِلَانِ	تُسَائِلُ	سَاءَلْنَ	سَاءَلَتَا	سَاءَلَتْ

	Jussive	*yusā'il*		**Subjunctive**	*yusā'ila*
نُسَائِلْ		أُسَائِلْ	نُسَائِلَ		أُسَائِلَ
تُسَائِلُوا	تُسَائِلَا	تُسَائِلْ	تُسَائِلُوا	تُسَائِلَا	تُسَائِلَ
تُسَائِلْنَ	تُسَائِلَا	تُسَائِلِي	تُسَائِلْنَ	تُسَائِلَا	تُسَائِلِي
يُسَائِلُوا	يُسَائِلَا	يُسَائِلْ	يُسَائِلُوا	يُسَائِلَا	يُسَائِلَ
يُسَائِلْنَ	تُسَائِلَا	تُسَائِلْ	يُسَائِلْنَ	تُسَائِلَا	تُسَائِلَ

Verbal Noun مُسَاءَلَة *musā'ala* **Participle** مُسَائِل *musā'il*

Imperative سَائِلْ، سَائِلِي؛ سَائِلَا؛ سَائِلُوا، سَائِلْنَ *sā'il, -ī; -ā; -ū, -na*

PASSIVE **Present** يُسَاءَلُ *yusā'alu* **Past** سُوئِلَ *sū'ila*

Participle مُسَاءَل *musā'al*

See **37**

42 | **IV** | أَكْأَبَ يُكْئِبُ *'ak'aba yuk'ibu* to sadden ه | **كأب**

ACTIVE	**Present**	*yuk'ibu*		**Past**	*'ak'aba*
نُكْئِبُ		أُكْئِبُ	أَكْأَبْنَا		أَكْأَبْتُ
تُكْئِبُونَ	تُكْئِبَانِ	تُكْئِبُ	أَكْأَبْتُمْ	أَكْأَبْتُمَا	أَكْأَبْتَ
تُكْئِبْنَ	تُكْئِبَانِ	تُكْئِبِينَ	أَكْأَبْتُنَّ	أَكْأَبْتُمَا	أَكْأَبْتِ
يُكْئِبُونَ	يُكْئِبَانِ	يُكْئِبُ	أَكْأَبُوا	أَكْأَبَا	أَكْأَبَ
يُكْئِبْنَ	تُكْئِبَانِ	تُكْئِبُ	أَكْأَبْنَ	أَكْأَبَتَا	أَكْأَبَتْ

	Jussive	*yuk'ib*		**Subjunctive**	*yuk'iba*
نُكْئِبْ		أُكْئِبْ	نُكْئِبَ		أُكْئِبَ
تُكْئِبُوا	تُكْئِبَا	تُكْئِبْ	تُكْئِبُوا	تُكْئِبَا	تُكْئِبَ
تُكْئِبْنَ	تُكْئِبَا	تُكْئِبِي	تُكْئِبْنَ	تُكْئِبَا	تُكْئِبِي
يُكْئِبُوا	يُكْئِبَا	يُكْئِبْ	يُكْئِبُوا	يُكْئِبَا	يُكْئِبَ
يُكْئِبْنَ	تُكْئِبَا	تُكْئِبْ	يُكْئِبْنَ	تُكْئِبَا	تُكْئِبَ

Verbal Noun اِكْآب *ik'āb* **Participle** مُكْئِب *muk'ib*

Imperative أَكْئِبْ، أَكْئِبِي؛ أَكْئِبَا؛ أَكْئِبُوا، أَكْئِبْنَ *'ak'ib, -ī; -ā; -ū, -na*

PASSIVE **Present** يُكْأَبُ *yuk'abu* **Past** أُكْئِبَ *'uk'iba*

Participle مُكْأَب *muk'ab*

I/VIII كَئِبَ يَكْأَبُ (كَأْب) \ اِكْتَأَبَ to be sad about على 39/45

كَأْب \ اِكْتِئَاب sorrow كَئِب \ كَئِيب \ مُكْتَئِب sorrowful

43 V تَرَأَّسَ يَتَرَأَّسُ *tara''asa yatara''asu* — رأس

to be appointed head/chairman, to take the chair

ACTIVE Present *yatara''asu*

نَتَرَأَّسُ		أَتَرَأَّسُ
تَتَرَأَّسُونَ	تَتَرَأَّسَانِ	تَتَرَأَّسُ
تَتَرَأَّسْنَ	تَتَرَأَّسَانِ	تَتَرَأَّسِينَ
يَتَرَأَّسُونَ	يَتَرَأَّسَانِ	يَتَرَأَّسُ
يَتَرَأَّسْنَ	تَتَرَأَّسَانِ	تَتَرَأَّسُ

Past *tara''asa*

تَرَأَّسْنَا		تَرَأَّسْتُ
تَرَأَّسْتُمْ	تَرَأَّسْتُمَا	تَرَأَّسْتَ
تَرَأَّسْتُنَّ	تَرَأَّسْتُمَا	تَرَأَّسْتِ
تَرَأَّسُوا	تَرَأَّسَا	تَرَأَّسَ
تَرَأَّسْنَ	تَرَأَّسَتَا	تَرَأَّسَتْ

Jussive *yatara''as*

نَتَرَأَّسْ		أَتَرَأَّسْ
تَتَرَأَّسُوا	تَتَرَأَّسَا	تَتَرَأَّسْ
تَتَرَأَّسْنَ	تَتَرَأَّسَا	تَتَرَأَّسِي
يَتَرَأَّسُوا	يَتَرَأَّسَا	يَتَرَأَّسْ
يَتَرَأَّسْنَ	تَتَرَأَّسَا	تَتَرَأَّسْ

Subjunctive *yatara''asa*

نَتَرَأَّسَ		أَتَرَأَّسَ
تَتَرَأَّسُوا	تَتَرَأَّسَا	تَتَرَأَّسَ
تَتَرَأَّسْنَ	تَتَرَأَّسَا	تَتَرَأَّسِي
يَتَرَأَّسُوا	يَتَرَأَّسَا	يَتَرَأَّسَ
يَتَرَأَّسْنَ	تَتَرَأَّسَا	تَتَرَأَّسَ

Verbal Noun يَتَرَأُّس *tara''us* **Participle** مُتَرَئِّس *mutara''is*

Imperative تَرَأَّسْ، تَرَأَّسِي؛ تَرَأَّسَا؛ تَرَأَّسُوا، تَرَأَّسْنَ
tara''as, -ī; -ā; -ū, -na

PASSIVE° Present يُتَرَأَّسُ *yutara''asu* **Past** تُرُئِّسَ *turu''isa*

See **40**

44 | **VI** | تَفاءَلَ يَتَفاءَلُ *tafā'ala yatafā'alu* to be optimistic | **فأل**

ACTIVE

Present *yatafā'alu*

نَتَفاءَلُ		أَتَفاءَلُ
تَتَفاءَلُونَ	تَتَفاءَلانِ	تَتَفاءَلُ
تَتَفاءَلْنَ	تَتَفاءَلانِ	تَتَفاءَلِينَ
يَتَفاءَلُونَ	يَتَفاءَلانِ	يَتَفاءَلُ
يَتَفاءَلْنَ	تَتَفاءَلانِ	تَتَفاءَلُ

Past *tafā'ala*

تَفاءَلْنا		تَفاءَلْتُ
تَفاءَلْتُمْ	تَفاءَلْتُما	تَفاءَلْتَ
تَفاءَلْتُنَّ	تَفاءَلْتُما	تَفاءَلْتِ
تَفاءَلُوا	تَفاءَلا	تَفاءَلَ
تَفاءَلْنَ	تَفاءَلَتا	تَفاءَلَتْ

Jussive *yatafā'al*

نَتَفاءَلْ		أَتَفاءَلْ
تَتَفاءَلُوا	تَتَفاءَلا	تَتَفاءَلْ
تَتَفاءَلْنَ	تَتَفاءَلا	تَتَفاءَلِي
يَتَفاءَلُوا	يَتَفاءَلا	يَتَفاءَلْ
يَتَفاءَلْنَ	تَتَفاءَلا	تَتَفاءَلْ

Subjunctive *yatafā'ala*

نَتَفاءَلَ		أَتَفاءَلَ
تَتَفاءَلُوا	تَتَفاءَلا	تَتَفاءَلَ
تَتَفاءَلْنَ	تَتَفاءَلا	تَتَفاءَلِي
يَتَفاءَلُوا	يَتَفاءَلا	يَتَفاءَلَ
يَتَفاءَلْنَ	تَتَفاءَلا	تَتَفاءَلَ

Verbal Noun تَفاؤُل *tafā'ul* **Participle** مُتَفائِل *mutafā'il*

Impv. تَفاءَلْ، تَفاءَلِي؛ تَفاءَلا؛ تَفاءَلُوا، تَفاءَلْنَ *tafā'al, -ī; -ā; -ū, -na*

PASSIVE° **Present** يُتَفاءَلُ *yutafā'alu* **Past** تُفُوئِلَ *tufū'ila*

فَأْل ج فُؤُول\أَفْؤُل good omen

تَفاؤُل optimism

مُتَفائِل optimist(ic)

قَرَأَ الفَأْل to tell ('read') fortunes

45 | VIII | الْتَأَمَ يَلْتَئِمُ *iltá'ama yaltá'imu* | لأم

to be convened/mended

ACTIVE **Present** *yaltá'imu*

نَلْتَئِمُ		أَلْتَئِمُ
تَلْتَئِمُونَ	تَلْتَئِمَانِ	تَلْتَئِمُ
تَلْتَئِمْنَ	تَلْتَئِمَانِ	تَلْتَئِمِينَ
يَلْتَئِمُونَ	يَلْتَئِمَانِ	يَلْتَئِمُ
يَلْتَئِمْنَ	تَلْتَئِمَانِ	تَلْتَئِمُ

Past *iltá'ama*

الْتَأَمْنَا		الْتَأَمْتُ
الْتَأَمْتُمْ	الْتَأَمْتُمَا	الْتَأَمْتَ
الْتَأَمْتُنَّ	الْتَأَمْتُمَا	الْتَأَمْتِ
الْتَأَمُوا	الْتَأَمَا	الْتَأَمَ
الْتَأَمْنَ	الْتَأَمَتَا	الْتَأَمَتْ

Jussive *yaltá'im*

نَلْتَئِمْ		أَلْتَئِمْ
تَلْتَئِمُوا	تَلْتَئِمَا	تَلْتَئِمْ
تَلْتَئِمْنَ	تَلْتَئِمَا	تَلْتَئِمِي
يَلْتَئِمُوا	يَلْتَئِمَا	يَلْتَئِمْ
يَلْتَئِمْنَ	تَلْتَئِمَا	تَلْتَئِمْ

Subjunctive *yaltá'ima*

نَلْتَئِمَ		أَلْتَئِمَ
تَلْتَئِمُوا	تَلْتَئِمَا	تَلْتَئِمَ
تَلْتَئِمْنَ	تَلْتَئِمَا	تَلْتَئِمِي
يَلْتَئِمُوا	يَلْتَئِمَا	يَلْتَئِمَ
يَلْتَئِمْنَ	تَلْتَئِمَا	تَلْتَئِمَ

Verbal Noun الْتِئَام *ilti'ām* **Participle** مُلْتَئِم *multá'im*

Imperative الْتَئِمْ، الْتَئِمِي؛ الْتَئِمَا؛ الْتَئِمُوا، الْتَئِمْنَ
iltá'im, -ī; -ā; -ū, -na

PASSIVE° **Present** يُلْتَأَمُ *yultá'amu* **Past** أُلْتُئِمَ *ultú'ima*

I لأَمَ يَلأَمُ (لأْم) to mend, bandage هـ 37 (no alternative subjunctive/jussive form); III لاءَمَ to suit ه هـ 41

لأْم repair, bandaging

مُلاءَمَة suitability

مُلائِم ل suitable for

46 | X | اِسْتَرْأَفَ يَسْتَرْئِفُ *istar'afa yastar'ifu* | رأف

to beg mercy of مِن

ACTIVE

Past *istar'afa*

اِسْتَرْأَفْتُ		اِسْتَرْأَفْنَا
اِسْتَرْأَفْتَ	اِسْتَرْأَفْتُمَا	اِسْتَرْأَفْتُمْ
اِسْتَرْأَفْتِ	اِسْتَرْأَفْتُمَا	اِسْتَرْأَفْتُنَّ
اِسْتَرْأَفَ	اِسْتَرْأَفَا	اِسْتَرْأَفُوا
اِسْتَرْأَفَتْ	اِسْتَرْأَفَتَا	اِسْتَرْأَفْنَ

Present *yastar'ifu*

أَسْتَرْئِفُ		نَسْتَرْئِفُ
تَسْتَرْئِفُ	تَسْتَرْئِفَانِ	تَسْتَرْئِفُونَ
تَسْتَرْئِفِينَ	تَسْتَرْئِفَانِ	تَسْتَرْئِفْنَ
يَسْتَرْئِفُ	يَسْتَرْئِفَانِ	يَسْتَرْئِفُونَ
تَسْتَرْئِفُ	تَسْتَرْئِفَانِ	يَسْتَرْئِفْنَ

Subjunctive *yastar'ifa*

أَسْتَرْئِفَ		نَسْتَرْئِفَ
تَسْتَرْئِفَ	تَسْتَرْئِفَا	تَسْتَرْئِفُوا
تَسْتَرْئِفِي	تَسْتَرْئِفَا	تَسْتَرْئِفْنَ
يَسْتَرْئِفَ	يَسْتَرْئِفَا	يَسْتَرْئِفُوا
تَسْتَرْئِفَ	تَسْتَرْئِفَا	يَسْتَرْئِفْنَ

Jussive *yastar'if*

أَسْتَرْئِفْ		نَسْتَرْئِفْ
تَسْتَرْئِفْ	تَسْتَرْئِفَا	تَسْتَرْئِفُوا
تَسْتَرْئِفِي	تَسْتَرْئِفَا	تَسْتَرْئِفْنَ
يَسْتَرْئِفْ	يَسْتَرْئِفَا	يَسْتَرْئِفُوا
تَسْتَرْئِفْ	تَسْتَرْئِفَا	يَسْتَرْئِفْنَ

Verbal Noun اِسْتِرْآف *istir'āf* **Participle** مُسْتَرْئِف *mustar'if*

Imperative اِسْتَرْئِفْ، اِسْتَرْئِفِي؛ اِسْتَرْئِفَا؛ اِسْتَرْئِفُوا، اِسْتَرْئِفْنَ
istar'if, -ī; -ā; -ū, -na

PASSIVE° **Present** يُسْتَرْأَفُ *yustar'afu* **Past** أُسْتُرْئِفَ *ustur'ifa*

Participle مُسْتَرْأَف *mustar'af*

I رَؤُفَ يَرْؤُفُ (رَأْفَة) to show mercy to ب 38

رَأْفَة\رَآفَة mercy, kindness

رَؤُوف merciful, kindly

47 | I | قَرَأَ يَقْرَأُ *qara'a yaqra'u* to read هـ | قرأ

ACTIVE

Present *yaqra'u*

نَقْرَأُ		أَقْرَأُ
تَقْرَأُونَ\تَقْرَؤُونَ	تَقْرَآنِ	تَقْرَأُ
تَقْرَأْنَ	تَقْرَآنِ	تَقْرَئِينَ
يَقْرَأُونَ\يَقْرَؤُونَ	يَقْرَآنِ	يَقْرَأُ
يَقْرَأْنَ	تَقْرَآنِ	تَقْرَأُ

Past *qara'a*

قَرَأْنَا		قَرَأْتُ
قَرَأْتُمْ	قَرَأْتُمَا	قَرَأْتَ
قَرَأْتُنَّ	قَرَأْتُمَا	قَرَأْتِ
قَرَأُوا\قَرَؤُوا	قَرَآ	قَرَأَ
قَرَأْنَ	قَرَأَتَا	قَرَأَتْ

Jussive *yaqra'*

نَقْرَأْ		أَقْرَأْ
تَقْرَأُوا\تَقْرَؤُوا	تَقْرَآ	تَقْرَأْ
تَقْرَأْنَ	تَقْرَآ	تَقْرَئِي
يَقْرَأُوا\يَقْرَؤُوا	يَقْرَآ	يَقْرَأْ
يَقْرَأْنَ	تَقْرَآ	تَقْرَأْ

Subjunctive *yaqra'a*

نَقْرَأَ		أَقْرَأَ
تَقْرَأُوا\تَقْرَؤُوا	تَقْرَآ	تَقْرَأَ
تَقْرَأْنَ	تَقْرَآ	تَقْرَئِي
يَقْرَأُوا\يَقْرَؤُوا	يَقْرَآ	يَقْرَأَ
يَقْرَأْنَ	تَقْرَآ	تَقْرَأَ

Verbal Noun قِرَاءَة *qirā'a* **Participle** قَارِئ *qāri'*

Imperative اِقْرَأْ ، اِقْرَئِي؛ اِقْرَآ؛ اِقْرَأُوا\اِقْرَؤُوا ، اِقْرَأْنَ

iqra', -ī; -ā; -ū, -na

PASSIVE **Present** يُقْرَأُ *yuqra'u* **Past** قُرِئَ *quri'a*

Participle مَقْرُوء *maqrū'*

X اِسْتَقْرَأَ to investigate هـ 57

القُرْآن the Koran/Qur'an

قِرَاءَة reading

قَارِئ ج قُرَّاء reader, Koranic reciter

قُرْآنِي Koranic

مَقْرُوء read, legible

اِسْتِقْرَاء investigation

48 | **I** | بَطُؤَ يَبْطُؤُ *baṭu'a yabṭu'u* to be slow | **بطأ**

ACTIVE

Present *yabṭu'u*

نَبْطُؤُ		أَبْطُؤُ
تَبْطُؤُونَ	تَبْطُؤَانِ	تَبْطُؤُ
تَبْطُؤْنَ	تَبْطُؤَانِ	تَبْطُئِينَ
يَبْطُؤُونَ	يَبْطُؤَانِ	يَبْطُؤُ
يَبْطُؤْنَ	تَبْطُؤَانِ	تَبْطُؤُ

Past *baṭu'a*

بَطُؤْنَا		بَطُؤْتُ
بَطُؤْتُمْ	بَطُؤْتُمَا	بَطُؤْتَ
بَطُؤْتُنَّ	بَطُؤْتُمَا	بَطُؤْتِ
بَطُؤُوا	بَطُؤَا	بَطُؤَ
بَطُؤْنَ	بَطُؤَتَا	بَطُؤَتْ

Jussive *yabṭu'*

نَبْطُؤْ		أَبْطُؤْ
تَبْطُؤُوا	تَبْطُؤَا	تَبْطُؤْ
تَبْطُؤْنَ	تَبْطُؤَا	تَبْطُئِي
يَبْطُؤُوا	يَبْطُؤَا	يَبْطُؤْ
يَبْطُؤْنَ	تَبْطُؤَا	تَبْطُؤْ

Subjunctive *yabṭu'a*

نَبْطُؤَ		أَبْطُؤَ
تَبْطُؤُوا	تَبْطُؤَا	تَبْطُؤَ
تَبْطُؤْنَ	تَبْطُؤَا	تَبْطُئِي
يَبْطُؤُوا	يَبْطُؤَا	يَبْطُؤَ
يَبْطُؤْنَ	تَبْطُؤَا	تَبْطُؤَ

Verbal Noun بُطْء *buṭ'* **Participle** بَاطِئ *bāṭi'*

Imperative أُبْطُؤْ، أُبْطُئِي؛ أُبْطُؤَا؛ أُبْطُؤُوا، أُبْطُؤْنَ *ubṭu', -ī; -ā; -ū, -na*

PASSIVE none

II بَطَّأَ to retard على ب 50; IV أَبْطَأَ to retard هـ 52;

V/VI تَبَطَّأَ \ تَبَاطَأَ 53/54 = I بَطُؤَ **48**; X اِسْتَبْطَأَ to find slow هـ ه 57

بُطْء \ تَبَاطُؤ slowness — إِبْطَاء retardation

بِبُطْء slowly — بَطِيء ج بِطَاء slow

دون إِبْطَاء without delay — بَطِيء التَرَدُّد low-frequency, LF

إِضْرَاب تَبَاطُؤ العَمَل go-slow (strike)

49 | I | بَرِئَ يَبْرَأُ *bari'a yabra'u* to be(come) free from من **برأ**

ACTIVE Present *yabra'u*

نَبْرَأُ		أَبْرَأُ
تَبْرَأُونَ\تَبْرَؤُونَ	تَبْرَآنِ	تَبْرَأُ
تَبْرَأْنَ	تَبْرَآنِ	تَبْرَئِينَ
يَبْرَأُونَ\يَبْرَؤُونَ	يَبْرَآنِ	يَبْرَأُ
يَبْرَأْنَ	تَبْرَآنِ	تَبْرَأُ

Past *bari'a*

بَرِئْنَا		بَرِئْتُ
بَرِئْتُمْ	بَرِئْتُمَا	بَرِئْتَ
بَرِئْتُنَّ	بَرِئْتُمَا	بَرِئْتِ
بَرِئُوا	بَرِئَا	بَرِئَ
بَرِئْنَ	بَرِئَتَا	بَرِئَتْ

Jussive *yabra'*

نَبْرَأْ		أَبْرَأْ
تَبْرَأُوا\تَبْرَؤُوا	تَبْرَآ	تَبْرَأْ
تَبْرَأْنَ	تَبْرَآ	تَبْرَئِي
يَبْرَأُوا\يَبْرَؤُوا	يَبْرَآ	يَبْرَأْ
يَبْرَأْنَ	تَبْرَآ	تَبْرَأْ

Subjunctive *yabra'a*

نَبْرَأَ		أَبْرَأَ
تَبْرَأُوا\تَبْرَؤُوا	تَبْرَآ	تَبْرَأَ
تَبْرَأْنَ	تَبْرَآ	تَبْرَئِي
يَبْرَأُوا\يَبْرَؤُوا	يَبْرَآ	يَبْرَأَ
يَبْرَأْنَ	تَبْرَآ	تَبْرَأَ

Verbal Noun بَرَاءَة *barā'a* **Participle** بَارِئ *bāri'*

Imperative اِبْرَأْ ، اِبْرَئِي؛ اِبْرَآ؛ اِبْرَأُوا\اِبْرَؤُوا ، اِبْرَأْنَ *ibra', -ī; -ā; -ū, -na*

PASSIVE° Present يُبْرَأُ *yubra'u* **Past** بُرِئَ *buri'a*

Participle مَبْرُوء *mabrū'*

II/IV بَرَّأَ\أَبْرَأَ to absolve from ه من 50/52; V تَبَرَّأَ to clear o.s. of من 53

بَرَاء من free/exempt from

إِبْرَاء acquittal

بَرِيء ج أَبْرِيَاء من free of

على بَرَاءَة innocent

تَبْرِئَة discharge, exemption

بَرَاءَة being free, innocence, diploma, patent

50 | II — هَنَّأَ يُهَنِّئُ *hanna'a yuhanni'u* — **هنأ**

to congratulate on ه ب\على

ACTIVE

Past *hanna'a*

هَنَّأْتُ		هَنَّأْنَا
هَنَّأْتَ	هَنَّأْتُمَا	هَنَّأْتُمْ
هَنَّأْتِ	هَنَّأْتُمَا	هَنَّأْتُنَّ
هَنَّأَ	هَنَّآ	هَنَّأُوا\هَنَّؤُوا
هَنَّأَتْ	هَنَّأَتَا	هَنَّأْنَ

Present *yuhanni'u*

أُهَنِّئُ		نُهَنِّئُ
تُهَنِّئُ	تُهَنِّئَانِ	تُهَنِّئُونَ
تُهَنِّئِينَ	تُهَنِّئَانِ	تُهَنِّئْنَ
يُهَنِّئُ	يُهَنِّئَانِ	يُهَنِّئُونَ
تُهَنِّئُ	تُهَنِّئَانِ	يُهَنِّئْنَ

Subjunctive *yuhanni'a*

أُهَنِّئَ		نُهَنِّئَ
تُهَنِّئَ	تُهَنِّئَا	تُهَنِّئُوا
تُهَنِّئِي	تُهَنِّئَا	تُهَنِّئْنَ
يُهَنِّئَ	يُهَنِّئَا	يُهَنِّئُوا
تُهَنِّئَ	تُهَنِّئَا	يُهَنِّئْنَ

Jussive *yuhanni'*

أُهَنِّئْ		نُهَنِّئْ
تُهَنِّئْ	تُهَنِّئَا	تُهَنِّئُوا
تُهَنِّئِي	تُهَنِّئَا	تُهَنِّئْنَ
يُهَنِّئْ	يُهَنِّئَا	يُهَنِّئُوا
تُهَنِّئْ	تُهَنِّئَا	يُهَنِّئْنَ

Verbal Noun تَهْنِئَة *tahni'a* **Participle** مُهَنِّئ *muhanni'*

Imperative هَنِّئْ، هَنِّئِي؛ هَنِّئَا؛ هَنِّئُوا، هَنِّئْنَ *hanni', -ī; -ā; -ū, -na*

PASSIVE **Present** يُهَنَّأُ *yuhanna'u* **Past** هُنِّئَ *hunni'a*

Participle مُهَنَّأ *muhanna'*

I (هَنَأَ) هَنَأَ يَهْنَأُ\يَهْنُؤُ\يَهْنِئُ to do good to/for ه ل 47 (also ...\...ُ ...ِ -u-/-i- in present tenses); V تَهَنَّأَ to enjoy ب 53

مُهَنِّئ wellwisher	تَهْنِئَة ج تَهَانِئ congratulation
هَانِئ happy	هَنَاء wellbeing
هَنِيء wholesome	هَنِئَة servant-girl
الله يُهَنِّئُكَ! same to you! (reply)	هَنِيئًا! good health! bon appétit!

51 III كَافَأَ يُكَافِئُ *kāfa'a yukāfi'u* to reward ه ـ **كفأ**

ACTIVE	**Present**	*yukāfi'u*		**Past**	*hanna'a*
نُكَافِئُ		أُكَافِئُ	كَافَأْنَا		كَافَأْتُ
تُكَافِئُونَ	تُكَافِئَانِ	تُكَافِئُ	كَافَأْتُمْ	كَافَأْتُمَا	كَافَأْتَ
تُكَافِئْنَ	تُكَافِئَانِ	تُكَافِئِينَ	كَافَأْتُنَّ	كَافَأْتُمَا	كَافَأْتِ
يُكَافِئُونَ	يُكَافِئَانِ	يُكَافِئُ	كَافَأُوا\كَافَؤُوا	كَافَآ	كَافَأَ
يُكَافِئْنَ	تُكَافِئَانِ	تُكَافِئُ	كَافَأْنَ	كَافَأَتَا	كَافَأَتْ

	Jussive	*yukāfi'*		**Subjunctive**	*yukāfi'a*
نُكَافِئْ		أُكَافِئْ	نُكَافِئَ		أُكَافِئَ
تُكَافِئُوا	تُكَافِئَا	تُكَافِئْ	تُكَافِئُوا	تُكَافِئَا	تُكَافِئَ
تُكَافِئْنَ	تُكَافِئَا	تُكَافِئِي	تُكَافِئْنَ	تُكَافِئَا	تُكَافِئِي
يُكَافِئُوا	يُكَافِئَا	يُكَافِئْ	يُكَافِئُوا	يُكَافِئَا	يُكَافِئَ
يُكَافِئْنَ	تُكَافِئَا	تُكَافِئْ	يُكَافِئْنَ	تُكَافِئَا	تُكَافِئَ

Verbal Noun مُكَافَأَة *mukāfa'a* **Participle** مُكَافِئ *mukāfi'*

Imperative كَافِئْ، كَافِئِي؛ كَافِئَا؛ كَافِئُوا، كَافِئْنَ *kāfi', -ī; -ā; -ū, -na*

PASSIVE **Present** يُكَافَأُ *yukāfa'u* **Past** كُوفِئَ *kūfi'a*

Participle مُكَافَأ *mukāfa'*

I كَفَأَ يَكْفَأُ (كَفْء) to invert ه ـ, to turn away from من 47;

IV أَكْفَأَ to invert ه ـ 52; VI تَكَافَأَ to be equal to e.o. 54;

VII اِنْكَفَأَ to be repelled **55**

مُكَافَأَة reward — مُتَكَافِئ corresponding

كَفْء ج أَكْفَاء ل equal to, suitable for — كَفَاءَة equality

تَكَافُؤ equivalence — مُكَافِئ equivalent (adj.) — كِفَاء an equivalent

52 | IV | أَنْشَأَ يُنْشِئُ *'ansha'a yunshi'u* | نشأ

to create, construct هـ

ACTIVE

Past *'ansha'a*

أَنْشَأْتُ		أَنْشَأْنَا
أَنْشَأْتَ	أَنْشَأْتُمَا	أَنْشَأْتُمْ
أَنْشَأْتِ	أَنْشَأْتُمَا	أَنْشَأْتُنَّ
أَنْشَأَ	أَنْشَآ	أَنْشَأُوا\أَنْشَؤُوا
أَنْشَأَتْ	أَنْشَأَتَا	أَنْشَأْنَ

Present *yunshi'u*

أُنْشِئُ		نُنْشِئُ
تُنْشِئُ	تُنْشِئَانِ	تُنْشِئُونَ
تُنْشِئِينَ	تُنْشِئَانِ	تُنْشِئْنَ
يُنْشِئُ	يُنْشِئَانِ	يُنْشِئُونَ
تُنْشِئُ	تُنْشِئَانِ	يُنْشِئْنَ

Subjunctive *yunshi'a*

أُنْشِئَ		نُنْشِئَ
تُنْشِئَ	تُنْشِئَا	تُنْشِئُوا
تُنْشِئِي	تُنْشِئَا	تُنْشِئْنَ
يُنْشِئَ	يُنْشِئَا	يُنْشِئُوا
تُنْشِئَ	تُنْشِئَا	يُنْشِئْنَ

Jussive *yunshi'*

أُنْشِئْ		نُنْشِئْ
تُنْشِئْ	تُنْشِئَا	تُنْشِئُوا
تُنْشِئِي	تُنْشِئَا	تُنْشِئْنَ
يُنْشِئْ	يُنْشِئَا	يُنْشِئُوا
تُنْشِئْ	تُنْشِئَا	يُنْشِئْنَ

Verbal Noun إِنْشَاء *'inshā'* **Participle** مُنْشِئ *munshi'*

Impv. أَنْشِئْ، أَنْشِئِي؛ أَنْشِئَا؛ أَنْشِئُوا، أَنْشِئْنَ *'anshi', -ī; -ā; -ū, -na*

PASSIVE Present يُنْشَأُ *yunsha'u* **Past** أُنْشِئَ *'unshi'a*

Participle مُنْشَأ *munsha'*

I نَشَأَ يَنْشَأُ (نَشْء) to arise 47; II نَشَّأَ to bring up (a child) ه 50

إِنْشَاء creation, construction, composition — نُشُوء evolution

إِنْشَائِي creative, editorial — مُنْشِئ creator, author — مَنْشَأ place of origin

مُنْشَأَة creation, production — نَشْء younger generation

نَشِئَ عن arising from — نَشْأَة\تَنْشِيء\تَنْشِئَة upbringing

53 | V | تَنَبَّأَ يَتَنَبَّأُ *tanabba'a yatanabba'u* to forecast ب | نبأ

ACTIVE Present *yatanabba'u*

أَتَنَبَّأُ		نَتَنَبَّأُ
تَتَنَبَّأُ	تَتَنَبَّآنِ	تَتَنَبَّأُونَ\تَتَنَبَّؤُونَ
تَتَنَبَّئِينَ	تَتَنَبَّآنِ	تَتَنَبَّأْنَ
يَتَنَبَّأُ	يَتَنَبَّآنِ	يَتَنَبَّأُونَ\يَتَنَبَّؤُونَ
تَتَنَبَّأُ	تَتَنَبَّآنِ	يَتَنَبَّأْنَ

Past *tanabba'a*

تَنَبَّأْتُ		تَنَبَّأْنَا
تَنَبَّأْتَ	تَنَبَّأْتُمَا	تَنَبَّأْتُمْ
تَنَبَّأْتِ	تَنَبَّأْتُمَا	تَنَبَّأْتُنَّ
تَنَبَّأَ	تَنَبَّآ	تَنَبَّأُوا\تَنَبَّؤُوا
تَنَبَّأَتْ	تَنَبَّأَتَا	تَنَبَّأْنَ

Jussive *yatanabba'*

أَتَنَبَّأْ		نَتَنَبَّأْ
تَتَنَبَّأْ	تَتَنَبَّآ	تَتَنَبَّأُوا\تَتَنَبَّؤُوا
تَتَنَبَّئِي	تَتَنَبَّآ	تَتَنَبَّأْنَ
يَتَنَبَّأْ	يَتَنَبَّآ	يَتَنَبَّأُوا\يَتَنَبَّؤُوا
تَتَنَبَّأْ	تَتَنَبَّآ	يَتَنَبَّأْنَ

Subjunctive *yatanabba'a*

أَتَنَبَّأَ		تَتَنَبَّأَ
تَتَنَبَّأَ	تَتَنَبَّآ	تَتَنَبَّأُوا\تَتَنَبَّؤُوا
تَتَنَبَّئِي	تَتَنَبَّآ	تَتَنَبَّأْنَ
يَتَنَبَّأَ	يَتَنَبَّآ	يَتَنَبَّأُوا\يَتَنَبَّؤُوا
تَتَنَبَّأَ	تَتَنَبَّآ	يَتَنَبَّأْنَ

Verbal Noun تَنَبُّؤ *tanabbu'* **Participle** مُتَنَبِّئ *mutanabbi'*

Imperative تَنَبَّأْ ، تَنَبَّئِي؛ تَنَبَّآ؛ تَنَبَّأُوا\تَنَبَّؤُوا ، تَنَبَّأْنَ
tanabba', -ī; -ā; -ū, -na

PASSIVE° **Present** يُتَنَبَّأُ *yutanabba'u* **Past** تُنُبِّئَ *tunubbi'a*
Participle مُتَنَبَّأ *mutanabba'*

II نَبَّأَ to inform ه ب\عن 50; IV أَنْبَأَ to inform ه ب 52;
X اِسْتَنْبَأَ to enquire after هـ 57

تَنَبُّؤ forecast — نَبَأ ج أَنْبَاء news

إِنْبَاء notification — نُبُوءَة prophecy

اِسْتِنْبَاء inquiry — تَنَبُّؤَات جَوِّيَة (pl.) weather forecast

54 | VI | تَبَاطَأَ يَتَبَاطَأُ *tabāṭa'a yatabāṭa'u* to be slow | **بطأ**

ACTIVE			**Present** *yatabāṭa'u*			**Past** *tabāṭa'a*
	نَتَبَاطَأُ		أَتَبَاطَأُ	تَبَاطَأْنَا		تَبَاطَأْتُ
	تَتَبَاطَأُونَ\تَتَبَاطَؤُونَ	تَتَبَاطَآنِ	تَتَبَاطَأُ	تَبَاطَأْتُمْ	تَبَاطَأْتُمَا	تَبَاطَأْتَ
	تَتَبَاطَأْنَ	تَتَبَاطَآنِ	تَتَبَاطَئِينَ	تَبَاطَأْتُنَّ	تَبَاطَأْتُمَا	تَبَاطَأْتِ
	يَتَبَاطَأُونَ\يَتَبَاطَؤُونَ	يَتَبَاطَآنِ	يَتَبَاطَأُ	تَبَاطَأُوا\تَبَاطَؤُوا	تَبَاطَآ	تَبَاطَأَ
	يَتَبَاطَأْنَ	تَتَبَاطَآنِ	تَتَبَاطَأُ	تَبَاطَأْنَ	تَبَاطَأَتَا	تَبَاطَأَتْ

	Jussive *yatabāṭa'*			**Subjunctive** *yatabāṭa'a*	
نَتَبَاطَأْ		أَتَبَاطَأْ	تَتَبَاطَأَ		أَتَبَاطَأَ
تَتَبَاطَأُوا\تَتَبَاطَؤُوا	تَتَبَاطَآ	تَتَبَاطَأْ	تَتَبَاطَأُوا\تَتَبَاطَؤُوا	تَتَبَاطَآ	تَتَبَاطَأَ
تَتَبَاطَأْنَ	تَتَبَاطَآ	تَتَبَاطَئِي	تَتَبَاطَأْنَ	تَتَبَاطَآ	تَتَبَاطَئِي
يَتَبَاطَأُوا\يَتَبَاطَؤُوا	يَتَبَاطَآ	يَتَبَاطَأْ	يَتَبَاطَأُوا\يَتَبَاطَؤُوا	يَتَبَاطَآ	يَتَبَاطَأَ
يَتَبَاطَأْنَ	تَتَبَاطَآ	تَتَبَاطَأْ	يَتَبَاطَأْنَ	تَتَبَاطَآ	تَتَبَاطَأَ

Verbal Noun تَبَاطُؤ *tabāṭu'* **Participle** مُتَبَاطِئ *mutabāṭi'*

Imperative تَبَاطَأْ ، تَبَاطَئِي؛ تَبَاطَآ؛ تَبَاطَأُوا\تَبَاطَؤُوا ، تَبَاطَأْنَ

tabāṭa', -ī; -ā; -ū, -na

PASSIVE none

See **48**

55 VII اِنْكَفَأَ يَنْكَفِئُ *inkáfa'a yankáfi'u* to be repelled — كفأ

ACTIVE	**Present**	*yankáfi'u*		**Past**	*inkáfa'a*
نَنْكَفِئُ		أَنْكَفِئُ	اِنْكَفَأْنَا		اِنْكَفَأْتُ
تَنْكَفِئُونَ	تَنْكَفِئَانِ	تَنْكَفِئُ	اِنْكَفَأْتُمْ	اِنْكَفَأْتُمَا	اِنْكَفَأْتَ
تَنْكَفِئْنَ	تَنْكَفِئَانِ	تَنْكَفِئِينَ	اِنْكَفَأْتُنَّ	اِنْكَفَأْتُمَا	اِنْكَفَأْتِ
يَنْكَفِئُونَ	يَنْكَفِئَانِ	يَنْكَفِئُ	اِنْكَفَأُوا\اِنْكَفَؤُوا	اِنْكَفَآ	اِنْكَفَأَ
يَنْكَفِئْنَ	تَنْكَفِئَانِ	تَنْكَفِئُ	اِنْكَفَأْنَ	اِنْكَفَأَتَا	اِنْكَفَأَتْ

	Jussive	*yankáfi'*		**Subjunctive**	*yankáfi'a*
نَنْكَفِئْ		أَنْكَفِئْ	نَنْكَفِئَ		أَنْكَفِئَ
تَنْكَفِئُوا	تَنْكَفِئَا	تَنْكَفِئْ	تَنْكَفِئُوا	تَنْكَفِئَا	تَنْكَفِئَ
تَنْكَفِئْنَ	تَنْكَفِئَا	تَنْكَفِئِي	تَنْكَفِئْنَ	تَنْكَفِئَا	تَنْكَفِئِي
يَنْكَفِئُوا	يَنْكَفِئَا	يَنْكَفِئْ	يَنْكَفِئُوا	يَنْكَفِئَا	يَنْكَفِئَ
يَنْكَفِئْنَ	تَنْكَفِئَا	تَنْكَفِئْ	يَنْكَفِئْنَ	تَنْكَفِئَا	تَنْكَفِئَ

Verbal Noun اِنْكِفَاء *inkifā'* **Participle** مُنْكَفِئ *munkáfi'*

Imperative اِنْكَفِئْ، اِنْكَفِئِي؛ اِنْكَفِئَا؛ اِنْكَفِئُوا، اِنْكَفِئْنَ

inkáfi', -ī; -ā; -ū, -na

PASSIVE none

See **51**

56 | VIII | ابْتَدَأَ يَبْتَدِئُ *ibtáda'a yabtádi'u* to begin ب | **بدأ**

ACTIVE

Past *ibtáda'a*

ابْتَدَأْتُ		ابْتَدَأْنَا
ابْتَدَأْتَ	ابْتَدَأْتُمَا	ابْتَدَأْتُمْ
ابْتَدَأْتِ	ابْتَدَأْتُمَا	ابْتَدَأْتُنَّ
ابْتَدَأَ	ابْتَدَآ	ابْتَدَأُوا\ابْتَدَؤُوا
ابْتَدَأَتْ	ابْتَدَأَتَا	ابْتَدَأْنَ

Present *yabtádi'u*

أَبْتَدِئُ		نَبْتَدِئُ
تَبْتَدِئُ	تَبْتَدِئَانِ	تَبْتَدِئُونَ
تَبْتَدِئِينَ	تَبْتَدِئَانِ	تَبْتَدِئْنَ
يَبْتَدِئُ	يَبْتَدِئَانِ	يَبْتَدِئُونَ
تَبْتَدِئُ	تَبْتَدِئَانِ	يَبْتَدِئْنَ

Subjunctive *yabtádi'a*

أَبْتَدِئَ		نَبْتَدِئَ
تَبْتَدِئَ	تَبْتَدِئَا	تَبْتَدِئُوا
تَبْتَدِئِي	تَبْتَدِئَا	تَبْتَدِئْنَ
يَبْتَدِئَ	يَبْتَدِئَا	يَبْتَدِئُوا
تَبْتَدِئَ	تَبْتَدِئَا	يَبْتَدِئْنَ

Jussive *yabtádi'*

أَبْتَدِئْ		نَبْتَدِئْ
تَبْتَدِئْ	تَبْتَدِئَا	تَبْتَدِئُوا
تَبْتَدِئِي	تَبْتَدِئَا	تَبْتَدِئْنَ
يَبْتَدِئْ	يَبْتَدِئَا	يَبْتَدِئُوا
تَبْتَدِئْ	تَبْتَدِئَا	يَبْتَدِئْنَ

Verbal Noun ابْتِدَاء *ibtidā'* **Participle** مُبْتَدِئ *mubtádi'*

Impv. ابْتَدِئْ، ابْتَدِئِي؛ ابْتَدِئَا؛ ابْتَدِئُوا، ابْتَدِئْنَ *ibtádi', -ī; -ā; -ū, -na*

PASSIVE° **Present** يُبْتَدَأُ *yubtáda'u* **Past** أُبْتُدِئَ *ubtúdi'a*

Participle مُبْتَدَأ *mubtáda'*

I بَدَأَ يَبْدَأُ (بَدْء) to begin ه\ب\في\π 47;

II بَدَّأَ to give priority over ه على 50

ابْتِدَاء\بَدْء\بِدَايَة\مُبْتَدَأ beginning (noun) — مُبْتَدِئ beginner

بَادِئ\مُبْتَدِئ beginning (adj.) — مَبْدَأ ج مَبَادِئ principle, origin

مَبْدَئِي fundamental, original — مَبْدَئِيًّا in principle, originally

ابْتِدَائِي initial, primary — ابْتِدَاءً من with effect from

من البِدَايَة from the beginning — تَعْلِيم ابْتِدَائِي primary education

57 | X | اِسْتَقْرَأَ يَسْتَقْرِئُ *istaqra'a yastaqri'u* to investigate هـ | **قرأ**

ACTIVE

Past *istaqra'a*

اِسْتَقْرَأْنَا		اِسْتَقْرَأْتُ
اِسْتَقْرَأْتُمْ	اِسْتَقْرَأْتُمَا	اِسْتَقْرَأْتَ
اِسْتَقْرَأْتُنَّ	اِسْتَقْرَأْتُمَا	اِسْتَقْرَأْتِ
اِسْتَقْرَأُوا\اِسْتَقْرَؤُوا	اِسْتَقْرَآ	اِسْتَقْرَأَ
اِسْتَقْرَأْنَ	اِسْتَقْرَأَتَا	اِسْتَقْرَأَتْ

Present *yastaqri'u*

نَسْتَقْرِئُ		أَسْتَقْرِئُ
تَسْتَقْرِئُونَ	تَسْتَقْرِئَانِ	تَسْتَقْرِئُ
تَسْتَقْرِئْنَ	تَسْتَقْرِئَانِ	تَسْتَقْرِئِينَ
يَسْتَقْرِئُونَ	يَسْتَقْرِئَانِ	يَسْتَقْرِئُ
يَسْتَقْرِئْنَ	تَسْتَقْرِئَانِ	تَسْتَقْرِئُ

Subjunctive *yastaqri'a*

نَسْتَقْرِئَ		أَسْتَقْرِئَ
تَسْتَقْرِئُوا	تَسْتَقْرِئَا	تَسْتَقْرِئَ
تَسْتَقْرِئْنَ	تَسْتَقْرِئَا	تَسْتَقْرِئِي
يَسْتَقْرِئُوا	يَسْتَقْرِئَا	يَسْتَقْرِئَ
يَسْتَقْرِئْنَ	تَسْتَقْرِئَا	تَسْتَقْرِئَ

Jussive *yastaqri'*

نَسْتَقْرِئْ		أَسْتَقْرِئْ
تَسْتَقْرِئُوا	تَسْتَقْرِئَا	تَسْتَقْرِئْ
تَسْتَقْرِئْنَ	تَسْتَقْرِئَا	تَسْتَقْرِئِي
يَسْتَقْرِئُوا	يَسْتَقْرِئَا	يَسْتَقْرِئْ
يَسْتَقْرِئْنَ	تَسْتَقْرِئَا	تَسْتَقْرِئْ

Verbal Noun اِسْتِقْرَاء *istiqrā'* **Participle** مُسْتَقْرِئ *mustaqri'*

Imperative اِسْنَقْرِئْ، اِسْنَقْرِئِي؛ اِسْنَقْرِئَا؛ اِسْنَقْرِئُوا، اِسْنَقْرِئْنَ

istaqri', -ī; -ā; -ū, -na

PASSIVE **Present** يُسْتَقْرَأُ *yustaqra'u* **Past** أُسْتُقْرِئَ *ustuqri'a*

Participle مُسْتَقْرَأ *mustaqra'*

See **47**

Doubled

Doubled verbs have identical middle and final root letters. These identical root letters are sound (i.e. not و , ي or ء). The initial root letter is mostly sound; one doubled verb has initial و and is listed here (no. **61**), as the و is mostly stable (i.e. becomes a consonant, *w*). Two important doubled roots have initial *hamza*, and are listed here (nos. **63** and **67**.) The sound patterns shown in §§ 7, 8, 17, 18, 21-23 and 26 apply to doubled verbs, with the exceptions shown below:

- The identical root letters fall together as a doubled letter when followed by a vowel in full-form pronunciation (§ 6):
  أمرُّ *'amurru* I pass ظلّوا *ẓallū* they remained
- The identical root letters are written and pronounced separately:
  - when not followed by a vowel in full-form pronunciation:
    مررْتُ *marartu* I passed †نمرُرْ *namrur*† we pass (jussive)
  - when separated by a long vowel: تقرير *taqrīr* 'report'.
- In all Forms except II and V there are two jussives and imperatives: a commoner 'contracted' pattern identical to the subjunctive, and a rarer 'uncontracted' pattern in which the identical root letters are separated when not followed by a vowel. Compare with no. **22** (sound, Form IX).
- The alternative uncontracted patterns are further found in the tenses of Forms III and VI (see nos. **64** and **66**).

Participles follow the sound rules, except that the *-i-* or *-a-* which in sound participles follows the middle root letter, follows the *initial* root letter in doubled Forms IV and X, and is *dropped* in doubled Forms I, VII and VIII, as also in the contracted patterns of III and VI.

Verbal nouns follow the sound rules, except that the contracted pattern of Form VI has no vowel *-u-* between the middle and final root letters.

The verbal noun of no. **65** (Form IV) is irregular; a regular Form IV model is e.g. إصرار *'iṣrār* 'insistence', from أصرّ *'aṣarra* IV 'to insist'.

58 | **I** | مَرَّ يَمُرُّ *marra yamurru* to pass ب\على, to continue π | **مرّ**

ACTIVE	**Present**	*yamurru*		**Past**	*marra*
نَمُرُّ		أَمُرُّ	مَرَرْنَا		مَرَرْتُ
تَمُرُّونَ	تَمُرَّانِ	تَمُرُّ	مَرَرْتُمْ	مَرَرْتُمَا	مَرَرْتَ
تَمْرُرْنَ	تَمُرَّانِ	تَمُرِّينَ	مَرَرْتُنَّ	مَرَرْتُمَا	مَرَرْتِ
يَمُرُّونَ	يَمُرَّانِ	يَمُرُّ	مَرُّوا	مَرَّا	مَرَّ
يَمْرُرْنَ	تَمُرَّانِ	تَمُرُّ	مَرَرْنَ	مَرَّتَا	مَرَّتْ

	Jussive (ii)†	*yamrur*	**Subjunc.+Jussive (i)**		*yamurra*
نَمْرُرْ		أَمْرُرْ	نَمُرَّ		أَمُرَّ
تَمُرُّوا	تَمُرَّا	تَمْرُرْ	تَمُرُّوا	تَمُرَّا	تَمُرَّ
تَمْرُرْنَ	تَمُرَّا	تَمُرِّي	تَمْرُرْنَ	تَمُرَّا	تَمُرِّي
يَمُرُّوا	يَمُرَّا	يَمْرُرْ	يَمُرُّوا	يَمُرَّا	يَمُرَّ
يَمْرُرْنَ	تَمُرَّا	تَمْرُرْ	يَمْرُرْنَ	تَمُرَّا	تَمُرَّ

Verbal Noun مُرُور *murūr* **Participle** مَارّ *mārr*

Imperative مُرَّ\أُمْرُرْ † ، مُرِّي؛ مُرَّا؛ مُرُّوا ، أُمْرُرْنَ

murra/umrur†, murrī; murrā; murrū, umrurna

PASSIVE° **Present** يُمَرُّ *yumarru* **Past** مُرَّ *murra*

Participle مَمْرُور *mamrūr*

II/IV مَرَّرَ\أَمَرَّ to let pass ه هـ 62/65; X اِسْتَمَرَّ to continue π\في\على 72

مَارّ passing, passer-by إِمْرَار insertion مُسْتَمِرّ continuous

اِسْتِمْرَار continuity بِاسْتِمْرَار\مُسْتَمِرًّا continually مَرَّة (وَاحِدَة) once

(عِدَّة) مَرَّات often مَرَّة جَدِيدَة\ثَانِيَة\أُخْرَى again مَرَّتَيْن twice

لأَوَّل\لآخر مَرَّة for the first/last time تَذْكَرَة المُرُور laissez-passer

مع مُرُور الزَمَن with the passage of time إِشَارَة مُرُور traffic signal

59 **I** ظَلَّ يَظَلُّ *ẓalla yaẓallu* to become, remain ١ً, to continue π **ظلّ**

ACTIVE	**Present**	*yaẓallu*		**Past**	*ẓalla*
نَظَلُّ		أَظَلُّ	ظَلَلْنَا		ظَلَلْتُ
تَظَلُّونَ	تَظَلاَّنِ	تَظَلُّ	ظَلَلْتُمْ	ظَلَلْتُمَا	ظَلَلْتَ
تَظْلَلْنَ	تَظَلاَّنِ	تَظَلِّينَ	ظَلَلْتُنَّ	ظَلَلْتُمَا	ظَلَلْتِ
يَظَلُّونَ	يَظَلاَّنِ	يَظَلُّ	ظَلُّوا	ظَلاَّ	ظَلَّ
يَظْلَلْنَ	تَظَلاَّنِ	تَظَلُّ	ظَلَلْنَ	ظَلَّتَا	ظَلَّتْ
	Jussive (ii)†	*yaẓlal*	**Subjunc.+ Jussive (i)**		*yaẓalla*
نَظْلَلْ		أَظْلَلْ	نَظَلَّ		أَظَلَّ
تَظَلُّوا	تَظَلاَّ	تَظْلَلْ	تَظَلُّوا	تَظَلاَّ	تَظَلَّ
تَظْلَلْنَ	تَظَلاَّ	تَظَلِّي	تَظْلَلْنَ	تَظَلاَّ	تَظَلِّي
يَظَلُّوا	يَظَلاَّ	يَظْلَلْ	يَظَلُّوا	يَظَلاَّ	يَظَلَّ
يَظْلَلْنَ	تَظَلاَّ	تَظْلَلْ	يَظْلَلْنَ	تَظَلاَّ	تَظَلَّ

Verbal Noun ظَلّ *ẓall* **Participle** ظَالّ *ẓāll*

Imperative ظَلَّ\اِظْلَلْ†، ظَلِّي؛ ظَلاَّ؛ ظَلُّوا، اِظْلَلْنَ
ẓalla/iẓlal†, ẓallī; ẓallā; ẓallū, iẓlalna

PASSIVE none

II/IV ظَلَّلَ\أَظَلَّ to overshadow ـه ه 62/65; V تَظَلَّلَ to be overshadowed by بـ 66; X اِسْتَظَلَّ to seek the protection of بـ 72

ظِلّ ج ظِلاَل\ظُلُول shade, shadow, patronage ظَلِيل shaded

مِظَلَّة sunshade, parachute مِظَلِّي paratrooper

مُظَلّ approved في\تحت ظِلّ under the patronage of

ظَلَّ على رَأْيِه أنّ to maintain the opinion that

ظَلَّ يَدْرُسُ الهَنْدَسَة. He continued to study engineering.

60 | **I** | تَمَّ يَتِمُّ *tamma yatimmu* to come to an end | **تمّ**

ACTIVE **Past** *tamma*

Singular	Dual	Plural
تَمَمْتُ		تَمَمْنَا
تَمَمْتَ	تَمَمْتُمَا	تَمَمْتُمْ
تَمَمْتِ	تَمَمْتُمَا	تَمَمْتُنَّ
تَمَّ	تَمَّا	تَمُّوا
تَمَّتْ	تَمَّتَا	تَمَمْنَ

Present *yatimmu*

Singular	Dual	Plural
أَتِمُّ		نَتِمُّ
تَتِمُّ	تَتِمَّانِ	تَتِمُّونَ
تَتِمِّينَ	تَتِمَّانِ	تَتْمِمْنَ
يَتِمُّ	يَتِمَّانِ	يَتِمُّونَ
تَتِمُّ	تَتِمَّانِ	يَتْمِمْنَ

Subjunc.+Jussive (i) *yatimma*

Singular	Dual	Plural
أَتِمَّ		نَتِمَّ
تَتِمَّ	تَتِمَّا	تَتِمُّوا
تَتِمِّي	تَتِمَّا	تَتْمِمْنَ
يَتِمَّ	يَتِمَّا	يَتِمُّوا
تَتِمَّ	تَتِمَّا	يَتْمِمْنَ

Jussive (ii)† *yatmim*

Singular	Dual	Plural
أَتْمِمْ		نَتْمِمْ
تَتْمِمْ	تَتِمَّا	تَتِمُّوا
تَتِمِّي	تَتِمَّا	تَتْمِمْنَ
يَتْمِمْ	يَتِمَّا	يَتِمُّوا
تَتْمِمْ	تَتِمَّا	يَتْمِمْنَ

Verbal Noun تَمَام *tamām* **Participle** تَامّ *tāmm*

Imperative تِمَّ\اِتْمِمْ†، تِمِّي؛ تِمَّا؛ تِمُّوا، اِتْمِمْنَ

timma/itmim†, timmī; timmā; timmū, itmimna

PASSIVE° **Present** يُتَمُّ *yutammu* **Past** تُمَّ *tumma*

II/IV تَمَّمَ\أَتَمَّ to finish هـ 62/65

تَامّ complete, perfect

تَمَام complete(ness), perfect(ion)

تَتْمِيم\إِتْمَام completion

تَمَامًا\بِالتَّمَام completely, perfectly

فِي تَمَامِ السَّاعَةِ الثَّالِثَة at 3 o'clock sharp

قَمَر تَمَام full moon

فِي تَمَامِ مَعْنَى الإِبَارَة in the full meaning of the word ('expression')

تَمَّ وُصُول إِلى اتِّفَاقِيَّة a decision was arrived at

تَمَّتْ دِرَاسَة المَوْضُوع the matter was studied

61 | **I** | وَدَّ يَوَدُّ *wadda yawaddu* to like, love ه هـ\أنْ | **ودّ**

ACTIVE	**Present**	*yawaddu*		**Past**	*wadda*
نَوَدُّ		أَوَدُّ	وَدِدْنَا		وَدِدْتُ
تَوَدُّونَ	تَوَدَّانِ	تَوَدُّ	وَدِدْتُمْ	وَدِدْتُمَا	وَدِدْتَ
تَوْدَدْنَ	تَوَدَّانِ	تَوَدِّينَ	وَدِدْتُنَّ	وَدِدْتُمَا	وَدِدْتِ
يَوَدُّونَ	يَوَدَّانِ	يَوَدُّ	وَدُّوا	وَدَّا	وَدَّ
يَوْدَدْنَ	تَوَدَّانِ	تَوَدُّ	وَدِدْنَ	وَدَّتَا	وَدَّتْ
	Jussive (ii)†	*yawdad*	**Subjunc.+ Jussive (i)**		*yawadda*
نَوْدَدْ		أَوْدَدْ	نَوَدَّ		أَوَدَّ
تَوَدُّوا	تَوَدَّا	تَوْدَدْ	تَوَدُّوا	تَوَدَّا	تَوَدَّ
تَوْدَدْنَ	تَوَدَّا	تَوَدِّي	تَوْدَدْنَ	تَوَدَّا	تَوَدِّي
يَوَدُّوا	يَوَدَّا	يَوْدَدْ	يَوَدُّوا	يَوَدَّا	يَوَدَّ
يَوْدَدْنَ	تَوَدَّا	تَوْدَدْ	يَوْدَدْنَ	تَوَدَّا	تَوَدَّ

Verbal Noun وَدّ *wadd* **Participle** وادّ *wādd*

Imperative وَدَّ\ايدَدْ†، وَدِّي؛ وَدَّا؛ وَدُّوا، ايدَدْنَ

wadda/īdad†, waddī; waddā; waddū, īdadna

PASSIVE **Present** يُوَدُّ *yuwaddu* **Past** وُدَّ *wudda*

Participle مَوْدُود *mawdūd*

III وَدَّدَ to befriend ه 64; V تَوَدَّدَ to court, ingratiate o.s. with ه\إلى 66;

VI تَوادَّ to be friends with e.o. 68

وَدّ\وِداد\مَوَدَّة friendship, love

وَدِّي\وُدِّي friendly

وَدّ ج أَوْداد affectionate

وَدُود\وَدِيد attached

تَوادّ friendly relations

أَوَدّ أَنْ أَقُول ... I would like to say ...

كان بِوَدِّي لَوْ ... I would be pleased if ...

مُنافَسَة وُدِّيَّة friendly contest

تَسْوِيَة وُدِّيَّة amicable settlement

وَدِدْتُ لَوْ كُنْتُ ... I wish I were ...

62 II قَرَّرَ يُقَرِّرُ *qarrara yuqarriru* to report, decide هـ

قرّ

ACTIVE

Present *yuqarriru*

نُقَرِّرُ		أُقَرِّرُ
تُقَرِّرُونَ	تُقَرِّرَانِ	تُقَرِّرُ
تُقَرِّرْنَ	تُقَرِّرَانِ	تُقَرِّرِينَ
يُقَرِّرُونَ	تُقَرِّرَانِ	يُقَرِّرُ
يُقَرِّرْنَ	تُقَرِّرَانِ	تُقَرِّرُ

Past *qarrara*

قَرَّرْنَا		قَرَّرْتُ
قَرَّرْتُمْ	قَرَّرْتُمَا	قَرَّرْتَ
قَرَّرْتُنَّ	قَرَّرْتُمَا	قَرَّرْتِ
قَرَّرُوا	قَرَّرَا	قَرَّرَ
قَرَّرْنَ	قَرَّرَتَا	قَرَّرَتْ

Jussive *yuqarrir*

نُقَرِّرْ		أُقَرِّرْ
تُقَرِّرُوا	تُقَرِّرَا	تُقَرِّرْ
تُقَرِّرْنَ	تُقَرِّرَا	تُقَرِّرِي
يُقَرِّرُوا	يُقَرِّرَا	يُقَرِّرْ
يُقَرِّرْنَ	تُقَرِّرَا	تُقَرِّرْ

Subjunctive *yuqarrira*

نُقَرِّرَ		أُقَرِّرَ
تُقَرِّرُوا	تُقَرِّرَا	تُقَرِّرَ
تُقَرِّرْنَ	تُقَرِّرَا	تُقَرِّرِي
يُقَرِّرُوا	يُقَرِّرَا	يُقَرِّرَ
يُقَرِّرْنَ	تُقَرِّرَا	تُقَرِّرَ

Verbal Noun تَقْرِير *taqrīr* **Participle** مُقَرِّر *muqarrir*

Imperative قَرِّرْ، قَرِّرِي؛ قَرِّرَا؛ قَرِّرُوا، قَرِّرْنَ *qarrir, -ī; -ā; -ū, -na*

PASSIVE **Present** يُقَرَّرُ *yuqarraru* **Past** قُرِّرَ *qurrira*

Participle مُقَرَّر *muqarrar*

I قَرَّ يَقَرُّ (قَرَار) to settle down 60; IV أَقَرَّ to settle, establish ه هـ 65; V تَقَرَّرَ to be decided 66; X اسْتَقَرَّ to become stable 72

قَرَار stability, fixedness — مَقَرّ ج مَقَارّ site, habitation, headquarters

تَقْرِير\قَرَار decision — تَقْرِير ج تَقَارِير report — مُقَرِّر reporter

مُقَرَّر decided, fixed — مُسْتَقَرّ stable, settled — اِسْتِقْرَار stability

إِقْرَار establishment, confirmation — قَارّ permanent

لَجْنَة قَارَّة standing committee — تَقْرِير المَصِير self-determination

63 | **II** | أَمَّمَ يُؤَمِّمُ *'ammama yu'ammimu* to nationalise هـ | **أمّ**

ACTIVE

Past *'ammama*

أَمَّمْتُ		أَمَّمْنَا
أَمَّمْتَ	أَمَّمْتُمَا	أَمَّمْتُمْ
أَمَّمْتِ	أَمَّمْتُمَا	أَمَّمْتُنَّ
أَمَّمَ	أَمَّمَا	أَمَّمُوا
أَمَّمَتْ	أَمَّمَتَا	أَمَّمْنَ

Present *yu'ammimu*

أُؤَمِّمُ		نُؤَمِّمُ
تُؤَمِّمُ	تُؤَمِّمَانِ	تُؤَمِّمُونَ
تُؤَمِّمِينَ	تُؤَمِّمَانِ	تُؤَمِّمْنَ
يُؤَمِّمُ	يُؤَمِّمَانِ	يُؤَمِّمُونَ
تُؤَمِّمُ	تُؤَمِّمَانِ	يُؤَمِّمْنَ

Subjunctive *yu'ammima*

أُؤَمِّمَ		نُؤَمِّمَ
تُؤَمِّمَ	تُؤَمِّمَا	تُؤَمِّمُوا
تُؤَمِّمِي	تُؤَمِّمَا	تُؤَمِّمْنَ
يُؤَمِّمَ	يُؤَمِّمَا	يُؤَمِّمُوا
تُؤَمِّمَ	تُؤَمِّمَا	يُؤَمِّمْنَ

Jussive *yu'ammim*

أُؤَمِّمْ		نُؤَمِّمْ
تُؤَمِّمْ	تُؤَمِّمَا	تُؤَمِّمُوا
تُؤَمِّمِي	تُؤَمِّمَا	تُؤَمِّمْنَ
يُؤَمِّمْ	يُؤَمِّمَا	يُؤَمِّمُوا
تُؤَمِّمْ	تُؤَمِّمَا	يُؤَمِّمْنَ

Verbal Noun تَأْمِيم *ta'mīm* **Participle** مُؤَمِّم *mu'ammim*

Imperative أَمِّمْ، أَمِّمِي؛ أَمِّمَا؛ أَمِّمُوا، أَمِّمْنَ *'ammim, -ī; -ā; -ū, -na*

PASSIVE **Present** يُؤَمَّمُ *yu'ammamu* **Past** أُمِّمَ *'ummima*

Participle مُؤَمَّم *mu'ammam*

I أَمَّ يَؤُمُّ (أَمّ) to go to هـ, to seek out هـ ه, to show the way to ه 58;

V تَأَمَّمَ to be nationalised, to go to هـ, to seek out هـ ه 67;

VIII اِئْتَمَّ to follow the example of ه 70

أُمّ ج أُمَّهَات mother, matrix | أُمُومَة motherhood | أُمَّة ج أُمَم nation

الأُمَم المُتَّحِدَة United Nations | أُمِّي illiterate | أُمِّيَّة illiteracy

أَمَامَ in front of | أَمَامِي front, forward (adj.) | إِلَى الأَمَام forwards

نُقْطَة أَمَامِي outpost | تَأْمِيم nationalisation | إِمَام ج أَئِمَّة imam

64 III حَاجَّ\حَاجَجَ يُحَاجُّ\يُحَاجِجُ *ḥājja/ḥājaja yuḥājju/yuḥājiju* to dispute with ه **حجّ**

ACTIVE Past* *ḥājja/ḥājaja†*

حَاجَجْتُ		حَاجَجْنَا
حَاجَجْتَ	حَاجَجْتُمَا	حَاجَجْتُمْ
حَاجَجْتِ	حَاجَجْتُمَا	حَاجَجْتُنَّ
حَاجَّ	حَاجَّا	حَاجُّوا
حَاجَّتْ	حَاجَّتَا	حَاجَجْنَ

Present* *yuḥājju/yuḥājiju†*

أُحَاجُّ\أُحَاجِجُ†		نُحَاجُّ
تُحَاجُّ	تُحَاجَّانِ	تُحَاجُّونَ
تُحَاجِّينَ	تُحَاجَّانِ	تُحَاجِجْنَ
يُحَاجُّ	يُحَاجَّانِ	يُحَاجُّونَ
تُحَاجُّ	تُحَاجَّانِ	يُحَاجِجْنَ

Subjunctive* + Jussive (i)* *yuḥājja/yuḥājija†*

أُحَاجَّ\أُحَاجِجَ†		نُحَاجَّ
تُحَاجَّ	تُحَاجَّا	تُحَاجُّوا
تُحَاجِّي	تُحَاجَّا	تُحَاجِجْنَ
يُحَاجَّ	يُحَاجَّا	يُحَاجُّوا
تُحَاجَّ	تُحَاجَّا	يُحَاجِجْنَ

Jussive (ii)†* *yuḥājij*

أُحَاجِجْ		نُحَاجِجْ
تُحَاجِجْ	تُحَاجَّا	تُحَاجُّوا
تُحَاجِّي	تُحَاجَّا	تُحَاجِجْنَ
يُحَاجِجْ	يُحَاجَّا	يُحَاجُّوا
تُحَاجِجْ	تُحَاجَّا	يُحَاجِجْنَ

* In the tenses and derivatives marked *, the contracted forms have a rarer uncontracted alternative† on the pattern shown for each one.

Verbal Noun* حِجَاج\مُحَاجَجَة† *ḥijāj/muḥājaja†*

Participle* مُحَاجّ\مُحَاجِج† *muḥājj/muḥājij†*

Imperative* حَاجَّ\حَاجِجْ†، حَاجِّي؛ حَاجَّا؛ حَاجُّوا، حَاجِجْنَ
ḥājj-a/ḥājij†, -ī; -ā; -ū, ḥājijna

PASSIVE Present* يُحَاجُّ\يُحَاجَجُ† *yuḥājju/yuḥājaju†*

Past حُوجِجَ *ḥūjija* **Participle*** مُحَاجّ\مُحَاجَج† *muḥājj/muḥājaj†*

I حَجَّ يَحُجُّ (حَجّ) to make the Mecca pilgrimage 58; VI تَحَاجَّ\تَحَاجَجَ† to dispute with e.o. 68; VIII اِحْتَجَّ to protest against على 70

حَجّ pilgrimage حَاجّ ج حُجَّاج pilgrim حَجَج dispute اِحْتِجَاج protest

65 | **IV** | أَحَبَّ يُحِبُّ *'aḥabba yuḥibbu* to like, love ه هـ\أنْ | **حبّ**

ACTIVE Present *yuḥibbu*

نُحِبُّ		أُحِبُّ
تُحِبُّونَ	تُحِبَّانِ	تُحِبُّ
تُحْبِبْنَ	تُحِبَّانِ	تُحِبِّينَ
يُحِبُّونَ	يُحِبَّانِ	يُحِبُّ
يُحْبِبْنَ	تُحِبَّانِ	تُحِبُّ

Past *ḥabba*

أَحْبَبْنَا		أَحْبَبْتُ
أَحْبَبْتُمْ	أَحْبَبْتُمَا	أَحْبَبْتَ
أَحْبَبْتُنَّ	أَحْبَبْتُمَا	أَحْبَبْتِ
أَحَبُّوا	أَحَبَّا	أَحَبَّ
أَحْبَبْنَ	أَحَبَّتَا	أَحَبَّتْ

Jussive(ii)† *yuḥbib*

نُحْبِبْ		أُحْبِبْ
تُحِبُّوا	تُحِبَّا	تُحْبِبْ
تُحْبِبْنَ	تُحِبَّا	تُحِبِّي
يُحِبُّوا	يُحِبَّا	يُحْبِبْ
يُحْبِبْنَ	تُحِبَّا	تُحْبِبْ

Subjunc.+ Jussive(i) *yuḥabba*

نُحِبَّ		أُحِبَّ
تُحِبُّوا	تُحِبَّا	تُحِبَّ
تُحْبِبْنَ	تُحِبَّا	تُحِبِّي
يُحِبُّوا	يُحِبَّا	يُحِبَّ
يُحْبِبْنَ	تُحِبَّا	تُحِبَّ

Vb. Noun مَحَبَّة *maḥabba* (irregular) **Participle** مُحِبّ *muḥibb*

Imperative أَحِبَّ\أَحْبِبْ†، أَحِبِّي؛ أَحِبَّا؛ أَحِبُّوا، أَحْبِبْنَ

'aḥibba/'aḥbib†, 'aḥibbī; 'aḥibbā; 'aḥibbū, 'aḥbibna

PASSIVE Present يُحَبُّ *yuḥabbu* **Past** أُحِبَّ *'uḥibba*

Participle مُحَبّ *muḥabb*

I (حُبّ) حَبَّ يَحِبُّ ه هـ\أنْ 60 = (but less common than) IV أَحَبَّ 65

حُبّ\مُحَبَّة love حُبِّي amicable (also in law) حُبِّيًّا amicably (also in law)

أَحَبّ preferable حَبِيبَة ج حَبَائِب (f.) حَبِيب ج أَحْبَاب (m.) beloved

مَحْبُوب beloved مُحَبّ lover, amateur مُحَبَّب agreeable

حُبًّا لِ for love of حُبّ الوَطَن patriotism مُحِبّ للوَطَن patriot(ic)

حُبّ الذات egoism مُحِبّ للذات egoist(ic) مُحِبّ للسَلَام peace-loving

66 | V | **تَرَدَّدَ يَتَرَدَّدُ** *taraddada yataraddadu* | **ردّ**

to hesitate in/to فِي\أَنْ , to keep coming back to على

ACTIVE Present *yataraddadu* — **Past** *taraddada*

نَتَرَدَّدُ		أَتَرَدَّدُ	تَرَدَّدْنَا		تَرَدَّدْتُ
تَتَرَدَّدُونَ	تَتَرَدَّدَانِ	تَتَرَدَّدُ	تَرَدَّدْتُمْ	تَرَدَّدْتُمَا	تَرَدَّدْتَ
تَتَرَدَّدْنَ	تَتَرَدَّدَانِ	تَتَرَدَّدِينَ	تَرَدَّدْتُنَّ	تَرَدَّدْتُمَا	تَرَدَّدْتِ
يَتَرَدَّدُونَ	يَتَرَدَّدَانِ	يَتَرَدَّدُ	تَرَدَّدُوا	تَرَدَّدَا	تَرَدَّدَ
يَتَرَدَّدْنَ	تَتَرَدَّدَانِ	تَتَرَدَّدُ	تَرَدَّدْنَ	تَرَدَّدَتَا	تَرَدَّدَتْ

Jussive *yataraddad* — **Subjunctive** *yataraddada*

نَتَرَدَّدْ		أَتَرَدَّدْ	نَتَرَدَّدَ		أَتَرَدَّدَ
تَتَرَدَّدُوا	تَتَرَدَّدَا	تَتَرَدَّدْ	تَتَرَدَّدُوا	تَتَرَدَّدَا	تَتَرَدَّدَ
تَتَرَدَّدْنَ	تَتَرَدَّدَا	تَتَرَدَّدِي	تَتَرَدَّدْنَ	تَتَرَدَّدَا	تَتَرَدَّدِي
يَتَرَدَّدُوا	يَتَرَدَّدَا	يَتَرَدَّدْ	يَتَرَدَّدُوا	يَتَرَدَّدَا	يَتَرَدَّدَ
يَتَرَدَّدْنَ	تَتَرَدَّدَا	تَتَرَدَّدْ	يَتَرَدَّدْنَ	تَتَرَدَّدَا	تَتَرَدَّدَ

Verbal Noun تَرَدُّد *taraddud* **Participle** مُتَرَدِّد *mutaraddid*

Impv. تَرَدَّدْ ، تَرَدَّدِي؛ تَرَدَّدَا؛ تَرَدَّدُوا ، تَرَدَّدْنَ *taraddad, -ī; -ā; -ū, -na*

PASSIVE° **Present** يُتَرَدَّدُ *yutaraddadu* **Past** تُرُدِّدَ *turuddida*

Participle مُتَرَدَّد *mutaraddad*

I رَدَّ يَرُدُّ (رَدّ ج رُدُود) to give/send back ه هـ, to reply to على 58;

II رَدَّدَ to repel ه هـ 62; VIII اِرْتَدَّ to abandon عن 70;

X اِسْتَرَدَّ to reclaim, retrieve, withdraw هـ 72

رَدّ ج رُدُود restitution تَرْدِيد reiteration تَرَدُّد hesitation, frequentation

اِرْتِدَاد desertion اِسْتِرْدَاد retrieval مَرْدُود (financial) yield

رَدّ فِعْل reaction رَدّ فِعْل شَدِيد اللَّهْجَة a strongly worded reply

دَلِيل لا يُرَدّ indisputable evidence مَرَدّ basis (for an argument)

67 **V** تَأَسَّسَ يَتَأَسَّسُ *ta'assasa yata'assasu* **أسّ**

to be established

ACTIVE Present *yata'assasu*

نَتَأَسَّسُ		أَتَأَسَّسُ
تَتَأَسَّسُونَ	تَتَأَسَّسَانِ	تَتَأَسَّسُ
تَتَأَسَّسْنَ	تَتَأَسَّسَانِ	تَتَأَسَّسِينَ
يَتَأَسَّسُونَ	يَتَأَسَّسَانِ	يَتَأَسَّسُ
يَتَأَسَّسْنَ	تَتَأَسَّسَانِ	تَتَأَسَّسُ

Past *ta'assasa*

تَأَسَّسْنَا		تَأَسَّسْتُ
تَأَسَّسْتُمْ	تَأَسَّسْتُمَا	تَأَسَّسْتَ
تَأَسَّسْتُنَّ	تَأَسَّسْتُمَا	تَأَسَّسْتِ
تَأَسَّسُوا	تَأَسَّسَا	تَأَسَّسَ
تَأَسَّسْنَ	تَأَسَّسَتَا	تَأَسَّسَتْ

Jussive *yata'assas*

نَتَأَسَّسْ		أَتَأَسَّسْ
تَتَأَسَّسُوا	تَتَأَسَّسَا	تَتَأَسَّسْ
تَتَأَسَّسْنَ	تَتَأَسَّسَا	تَتَأَسَّسِي
يَتَأَسَّسُوا	يَتَأَسَّسَا	يَتَأَسَّسْ
يَتَأَسَّسْنَ	تَتَأَسَّسَا	تَتَأَسَّسْ

Subjunctive *yata'assasa*

نَتَأَسَّسَ		أَتَأَسَّسَ
تَتَأَسَّسُوا	تَتَأَسَّسَا	تَتَأَسَّسَ
تَتَأَسَّسْنَ	تَتَأَسَّسَا	تَتَأَسَّسِي
يَتَأَسَّسُوا	يَتَأَسَّسَا	يَتَأَسَّسَ
يَتَأَسَّسْنَ	تَتَأَسَّسَا	تَتَأَسَّسَ

Vb. Noun تَأَسُّس *ta'assus* **Participle, Imperative** not used

PASSIVE not used

II أَسَّسَ to establish هـ 63

أَسَاس ج أُسُس basis

أَسَاسِي basic, fundamental

أَسَاسِيَات (pl.) (basic) principles

أَسَاسِيًّا basically, essentially

تَأْسِيس\تَأَسُّس founding

مُؤَسِّس founder

مُؤَسَّس founded, established

مُؤَسَّسَة institution

68 | VI | تَضَادَّ\تَضَادَدَ يَتَضَادُّ\يَتَضَادَدُ *taḍādda/taḍādada yataḍāddu/yataḍādadu* to contradict e.o. | ضدّ

ACTIVE

Past* *taḍādda/taḍādada†*

تَضَادَدْتُ		تَضَادَدْنَا
تَضَادَدْتَ	تَضَادَدْتُمَا	تَضَادَدْتُمْ
تَضَادَدْتِ	تَضَادَدْتُمَا	تَضَادَدْتُنَّ
تَضَادَّ	تَضَادَّا	تَضَادُّوا
تَضَادَّتْ	تَضَادَّتَا	تَضَادَدْنَ

Present* *yataḍāddu/yataḍādadu†*

أَتَضَادُّ\أَتَضَادَدُ†		نَتَضَادُّ
تَتَضَادُّ	تَتَضَادَّانِ	تَتَضَادُّونَ
تَتَضَادِّينَ	تَتَضَادَّانِ	تَتَضَادَدْنَ
يَتَضَادُّ	يَتَضَادَّانِ	يَتَضَادُّونَ
تَتَضَادُّ	تَتَضَادَّانِ	يَتَضَادَدْنَ

Subjunctive* *yataḍādda/* **+ Jussive (i)*** *yataḍādada†*

أَتَضَادَّ\أَتَضَادَدَ†		نَتَضَادَّ
تَتَضَادَّ	تَتَضَادَّا	تَتَضَادُّوا
تَتَضَادِّي	تَتَضَادَّا	تَتَضَادَدْنَ
يَتَضَادَّ	يَتَضَادَّا	يَتَضَادُّوا
تَتَضَادَّ	تَتَضَادَّا	يَتَضَادَدْنَ

Jussive (ii)†* *yataḍādad*

أَتَضَادَدْ		نَتَضَادَدْ
تَتَضَادَدْ	تَتَضَادَّا	تَتَضَادُّوا
تَتَضَادِّي	تَتَضَادَّا	تَتَضَادَدْنَ
يَتَضَادَدْ	يَتَضَادَّا	يَتَضَادُّوا
تَتَضَادَدْ	تَتَضَادَّا	يَتَضَادَدْنَ

* In the tenses and derivatives marked *, the contracted forms have a rarer uncontracted alternative ('†') on the pattern shown for each one.

Verbal Noun* تَضَادّ\تَضَادُد† *taḍādd/taḍādud†*

Participle* مُتَضَادّ\مُتَضَادِد† *mutaḍādd/mutaḍādid†*

Imperative* تَضَادَّ\تَضَادَدْ†، تَضَادِّي؛ تَضَادَّا؛ تَضَادُّوا، تَضَادَدْنَ
taḍādd-a/taḍādad†, -ī; -ā; -ū, taḍādadna

PASSIVE° **Present*** يُتَضَادُّ\يُتَضَادَدُ† *yutaḍāddu/yutaḍādadu†*

Past تُضُودِدَ *tuḍūdida*

III ضَادَّ to contravene, oppose ـه 64

ضِدّ against مُضَادّ\تَضَادّ contrast, contradiction ضِدِّيَة opposition

مُضَادّ contra-, anti- هُجُوم مُضَادّ counter-attack مُضَادّ حَيَوِي antibiotic

69 | VII | انْحَلَّ يَنْحَلُّ *inḥalla yanḥallu* to be (dis)solved/untied | حلّ

ACTIVE	**Present** *yanḥallu*			**Past**	*inḥalla*
نَنْحَلُّ		أَنْحَلُّ	انْحَلَلْنَا		انْحَلَلْتُ
تَنْحَلُّونَ	تَنْحَلاَّنِ	تَنْحَلُّ	انْحَلَلْتُمْ	انْحَلَلْتُمَا	انْحَلَلْتَ
تَنْحَلِلْنَ	تَنْحَلاَّنِ	تَنْحَلِّينَ	انْحَلَلْتُنَّ	انْحَلَلْتُمَا	انْحَلَلْتِ
يَنْحَلُّونَ	يَنْحَلاَّنِ	يَنْحَلُّ	انْحَلُّوا	انْحَلاَّ	انْحَلَّ
يَنْحَلِلْنَ	تَنْحَلاَّنِ	تَنْحَلُّ	انْحَلَلْنَ	انْحَلَّتَا	انْحَلَّتْ

	Jussive (ii)† *yanḥálil*		**Subjunc.+Jussive (i)**		*yanḥalla*
نَنْحَلِلْ		أَنْحَلِلْ	نَنْحَلَّ		أَنْحَلَّ
تَنْحَلُّو	تَنْحَلاَّ	تَنْحَلِلْ	تَنْحَلُّوا	تَنْحَلاَّ	تَنْحَلَّ
تَنْحَلِلْنَ	تَنْحَلاَّ	تَنْحَلِّي	تَنْحَلِلْنَ	تَنْحَلاَّ	تَنْحَلِّي
يَنْحَلُّوا	يَنْحَلاَّ	يَنْحَلِلْ	يَنْحَلُّوا	يَنْحَلاَّ	يَنْحَلَّ
يَنْحَلِلْنَ	تَنْحَلاَّ	تَنْحَلِلْ	يَنْحَلِلْنَ	تَنْحَلاَّ	تَنْحَلَّ

Verbal Noun انْحِلاَل *inḥilāl* **Participle** مُنْحَلّ *munḥall*

Imperative انْحَلَّ\انْحَلِلْ†، انْحَلِّي؛ انْحَلاَّ؛ انْحَلُّوا، انْحَلِلْنَ

inḥalla/inḥálil†, inḥallī; inḥallā; inḥallū, inḥalilna

PASSIVE none (active voice of Form VII has passive meaning)

I (حَلّ) حَلَّ يَحُلُّ to untie, (dis)solve ه, to release ه ه 58;

II حَلَّل to analyse, permit ه, to absolve ه 62;

IV أَحَلَّ to release, permit, relocate ه 65; VIII احْتَلَّ to occupy ه 70

حَلّ ج حُلُول (dis)solution انْحِلاَل (dis)solution مَحَلّ place

مَحْلُول\مُنْحَلّ (dis)solved مَحَلِّي local تَحْلِيل analysis

تَحْلِيلِي analytical احْتِلاَل occupation مُحْتَلّ occupying, occupied

حَلَّ مَحَلَّ to take the place of قَابِل للحَلّ soluble بِالتَّحْلِيل in detail

70 VIII امْتَدَّ يَمْتَدُّ *imtadda yamtaddu* to be extended — مدّ

ACTIVE **Past** *imtadda*

امْتَدَدْتُ		امْتَدَدْنَا
امْتَدَدْتَ	امْتَدَدْتُمَا	امْتَدَدْتُمْ
امْتَدَدْتِ	امْتَدَدْتُمَا	امْتَدَدْتُنَّ
امْتَدَّ	امْتَدَّا	امْتَدُّوا
امْتَدَّتْ	امْتَدَّتَا	امْتَدَدْنَ

Present *yamtaddu*

أَمْتَدُّ		نَمْتَدُّ
تَمْتَدُّ	تَمْتَدَّانِ	تَمْتَدُّونَ
تَمْتَدِّينَ	تَمْتَدَّانِ	تَمْتَدِدْنَ
يَمْتَدُّ	يَمْتَدَّانِ	يَمْتَدُّونَ
تَمْتَدُّ	تَمْتَدَّانِ	يَمْتَدِدْنَ

Subjunc.+Jussive(i) *yamtadda*

أَمْتَدَّ		نَمْتَدَّ
تَمْتَدَّ	تَمْتَدَّا	تَمْتَدُّوا
تَمْتَدِّي	تَمْتَدَّا	تَمْتَدِدْنَ
يَمْتَدَّ	يَمْتَدَّا	يَمْتَدُّوا
تَمْتَدَّ	تَمْتَدَّا	يَمْتَدِدْنَ

Jussive(ii)† *yamtádid*

أَمْتَدِدْ		نَمْتَدِدْ
تَمْتَدِدْ	تَمْتَدَّا	تَمْتَدُّوا
تَمْتَدِّي	تَمْتَدَّا	تَمْتَدِدْنَ
يَمْتَدِدْ	يَمْتَدَّا	يَمْتَدُّوا
تَمْتَدِدْ	تَمْتَدَّا	يَمْتَدِدْنَ

Verbal Noun امْتِدَاد *imtidād* **Participle** مُمْتَدّ *mumtadd*

Imperative امْتَدَّ\امْتَدِدْ†، امْتَدِّي؛ امْتَدَّا؛ امْتَدُّوا، امْتَدِدْنَ

imtadda/imtádid†, imtaddī; imtaddā; imtaddū, imtadidna

PASSIVE° **Present** يُمْتَدُّ *yumtaddu* **Past** أُمْتُدَّ *umtudda*

I/II مَدَّ يَمُدُّ (مَدّ)\مَدَّدَ to extend هـ 58/62;

IV أَمَدَّ to provide with ه ب هـ ب 65; V تَمَدَّدَ to extend 66

مَدّ ج مُدُود extension مُدَّة ج مُدَد period of time تَمْدِيد\تَمَدُّد extension

امْدَاد supply امْتِدَاد extension, extensibility مَادّ extending

مَادَّة ج مَوَادّ material, clause (of document) مَادِّي material(ist(ic))

مَمْدُود\مُمَدَّد\مُمْتَدّ extended مَوَادّ خَام raw materials

مَوَادّ تِجَارِيَة commodities مَدَّ يَدَهُ to hold out one's hand

71 | VIII | اِضْطَرَّ يَضْطَرُّ *iḍṭarra yaḍṭarru* to compel to ه إلى | ضرّ

ACTIVE	**Present**	*yaḍṭarru*		**Past**	*iḍṭarra*
نَضْطَرُّ		أَضْطَرُّ	اِضْطَرَرْنَا		اِضْطَرَرْتُ
تَضْطَرُّونَ	تَضْطَرَّانِ	تَضْطَرُّ	اِضْطَرَرْتُمْ	اِضْطَرَرْتُمَا	اِضْطَرَرْتَ
تَضْطَرِرْنَ	تَضْطَرَّانِ	تَضْطَرِّينَ	اِضْطَرَرْتُنَّ	اِضْطَرَرْتُمَا	اِضْطَرَرْتِ
يَضْطَرُّونَ	يَضْطَرَّانِ	يَضْطَرُّ	اِضْطَرُّوا	اِضْطَرَّا	اِضْطَرَّ
يَضْطَرِرْنَ	تَضْطَرَّانِ	تَضْطَرُّ	اِضْطَرَرْنَ	اِضْطَرَّتَا	اِضْطَرَّتْ

	Jussive (ii)†	*yaḍṭárir*	**Subjunc.+ Jussive (i)**		*yaḍṭarra*
نَضْطَرِرْ		أَضْطَرِرْ	نَضْطَرَّ		أَضْطَرَّ
تَضْطَرُّوا	تَضْطَرَّا	تَضْطَرِرْ	تَضْطَرُّوا	تَضْطَرَّا	تَضْطَرَّ
تَضْطَرِرْنَ	تَضْطَرَّا	تَضْطَرِّي	تَضْطَرِرْنَ	تَضْطَرَّا	تَضْطَرِّي
يَضْطَرُّوا	يَضْطَرَّا	يَضْطَرِرْ	يَضْطَرُّوا	يَضْطَرَّا	يَضْطَرَّ
يَضْطَرِرْنَ	تَضْطَرَّا	تَضْطَرِرْ	يَضْطَرِرْنَ	تَضْطَرَّا	تَضْطَرَّ

Verbal Noun اِضْطِرَار *iḍṭirār* **Participle** مُضْطَرّ *muḍṭarr*

Imperative اِضْطَرَّ\اِضْطَرِرْ†، اِضْطَرِّي؛ اِضْطَرَّا؛ اِضْطَرُّوا، اِضْطَرِرْنَ

iḍṭarra/iḍṭárir†, iḍṭarrī; iḍṭarrā; iḍṭarrū, iḍṭarirna

PASSIVE **Present** يُضْطَرُّ *yuḍṭarru* **Past** أُضْطُرَّ *uḍṭurra*

Participle مُضْطَرّ *muḍṭarr*

I ضَرَّ يَضُرُّ (ضَرّ) to damage ه هـ 58; IV أَضَرَّ to oblige to ه على 65;
VII اِنْضَرَّ to be damaged 69

ضَرّ damage ضَرَر ج أَضْرَار damage ضَارّ\مُضِرّ harmful

ضَرُورَة necessity, emergency ضَرُورِي necessary اِضْطِرَار compulsion

مُضْطَرّ إلى compelled to عِنْدَ الضَرُورَة if necessary, in an emergency

(لَيْسَ) من الضَرُورِي أنْ ... It is (not) necessary that ...

72 | X | يَسْتَحِقُّ اِسْتَحَقَّ *istaḥaqqa yastaḥiqqu* to deserve هـ | **حقّ**

ACTIVE

Present *yastaḥiqqu*			Past *istaḥaqqa*		
نَسْتَحِقُّ		أَسْتَحِقُّ	اِسْتَحْقَقْنَا		اِسْتَحْقَقْتُ
تَسْتَحِقُّونَ	تَسْتَحِقَّانِ	تَسْتَحِقُّ	اِسْتَحْقَقْتُمْ	اِسْتَحْقَقْتُمَا	اِسْتَحْقَقْتَ
تَسْتَحْقِقْنَ	تَسْتَحِقَّانِ	تَسْتَحِقِّينَ	اِسْتَحْقَقْتُنَّ	اِسْتَحْقَقْتُمَا	اِسْتَحْقَقْتِ
يَسْتَحِقُّونَ	يَسْتَحِقَّانِ	يَسْتَحِقُّ	اِسْتَحَقُّوا	اِسْتَحَقَّا	اِسْتَحَقَّ
يَسْتَحْقِقْنَ	تَسْتَحِقَّانِ	تَسْتَحِقُّ	اِسْتَحْقَقْنَ	اِسْتَحَقَّتَا	اِسْتَحَقَّتْ

Jussive (ii)† *yastaḥqiq*			Subjunc.+Jussive (i) *yastaḥiqqa*		
نَسْتَحْقِقْ		أَسْتَحْقِقْ	نَسْتَحِقَّ		أَسْتَحِقَّ
تَسْتَحِقُّوا	تَسْتَحِقَّا	تَسْتَحْقِقْ	تَسْتَحِقُّوا	تَسْتَحِقَّا	تَسْتَحِقَّ
تَسْتَحْقِقْنَ	تَسْتَحِقَّا	تَسْتَحِقِّي	تَسْتَحْقِقْنَ	تَسْتَحِقَّا	تَسْتَحِقِّي
يَسْتَحِقُّوا	يَسْتَحِقَّا	يَسْتَحْقِقْ	يَسْتَحِقُّوا	يَسْتَحِقَّا	يَسْتَحِقَّ
يَسْتَحْقِقْنَ	تَسْتَحِقَّا	تَسْتَحْقِقْ	يَسْتَحْقِقْنَ	تَسْتَحِقَّا	تَسْتَحِقَّ

Vb. Noun اِسْتِحْقَاق *istiḥqāq* **Participle** مُسْتَحِقّ *mustaḥiqq*

Impv. † اِسْتَحِقَّ\اِسْتَحْقِقْ†، اِسْتَحِقِّي؛ اِسْتَحِقَّا؛ اِسْتَحِقُّوا، اِسْتَحْقِقْنَ

istaḥiqqa/istaḥqiq†, istaḥiqqī; istaḥiqqā; istaḥiqqū, istaḥqiqna

---

PASSIVE Present يُسْتَحَقُّ *yustaḥaqqu* **Past** اُسْتُحِقَّ *ustuḥiqqa*

Participle مُسْتَحَقّ *mustaḥaqq*

I (حَقّ) حَقَّ يَحِقُّ to be true 60;

II حَقَّقَ to realise, implement, confirm هـ 62; IV أَحَقَّ to be right in في 65;

V تَحَقَّقَ to be convinced of هـ , to materialise 66

حَقّ ج حُقُوق right (noun) حَقِيقَة ج حَقَائِق truth, reality حَقِيقِي true

تَحْقِيق realisation, confirmation, identification تَحَقُّق verification

حُقُوق jurisprudence الحَقّ معه\عليه he is right/wrong مُحِقّ truthful

Assimilated

Assimilated verbs are the first sub-class of the weak class. They have a weak letter, و or ي , as initial root letter, and two sound root letters (in one or two less common roots, middle ء and a final sound root letter). All common assimilated verbs have initial و ; initial ي verbs are few and infrequently used.

One root with initial و and identical sound middle and final root letters is studied under the doubled verbs (no. **61**).

The sound patterns shown in §§ 7, 8, 17, 18, 21-23 and 26 apply to assimilated verbs, subject to the following provisions:

- In the active present tenses of Form I of all common verbs with initial و , this initial root letter and its vowel are dropped. In the affirmative imperative of such verbs, the initial root letter and its vowel, and also the imperative prefix, are dropped:

  وجد *wajada* he found   يجد *yajidu* he finds

  جد\جدي *jid, jidī* find (m. s./f. s.)

  In a few exceptional roots, however, the initial و remains consonantal in Form I and the verb follows the sound pattern. All assimilated verbs with initial root letter ي are sound in Form I.
- The theoretical combination *uw/uy* becomes و *ū* and the theoretical combination *iw/iy* becomes يـ *ī*:

  أستورد *ustūrida* it was imported   إيجاب *'ījāb* imposition
- In Forms II, III, V and VI the weak root letter stabilises as a consonant (*w* or *y*), and the conjugation follows the sound pattern completely.
- There are no assimilated verbs in Form VII.
- In Form VIII, the initial root letter و plus the ت *-t-* of the increased form are combined as تّـ *-tt-*:

  اتّحد *ittáḥada* to be united (from root وحد)

Verbs with initial و are listed, in all Forms, before verbs with initial ي .

73 | **I** | وَجَدَ يَجِدُ *wajada yajidu* to find هـ | **وجد**

ACTIVE	Present *yajidu*			Past *wajada*	
نَجِدُ		أَجِدُ	وَجَدْنَا		وَجَدْتُ
تَجِدُونَ	تَجِدَانِ	تَجِدُ	وَجَدْتُمْ	وَجَدْتُمَا	وَجَدْتَ
تَجِدْنَ	تَجِدَانِ	تَجِدِينَ	وَجَدْتُنَّ	وَجَدْتُمَا	وَجَدْتِ
يَجِدُونَ	يَجِدَانِ	يَجِدُ	وَجَدُوا	وَجَدَا	وَجَدَ
يَجِدْنَ	تَجِدَانِ	تَجِدُ	وَجَدْنَ	وَجَدَتَا	وَجَدَتْ

	Jussive *yajid*			Subjunctive *yajida*	
نَجِدْ		أَجِدْ	نَجِدَ		أَجِدَ
تَجِدُوا	تَجِدَا	تَجِدْ	تَجِدُوا	تَجِدَا	تَجِدَ
تَجِدْنَ	تَجِدَا	تَجِدِي	تَجِدْنَ	تَجِدَا	تَجِدِي
يَجِدُوا	يَجِدَا	يَجِدْ	يَجِدُوا	يَجِدَا	يَجِدَ
يَجِدْنَ	تَجِدَا	تَجِدْ	يَجِدْنَ	تَجِدَا	تَجِدَ

Verbal Noun وُجُود *wujūd* **Participle** وَاجِد *wājid*

Imperative جِدْ ، جِدِي؛ جِدَا؛ جِدُوا ، جِدْنَ *jid, -ī; -ā; -ū, -na*

PASSIVE **Present** يُوجَدُ *yūjadu* **Past** وُجِدَ *wujida*

Participle مَوْجُود *mawjūd*

I *passive* وُجِدَ يُوجَدُ to exist, be there **73**;

IV أَوْجَدَ to bring about, accomplish هـ 79

وُجُود existence مَوْجُود found, present مُوجِد originator

مَوْجُودَات سَائِلِيَة\ثَابِتَة liquid/fixed assets إِيجَاد production, supply

يُوجَدُ\تُوجَد there is/are (of things) وُجُودِي existentialist

إِنْ وُجِدَ\وُجِدَت if any, if applicable (in statistics, reports etc.) وَجْد passion

لا يُوجَدُ\تُوجَد there is/are none, nil (in statistics, reports etc.)

74 | I | وَضَعَ يَضَعُ *waḍaʿa yaḍaʿu* to place, set down هـ | **وضع**

ACTIVE

Past *waḍaʿa*

وَضَعْتُ		وَضَعْنَا
وَضَعْتَ	وَضَعْتُمَا	وَضَعْتُمْ
وَضَعْتِ	وَضَعْتُمَا	وَضَعْتُنَّ
وَضَعَ	وَضَعَا	وَضَعُوا
ضَعَتْ	وَضَعَتَا	وَضَعْنَ

Present *yaḍaʿu*

أَضَعُ		نَضَعُ
تَضَعُ	تَضَعَانِ	تَضَعُونَ
تَضَعِينَ	تَضَعَانِ	تَضَعْنَ
يَضَعُ	يَضَعَانِ	يَضَعُونَ
تَضَعُ	تَضَعَانِ	يَضَعْنَ

Subjunctive *yaḍaʿa*

أَضَعَ		نَضَعَ
تَضَعَ	تَضَعَا	تَضَعُوا
تَضَعِي	تَضَعَا	تَضَعْنَ
يَضَعَ	يَضَعَا	يَضَعُوا
تَضَعَ	تَضَعَا	يَضَعْنَ

Jussive *yaḍaʿ*

أَضَعْ		نَضَعْ
تَضَعْ	تَضَعَا	تَضَعُوا
تَضَعِي	تَضَعَا	تَضَعْنَ
يَضَعْ	يَضَعَا	يَضَعُوا
تَضَعْ	تَضَعَا	يَضَعْنَ

Verbal Noun وَضْع *waḍʿ* **Participle** وَاضِع *wāḍiʿ*

Imperative ضَعْ ، ضَعِي؛ ضَعَا؛ ضَعُوا ، ضَعْنَ *ḍaʿ, -ī; -ā; -ū, -na*

PASSIVE **Present** يُوضَعُ *yūḍaʿu* **Past** وُضِعَ *wuḍiʿa*

Participle مَوْضُوع *mawḍūʿ*

VI/VIII تَوَضَعَ\اِتَّضَعَ to humble oneself 81/82

تَوَاضُع\اِتِّضَاع humility

وَضْع ج أَوْضَاع setting down, position, situation

وَضَعَ تَقْرِيراً to make a report

مَوْضُوع ج مَوَاضِيع subject, topic

مَوْضِع ج مَوَاضِع place, passage (of text)

مَوْضُوعِي objective (adj.)

وَضَعَ يَدَهُ على to lay hands on

وَضَعَ سِلاَحَهُ to lay down one's arms

في مَوْضِعِه in its place

شَكْلاً وَمَوْضُوعًا in form and substance

وَضِيع ج وُضَعَاء vulgar, low

مَوْضِع الاِهْتِمَام focus of attention

75 I وَرِثَ يَرِثُ *waritha yarithu* to inherit from ه\عن\من هـ **ورث**

ACTIVE	**Present** *yarithu*		**Past** *waritha*		
نَرِثُ		أَرِثُ	وَرِثْنَا		وَرِثْتُ
تَرِثُونَ	تَرِثَانِ	تَرِثُ	وَرِثْتُمْ	وَرِثْتُمَا	وَرِثْتَ
تَرِثْنَ	تَرِثَانِ	تَرِثِينَ	وَرِثْتُنَّ	وَرِثْتُمَا	وَرِثْتِ
يَرِثُونَ	يَرِثَانِ	يَرِثُ	وَرِثُوا	وَرِثَا	وَرِثَ
يَرِثْنَ	تَرِثَانِ	تَرِثُ	وَرِثْنَ	وَرِثَتَا	وَرِثَتْ
	Jussive *yarith*		**Subjunctive** *yaritha*		
نَرِثْ		أَرِثْ	نَرِثَ		أَرِثَ
تَرِثُوا	تَرِثَا	تَرِثْ	تَرِثُوا	تَرِثَا	تَرِثَ
تَرِثْنَ	تَرِثَا	تَرِثِي	تَرِثْنَ	تَرِثَا	تَرِثِي
يَرِثُوا	يَرِثَا	يَرِثْ	يَرِثُوا	يَرِثَا	يَرِثَ
يَرِثْنَ	تَرِثَا	تَرِثْ	يَرِثْنَ	تَرِثَا	تَرِثَ

Verbal Noun وِرْث\وِرَاثَة *wirth/wirātha* **Participle** وَارِث *warith*

Imperative رِثْ ، رِثِي؛ رِثَا؛ رِثُوا ، رِثْنَ *rith, -ī; -ā; -ū, -na*

PASSIVE **Present** يُورَثُ *yūrathu* **Past** وُرِثَ *wuritha*

Participle مَوْرُوث *mawrūth*

II/IV وَرَّثَ\أَوْرَثَ to appoint as heir ه, to bequeath to ه هـ 77/79;

VI تَوَارَثَ to hold as a bequest هـ 81

وِرْث legacy وِرَاثِي hereditary وَرِيث ج وُرَثَاء heir

وَارِث ج وَرَثَة heir مُوَرِّث\مُورِث testator مَوْرُوث inherited, traditional

مُتَوَارَث inherited تَوَارُث heredity وِرَاثَة\تُرَاث inheritance, heritage

76 | **I** | وَجُهَ يَوْجُهُ *wajuha yawjuhu* to be distinguished | **وجه**

ACTIVE	**Present**	*yawjuhu*	**Past**		*wajuha*
نَوْجُهُ		أَوْجُهُ	وَجُهْنَا		وَجُهْتُ
تَوْجُهُونَ	تَوْجُهَانِ	تَوْجُهُ	وَجُهْتُمْ	وَجُهْتُمَا	وَجُهْتَ
تَوْجُهْنَ	تَوْجُهَانِ	تَوْجُهِينَ	وَجُهْتُنَّ	وَجُهْتُمَا	وَجُهْتِ
يَوْجُهُونَ	يَوْجُهَانِ	يَوْجُهُ	وَجُهُوا	وَجُهَا	وَجُهَ
يَوْجُهْنَ	تَوْجُهَانِ	تَوْجُهُ	وَجُهْنَ	وَجُهَتَا	وَجُهَتْ

	Jussive	*yawjuh*	**Subjunctive**		*yawjuha*
نَوْجُهْ		أَوْجُهْ	نَوْجُهَ		أَوْجُهَ
تَوْجُهُوا	تَوْجُهَا	تَوْجُهْ	تَوْجُهُوا	تَوْجُهَا	تَوْجُهَ
تَوْجُهْنَ	تَوْجُهَا	تَوْجُهِي	تَوْجُهْنَ	تَوْجُهَا	تَوْجُهِي
يَوْجُهُوا	يَوْجُهَا	يَوْجُهْ	يَوْجُهُوا	يَوْجُهَا	يَوْجُهَ
يَوْجُهْنَ	تَوْجُهَا	تَوْجُهْ	يَوْجُهْنَ	تَوْجُهَا	تَوْجُهَ

Verbal Noun وَجَاهَة *wajāha* **Participle** وَاجِه *wājih*

Imperative أُوجُهْ ، أُوجُهِي؛ أُوجُهَا؛ أُوجُهُوا ، أُوجُهْنَ *ūjuh, -ī; -ā; -ū, -na*

PASSIVE none

II وَجَّهَ to turn towards (هـ) إلى 77; III وَاجَهَ to face ه هـ 78;

V تَوَجَّهَ to head for ل\إلى 80; VI تَوَاجَهَ to face e.o. **81**;

VIII اِتَّجَهَ to be directed at إلى 82

وَجْه ج وُجُوه face (also fig.) جِهَة side, direction مُوَاجَهَة confrontation

وِجْهَة\اتِّجَاه direction, trend تُجَاهَ opposite (prep.) تَوْجِيه guidance

وُجْهَة نَظَر point of view من جِهَة أُخْرَى on the other hand

من جِهَتِي for my part من كُلّ جِهَة on all sides بوَجْه خَاصّ especially

من كُلّ وُجْهَة in every respect (شَهَادَة) تَوْجِيهِيَّة school-leaving cert.

77 **II** **وَصَّلَ يُوَصِّلُ** *waṣṣala yuwaṣṣilu* to convey ه ه , to connect ... with هـ ب **وصل**

ACTIVE

Past *waṣṣala*			Present *yuwaṣṣilu*		
وَصَّلْتُ		وَصَّلْنَا	أُوَصِّلُ		نُوَصِّلُ
وَصَّلْتَ	وَصَّلْتُمَا	وَصَّلْتُمْ	تُوَصِّلُ	تُوَصِّلاَنِ	تُوَصِّلُونَ
وَصَّلْتِ	وَصَّلْتُمَا	وَصَّلْتُنَّ	تُوَصِّلِينَ	تُوَصِّلاَنِ	تُوَصِّلْنَ
وَصَّلَ	وَصَّلاَ	وَصَّلُوا	يُوَصِّلُ	يُوَصِّلاَنِ	يُوَصِّلُونَ
وَصَّلَتْ	وَصَّلَتَا	وَصَّلْنَ	تُوَصِّلُ	تُوَصِّلاَنِ	يُوَصِّلْنَ

Subjunctive *yuwaṣṣila*			Jussive *yuwaṣṣil*		
أُوَصِّلَ		نُوَصِّلَ	أُوَصِّلْ		نُوَصِّلْ
تُوَصِّلَ	تُوَصِّلاَ	تُوَصِّلُوا	تُوَصِّلْ	تُوَصِّلاَ	تُوَصِّلُوا
تُوَصِّلِي	تُوَصِّلاَ	تُوَصِّلْنَ	تُوَصِّلِي	تُوَصِّلاَ	تُوَصِّلْنَ
يُوَصِّلَ	يُوَصِّلاَ	يُوَصِّلُوا	يُوَصِّلْ	يُوَصِّلاَ	يُوَصِّلُوا
تُوَصِّلَ	تُوَصِّلاَ	يُوَصِّلْنَ	تُوَصِّلْ	تُوَصِّلاَ	يُوَصِّلْنَ

Verbal Noun تَوْصِيل *tawṣīl* **Participle** مُوَصِّل *muwaṣṣil*

Imperative وَصِّلْ، وَصِّلِي؛ وَصِّلاَ؛ وَصِّلُوا، وَصِّلْنَ *waṣṣil, -ī; -ā; -ū, -na*

PASSIVE **Present** يُوَصَّلُ *yuwaṣṣalu* **Past** وُصِّلَ *wuṣṣila*

Participle مُوَصَّل *muwaṣṣal*

I وَصَلَ يَصِلُ (وُصُول) to arrive at ه هـ\إلى 73; III وَاصَلَ to be connected with هـ 78; IV أَوْصَلَ 79 = II وَصَّلَ 77; V تَوَصَّلَ to gain access to إلى 80; VI تَوَاصَلَ to be interconnected 81; VIII اِتَّصَلَ to contact ب 82

وَصْل\صِلَة\وَصْلَة ج وُصَل connexion

وُصُول إلى arrival at

اِتِّصَال contact, (written) receipt

مُوَصَلاَت (pl.) communications

تَوَاصُل continuity

مُتَّصِل\مُتَوَاصِل continuous

مَوْصُول ب fixed to

مُوَصِّل (electrical) conductor

تَوَصُّل إلى attainment of

78 | **III** — وَافَقَ يُوَافِقُ *wāfaqa yuqāfiqu* to suit ه , to agree with ... on/to ه على — **وفق**

ACTIVE

Present *yuwāfiqu*

نُوَافِقُ		أُوَافِقُ
تُوَافِقُونَ	تُوَافِقَانِ	تُوَافِقُ
تُوَافِقْنَ	تُوَافِقَانِ	تُوَافِقِينَ
يُوَافِقُونَ	يُوَافِقَانِ	يُوَافِقُ
يُوَافِقْنَ	تُوَافِقَانِ	تُوَافِقُ

Past *wāfaqa*

وَافَقْنَا		وَافَقْتُ
وَافَقْتُمْ	وَافَقْتُمَا	وَافَقْتَ
وَافَقْتُنَّ	وَافَقْتُمَا	وَافَقْتِ
وَافَقُوا	وَافَقَا	وَافَقَ
وَافَقْنَ	وَافَقَتَا	وَافَقَتْ

Jussive *yuwāfiq*

نُوَافِقْ		أُوَافِقْ
تُوَافِقُوا	تُوَافِقَا	تُوَافِقْ
تُوَافِقْنَ	تُوَافِقَا	تُوَافِقِي
يُوَافِقُوا	يُوَافِقَا	يُوَافِقْ
يُوَافِقْنَ	تُوَافِقَا	تُوَافِقْ

Subjunctive *yuwāfiqa*

نُوَافِقَ		أُوَافِقَ
تُوَافِقُوا	تُوَافِقَا	تُوَافِقَ
تُوَافِقْنَ	تُوَافِقَا	تُوَافِقِي
يُوَافِقُوا	يُوَافِقَا	يُوَافِقَ
يُوَافِقْنَ	تُوَافِقَا	تُوَافِقَ

Vb. Noun مُوَافَقَة\وِفَاق *muwāfaqa/wifāq* **Participle** مُوَافِق *muwāfiq*

Imperative وَافِقْ، وَافِقِي؛ وَافِقَا؛ وَافِقُوا، وَافِقْنَ *wāfiq, -ī; -ā; -ū, -na*

PASSIVE **Present** يُوَافَقُ *yuwāfaqu* **Past** وُوفِقَ *wūfiqa*

Participle مُوَافَق *muwāfaq*

I (وَفْق) وَفِقَ يَفِقُ to be suitable 75; II وَفَّقَ to adjust هـ, to reconcile بين ...وبين , *passive* وُفِّقَ to succeed in ل\إلى 77;

VIII اِتَّفَقَ to agree with ... on مع على , to happen by chance 82

مُوَافَقَة\وَفْق agreement, conformity, (diplomatic) agrément

وِفَاق agreement تَوْفِيق adjustment, reconciliation مُوَفَّق successful

اِتِّفَاق agreement, coincidence اِتِّفَاقًا by chance مُوَافِق appropriate

اِتِّفَاقِيَّة written agreement, treaty وِفْقًا ل in accordance with

79 IV أَوْجَبَ يُوجِبُ *'awjaba yūjibu* to impose on على هـ   **وجب**

ACTIVE **Present** *yūjibu*

نُوجِبُ		أُوجِبُ
تُوجِبُونَ	تُوجِبَانِ	تُوجِبُ
تُوجِبْنَ	تُوجِبَانِ	تُوجِبِينَ
يُوجِبُونَ	يُوجِبَانِ	يُوجِبُ
يُوجِبْنَ	تُوجِبَانِ	تُوجِبُ

Past *'awjaba*

أَوْجَبْنَا		أَوْجَبْتُ
أَوْجَبْتُمْ	أَوْجَبْتُمَا	أَوْجَبْتَ
أَوْجَبْتُنَّ	أَوْجَبْتُمَا	أَوْجَبْتِ
أَوْجَبُوا	أَوْجَبَا	أَوْجَبَ
أَوْجَبْنَ	أَوْجَبَتَا	أَوْجَبَتْ

Jussive *yūjib*

نُوجِبْ		أُوجِبْ
تُوجِبُوا	تُوجِبَا	تُوجِبْ
تُوجِبْنَ	تُوجِبَا	تُوجِبِي
يُوجِبُوا	يُوجِبَا	يُوجِبْ
يُوجِبْنَ	تُوجِبَا	تُوجِبْ

Subjunctive *yūjiba*

نُوجِبَ		أُوجِبَ
تُوجِبُوا	تُوجِبَا	تُوجِبَ
تُوجِبْنَ	تُوجِبَا	تُوجِبِي
يُوجِبُوا	يُوجِبَا	يُوجِبَ
يُوجِبْنَ	تُوجِبَا	تُوجِبَ

Verbal Noun إِيجَاب *'ījāb*   **Participle** مُوجِب *mūjib*

Imperative أَوْجِبْ، أَوْجِبِي؛ أَوْجِبَا؛ أَوْجِبُوا، أَوْجِبْنَ *'awjib, -ī; -ā; -ū, -na*

PASSIVE **Present** يُوجَبُ *yūjabu*   **Past** أُوجِبَ *'ūjiba*

Participle مُوجَب *mūjab*

I وَجَبَ يَجِبُ (وُجُوب) to be necessary على أَنْ 73;

II وَجَّبَ 77 = IV أَوْجَبَ **79**

إِيجَاب obligation   إِيجَابِي positive   وَاجِب necessary, duty

مَوْجُوب moral duty   مُوجِب compelling, exigency   مُوجَب obligatory

مُوجِبَة motive   على مُوجَب on the basis of

(كَان) يَجِب (عليه) أنْ يَحْضُرَ.
(كَان) يَجِب (عليه) الحُضُور.
} He has to/had to attend.

80 | **V** | تَوَسَّعَ يَتَوَسَّعُ *tawassaʿa yatawassaʿu* to expand | **وسع**

ACTIVE Past *tawassaʿa*

تَوَسَّعْتُ		تَوَسَّعْنَا
تَوَسَّعْتَ	تَوَسَّعْتُمَا	تَوَسَّعْتُمْ
تَوَسَّعْتِ	تَوَسَّعْتُمَا	تَوَسَّعْتُنَّ
تَوَسَّعَ	تَوَسَّعَا	تَوَسَّعُوا
تَوَسَّعَتْ	تَوَسَّعَتَا	تَوَسَّعْنَ

Present *yatawassaʿu*

أَتَوَسَّعُ		نَتَوَسَّعُ
تَتَوَسَّعُ	تَتَوَسَّعَانِ	تَتَوَسَّعُونَ
تَتَوَسَّعِينَ	تَتَوَسَّعَانِ	تَتَوَسَّعْنَ
يَتَوَسَّعُ	يَتَوَسَّعَانِ	يَتَوَسَّعُونَ
تَتَوَسَّعُ	تَتَوَسَّعَانِ	يَتَوَسَّعْنَ

Subjunctive *yatawassaʿa*

أَتَوَسَّعَ		نَتَوَسَّعَ
تَتَوَسَّعَ	تَتَوَسَّعَا	تَتَوَسَّعُوا
تَتَوَسَّعِي	تَتَوَسَّعَا	تَتَوَسَّعْنَ
يَتَوَسَّعَ	يَتَوَسَّعَا	يَتَوَسَّعُوا
تَتَوَسَّعَ	تَتَوَسَّعَا	يَتَوَسَّعْنَ

Jussive *yatawassaʿ*

أَتَوَسَّعْ		نَتَوَسَّعْ
تَتَوَسَّعْ	تَتَوَسَّعَا	تَتَوَسَّعُوا
تَتَوَسَّعِي	تَتَوَسَّعَا	تَتَوَسَّعْنَ
يَتَوَسَّعْ	يَتَوَسَّعَا	يَتَوَسَّعُوا
تَتَوَسَّعْ	تَتَوَسَّعَا	يَتَوَسَّعْنَ

Verbal Noun تَوَسُّع *tawassuʿ* **Participle** مُتَوَسِّع *mutawassiʿ*

Impv. تَوَسَّعْ، تَوَسَّعِي؛ تَوَسَّعَا؛ تَوَسَّعُوا، تَوَسَّعْنَ *tawassaʿ, -ī; -ā; -ū, -na*

PASSIVE° **Present** يُتَوَسَّعُ *yutawassaʿu* **Past** تُوُسِّعَ *tuwussiʿa*

I وَسِعَ يَسَعُ (سَعَة) to be wide/roomy, to be wide/roomy enough for ه هـ *past* 75, *present* 74; II/IV وَسَّعَ\أَوْسَعَ to broaden هـ 77/79; VIII اِتَّسَعَ to be expanded, to be wide/roomy enough for لـ 82

تَوَسُّع expansion تَوَسُّعِي expansionist تَوَسُّعِيَّة expansionism

وَسِع\وَسِيع ج وِسَاع wide, roomy تَوْسِيع broadening مُتَّسِع extensive

سَعَة capacity (also mechanical/electrical) مُتَّسَع space

وُسْعَة wideness, roominess اِتِّسَاع extensiveness, extent

مع التَوَسُّع by extension في سَعَتِي within my capacity

81 | VI | تَوَاجَهَ يَتَوَاجَهُ *tawājaha yatawājahu* to face e.o. | **وجه**

ACTIVE

Past *tawājaha*

تَوَاجَهْتُ		تَوَاجَهْنَا
تَوَاجَهْتَ	تَوَاجَهْتُمَا	تَوَاجَهْتُمْ
تَوَاجَهْتِ	تَوَاجَهْتُمَا	تَوَاجَهْتُنَّ
تَوَاجَهَ	تَوَاجَهَا	تَوَاجَهُوا
تَوَاجَهَتْ	تَوَاجَهَتَا	تَوَاجَهْنَ

Present *yatawājahu*

أَتَوَاجَهُ		نَتَوَاجَهُ
تَتَوَاجَهُ	تَتَوَاجَهَانِ	تَتَوَاجَهُونَ
تَتَوَاجَهِينَ	تَتَوَاجَهَانِ	تَتَوَاجَهْنَ
يَتَوَاجَهُ	يَتَوَاجَهَانِ	يَتَوَاجَهُونَ
تَتَوَاجَهُ	تَتَوَاجَهَانِ	يَتَوَاجَهْنَ

Subjunctive *yatawājaha*

أَتَوَاجَهَ		نَتَوَاجَهَ
تَتَوَاجَهَ	تَتَوَاجَهَا	تَتَوَاجَهُوا
تَتَوَاجَهِي	تَتَوَاجَهَا	تَتَوَاجَهْنَ
يَتَوَاجَهَ	يَتَوَاجَهَا	يَتَوَاجَهُوا
تَتَوَاجَهَ	تَتَوَاجَهَا	يَتَوَاجَهْنَ

Jussive *yatawājah*

أَتَوَاجَهْ		نَتَوَاجَهْ
تَتَوَاجَهْ	تَتَوَاجَهَا	تَتَوَاجَهُوا
تَتَوَاجَهِي	تَتَوَاجَهَا	تَتَوَاجَهْنَ
يَتَوَاجَهْ	يَتَوَاجَهَا	يَتَوَاجَهُوا
تَتَوَاجَهْ	تَتَوَاجَهَا	يَتَوَاجَهْنَ

Verbal Noun تَوَاجُه *tawājuh* **Participle** مُتَوَاجِه *mutawājih*

Impv. تَوَاجَهْ، تَوَاجَهِي؛ تَوَاجَهَا؛ تَوَاجَهُوا، تَوَاجَهْنَ *tawājah, -ī; -ā; -ū, -na*

PASSIVE° **Present** يُتَوَاجَهُ *yutawājahu* **Past** تُوُوجِهَ *tuwūjiha*

See **76**

82 | **VIII** اتَّفَقَ يَتَّفِقُ *ittáfaqa yattáfiqu* | **وفق**

to agree with ... on مع على, to happen by chance

ACTIVE **Present** *yattáfiqu* **Past** *ittáfaqa*

نَتَّفِقُ		أَتَّفِقُ	اتَّفَقْنَا		اتَّفَقْتُ
تَتَّفِقُونَ	تَتَّفِقَانِ	تَتَّفِقُ	اتَّفَقْتُمْ	اتَّفَقْتُمَا	اتَّفَقْتَ
تَتَّفِقْنَ	تَتَّفِقَانِ	تَتَّفِقِينَ	اتَّفَقْتُنَّ	اتَّفَقْتُمَا	اتَّفَقْتِ
يَتَّفِقُونَ	يَتَّفِقَانِ	يَتَّفِقُ	اتَّفَقُوا	اتَّفَقَا	اتَّفَقَ
يَتَّفِقْنَ	تَتَّفِقَانِ	تَتَّفِقُ	اتَّفَقْنَ	اتَّفَقَتَا	اتَّفَقَتْ

Jussive *yattáfiq* **Subjunctive** *yattáfiqa*

نَتَّفِقْ		أَتَّفِقْ	نَتَّفِقَ		أَتَّفِقَ
تَتَّفِقُوا	تَتَّفِقَا	تَتَّفِقْ	تَتَّفِقُوا	تَتَّفِقَا	تَتَّفِقَ
تَتَّفِقْنَ	تَتَّفِقَا	تَتَّفِقِي	تَتَّفِقْنَ	تَتَّفِقَا	تَتَّفِقِي
يَتَّفِقُوا	يَتَّفِقَا	يَتَّفِقْ	يَتَّفِقُوا	يَتَّفِقَا	يَتَّفِقَ
يَتَّفِقْنَ	تَتَّفِقَا	تَتَّفِقْ	يَتَّفِقْنَ	تَتَّفِقَا	تَتَّفِقَ

Verbal Noun اِتِّفَاق *ittifāq* **Participle** مُتَّفِق *muttáfiq*

Imperative اِتَّفِقْ، اِتَّفِقِي؛ اِتَّفِقَا؛ اِتَّفِقُوا، اِتَّفِقْنَ *ittáfiq, -ī; -ā; -ū, -na*

PASSIVE° **Present** يُتَّفَقُ *yuttáfaqu* **Past** أُتُّفِقَ *uttúfiqa*

Participle مُتَّفَق *muttáfaq*

See **78**

83 | X | اِسْتَوْرَدَ يَسْتَوْرِدُ *istawrada yastawridu* to import هـ | ورد

ACTIVE

Past *istawrada*

اِسْتَوْرَدْتُ		اِسْتَوْرَدْنَا
اِسْتَوْرَدْتَ	اِسْتَوْرَدْتُمَا	اِسْتَوْرَدْتُمْ
اِسْتَوْرَدْتِ	اِسْتَوْرَدْتُمَا	اِسْتَوْرَدْتُنَّ
اِسْتَوْرَدَ	اِسْتَوْرَدَا	اِسْتَوْرَدُوا
اِسْتَوْرَدَتْ	اِسْتَوْرَدَتَا	اِسْتَوْرَدْنَ

Present *yastawridu*

أَسْتَوْرِدُ		نَسْتَوْرِدُ
تَسْتَوْرِدُ	تَسْتَوْرِدَانِ	تَسْتَوْرِدُونَ
تَسْتَوْرِدِينَ	تَسْتَوْرِدَانِ	تَسْتَوْرِدْنَ
يَسْتَوْرِدُ	يَسْتَوْرِدَانِ	يَسْتَوْرِدُونَ
تَسْتَوْرِدُ	تَسْتَوْرِدَانِ	يَسْتَوْرِدْنَ

Subjunctive *yastawrida*

أَسْتَوْرِدَ		نَسْتَوْرِدَ
تَسْتَوْرِدَ	تَسْتَوْرِدَا	تَسْتَوْرِدُوا
تَسْتَوْرِدِي	تَسْتَوْرِدَا	تَسْتَوْرِدْنَ
يَسْتَوْرِدَ	يَسْتَوْرِدَا	يَسْتَوْرِدُوا
تَسْتَوْرِدَ	تَسْتَوْرِدَا	يَسْتَوْرِدْنَ

Jussive *yastawrid*

أَسْتَوْرِدْ		نَسْتَوْرِدْ
تَسْتَوْرِدْ	تَسْتَوْرِدَا	تَسْتَوْرِدُوا
تَسْتَوْرِدِي	تَسْتَوْرِدَا	تَسْتَوْرِدْنَ
يَسْتَوْرِدْ	يَسْتَوْرِدَا	يَسْتَوْرِدُوا
تَسْتَوْرِدْ	تَسْتَوْرِدَا	يَسْتَوْرِدْنَ

Vb. Noun اِسْتِيرَاد *istīrād* **Participle** مُسْتَوْرِد *mustawrid*

Imperative اِسْتَوْرِدْ، اِسْتَوْرِدِي؛ اِسْتَوْرِدَا؛ اِسْتَوْرِدُوا، اِسْتَوْرِدْنَ
istawrid, -ī; -ā; -ū, -na

PASSIVE **Present** يُسْتَوْرَدُ *yustawradu* **Past** أُسْتُورِدُ *ustūrida*

Participle مُسْتَوْرَد *mustawrad*

I وَرَدَ يَرِدُ (وُرُود) to arrive at هـ\إلى , to appear 73;

II وَرَّدَ to supply with ب هـ 77; IV أَوْرَدَ to transfer, import, quote هـ 79

اِسْتِيرَاد importation مُسْتَوْرِد importer مُسْتَوْرَد import (goods)

إِيرَاد quotation, importation, revenue مُوَرِّد supplier تَوْرِيد supply

مَوْرِد ج مَوَارِد source, revenue وَارِد ج وُرَّاد arriving, import, income

وَارِدَات وَصَادِرَات imports and exports مَوَارِد صَافِيَة net revenue

84 | I | يَبِسَ يَيْبَسُ *yabisa yaybasu* to be(come) dry | **يبس**

ACTIVE

Past *yabisa*

يَبِسْتُ		يَبِسْنَا
يَبِسْتَ	يَبِسْتُمَا	يَبِسْتُمْ
يَبِسْتِ	يَبِسْتُمَا	يَبِسْتُنَّ
يَبِسَ	يَبِسَا	يَبِسُوا
يَبِسَتْ	يَبِسَتَا	يَبِسْنَ

Present *yaybasu*

أَيْبَسُ		نَيْبَسُ
تَيْبَسُ	تَيْبَسَانِ	تَيْبَسُونَ
تَيْبَسِينَ	تَيْبَسَانِ	تَيْبَسْنَ
يَيْبَسُ	يَيْبَسَانِ	يَيْبَسُونَ
تَيْبَسُ	تَيْبَسَانِ	يَيْبَسْنَ

Subjunctive *yaybasa*

أَيْبَسَ		نَيْبَسَ
تَيْبَسَ	تَيْبَسَا	تَيْبَسُوا
تَيْبَسِي	تَيْبَسَا	تَيْبَسْنَ
يَيْبَسَ	يَيْبَسَا	يَيْبَسُوا
تَيْبَسَ	تَيْبَسَا	يَيْبَسْنَ

Jussive *yaybas*

أَيْبَسْ		نَيْبَسْ
تَيْبَسْ	تَيْبَسَا	تَيْبَسُوا
تَيْبَسِي	تَيْبَسَا	تَيْبَسْنَ
يَيْبَسْ	يَيْبَسَا	يَيْبَسُوا
تَيْبَسْ	تَيْبَسَا	يَيْبَسْنَ

Verbal Noun يَبْس *yabs* **Participle** يَابِس *yābis*

Imperative اِيبَسْ ، اِيبَسِي؛ اِيبَسَا؛ اِيبَسُوا، اِيبَسْنَ *ības, -ī; -ā; -ū, -na*

PASSIVE none

II/IV يَبَّسَ\أَيْبَسَ to dry هـ 85/87

يَبْس dryness, dried, arid

يَابِس dry, arid

اليَبْس\اليَابِس terra firma

85 **II** — يَسَّرَ يُيَسِّرُ *yassara yuyassiru* — **يسر**

to facilitate, ease على ه

ACTIVE

Present *yuyassiru*

أُيَسِّرُ		نُيَسِّرُ
تُيَسِّرُ	تُيَسِّرَانِ	تُيَسِّرُونَ
تُيَسِّرِينَ	تُيَسِّرَانِ	تُيَسِّرْنَ
يُيَسِّرُ	يُيَسِّرَانِ	يُيَسِّرُونَ
تُيَسِّرُ	تُيَسِّرَانِ	يُيَسِّرْنَ

Past *yassara*

يَسَّرْتُ		يَسَّرْنَا
يَسَّرْتَ	يَسَّرْتُمَا	يَسَّرْتُمْ
يَسَّرْتِ	يَسَّرْتُمَا	يَسَّرْتُنَّ
يَسَّرَ	يَسَّرَا	يَسَّرُوا
يَسَّرَتْ	يَسَّرَتَا	يَسَّرْنَ

Jussive *yuyassir*

أُيَسِّرْ		نُيَسِّرْ
تُيَسِّرْ	تُيَسِّرَا	تُيَسِّرُوا
تُيَسِّرِي	تُيَسِّرَا	تُيَسِّرْنَ
يُيَسِّرْ	يُيَسِّرَا	يُيَسِّرُوا
تُيَسِّرْ	تُيَسِّرَا	يُيَسِّرْنَ

Subjunctive *yuyassira*

أُيَسِّرَ		نُيَسِّرَ
تُيَسِّرَ	تُيَسِّرَا	تُيَسِّرُوا
تُيَسِّرِي	تُيَسِّرَا	تُيَسِّرْنَ
يُيَسِّرَ	يُيَسِّرَا	يُيَسِّرُوا
تُيَسِّرَ	تُيَسِّرَا	يُيَسِّرْنَ

Verbal Noun تَيْسِير *taysīr* **Participle** مُيَسِّر *muyassir*

Imperative يَسِّرْ، يَسِّرِي؛ يَسِّرَا؛ يَسِّرُوا، يَسِّرْنَ *yassir, -ī; -ā; -ū, -na*

PASSIVE **Present** يُيَسَّرُ *yuyassaru* **Past** يُسِّرَ *yussira*

Participle مُيَسَّر *muyassar*

I يَسَرَ يَيْسَرُ (يَسَرَ) to be(come) easy 84; III يَاسَرَ to indulge ه **86**;

V تَيَسَّرَ to flourish 88

يَسَار	ease, left(-hand)	يَسَارِي	left-wing
تَيْسِير	facilitation	يَسِير إلى	easy for
مَيْسُور ج مَيَاسِير	easy to do, prosperous	مُيَسَّر	facilitated
على اليَسَار	on the left	مُتَيَسِّر\مُوسِر ج مَيَاسِير	prosperous

86 | III | يَاسَرَ يُيَاسِرُ *yāsara yuyāsiru* to indulge ه | **يسر**

ACTIVE	**Present** *yuyāsiru*			**Past**	*yāsara*
نُيَاسِرُ		أُيَاسِرُ	يَاسَرْنَا		يَاسَرْتُ
تُيَاسِرُونَ	تُيَاسِرَانِ	تُايَسِرُ	يَاسَرْتُمْ	يَاسَرْتُمَا	يَاسَرْتَ
تُيَاسِرْنَ	تُيَاسِرَانِ	تُيَاسِرِينَ	يَاسَرْتُنَّ	يَاسَرْتُمَا	يَاسَرْتِ
يُيَاسِرُونَ	يُيَاسِرَانِ	يُيَاسِرُ	يَاسَرُوا	يَاسَرَا	يَاسَرَ
يُيَاسِرْنَ	تُيَاسِرَانِ	تُيَاسِرُ	يَاسَرْنَ	يَاسَرَتَا	يَاسَرَتْ
	Jussive	*yuyāsir*	**Subjunctive**		*yuyāsira*
نُيَاسِرْ		أُيَاسِرْ	نُيَاسِرَ		أُيَاسِرَ
تُيَاسِرُوا	تُيَاسِرَا	تُيَاسِرْ	تُيَاسِرُوا	تُيَاسِرَا	تُيَاسِرَ
تُيَاسِرْنَ	تُيَاسِرَا	تُيَاسِرِي	تُيَاسِرْنَ	تُيَاسِرَا	تُيَاسِرِي
يُيَاسِرُوا	يُيَاسِرَا	يُيَاسِرْ	يُيَاسِرُوا	يُيَاسِرَا	يُيَاسِرَ
يُيَاسِرْنَ	تُيَاسِرَا	تُيَاسِرْ	يُيَاسِرْنَ	تُيَاسِرَا	تُيَاسِرَ

Verbal Noun مُيَاسَرَة *muyāsara* **Participle** مُوَيَاسِر *muyāsir*

Imperative يَاسِرْ، يَاسِرِي؛ يَاسِرَا؛ يَاسِرُوا، يَاسِرْنَ *yāsir, -ī; -ā; -ū, -na*

PASSIVE **Present** يُيَاسَرُ *yuyāsaru* **Past** يُوسِرَ *yūsira*

Participle مُوَيَاسَر *muyāsar*

See **85**

87 IV أَيْقَنَ يُوقِنُ *'ayqana yūqinu* to ascertain هـ\ب **يقن**

ACTIVE

Present *yūqinu*			Past *'ayqana*		
نُوقِنُ		أُوقِنُ	أَيْقَنَّا		أَيْقَنْتُ
تُوقِنُونَ	تُوقِنَانِ	تُوقِنُ	أَيْقَنْتُمْ	أَيْقَنْتُمَا	أَيْقَنْتَ
تُوقِنَّ	تُوقِنَانِ	تُوقِنِينَ	أَيْقَنْتُنَّ	أَيْقَنْتُمَا	أَيْقَنْتِ
يُوقِنُونَ	يُوقِنَانِ	يُوقِنُ	أَيْقَنُوا	أَيْقَنَا	أَيْقَنَ
يُوقِنَّ	تُوقِنَانِ	تُوقِنُ	أَيْقَنَّ	أَيْقَنَتَا	أَيْقَنَتْ
Jussive *yūqin*			**Subjunctive** *yūqina*		
نُوقِنْ		أُوقِنْ	نُوقِنَ		أُوقِنَ
تُوقِنُوا	تُوقِنَا	تُوقِنْ	تُوقِنُوا	تُوقِنَا	تُوقِنَ
تُوقِنَّ	تُوقِنَا	تُوجِبِي	تُوقِنَّ	تُوقِنَا	تُوجِبِي
يُوقِنُوا	يُوقِنَا	يُوقِنْ	يُوقِنُوا	يُوقِنَا	يُوقِنَ
يُوقِنَّ	تُوقِنَا	تُوقِنْ	يُوقِنَّ	تُوقِنَا	تُوقِنَ

Verbal Noun إِيقَان *'īqān* **Participle** مُوقِن *mūqin*

Imperative أَيْقِنْ، أَيْقِنِي؛ أَيْقِنَا؛ أَيْقِنُوا، أَيْقِنَّ *'ayqin, -ī; -ā; -ū, -na*

PASSIVE **Present** يُوقَنُ *yūqanu* **Past** أُوقِنَ *'ūqina*

Participle مُوقَن *mūqan*

I (يَقْن) يَقِنَ يَيْقَنُ to be sure of هـ\ب 84;

V/X تَيَقَّنَ\اِسْتَيْقَنَ هـ\ب 88/89 = IV أَيْقَنَ **87**

يَقِين ب\يَقْن ب certainty of مُوقِن ب\على ، يَقِين من certain of

مُتَيَقِّن convinced يَقِينِي indisputable

88 | V | تَيَقَّظَ يَتَيَقَّظُ *tayaqqaẓa yatayaqqaẓu* to be vigilant | يقظ

ACTIVE Present *yatayaqqaẓu* | **Past** *tayaqqaẓa*

نَتَيَقَّظُ		أَتَيَقَّظُ	تَيَقَّظْنَا		تَيَقَّظْتُ
تَتَيَقَّظُونَ	تَتَيَقَّظَانِ	تَتَيَقَّظُ	تَيَقَّظْتُمْ	تَيَقَّظْتُمَا	تَيَقَّظْتَ
تَتَيَقَّظْنَ	تَتَيَقَّظَانِ	تَتَيَقَّظِينَ	تَيَقَّظْتُنَّ	تَيَقَّظْتُمَا	تَيَقَّظْتِ
يَتَيَقَّظُونَ	يَتَيَقَّظَانِ	يَتَيَقَّظُ	تَيَقَّظُوا	تَيَقَّظَا	تَيَقَّظَ
يَتَيَقَّظْنَ	تَتَيَقَّظَانِ	تَتَيَقَّظُ	تَيَقَّظْنَ	تَيَقَّظَتَا	تَيَقَّظَتْ

Jussive *yatayaqqaẓ* | **Subjunctive** *yatayaqqaẓa*

نَتَيَقَّظْ		أَتَيَقَّظْ	نَتَيَقَّظَ		أَتَيَقَّظَ
تَتَيَقَّظُوا	تَتَيَقَّظَا	تَتَيَقَّظْ	تَتَيَقَّظُوا	تَتَيَقَّظَا	تَتَيَقَّظَ
تَتَيَقَّظْنَ	تَتَيَقَّظَا	تَتَيَقَّظِي	تَتَيَقَّظْنَ	تَتَيَقَّظَا	تَتَيَقَّظِي
يَتَيَقَّظُوا	يَتَيَقَّظَا	يَتَيَقَّظْ	يَتَيَقَّظُوا	يَتَيَقَّظَا	يَتَيَقَّظَ
يَتَيَقَّظْنَ	تَتَيَقَّظَا	تَتَيَقَّظْ	يَتَيَقَّظْنَ	تَتَيَقَّظَا	تَتَيَقَّظَ

Verbal Noun تَيَقُّظ *tayaqquẓ* **Participle** مُتَيَقِّظ *mutayaqqiẓ*

Impv. تَيَقَّظْ، تَيَقَّظِي؛ تَيَقَّظَا؛ تَيَقَّظُوا، تَيَقَّظْنَ *tayaqqaẓ, -ī; -ā; -ū, -na*

PASSIVE° **Present** يُتَيَقَّظُ *yutayaqqaẓu* **Past** تُيُقِّظَ *tuyuqqiẓa*

I/X يَقِظَ يَيْقَظُ (يَقُظَ)\اسْتَيْقَظَ to (be) awake 84/**89**

II/IV يَقَّظَ\أَيْقَظَ to waken ه 85/87

تَيَقُّظ vigilance | مُتَيَقِّظ\يَقِظ ج أَيْقَاظ vigilant

مُسْتَيْقِظ awake | إِيقَاظ awaking

يَقْظَان (m.) vigilant، يَقْظَى (f.)، ج يَقَاظَى (m./f.)

89 | X | اِسْتَيْقَظَ يَسْتَيْقِظُ *istayqaẓa yastayqiẓu* to (be) awake | **يقظ**

ACTIVE

Present *yastayqiẓu*

نَسْتَيْقِظُ		أَسْتَيْقِظُ
تَسْتَيْقِظُونَ	تَسْتَيْقِظَانِ	تَسْتَيْقِظُ
تَسْتَيْقِظْنَ	تَسْتَيْقِظَانِ	تَسْتَيْقِظِينَ
يَسْتَيْقِظُونَ	يَسْتَيْقِظَانِ	يَسْتَيْقِظُ
يَسْتَيْقِظْنَ	تَسْتَيْقِظَانِ	تَسْتَيْقِظُ

Past *istayqaẓa*

اِسْتَيْقَظْنَا		اِسْتَيْقَظْتُ
اِسْتَيْقَظْتُمْ	اِسْتَيْقَظْتُمَا	اِسْتَيْقَظْتَ
اِسْتَيْقَظْتُنَّ	اِسْتَيْقَظْتُمَا	اِسْتَيْقَظْتِ
اِسْتَيْقَظُوا	اِسْتَيْقَظَا	اِسْتَيْقَظَ
اِسْتَيْقَظْنَ	اِسْتَيْقَظَتَا	اِسْتَيْقَظَتْ

Jussive *yastayqiẓ*

نَسْتَيْقِظْ		أَسْتَيْقِظْ
تَسْتَيْقِظُوا	تَسْتَيْقِظَا	تَسْتَيْقِظْ
تَسْتَيْقِظْنَ	تَسْتَيْقِظَا	تَسْتَيْقِظِي
يَسْتَيْقِظُوا	يَسْتَيْقِظَا	يَسْتَيْقِظْ
يَسْتَيْقِظْنَ	تَسْتَيْقِظَا	تَسْتَيْقِظْ

Subjunctive *yastayqiẓa*

نَسْتَيْقِظَ		أَسْتَيْقِظَ
تَسْتَيْقِظُوا	تَسْتَيْقِظَا	تَسْتَيْقِظَ
تَسْتَيْقِظْنَ	تَسْتَيْقِظَا	تَسْتَيْقِظِي
يَسْتَيْقِظُوا	يَسْتَيْقِظَا	يَسْتَيْقِظَ
يَسْتَيْقِظْنَ	تَسْتَيْقِظَا	تَسْتَيْقِظَ

Vb. Noun اِسْتِيقَاظ *istīqāẓ* **Participle** مُسْتَيْقِظ *mustayqiẓ*

Imperative اِسْتَيْقِظْ، اِسْتَيْقِظِي؛ اِسْتَيْقِظَا؛ اِسْتَيْقِظُوا، اِسْتَيْقِظْنَ

istayqiẓ, -ī; -ā; -ū, -na

PASSIVE none

See **88**

Hollow

Hollow verbs are the second sub-class of the weak verbs. They are those with a weak letter, و or ي , as middle root letter. The other two root letters are sound; a few roots (e.g. no. **91**, also no. **29** in the hamzated tables) have initial ء and a sound final root letter. A few roots have alternative middle root letters و\ي, most following the و pattern.

Active voice. In the active voice, hollow verbs follow the sound patterns shown in §§ 7, 8, 17, 18 and 21-23, with these exceptions:

- In Form I tenses and imperative, the weak middle root letter vocalises, i.e. becomes a vowel: middle و becomes short *-u-*, long و *-ū-* or ا *-ā-*, middle ي becomes short *-i-*, long يـ *-ī-* or ا *-ā*:

  سقت *suqtu* I drove — يسوق *yasūqu* he drives
  ساق *sāqa* he drove — سق *suq* drive (m. s.)
  بعنا *bi'na* we sold — نبيع *nabī'u* we sell
  باعوا *bā'ū* they sold — بيعوا *bī'ū* sell (m. pl.)

  One small but important group of middle-و verbs is anomalous, with the و becoming short *-i-*, short *-a-* or long ا *-ā-*:

  خفت *khiftu* I feared — خاف *khāfa* he feared
  نخاف *nakhāfu* we fear — خف *khaf* fear (m. s.)

  In the participle, the middle و\ي becomes *hamza*:

  نائم *nā'im* sleeping — زائد *zā'id* increasing

- In Forms IV, VII, VIII and X the middle و\ي vocalises:
  - in Forms IV and X, middle و\ي becomes *-a-/-ā-* in the past, *-i-/-ī-* in the present tenses and imperative, *-ī-* in the participle:

    IV أضاف *'aḍāfa* he added — أضفنا *'aḍafna* we added
    X نستريح *nastarīḥ* we rest — استرح *istariḥ* rest (m. s.)
    IV مضيف *muḍīf* adding — X مستريح *mustarīḥ* resting

    In the verbal noun the middle و\ي disappears, and final ...ة *-a* is added after the final root letter:

    IV إضافة *'iḍāfa* addition — X استراحة *istirāḥa* rest, repose

- in Forms VII and VIII, middle و\ي becomes *-a-/-ā-* in the tenses, imperative and participle; and *-y-* in the verbal noun:
  VIII ازداد *izdāda* it increased ازدياد *izdiyād* increase

- When the middle root letter vocalises as indicated above, that vowel is long whenever the final root letter is followed by a vowel in full-form pronunciation (§ 6); otherwise it is short.
- In Forms II, III, V and VI, and in a few anomalous verbs in Forms IV, VIII and X, the middle و\ي stabilises as a consonant *-w-* or *-y-*, and the verb follows the sound pattern completely.
- In Form IX (nos. **112** and **113**) the middle و or ي stabilises and the verb follows the pattern of the doubled verbs (see page 123).

Passive voice. The sound patterns for the هو person of the passive tenses (§ 26) and for the passive participle (§ 17) apply completely to those increased forms (II, III, V and VI, and the few anomalous verbs in IV, VIII and X) in which the middle root letter stabilises. For the rest, the sound patterns apply to everything except the weak middle root letter, which takes the following forms:

- Form I tenses: ي *ī* in the past, ا *ā* in the present, for all verbs:
  بيع *bī'a* it was sold   يباع *yubā'u* it is sold
  Form I participles: middle و vocalises as *-ū-*, middle ي as *-ī-*:
  مسوق *masūq* driven   مبيع *mabī'* sold
- Form IV, VII (impersonal passive), VIII and X: ي *ī* in the past tense, ا *ā* in the present tense and the participle.
  IV أضيف *'uḍīfa* it was added مذاع *mudhā'* broadcast
  VIII يحتاج إليه *yuḥtāj 'ilayhi* it is needed
  محتاج إلية *muḥtāj 'ilayhi* needed

Using a dictionary. When searching for a hollow verb in a root-based dictionary (§ 16), remember that the middle root letter will be either و or ي (or both as alternatives); ا *'alif* is not a root letter.

The tables list و and ي verbs together (و first) in each Form (I to X).

90 **I** سَاقَ يَسُوقُ *sāqa yasūqu* to drive هـ **سوق**

ACTIVE	**Present** *yasūqu*		**Past**		*sāqa*
نَسُوقُ		أَسُوقُ	سُقْنَا		سُقْتُ
تَسُوقُونَ	تَسُوقَانِ	تَسُوقُ	سُقْتُمْ	سُقْتُمَا	سُقْتَ
تَسُقْنَ	تَسُوقَانِ	تَسُوقِينَ	سُقْتُنَّ	سُقْتُمَا	سُقْتِ
يَسُوقُونَ	يَسُوقَانِ	يَسُوقُ	سَاقُوا	سَاقَا	سَاقَ
يَسُقْنَ	تَسُوقَانِ	تَسُوقُ	سُقْنَ	سَاقَتَا	سَاقَتْ

	Jussive	*yasuq*	**Subjunctive**		*yasūqa*
نَسُقْ		أَسُقْ	نَسُوقَ		أَسُوقَ
تَسُوقُوا	تَسُوقَا	تَسُقْ	تَسُوقُوا	تَسُوقَا	تَسُوقَ
تَسُقْنَ	تَسُوقَا	تَسُوقِي	تَسُقْنَ	تَسُوقَا	تَسُوقِي
يَسُوقُوا	يَسُوقَا	يَسُقْ	يَسُوقُوا	يَسُوقَا	يَسُوقَ
يَسُقْنَ	تَسُوقَا	تَسُقْ	يَسُقْنَ	تَسُوقَا	تَسُوقَ

Verbal Noun سِيَاقَة *siyāqa* **Participle** سَائِق *sā'iq*

Impv. سُقْ، سُوقِي؛ سُوقَا؛ سُوقُوا، سُقْنَ *suq, sūqī; sūqā; sūqū, suqna*

PASSIVE **Present** يُسَاقُ *yusāqu* **Past** سِيقَ *sīqa*

Participle مَسُوق *masūq*

II سَوَّقَ to market هـ 95; III سَاوَقَ to accompany ه 97;

V تَسَوَّقَ to deal in the market 102; VI تَسَاوَقَ to form a series 104;

VII انْسَاقَ to be driven 106; VIII اسْتَاقَ to herd هـ 108

(f./m.) سُوق ج أَسْوَاق market سَائِق driver مَسَاق course, trend

السُوق الحُرَّة\السَوْدَاء the free/black market تَسْوِيق marketing

السُوق الأُرُبِّيَة المُشْتَرَكَة Common Market رُخْصَة سِيَاقَة driving licence

سَاقَ حَدِيثًا to pursue a discussion مَسَاقُهُ إلى هذا it comes down to this

91 | **I** | آبَ يَؤُوبُ *'āba ya'ūbu* to return, to incur, be left with بِ | **أوب**

ACTIVE

Past *'āba*

أُبْتُ		أُبْنَا
أُبْتَ	أُبْتُمَا	أُبْتُمْ
أُبْتِ	أُبْتُمَا	أُبْتُنَّ
آبَ	آبَا	آبُوا
آبَتْ	آبَتَا	أُبْنَ

Present *ya'ūbu*

أَؤُوبُ		نَؤُوبُ
تَؤُوبُ	تَؤُوبَانِ	تَؤُوبُونَ
تَؤُوبِينَ	تَؤُوبَانِ	تَؤُبْنَ
يَؤُوبُ	يَؤُوبَانِ	يَؤُوبُونَ
تَؤُوبُ	تَؤُوبَانِ	يَؤُبْنَ

Subjunctive *ya'ūba*

أَؤُوبَ		نَؤُوبَ
تَؤُوبَ	تَؤُوبَا	تَؤُوبُوا
تَؤُوبِي	تَؤُوبَا	تَؤُبْنَ
يَؤُوبَ	يَؤُوبَا	يَؤُوبُوا
تَؤُوبَ	تَؤُوبَا	يَؤُبْنَ

Jussive *ya'ub*

أَؤُبْ		نَؤُبْ
تَؤُبْ	تَؤُوبَا	تَؤُوبُوا
تَؤُوبِي	تَؤُوبَا	تَؤُبْنَ
يَؤُبْ	يَؤُوبَا	يَؤُوبُوا
تَؤُبْ	تَؤُوبَا	يَؤُبْنَ

Vb. Noun إِيَاب\أَوْب\أَوْبَة *'iyāb/'awb(a)* **Participle** آئِب *'ā'ib*

Imperative أُبْ، أُوبِي؛ أُوبَا؛ أُوبُوا، أُبْنَ *'ub, 'ūbī; 'ūbā; 'ūbū, 'ubna*

PASSIVE none

ذَهَابًا وإِيَابًا there and back

مَآب homecoming

ذُهُوب ومَآب coming and going

من كُلّ أَوْب on/from every side

تَذْكَرَة ذَهَاب وإِيَاب return ticket

92 | I | خَافَ يَخَافُ *khāfa yakhāfu* to fear ه\من هـ\من | خوف

ACTIVE	**Present** *yakhāfu*		**Past**	*khāfa*	
نَخَافُ		أَخَافُ	خِفْنَا		خِفْتُ
تَخَافُونَ	تَخَافَانِ	تَخَافُ	خِفْتُمْ	خِفْتُمَا	خِفْتَ
تَخَفْنَ	تَخَافَانِ	تَخَافِينَ	خِفْتُنَّ	خِفْتُمَا	خِفْتِ
يَخَافُونَ	يَخَافَانِ	يَخَافُ	خَافُوا	خَافَا	خَافَ
يَخَفْنَ	تَخَافَانِ	تَخَافُ	خِفْنَ	خَافَتَا	خَافَتْ

	Jussive *yakhaf*		**Subjunctive** *yakhāfa*		
نَخَفْ		أَخَفْ	نَخَافَ		أَخَافَ
تَخَافُوا	تَخَافَا	تَخَفْ	تَخَافُوا	تَخَافَا	تَخَافَ
تَخَفْنَ	تَخَافَا	تَخَافِي	تَخَفْنَ	تَخَافَا	تَخَافِي
يَخَافُوا	يَخَافَا	يَخَفْ	يَخَافُوا	يَخَافَا	يَخَافَ
يَخَفْنَ	تَخَافَا	تَخَفْ	يَخَفْنَ	تَخَافَا	تَخَافَ

Vb. Noun خَوْف\مُخَافَة *khawf/mukhāfa* **Participle** خَائِف *khā'if*

Impv. خَفْ، خَافِي؛ خَافَا؛ خَافُوا، خَفْنَ *khaf, khāfī; khāfā; khāfū, khafna*

PASSIVE **Present** يُخَافُ *yukhāfu* **Past** خِيفَ *khīfa*

Participle مَخُوف *makhūf*

II/IV خَوَّفَ\أَخَافَ to frighten ه هـ 95/99; V تَخَوَّفَ 102 = I خَافَ 92

خَوْف من fear of	مُخَافَة ج مُخَاوِف من fear of	مَخُوف feared
تَخْوِيف\إِخَافَة intimidation	مُخِيف dreadful	خَوْفًا على fearing for
خَوْفًا من for fear of	مُخَافَةَ أَنْ for fear that	تَخَوُّف dread
خَائِف ج خُوَّاف من frightened of		خَائِف ج خُوَّاف على anxious for

93 I زَادَ يَزِيدُ *zāda yazīdu* to increase (هـ) زيد

ACTIVE	**Present**	*yazīdu*		**Past**	*zāda*
نَزِيدُ		أَزِيدُ	زِدْنَا		زِدْتُ
تَزِيدُونَ	تَزِيدَانِ	تَزِيدُ	زِدْتُمْ	زِدْتُمَا	زِدْتَ
تَزِدْنَ	تَزِيدَانِ	تَزِيدِينَ	زِدْتُنَّ	زِدْتُمَا	زِدْتِ
يَزِيدُونَ	يَزِيدَانِ	يَزِيدُ	زَادُوا	زَادَا	زَادَ
يَزِدْنَ	تَزِيدَانِ	تَزِيدُ	زِدْنَ	زَادَتَا	زَادَتْ
	Jussive	*yazid*		**Subjunctive**	*yazīda*
نَزِدْ		أَزِدْ	نَزِيدَ		أَزِيدَ
تَزِيدُوا	تَزِيدَا	تَزِدْ	تَزِيدُوا	تَزِيدَا	تَزِيدَ
تَزِدْنَ	تَزِيدَا	تَزِيدِي	تَزِدْنَ	تَزِيدَا	تَزِيدِي
يَزِيدُوا	يَزِيدَا	يَزِدْ	يَزِيدُوا	يَزِيدَا	يَزِيدَ
يَزِدْنَ	تَزِيدَا	تَزِدْ	يَزِدْنَ	تَزِيدَا	تَزِيدَ

Verbal Noun زِيَادَة *ziyāda* **Participle** زَائِد *zā'id*

Imperative زِدْ ، زِيدِي؛ زِيدَا؛ زِيدُوا ، زِدْنَ *zid, zīdī; zīdā; zīdū, zidna*

PASSIVE **Present** يُزَادُ *yuzādu* **Past** زِيدَ *zīda*

Participle مَزِيد *mazīd*

II زَيَّدَ to increase هـ 96; III زَايَدَ to outbid ه 98; V تَزَيَّدَ to increase, exaggerate 103; VI تَزَايَدَ to intensify **105**; VIII اِزْدَادَ to increase **111**; X اِسْتَزَادَ to aim for more هـ , to demand more of ه 116

زِيَادَة\اِزْدِيَاد increase مَزَاد\مُزَايَدَة auction تَزَايُد increment
تَزَيُّد exaggeration زِيَادَةً additionally مَزِيد excess, increased vb. form
زَائِدَة ج زَوَائِد appendix, appendage زِيَادَةً على ذلك moreover

94 I — لَيْسَ *laysa* not to be ا\ب ً — **ليس**

ACTIVE — **Past** *laysa*

- See § 13 and end of § 26.
- This past tense has present meaning.
- Full pronunciation (§ 6) always used.
- For the future and past, use كان يكون *kāna yakūnu* I
- For present affirmative, see § 2.

لَسْتُ		لَسْنَا
لَسْتَ	لَسْتُمَا	لَسْتُمْ
لَسْتِ	لَسْتُمَا	لَسْتُنَّ
لَيْسَ	لَيْسَا	لَيْسُوا
لَيْسَتْ	لَيْسَتَا	لَسْنَ

Present tenses, **Imperative**, **Participle**, **Verbal Noun** none

PASSIVE none

لَيْسَ ... بَلْ ... not only … but also …

أَلَيْسَ كَذلك؟ is that not so?

لَيْسَ\لَيْسَتْ هُنَاك there is no

لَيْسَ\لَيْسَتْ لَهُ he has not/no

لَيْسَ بِقَائِلِ he cannot say

95 II مَوَّلَ يُمَوِّلُ *mawwala yumawwilu* to finance هـ, to enrich ه — مول

ACTIVE Present *yumawwilu*

أُمَوِّلُ		نُمَوِّلُ
تُمَوِّلُ	تُمَوِّلاَنِ	تُمَوِّلُونَ
تُمَوِّلِينَ	تُمَوِّلاَنِ	تُمَوِّلْنَ
يُمَوِّلُ	يُمَوِّلاَنِ	يُمَوِّلُونَ
تُمَوِّلُ	تُمَوِّلاَنِ	يُمَوِّلْنَ

Past *mawwala*

مَوَّلْتُ		مَوَّلْنَا
مَوَّلْتَ	مَوَّلْتُمَا	مَوَّلْتُمْ
مَوَّلْتِ	مَوَّلْتُمَا	مَوَّلْتُنَّ
مَوَّلَ	مَوَّلاَ	مَوَّلُوا
مَوَّلَتْ	مَوَّلَتَا	مَوَّلْنَ

Jussive *yumawwil*

أُمَوِّلْ		نُمَوِّلْ
تُمَوِّلْ	تُمَوِّلاَ	تُمَوِّلُوا
تُمَوِّلِي	تُمَوِّلاَ	تُمَوِّلْنَ
يُمَوِّلْ	يُمَوِّلاَ	يُمَوِّلُوا
تُمَوِّلْ	تُمَوِّلاَ	يُمَوِّلْنَ

Subjunctive *yumawwila*

أُمَوِّلَ		نُمَوِّلَ
تُمَوِّلَ	تُمَوِّلاَ	تُمَوِّلُوا
تُمَوِّلِي	تُمَوِّلاَ	تُمَوِّلْنَ
يُمَوِّلَ	يُمَوِّلاَ	يُمَوِّلُوا
تُمَوِّلَ	تُمَوِّلاَ	يُمَوِّلْنَ

Verbal Noun تَمْوِيل *tamwīl* **Participle** مُمَوِّل *mumawwil*

Imperative مَوِّلْ، مَوِّلِي؛ مَوِّلاَ؛ مَوِّلُوا، مَوِّلْنَ *mawwil, -ī; -ā; -ū, -na*

PASSIVE **Present** يُمَوَّلُ *yumawwalu* **Past** مُوِّلَ *muwwila*

Participle مُمَوَّل *mumawwal*

V تَمَوَّلَ to be financed, become rich 102;

X اسْتَمَالَ to become rich 114

مَال ج أَمْوَال wealth, property مَالِي financial مُمَوِّل financier

مُمَوَّل\ذو مَال wealthy تَمْوِيل financing سَنَة مَالِيَّة financial year

تَضَخُّم مَالِي inflation مُؤَسَّسَة كَثِيرَة المَال a wealthy foundation

مَال ثَابِت\نَقْلِي fixed/movable asset وَضْع مَالِي financial status

وِزَارَة\وَزِير (الأُمُور) المَالِيَّة Ministry/Minister of Finance

96 II **مَيَّلَ يُمَيِّلُ** *mayyala yumayyilu* to incline/predispose towards ه إلى\نحو هـ إلى\نحو **ميل**

ACTIVE Present *yumayyilu* **Past** *mayyala*

نُمَيِّلُ		أُمَيِّلُ	مَيَّلْنَا		مَيَّلْتُ
تُمَيِّلُونَ	تُمَيِّلاَنِ	تُمَيِّلُ	مَيَّلْتُمْ	مَيَّلْتُمَا	مَيَّلْتَ
تُمَيِّلْنَ	تُمَيِّلاَنِ	تُمَيِّلِينَ	مَيَّلْتُنَّ	مَيَّلْتُمَا	مَيَّلْتِ
يُمَيِّلُونَ	يُمَيِّلاَنِ	يُمَيِّلُ	مَيَّلُوا	مَيَّلاَ	مَيَّلَ
يُمَيِّلْنَ	تُمَيِّلاَنِ	تُمَيِّلُ	مَيَّلْنَ	مَيَّلَتَا	مَيَّلَتْ

Jussive *yumayyil* **Subjunctive** *yumayyila*

نُمَيِّلْ		أُمَيِّلْ	نُمَيِّلَ		أُمَيِّلَ
تُمَيِّلُوا	تُمَيِّلاَ	تُمَيِّلْ	تُمَيِّلُوا	تُمَيِّلاَ	تُمَيِّلَ
تُمَيِّلْنَ	تُمَيِّلاَ	تُمَيِّلِي	تُمَيِّلْنَ	تُمَيِّلاَ	تُمَيِّلِي
يُمَيِّلُوا	يُمَيِّلاَ	يُمَيِّلْ	يُمَيِّلُوا	يُمَيِّلاَ	يُمَيِّلَ
يُمَيِّلْنَ	تُمَيِّلاَ	تُمَيِّلْ	يُمَيِّلْنَ	تُمَيِّلاَ	تُمَيِّلَ

Verbal Noun تَمْيِيل *tamyīl* **Participle** مُمَيِّل *mumayyil*

Imperative مَيِّلْ، مَيِّلِي؛ مَيِّلاَ؛ مَيِّلُوا، مَيِّلْنَ *mayyil, -ī; -ā; -ū, -na*

PASSIVE Present يُمَيَّلُ *yumayyalu* **Past** مُيِّلَ *muyyila*

Participle مُمَيَّل *mumayyal*

I مَالَ يَمِيلُ (مَيْل) to incline towards إلى 93; IV أَمَالَ 99 = II مَيَّلَ 96;

V/VI تَمَيَّلَ\تَمَايَلَ to sway 103/105;

X اِسْتَمَالَ to attract towards ه إلى هـ إلى 114

مَيْل ج مُيُول\أَمْيَال inclination, trend

مَيَّال ألى biased towards

مَائِل إلى tending towards

أَمْيَل ألى more in favour of

97 | III | حَاوَلَ يُحَاوِلُ *ḥāwala yuḥāwilu* to try هـ\أنْ | حول\حيل

ACTIVE Present *yuḥāwilu*

نُحَاوِلُ		أُحَاوِلُ
تُحَاوِلُونَ	تُحَاوِلاَنِ	تُحَاوِلُ
تُحَاوِلْنَ	تُحَاوِلاَنِ	تُحَاوِلِينَ
يُحَاوِلُونَ	يُحَاوِلاَنِ	يُحَاوِلُ
يُحَاوِلْنَ	تُحَاوِلاَنِ	تُحَاوِلُ

Past *ḥāwala*

حَاوَلْنَا		حَاوَلْتُ
حَاوَلْتُمْ	حَاوَلْتُمَا	حَاوَلْتَ
حَاوَلْتُنَّ	حَاوَلْتُمَا	حَاوَلْتِ
حَاوَلُوا	حَاوَلاَ	حَاوَلَ
حَاوَلْنَ	حَاوَلَتَا	حَاوَلَتْ

Jussive *yuḥāwil*

نُحَاوِلْ		أُحَاوِلْ
تُحَاوِلُوا	تُحَاوِلاَ	تُحَاوِلْ
تُحَاوِلْنَ	تُحَاوِلاَ	تُحَاوِلِي
يُحَاوِلُوا	يُحَاوِلاَ	يُحَاوِلْ
يُحَاوِلْنَ	تُحَاوِلاَ	تُحَاوِلْ

Subjunctive *yuḥāwila*

نُحَاوِلَ		أُحَاوِلَ
تُحَاوِلُوا	تُحَاوِلاَ	تُحَاوِلَ
تُحَاوِلْنَ	تُحَاوِلاَ	تُحَاوِلِي
يُحَاوِلُوا	يُحَاوِلاَ	يُحَاوِلَ
يُحَاوِلْنَ	تُحَاوِلاَ	تُحَاوِلَ

Verbal Noun مُحَاوَلَة *muḥāwala* **Participle** مُحَاوِل *muḥāwil*

Imperative حَاوِلْ، حَاوِلِي؛ حَاوِلاَ؛ حَاوِلُوا، حَاوِلْنَ *ḥāwil, -ī; -ā; -ū, -na*

PASSIVE Present يُحَاوَلُ *yuḥāwalu* **Past** حُووِلَ *ḥūwila*
Participle مُحَاوَل *muḥāwal*

I حَالَ يَحُولُ (حَال) to be changed into هـ\ألى , (حَيْلُولَة) to prevent دون 90; II حَوَّلَ to transfer هـ 95; II/IV حَوَّلَ\أَحَالَ to transform from ... to هـ\ألى 95\99; V تَحَوَّلَ to be transferred/transformed to/into إلى 102; VI تَحَاوَلَ to strive for على 104; VIII احْتَالَ to deceive على 108; IX احْوَلَّ to squint 112; X اسْتَحَالَ to be transformed into إلى 114

حَال ج أَحْوَال condition, state حَالَة case حَالِي present, actual حَوْلَ\حَوَالَى\حَوَالِي about حَالِيًا at present على كُلِّ حَال in any case

98 **III** بَايَعَ يُبَايِعُ *bāya'a yubāyi'u* to make a contract with ه **بيع**

ACTIVE **Present** *yubāyi'u*

أُبَايِعُ		نُبَايِعُ
تُبَايِعُ	تُبَايِعَانِ	تُبَايِعُونَ
تُبَايِعِينَ	تُبَايِعَانِ	تُبَايِعْنَ
يُبَايِعُ	يُبَايِعَانِ	يُبَايِعُونَ
تُبَايِعُ	تُبَايِعَانِ	يُبَايِعْنَ

Past *bāya'a*

بَايَعْتُ		بَايَعْنَا
بَايَعْتَ	بَايَعْتُمَا	بَايَعْتُمْ
بَايَعْتِ	بَايَعْتُمَا	بَايَعْتُنَّ
بَايَعَ	بَايَعَا	بَايَعُوا
بَايَعَتْ	بَايَعَتَا	بَايَعْنَ

Jussive *yubāyi'*

أُبَايِعْ		نُبَايِعْ
تُبَايِعْ	تُبَايِعَا	تُبَايِعُوا
تُبَايِعِي	تُبَايِعَا	تُبَايِعْنَ
يُبَايِعْ	يُبَايِعَا	يُبَايِعُوا
تُبَايِعْ	تُبَايِعَا	يُبَايِعْنَ

Subjunctive *yubāyi'a*

أُبَايِعَ		نُبَايِعَ
تُبَايِعَ	تُبَايِعَا	تُبَايِعُوا
تُبَايِعِي	تُبَايِعَا	تُبَايِعْنَ
يُبَايِعَ	يُبَايِعَا	يُبَايِعُوا
تُبَايِعَ	تُبَايِعَا	يُبَايِعْنَ

Verbal Noun مُبَايَعَة *mubāya'a* **Participle** مُبَايِع *mubāyi'*

Imperative بَايِعْ، بَايِعِي؛ بَايِعَا؛ بَايِعُوا، بَايِعْنَ *bāyi', -ī; -ā; -ū, -na*

PASSIVE **Present** يُبَايَعُ *yubāya'u* **Past** بُويِعَ *būyi'a*

Participle مُبَايَع *mubāya'*

I بَاعَ يَبِيعُ (بَيْع) to sell ه\إلى ه 93; IV أَبَاعَ to offer for sale ه 101;
VI تَبَايَعَ to conclude a deal 105; VII اِنْبَاعَ to be sold **107**;
VIII اِبْتَاعَ to buy ه\من ه 110

بَيْع ج بُيُوع sale بَائِع ج بَاعَة seller بَيْعَة\مُبَايَعَة transaction
بَيَّاع salesman مَبِيع sale, sold لِلْبَيْع for sale
مُبْتَاع buyer اِبْتِيَاع purchase شُرُوط البَيْع terms/conditions of sale
بَيْع بِالجُمْلَة wholesale بَيْع بِالفَرْد retail

99 | **IV** — أَقَامَ يُقِيمُ *'aqāma yuqīmu* — **قوم**

to organise, rectfy, raise هـ , to reside

ACTIVE Present		*yuqīmu*	**Past**		*'aqāma*
نُقِيمُ		أُقِيمُ	أَقَمْنَا		أَقَمْتُ
تُقِيمُونَ	تُقِيمَانِ	تُقِيمُ	أَقَمْتُمْ	أَقَمْتُمَا	أَقَمْتَ
تُقِمْنَ	تُقِيمَانِ	تُقِيمِينَ	أَقَمْتُنَّ	أَقَمْتُمَا	أَقَمْتِ
يُقِيمُونَ	يُقِيمَانِ	يُقِيمُ	أَقَامُوا	أَقَامَا	أَقَامَ
يُقِمْنَ	تُقِيمَانِ	تُقِيمُ	أَقَمْنَ	أَقَامَتَا	أَقَامَتْ

Jussive		*yuqim*	**Subjunctive**		*yuqīma*
نُقِمْ		أُقِمْ	نُقِيمَ		أُقِيمَ
تُقِيمُوا	تُقِيمَا	تُقِمْ	تُقِيمُوا	تُقِيمَا	تُقِيمَ
تُقِمْنَ	تُقِيمَا	تُقِيمِي	تُقِمْنَ	تُقِيمَا	تُقِيمِي
يُقِيمُوا	يُقِيمَا	يُقِمْ	يُقِيمُوا	يُقِيمَا	يُقِيمَ
يُقِمْنَ	تُقِيمَا	تُقِمْ	يُقِمْنَ	تُقِيمَا	تُقِيمَ

Verbal Noun إِقَامَة *'iqāma* **Participle** مُقِيم *muqīm*

Imperative أَقِمْ، أَقِيمِي؛ أَقِيمَا؛ أَقِيمُوا، أَقِمْنَ
'aqim, 'aqīmī; 'aqīmā; 'aqīmū, 'aqimna

PASSIVE Present يُقَامُ *yuqāmu* **Past** أُقِيمَ *'uqīma*

Participle مُقَام *muqām*

I قَامَ يَقُومُ (قِيَامَة\قَوْمَة) to rise, to undertake ب , to take charge of على 90; II قَوَّمَ to raise, evaluate, adjust هـ 95; III قَاوَمَ to resist هـ ه 97; X اِسْتَقَامَ to stand up 114

قَوْم ج أَقْوَام nation قَوْمِي national(ist) قِيمَة ج قِيَم value
قِيَام uprising قَائِم ج قُوَّام upright, rising قَائِمَة ج قَوَائِم list, register
إِقَامَة raising, residence مَقَام site قَائِم بِالأَعْمَال chargé d'affaires

100 | IV | أَحْوَجَ يُحْوِجُ *'aḥwaja yuḥwiju* to need إلى , to compel ه إلى , to impoverish ه | حوج

ACTIVE	**Present** *yuḥwiju*			**Past** *'aḥwaja*	
نُحْوِجُ		أُحْوِجُ	أَحْوَجْنَا		أَحْوَجْتُ
تُحْوِجُونَ	تُحْوِجَانِ	تُحْوِجُ	أَحْوَجْتُمْ	أَحْوَجْتُمَا	أَحْوَجْتَ
تُحْوِجْنَ	تُحْوِجَانِ	تُحْوِجِينَ	أَحْوَجْتُنَّ	أَحْوَجْتُمَا	أَحْوَجْتِ
يُحْوِجُونَ	يُحْوِجَانِ	يُحْوِجُ	أَحْوَجُوا	أَحْوَجَا	أَحْوَجَ
يُحْوِجْنَ	تُحْوِجَانِ	تُحْوِجُ	أَحْوَجْنَ	أَحْوَجَتَا	أَحْوَجَتْ

	Jussive *yuḥwij*			**Subjunctive** *yuḥwija*	
نُحْوِجْ		أُحْوِجْ	نُحْوِجَ		أُحْوِجَ
تُحْوِجُوا	تُحْوِجَا	تُحْوِجْ	تُحْوِجُوا	تُحْوِجَا	تُحْوِجَ
تُحْوِجْنَ	تُحْوِجَا	تُحْوِجِي	تُحْوِجْنَ	تُحْوِجَا	تُحْوِجِي
يُحْوِجُوا	يُحْوِجَا	يُحْوِجْ	يُحْوِجُوا	يُحْوِجَا	يُحْوِجَ
يُحْوِجْنَ	تُحْوِجَا	تُحْوِجْ	يُحْوِجْنَ	تُحْوِجَا	تُحْوِجَ

Verbal Noun إِحْوَاج *'iḥwāj* **Participle** مُحْوِجْ *muḥwij*

Impv. أَحْوِجْ، أَحْوِجِي؛ أَحْوِجَا؛ أَحْوِجُوا، أَحْوِجْنَ *'aḥwij, -ī; -ā; -ū, -na*

PASSIVE **Present** يُحْوَجُ *yuḥwaju* **Past** أُحْوِجَ *'uḥwija*

Participle مُحْوَجْ *muḥwaj*

VIII اِحْتَاجَ to need إلى **108**

مُحْتَاج needy مُحْتَاج إليه needed اِحْتِيَاج إلى need of

حَوْج need, destitution حَاجَة إلى necessity for عند الحَاجَة if need be

حَاجَة ج حَوَائِج necessity (thing needed) حَاجِيَات (basic) necessities

ما نَحْتَاجُ إليه من التمْوِيل the ('whatever') financing we need

101 IV **أَذَاعَ يُذِيعُ** *'adhā'a yudhī'u* to broadcast هـ\ب **ذيع**

ACTIVE

Present *yudhī'u*			Past *'adhā'a*		
نُذِيعُ		أُذِيعُ	أَذَعْنَا		أَذَعْتُ
تُذِيعُونَ	تُذِيعَانِ	تُذِيعُ	أَذَعْتُمْ	أَذَعْتُمَا	أَذَعْتَ
تُذِعْنَ	تُذِيعَانِ	تُذِيعِينَ	أَذَعْتُنَّ	أَذَعْتُمَا	أَذَعْتِ
يُذِيعُونَ	يُذِيعَانِ	يُذِيعُ	أَذَاعُوا	أَذَاعَا	أَذَاعَ
يُذِعْنَ	تُذِيعَانِ	تُذِيعُ	أَذَعْنَ	أَذَاعَتَا	أَذَاعَتْ

Jussive *yudhi'*			Subjunctive *yudhī'a*		
نُذِعْ		أُذِعْ	نُذِيعَ		أُذِيعَ
تُذِيعُوا	تُذِيعَا	تُذِعْ	تُذِيعُوا	تُذِيعَا	تُذِيعَ
تُذِعْنَ	تُذِيعَا	تُذِيعِي	تُذِعْنَ	تُذِيعَا	تُذِيعِي
يُذِيعُوا	يُذِيعَا	يُذِعْ	يُذِيعُوا	يُذِيعَا	يُذِيعَ
يُذِعْنَ	تُذِيعَا	تُذِعْ	يُذِعْنَ	تُذِيعَا	تُذِيعَ

Verbal Noun إِذَاعَة *'idhā'a* **Participle** مُذِيع *mudhī'*

Imperative أَذِعْ، أَذِيعِي؛ أَذِيعَا؛ أَذِيعُوا، أَذِعْنَ

'adhi', 'adhī'ī; 'adhī'ā; 'adhī'ū, 'adhi'na

PASSIVE **Present** يُذَاعُ *yudhā'u* **Past** أُذِيعَ *'udhī'a*

Participle مُذَاع *mudhā'*

I ذَاعَ يَذِيعُ (ذُيُوع) to spread (o.s.) 93

ذُيُوع diffusion, circulation إِذَاعَة broadcast(ing) ذَائِع widespread

مُذِيع transmitter, announcer مِذْيَاع ج مَذَايِيع microphone

إِذَاعَة الأَخْبَار\تَلْفَزِيَّة\لا سِلْكِيَّة news/television/radio broadcast(ing)

102 V **تَصَوَّرَ يَتَصَوَّرُ** *taṣawwara yataṣawwaru* **صور**

to imagine هـ , to be portrayed

ACTIVE Present *yataṣawwaru* | **Past** *taṣawwara*

نَتَصَوَّرُ		أَتَصَوَّرُ	تَصَوَّرْنَا		تَصَوَّرْتُ
تَتَصَوَّرُونَ	تَتَصَوَّرَانِ	تَتَصَوَّرُ	تَصَوَّرْتُمْ	تَصَوَّرْتُمَا	تَصَوَّرْتَ
تَتَصَوَّرْنَ	تَتَصَوَّرَانِ	تَتَصَوَّرِينَ	تَصَوَّرْتُنَّ	تَصَوَّرْتُمَا	تَصَوَّرْتِ
يَتَصَوَّرُونَ	يَتَصَوَّرَانِ	يَتَصَوَّرُ	تَصَوَّرُوا	تَصَوَّرَا	تَصَوَّرَ
يَتَصَوَّرْنَ	تَتَصَوَّرَانِ	تَتَصَوَّرُ	تَصَوَّرْنَ	تَصَوَّرَتَا	تَصَوَّرَتْ

Jussive *yataṣawwar* | **Subjunctive** *yataṣawwara*

نَتَصَوَّرْ		أَتَصَوَّرْ	نَيَتَصَوَّرَ		أَتَصَوَّرَ
تَتَصَوَّرُوا	تَتَصَوَّرَا	تَتَصَوَّرْ	تَتَصَوَّرُوا	تَتَصَوَّرَا	تَتَصَوَّرَ
تَتَصَوَّرْنَ	تَتَصَوَّرَا	تَتَصَوَّرِي	تَتَصَوَّرْنَ	تَتَصَوَّرَا	تَتَصَوَّرِي
يَتَصَوَّرُوا	يَتَصَوَّرَا	يَتَصَوَّرْ	يَتَصَوَّرُوا	يَتَصَوَّرَا	يَتَصَوَّرَ
يَتَصَوَّرْنَ	تَتَصَوَّرَا	تَتَصَوَّرْ	يَتَصَوَّرْنَ	تَتَصَوَّرَا	تَتَصَوَّرَ

Verbal Noun يَتَصَوُّر *taṣawwur* **Participle** مُتَصَوِّر *mutaṣawwir*

Imperative تَصَوَّرْ، تَصَوَّرِي؛ تَصَوَّرَا؛ تَصَوَّرُوا، تَصَوَّرْنَ
taṣawwar, -ī; -ā; -ū, -na

PASSIVE Present يُتَصَوَّرُ *yutaṣawwaru* **Past** تُصُوِّرَ *tusuwwira*

II صَوَّرَ to depict, photograph هـ ه 95

صُرَة ج صُوَر picture, form, photograph تَصْوِير depiction, photography

مُصَوِّر photographer مُصَوِّرَة camera تَصَوُّر imagination

تَصَوُّرِي imaginary مُصَوَّر illustrated صُورِي formal, artificial

بِصُورَة (غَيْر) رَسْمِيَّة (un)officially بِصُورَة عَامَّة generally

بِصُورَة خَاصَّة especially (غَيْرُ) قَابِل لِلتَّصَوُّر (un)imaginable

بِصُورَة أَوْضَح more clearly ضَعِيف ج ضُعَفَاء التَّصَوُّر unimaginative

103 | V | تَغَيَّرَ يَتَغَيَّرُ *taghayyara yataghayyaru* to change | **غير**

ACTIVE Present *yataghayyaru* — **Past** *taghayyara*

نَتَغَيَّرُ		أَتَغَيَّرُ	تَغَيَّرْنَا		تَغَيَّرْتُ
تَتَغَيَّرُونَ	تَتَغَيَّرَانِ	تَتَغَيَّرُ	تَغَيَّرْتُمْ	تَغَيَّرْتُمَا	تَغَيَّرْتَ
تَتَغَيَّرْنَ	تَتَغَيَّرَانِ	تَتَغَيَّرِينَ	تَغَيَّرْتُنَّ	تَغَيَّرْتُمَا	تَغَيَّرْتِ
يَتَغَيَّرُونَ	يَتَغَيَّرَانِ	يَتَغَيَّرُ	تَغَيَّرُوا	تَغَيَّرَا	تَغَيَّرَ
يَتَغَيَّرْنَ	تَتَغَيَّرَانِ	تَتَغَيَّرُ	تَغَيَّرْنَ	تَغَيَّرَتَا	تَغَيَّرَتْ

Jussive *yataghayyar* — **Subjunctive** *yataghayyara*

نَتَغَيَّرْ		أَتَغَيَّرْ	نَتَغَيَّرَ		أَتَغَيَّرَ
تَتَغَيَّرُوا	تَتَغَيَّرَا	تَتَغَيَّرْ	تَتَغَيَّرُوا	تَتَغَيَّرَا	تَتَغَيَّرَ
تَتَغَيَّرْنَ	تَتَغَيَّرَا	تَتَغَيَّرِي	تَتَغَيَّرْنَ	تَتَغَيَّرَا	تَتَغَيَّرِي
يَتَغَيَّرُوا	يَتَغَيَّرَا	يَتَغَيَّرْ	يَتَغَيَّرُوا	يَتَغَيَّرَا	يَتَغَيَّرَ
يَتَغَيَّرْنَ	تَتَغَيَّرَا	تَتَغَيَّرْ	يَتَغَيَّرْنَ	تَتَغَيَّرَا	تَتَغَيَّرَ

Verbal Noun يتغيُّر *taghayyur* **Participle** مُتَغَيِّر *mutaghayyir*

Impv. تَغَيَّرْ، تَغَيَّرِي؛ تَغَيَّرَا؛ تَغَيَّرُوا، تَغَيَّرْنَ *taghayyar, -ī; -ā; -ū, -na*

PASSIVE° **Present** يُتَغَيَّرُ *yutaghayyaru* **Past** تُغُيِّرَ *tughuyyira*

I غَارَ يَغِيرُ (غَيْرَة) to be jealous of من 93; II غَيَّرَ to change هـ 96;

III غَايَرَ to differ from ه هـ , to compete with ه 98;

IV أَغَارَ to make jealous ه 101; VI تَغَايَرَ to be varied 105

غَيْرُ other than, dis-, un- غَيْرَ except for الغَيْر other people, others

وغَيْرُهُ etc. تَغْيِير change مُتَغَيِّر variable غَيْرِي altruist(ic)

غَيْرِيَّة altruism تَغَيُّر alteration غَيْر مَعْرُوف unknown

غَيْر مَقْبُول unacceptable غَيْر مَعْقُول unreasonable

غَيْر أَنَّ except that غَيْر هذا moreover بغَيْر\من غَيْر without

104 VI تَعاوَنَ يَتَعاوَنُ *taʿāwana yataʿāwanu* to cooperate عون

ACTIVE Present *yataʿāwanu*

أَتَعاوَنُ		نَتَعاوَنُ
تَتَعاوَنُ	تَتَعاوَنانِ	تَتَعاوَنُونَ
تَتَعاوَنِينَ	تَتَعاوَنانِ	تَتَعاوَنَّ
يَتَعاوَنُ	يَتَعاوَنانِ	يَتَعاوَنُونَ
تَتَعاوَنُ	تَتَعاوَنانِ	يَتَعاوَنَّ

Past *taʿāwana*

تَعاوَنْتُ		تَعاوَنّا
تَعاوَنْتَ	تَعاوَنْتُما	تَعاوَنْتُمْ
تَعاوَنْتِ	تَعاوَنْتُما	تَعاوَنْتُنَّ
تَعاوَنَ	تَعاوَنا	تَعاوَنُوا
تَعاوَنَتْ	تَعاوَنَتا	تَعاوَنَّ

Jussive *yataʿāwan*

أَتَعاوَنْ		نَتَعاوَنْ
تَتَعاوَنْ	تَتَعاوَنا	تَتَعاوَنُوا
تَتَعاوَنِي	تَتَعاوَنا	تَتَعاوَنَّ
يَتَعاوَنْ	يَتَعاوَنا	يَتَعاوَنُوا
تَتَعاوَنْ	تَتَعاوَنا	يَتَعاوَنَّ

Subjunctive *yataʿāwana*

أَتَعاوَنَ		نَتَعاوَنَ
تَتَعاوَنَ	تَتَعاوَنا	تَتَعاوَنُوا
تَتَعاوَنِي	تَتَعاوَنا	تَتَعاوَنَّ
يَتَعاوَنَ	يَتَعاوَنا	يَتَعاوَنُوا
تَتَعاوَنَ	تَتَعاوَنا	يَتَعاوَنَّ

Verbal Noun تَعاوُن *taʿāwun* **Participle** مُتَعاوِن *mutaʿāwin*

Impv. تَعاوَنْ، تَعاوَنِي؛ تَعاوَنا؛ تَعاوَنُوا، تَعاوَنَّ *taʿāwan, -ī; -ā; -ū, -na*

PASSIVE° **Present** يُتَعاوَنُ *yutaʿāwanu* **Past** تُعُووِنَ *tuʿūwina*

III/IV عاوَنَ\أَعانَ to help ه 97/99;

X اِسْتَعانَ to ask for help against ه على 114

عَوْن\مُعاوَنَة help
عَوْن ج أَعْوان assistant
تَعاوُن cooperation
تَعاوُني cooperative
إِعانَة subsidy
مُعاوِن assistant, adjutant
عَدَم التَعاوُن noncooperation
عَديم التَعاوُن uncooperative
تَعاوُن على التَنْمِيَة development cooperation
مُعْطِي العَوْن aid donor
عَوْن غِذائي food aid
عَوْن الطَوارِئ emergency aid
شَرِكَة تَعاوُنِيَّة cooperative society

105 | VI | تَزَايَدَ يَتَزَايَدُ *tazāyada yatazāyadu* to intensify | **زيد**

ACTIVE Present *yatazāyadu*			**Past** *tazāyada*		
نَتَزَايَدُ		أَتَزَايَدُ	تَزَايَدْنَا		تَزَايَدْتُ
تَتَزَايَدُونَ	تَتَزَايَدَانِ	تَتَزَايَدُ	تَزَايَدْتُمْ	تَزَايَدْتُمَا	تَزَايَدْتَ
تَتَزَايَدْنَ	تَتَزَايَدَانِ	تَتَزَايَدِينَ	تَزَايَدْتُنَّ	تَزَايَدْتُمَا	تَزَايَدْتِ
يَتَزَايَدُونَ	يَتَزَايَدَانِ	يَتَزَايَدُ	تَزَايَدُوا	تَزَايَدَا	تَزَايَدَ
يَتَزَايَدْنَ	تَتَزَايَدَانِ	تَتَزَايَدُ	تَزَايَدْنَ	تَزَايَدَتَا	تَزَايَدَتْ

Jussive *yatazāyad*			**Subjunctive** *yatazāyada*		
نَتَزَايَدْ		أَتَزَايَدْ	نَتَزَايَدَ		أَتَزَايَدَ
تَتَزَايَدُوا	تَتَزَايَدَا	تَتَزَايَدْ	تَتَزَايَدُوا	تَتَزَايَدَا	تَتَزَايَدَ
تَتَزَايَدْنَ	تَتَزَايَدَا	تَتَزَايَدِي	تَتَزَايَدْنَ	تَتَزَايَدَا	تَتَزَايَدِي
يَتَزَايَدُوا	يَتَزَايَدَا	يَتَزَايَدْ	يَتَزَايَدُوا	يَتَزَايَدَا	يَتَزَايَدَ
يَتَزَايَدْنَ	تَتَزَايَدَا	تَتَزَايَدْ	يَتَزَايَدْنَ	تَتَزَايَدَا	تَتَزَايَدَ

Verbal Noun تَزَايُد *tazāyud* **Participle** مُتَزَايِد *mutazāyid*

Impv. تَزَايَدْ، تَزَايَدِي؛ تَزَايَدَا؛ تَزَايَدُوا، تَزَايَدْنَ *tazāyad, -ī; -ā; -ū, -na*

PASSIVE° **Present** يُتَزَايَدُ *yutazāyadu* **Past** تُزُويِدَ *tuzūyida*

See **93**

106 VII انْحَازَ يَنْحَازُ *inḥāza yanḥāzu* حوز\حيز

to withdraw from عن\من, to join إلى

ACTIVE	**Present**	*yanḥāzu*		**Past**	*inḥāza*
نَنْحَازُ		أَنْحَازُ	انْحَزْنَا		انْحَزْتُ
تَنْحَازُونَ	تَنْحَازَانِ	تَنْحَازُ	انْحَزْتُمْ	انْحَزْتُمَا	انْحَزْتَ
تَنْحَزْنَ	تَنْحَازَانِ	تَنْحَازِينَ	انْحَزْتُنَّ	انْحَزْتُمَا	انْحَزْتِ
يَنْحَازُونَ	يَنْحَازَانِ	يَنْحَازُ	انْحَازُوا	انْحَازَا	انْحَازَ
يَنْحَزْنَ	تَنْحَازَانِ	تَنْحَازُ	انْحَزْنَ	انْحَازَتَا	انْحَازَتْ

	Jussive	*yanḥáz*	**Subjunctive**		*yanḥāza*
نَنْحَزْ		أَنْحَزْ	نَنْحَازَ		أَنْحَازَ
تَنْحَازُوا	تَنْحَازَا	تَنْحَزْ	تَنْحَازُوا	تَنْحَازَا	تَنْحَازَ
تَنْحَزْنَ	تَنْحَازَا	تَنْحَازِي	تَنْحَزْنَ	تَنْحَازَا	تَنْحَازِي
يَنْحَازُوا	يَنْحَازَا	يَنْحَزْ	يَنْحَازُوا	يَنْحَازَا	يَنْحَازَ
يَنْحَزْنَ	تَنْحَازَا	تَنْحَزْ	يَنْحَزْنَ	تَنْحَازَا	تَنْحَازَ

Verbal Noun انْحِيَاز *inḥiyāz* **Participle** مُنْحَاز *munḥāz*

Imperative انْحَزْ، انْحَازِي؛ انْحَازَا؛ انْحَازُوا، انْحَزْنَ
inḥáz, inḥāzī; inḥāzā; inḥāzū, inḥazna

PASSIVE° **Present** يُنْحَازُ *yunḥāzu* **Past** أُنْحِيزَ *unḥīza*
Participle مُنْحَاز *munḥāz*

I حَازَ يَحُوزُ (حِيَازَة) to gain هـ 90;

V تَحَوَّزَ\تَحَيَّزَ 102/103 = VII انْحَازَ **103**; VIII احْتَازَ to possess هـ 108

حَوْز\حَوْزَة\حِيَازَة possession, tenure — حَائِز possessor, tenant

تَحَيُّز partiality, bias — انْحِيَاز isolation

مُتَحَيِّز partial, biased — مُنْحَاز isolated, outsider

حَيْز ج أَحْيَاز range — في حَيْز الإمْكَان as far as possible

107 VII انْبَاعَ يَنْبَاعُ *inbāʿa yanbāʿu* to be sold **بيع**

ACTIVE	**Present**	*yanbāʿu*		**Past**	*inbāʿa*
نَنْبَاعُ		أَنْبَاعُ	انْبَعْنَا		انْبَعْتُ
تَنْبَاعُونَ	تَنْبَاعَانِ	تَنْبَاعُ	انْبَعْتُمْ	انْبَعْتُمَا	انْبَعْتَ
تَنْبَعْنَ	تَنْبَاعَانِ	تَنْبَاعِينَ	انْبَعْتُنَّ	انْبَعْتُمَا	انْبَعْتِ
يَنْبَاعُونَ	يَنْبَاعَانِ	يَنْبَاعُ	انْبَاعُوا	انْبَاعَا	انْبَاعَ
يَنْبَعْنَ	تَنْبَاعَانِ	تَنْبَاعُ	انْبَعْنَ	انْبَاعَتَا	انْبَاعَتْ
	Jussive	*yanbaʿ*	**Subjunctive**		*yanbāʿa*
نَنْبَعْ		أَنْبَعْ	نَنْبَاعَ		أَنْبَاعَ
تَنْبَاعُوا	تَنْبَاعَا	تَنْبَعْ	تَنْبَاعُوا	تَنْبَاعَا	تَنْبَاعَ
تَنْبَعْنَ	تَنْبَاعَا	تَنْبَاعِي	تَنْبَعْنَ	تَنْبَاعَا	تَنْبَاعِي
يَنْبَاعُوا	يَنْبَاعَا	يَنْبَعْ	يَنْبَاعُوا	يَنْبَاعَا	يَنْبَاعَ
يَنْبَعْنَ	تَنْبَاعَا	تَنْبَعْ	يَنْبَعْنَ	تَنْبَاعَا	تَنْبَاعَ

Verbal Noun انْبِيَاع *inbiyāʿ* **Participle** مُنْبَاع *munbāʿ*

Imperative انْبَعْ، انْبَاعِي؛ انْبَاعَا؛ انْبَاعُوا، انْبَعْنَ

inbaʿ, inbāʿī; inbāʿā; inbāʿū, inbaʿna

PASSIVE none (active verb has passive meaning)

See **98**

108 VIII اِحْتَاجَ يَحْتَاجُ *iḥtāja yaḥtāju* to need إلى **حوج**

ACTIVE **Present** *yaḥtāju*

نَحْتَاجُ		أَحْتَاجُ
تَحْتَاجُونَ	تَحْتَاجَانِ	تَحْتَاجُ
تَحْتَجْنَ	تَحْتَاجَانِ	تَحْتَاجِينَ
يَحْتَاجُونَ	يَحْتَاجَانِ	يَحْتَاجُ
يَحْتَجْنَ	تَحْتَاجَانِ	تَحْتَاجُ

Past *iḥtāja*

اِحْتَجْنَا		اِحْتَجْتُ
اِحْتَجْتُمْ	اِحْتَجْتُمَا	اِحْتَجْتَ
اِحْتَجْتُنَّ	اِحْتَجْتُمَا	اِحْتَجْتِ
اِحْتَاجُوا	اِحْتَاجَا	اِحْتَاجَ
اِحْتَجْنَ	اِحْتَاجَتَا	اِحْتَاجَتْ

Jussive *yaḥtáj*

نَحْتَجْ		أَحْتَجْ
تَحْتَاجُوا	تَحْتَاجَا	تَحْتَجْ
تَحْتَجْنَ	تَحْتَاجَا	تَحْتَاجِي
يَحْتَاجُوا	يَحْتَاجَا	يَحْتَجْ
يَحْتَجْنَ	تَحْتَاجَا	تَحْتَجْ

Subjunctive *yaḥtāja*

نَحْتَاجَ		أَحْتَاجَ
تَحْتَاجُوا	تَحْتَاجَا	تَحْتَاجَ
تَحْتَجْنَ	تَحْتَاجَا	تَحْتَاجِي
يَحْتَاجُوا	يَحْتَاجَا	يَحْتَاجَ
يَحْتَجْنَ	تَحْتَاجَا	تَحْتَاجَ

Verbal Noun اِحْتِيَاج *iḥtiyāj* **Participle** مُحْتَاج *muḥtāj*

Imperative اِحْتَجْ، اِحْتَاجِي؛ اِحْتَاجَا؛ اِحْتَاجُوا، اِحْتَجْنَ
iḥtáj, iḥtājī; iḥtājā; iḥtājū, iḥtajna

PASSIVE° **Present** يُحْتَاجُ *yuḥtāju* **Past** أُحْتِيجَ *uḥtīja*
Participle مُحْتَاج *muḥtāj*

See **100**

109 | VIII | اِتَّفَقَ يَتَّفِقُ *izdáwaja yazdáwiju* to be in pairs | زوج

ACTIVE

Present *yazdáwiju*			Past *izdáwaja*		
نَزْدَوِجُ		أَزْدَوِجُ	اِزْدَوَجْنَا		اِزْدَوَجْتُ
تَزْدَوِجُونَ	تَزْدَوِجَانِ	تَزْدَوِجُ	اِزْدَوَجْتُمْ	اِزْدَوَجْتُمَا	اِزْدَوَجْتَ
تَزْدَوِجْنَ	تَزْدَوِجَانِ	تَزْدَوِجِينَ	اِزْدَوَجْتُنَّ	اِزْدَوَجْتُمَا	اِزْدَوَجْتِ
يَزْدَوِجُونَ	يَزْدَوِجَانِ	يَزْدَوِجُ	اِزْدَوَجُوا	اِزْدَوَجَا	اِزْدَوَجَ
يَزْدَوِجْنَ	تَزْدَوِجَانِ	تَزْدَوِجُ	اِزْدَوَجْنَ	اِزْدَوَجَتَا	اِزْدَوَجَتْ

Jussive *yazdáwij*			Subjunctive *yazdáwija*		
نَزْدَوِجْ		أَزْدَوِجْ	نَزْدَوِجَ		أَزْدَوِجَ
تَزْدَوِجُوا	تَزْدَوِجَا	تَزْدَوِجْ	تَزْدَوِجُوا	تَزْدَوِجَا	تَزْدَوِجَ
تَزْدَوِجْنَ	تَزْدَوِجَا	تَزْدَوِجِي	تَزْدَوِجْنَ	تَزْدَوِجَا	تَزْدَوِجِي
يَزْدَوِجُوا	يَزْدَوِجَا	يَزْدَوِجْ	يَزْدَوِجُوا	يَزْدَوِجَا	يَزْدَوِجَ
يَزْدَوِجْنَ	تَزْدَوِجَا	تَزْدَوِجْ	يَزْدَوِجْنَ	تَزْدَوِجَا	تَزْدَوِجَ

Verbal Noun اِزْدِوَج *izdiwāj* **Participle** مُزْدَوِج *muzdáwij*

Imperative اِزْدَوِجْ، اِزْدَوِجِي؛ اِزْدَوِجَا؛ اِزْدَوِجُوا، اِزْدَوِجْنَ
izdáwij, -ī; -ā; -ū, -na

PASSIVE none

II زَوَّجَ to pair هـ 95; III زَاوَجَ to pair هـ , to join in marriage ه 97;
V تَزَوَّجَ to get married to ه\على\ب 102;
VI تَزَاوَجَ to intermarry, to be in pairs 104

زَوْج ج أَزْوَاج husband, couple زَوْجَة wife اِزْدِوَاج duality
مُزْدَوِج double(d) تَزَوُّج marriage
زَوَاج (من) wedding, marriage (to) مُتَزَوِّج married
زَوْجِيَّة matrimony مُزَاوَجَة duplication زِوَاج duplication

110 | VIII | امْتَازَ يَمْتَازُ *imtāza yamtāzu* to be distinguished | ميز

ACTIVE

Present *yamtāzu*

نَمْتَازُ		أَمْتَازُ
تَمْتَازُونَ	تَمْتَازَانِ	تَمْتَازُ
تَمْتَزْنَ	تَمْتَازَانِ	تَمْتَازِينَ
يَمْتَازُونَ	يَمْتَازَانِ	يَمْتَازُ
يَمْتَزْنَ	تَمْتَازَانِ	تَمْتَازُ

Past *imtāza*

اِمْتَزْنَا		اِمْتَزْتُ
اِمْتَزْتُمْ	اِمْتَزْتُمَا	اِمْتَزْتَ
اِمْتَزْتُنَّ	اِمْتَزْتُمَا	اِمْتَزْتِ
اِمْتَازُوا	اِمْتَازَا	اِمْتَازَ
اِمْتَزْنَ	اِمْتَازَتَا	اِمْتَازَتْ

Jussive *yamtáz*

نَمْتَزْ		أَمْتَزْ
تَمْتَازُوا	تَمْتَازَا	تَمْتَزْ
تَمْتَزْنَ	تَمْتَازَا	تَمْتَازِي
يَمْتَازُوا	يَمْتَازَا	يَمْتَزْ
يَمْتَزْنَ	تَمْتَازَا	تَمْتَزْ

Subjunctive *yamtāza*

نَمْتَازَ		أَمْتَازَ
تَمْتَازُوا	تَمْتَازَا	تَمْتَازَ
تَمْتَزْنَ	تَمْتَازَا	تَمْتَازِي
يَمْتَازُوا	يَمْتَازَا	يَمْتَازَ
يَمْتَزْنَ	تَمْتَازَا	تَمْتَازَ

Verbal Noun اِمْتِيَاز *imtiyāz* **Participle** مُمْتَاز *mumtāz*

Imperative اِمْتَزْ، اِمْتَازِي؛ اِمْتَازَا؛ اِمْتَازُوا، اِمْتَزْنَ

imtáz, imtāzī; imtāzā; imtāzū, imtazna

PASSIVE none

I/IV مَازَ يَمِيزُ (مَيْز) \ أَمَازَ to differentiate هـ 93/101;

II مَيَّزَ to distinguish هـ ه 96; V تَمَيَّزَ 103 = VIII اِمْتَازَ **110**;

VI تَمَايَزَ to differ 105

مَيْز preferment أَمْيَز على preferable to تَمْيِيز distinction, preference

اِمْتِيَاز distinction, honour, concession مُمَيَّز \ مُتَمَيِّز distinguished

مُمْتَاز outstanding مُمَيِّزَة peculiarity تَمْيِيز الجِنْس sex discrimination

تَمْيِيز عُنْصُرِي racial discrimination صَاحِب الامْتِيَاز concession holder

111 VIII اِزْدَادَ يَزْدَادُ *izdāda yazdādu* to increase زيد

ACTIVE **Present** *yazdādu*

أَزْدَادُ		نَزْدَادُ
تَزْدَادُ	تَزْدَادَانِ	تَزْدَادُونَ
تَزْدَادِينَ	تَزْدَادَانِ	تَزْدَدْنَ
يَزْدَادُ	يَزْدَادَانِ	يَزْدَادُونَ
تَزْدَادُ	تَزْدَادَانِ	يَزْدَدْنَ

Past *izdāda*

اِزْدَدْتُ		اِزْدَدْنَا
اِزْدَدْتَ	اِزْدَدْتُمَا	اِزْدَدْتُمْ
اِزْدَدْتِ	اِزْدَدْتُمَا	اِزْدَدْتُنَّ
اِزْدَادَ	اِزْدَادَا	اِزْدَادُوا
اِزْدَادَتْ	اِزْدَادَتَا	اِزْدَدْنَ

Jussive *yazdád*

أَزْدَدْ		نَزْدَدْ
تَزْدَدْ	تَزْدَادَا	تَزْدَادُوا
تَزْدَادِي	تَزْدَادَا	تَزْدَدْنَ
يَزْدَدْ	يَزْدَادَا	يَزْدَادُوا
تَزْدَدْ	تَزْدَادَا	يَزْدَدْنَ

Subjunctive *yazdāda*

أَزْدَادَ		نَزْدَادَ
تَزْدَادَ	تَزْدَادَا	تَزْدَادُوا
تَزْدَادِي	تَزْدَادَا	تَزْدَدْنَ
يَزْدَادَ	يَزْدَادَا	يَزْدَادُوا
تَزْدَادَ	تَزْدَادَا	يَزْدَدْنَ

Verbal Noun اِزْدِيَاد *izdiyād* **Participle** مُزْدَاد *muzdād*

Imperative اِزْدَدْ، اِزْدَادِي؛ اِزْدَادَا؛ اِزْدَادُوا، اِزْدَدْنَ

izdád, izdādī; izdādā; izdādū, izdadna

PASSIVE° **Present** يُزْدَادُ *yuzdādu* **Past** أُزْدِيدَ *uzdīda*

Participle مُزْدَاد *muzdād*

See 93

112 IX اِسْوَدَّ يَسْوَدُّ *iswadda yaswaddu* to be/turn black سود

ACTIVE **Past** *iswadda*

اِسْوَدَدْتُ		اِسْوَدَدْنَا
اِسْوَدَدْتَ	اِسْوَدَدْتُمَا	اِسْوَدَدْتُمْ
اِسْوَدَدْتِ	اِسْوَدَدْتُمَا	اِسْوَدَدْتُنَّ
اِسْوَدَّ	اِسْوَدَّا	اِسْوَدُّوا
اِسْوَدَّتْ	اِسْوَدَّتَا	اِسْوَدَدْنَ

Present *yaswaddu*

أَسْوَدُّ		نَسْوَدُّ
تَسْوَدُّ	تَسْوَدَّانِ	تَسْوَدُّونَ
تَسْوَدِّينَ	تَسْوَدَّانِ	تَسْوَدِدْنَ
يَسْوَدُّ	يَسْوَدَّانِ	يَسْوَدُّونَ
تَسْوَدُّ	تَسْوَدَّانِ	يَسْوَدِدْنَ

Subjunc.+ Jussive (i) *yaswadda*

أَسْوَدَّ		نَسْوَدَّ
تَسْوَدَّ	تَسْوَدَّا	تَسْوَدُّوا
تَسْوَدِّي	تَسْوَدَّا	تَسْوَدِدْنَ
يَسْوَدَّ	يَسْوَدَّا	يَسْوَدُّوا
تَسْوَدَّ	تَسْوَدَّا	يَسْوَدِدْنَ

Jussive (ii)† *yaswadid*

أَسْوَدِدْ		نَسْوَدِدْ
تَسْوَدِدْ	تَسْوَدَّا	تَسْوَدُّوا
تَسْوَدِّي	تَسْوَدَّا	تَسْوَدِدْنَ
يَسْوَدِدْ	يَسْوَدَّا	يَسْوَدُّوا
تَسْوَدِدْ	تَسْوَدَّا	يَسْوَدِدْنَ

Verbal Noun اِسْوِدَاد *iswidād* **Participle** مُسْوَدّ *muswadd*

Imperative اِسْوَدَّ\اِسْوَدِدْ †، اِسْوَدِّي؛ اِسْوَدَّا؛ اِسْوَدُّوا، اِسْوَدِدْنَ

iswadda/iswadid†, iswaddī; iswaddā; iswaddū, iswadidna

PASSIVE does not exist in Form IX

II سَوَّدَ to blacken, draft هـ 95

اِسْوِدَاد blackening — أَسْوَد (m.)، سَوْدَاء (f.)، سُود (an. pl.) black

مُسَوَّدَة draft (of a document) — السُّودَان Sudan

تَسْوِيد drafting — سَوَاد blackness

سَوْدَاوِي depressed — أَكْثَر سَوَاداً blacker

113 IX اِبْيَضَّ يَبْيَضُّ *ibyaḍḍa yabyaḍḍu* to be/turn white, to blanch **بيض**

ACTIVE

Present *yabyaḍḍu*					**Past** *ibyaḍḍa*
نَبْيَضُّ		أَبْيَضُّ	اِبْيَضَضْنَا		اِبْيَضَضْتُ
تَبْيَضُّونَ	تَبْيَضَّانِ	تَبْيَضُّ	اِبْيَضَضْتُمْ	اِبْيَضَضْتُمَا	اِبْيَضَضْتَ
تَبْيَضِضْنَ	تَبْيَضَّانِ	تَبْيَضِّينَ	اِبْيَضَضْتُنَّ	اِبْيَضَضْتُمَا	اِبْيَضَضْتِ
يَبْيَضُّونَ	يَبْيَضَّانِ	يَبْيَضُّ	اِبْيَضُّوا	اِبْيَضَّا	اِبْيَضَّ
يَبْيَضِضْنَ	تَبْيَضَّانِ	تَبْيَضُّ	اِبْيَضَضْنَ	اِبْيَضَّتَا	اِبْيَضَّتْ

Jussive (ii)† *yabyaḍiḍ*			**Subjunc.+ Jussive (i)** *yabyaḍḍa*		
نَبْيَضِضْ		أَبْيَضِضْ	نَبْيَضَّ		أَبْيَضَّ
تَبْيَضُّوا	تَبْيَضَّا	تَبْيَضِضْ	تَبْيَضُّوا	تَبْيَضَّا	تَبْيَضَّ
تَبْيَضِضْنَ	تَبْيَضَّا	تَبْيَضِّي	تَبْيَضِضْنَ	تَبْيَضَّا	تَبْيَضِّي
يَبْيَضُّوا	يَبْيَضَّا	يَبْيَضِضْ	يَبْيَضُّوا	يَبْيَضَّا	يَبْيَضَّ
يَبْيَضِضْنَ	تَبْيَضَّا	تَبْيَضِضْ	يَبْيَضِضْنَ	تَبْيَضَّا	تَبْيَضَّ

Verbal Noun اِبْيِضَاض *ibyiḍāḍ* **Participle** مُبْيَضّ *mubyaḍḍ*

Imperative اِبْيَضَّ\اِبْيَضِضْ †، اِبْيَضِّي؛ اِبْيَضَّا؛ اِبْيَضُّوا، اِبْيَضِضْنَ
ibyaḍḍa/ibyaḍiḍ†, *ibyaḍḍī; ibyaḍḍā; ibyaḍḍū, ibyaḍiḍna*

PASSIVE does not exist in Form IX

I بَاضَ يَبِيضُ to lay (eggs) هـ , to settle down 93;

II بَيَّضَ to whiten, make a fair copy of هـ 96;

V تَبَيَّضَ to be whitened 103

بِيض (an. pl.) بَيْضَاء، (f.) أَبْيَض، (m.) white اِبْيِضَاض whitening

بَيْض eggs (collective) بَيْضَة an egg

بَيْضِي\بَيْضَوِي oval بَيَاض whiteness, a blank

أَكْثَر بَيَاضًا whiter تَبْيِيضَة\مُبَيَّض fair copy

114 X اِسْتَرَاحَ يَسْتَرِيحُ *istarāḥa yastarīḥu* to rest روح\ريح

ACTIVE

Past *istarāḥa*

اِسْتَرَحْتُ		اِسْتَرَحْنَا
اِسْتَرَحْتَ	اِسْتَرَحْتُمَا	اِسْتَرَحْتُمْ
اِسْتَرَحْتِ	اِسْتَرَحْتُمَا	اِسْتَرَحْتُنَّ
اِسْتَرَاحَ	اِسْتَرَاحَا	اِسْتَرَاحُوا
اِسْتَرَاحَتْ	اِسْتَرَاحَتَا	اِسْتَرَحْنَ

Present *yastarīḥu*

أَسْتَرِيحُ		نَسْتَرِيحُ
تَسْتَرِيحُ	تَسْتَرِيحَانِ	تَسْتَرِيحُونَ
تَسْتَرِيحِينَ	تَسْتَرِيحَانِ	تَسْتَرِحْنَ
يَسْتَرِيحُ	يَسْتَرِيحَانِ	يَسْتَرِيحُونَ
تَسْتَرِيحُ	تَسْتَرِيحَانِ	يَسْتَرِحْنَ

Subjunctive *yastarīḥa*

أَسْتَرِيحَ		نَسْتَرِيحَ
تَسْتَرِيحَ	تَسْتَرِيحَا	تَسْتَرِيحُوا
تَسْتَرِيحِي	تَسْتَرِيحَا	تَسْتَرِحْنَ
يَسْتَرِيحَ	يَسْتَرِيحَا	يَسْتَرِيحُوا
تَسْتَرِيحَ	تَسْتَرِيحَا	يَسْتَرِحْنَ

Jussive *yastariḥ*

أَسْتَرِحْ		نَسْتَرِحْ
تَسْتَرِحْ	تَسْتَرِيحَا	تَسْتَرِيحُوا
تَسْتَرِيحِي	تَسْتَرِيحَا	تَسْتَرِحْنَ
يَسْتَرِحْ	يَسْتَرِيحَا	يَسْتَرِيحُوا
تَسْتَرِحْ	تَسْتَرِيحَا	يَسْتَرِحْنَ

Vb. Noun اِسْتِرَاحَة *istirāḥa* **Participle** مُسْتَرِيح *mustarīḥ*

Imperative اِسْتَرِحْ، اِسْتَرِيحِي؛ اِسْتَرِيحَا؛ اِسْتَرِيحُوا، اِسْتَرِحْنَ

istariḥ, istarīḥī; istarīḥā; istarīḥū, istariḥna

PASSIVE Present يُسْتَرَاحُ *yustarāḥu* **Past** أُسْتُرِيحَ *usturīḥa*

Participle مُسْتَرَاح *mustarāḥ*

I رَاحَ يَرُوحُ (رَوَاح) to depart 90; II رَوَّحَ to revive هـ 95, رَيَّحَ to rest هـ ه 96;

IV أَرَاحَ to comfort ه 99; VI تَرَاوَحَ to fluctuate between بين 104;

VIII اِرْتَاحَ to be content with إلى , to rest 108

رَاحَة\اِسْتِرَاحَة repose — رِيح ج رِيَاح\أَرْيَاح (m./f.) wind

رُوح ج أَرْوَاح (m./f.) soul, spirit (also liquid) — رُوحِي spiritual, spirituous

مُرْتَاح\مُسْتَرِيح relaxing — مُسْتَرَاح lavatory — مَرِيح restful

115 X **اِسْتَجْوَبَ يَسْتَجْوِبُ** *istajwaba yastajwibu* **جوب**

to interrogate ه

ACTIVE Present *yastajwibu* **Past** *istajwaba*

نَسْتَجْوِبُ		أَسْتَجْوِبُ	اِسْتَجْوَبْنَا		اِسْتَجْوَبْتُ
تَسْتَجْوِبُونَ	تَسْتَجْوِبَانِ	تَسْتَجْوِبُ	اِسْتَجْوَبْتُمْ	اِسْتَجْوَبْتُمَا	اِسْتَجْوَبْتَ
تَسْتَجْوِبْنَ	تَسْتَجْوِبَانِ	تَسْتَجْوِبِينَ	اِسْتَجْوَبْتُنَّ	اِسْتَجْوَبْتُمَا	اِسْتَجْوَبْتِ
يَسْتَجْوِبُونَ	يَسْتَجْوِبَانِ	يَسْتَجْوِبُ	اِسْتَجْوَبُوا	اِسْتَجْوَبَا	اِسْتَجْوَبَ
يَسْتَجْوِبْنَ	تَسْتَجْوِبَانِ	تَسْتَجْوِبُ	اِسْتَجْوَبْنَ	اِسْتَجْوَبَتَا	اِسْتَجْوَبَتْ

Jussive *yastajwib* **Subjunctive** *yastajwiba*

نَسْتَجْوِبْ		أَسْتَجْوِبْ	نَسْتَجْوِبَ		أَسْتَجْوِبَ
تَسْتَجْوِبُوا	تَسْتَجْوِبَا	تَسْتَجْوِبْ	تَسْتَجْوِبُوا	تَسْتَجْوِبَا	تَسْتَجْوِبَ
تَسْتَجْوِبْنَ	تَسْتَجْوِبَا	تَسْتَجْوِبِي	تَسْتَجْوِبْنَ	تَسْتَجْوِبَا	تَسْتَجْوِبِي
يَسْتَجْوِبُوا	يَسْتَجْوِبَا	يَسْتَجْوِبْ	يَسْتَجْوِبُوا	يَسْتَجْوِبَا	يَسْتَجْوِبَ
يَسْتَجْوِبْنَ	تَسْتَجْوِبَا	تَسْتَجْوِبْ	يَسْتَجْوِبْنَ	تَسْتَجْوِبَا	تَسْتَجْوِبَ

Vb. Noun اِسْتِجْوَاب *istījwāb* **Participle** مُسْتَجْوِب *mustajwib*

Imperative اِسْتَجْوِبْ، اِسْتَجْوِبِي؛ اِسْتَجْوِبَا؛ اِسْتَجْوِبُوا، اِسْتَجْوِبْنَ

istajwib, -ī; -ā; -ū, -na

PASSIVE Present يُسْتَجْوَبُ *yustajwabu* **Past** اُسْتُجْوِبَ *ustujwiba*

Participle مُسْتَجْوَب *mustajwab*

I جَابَ يَجُوبُ (جَوْب) to explore ﻫ 90; III جَاوَبَ to answer ه على 97;

IV أَجَابَ to answer ه\إلى على 99; VI تَجَاوَبَ to harmonise 104;

VII اِنْجَابَ to be dispelled 106; X اِسْتَجَابَ to grant (a request) ﻫ 114

جَوَاب ج أَجْوِبَة answer اِسْتِجْوَاب interrogation مُسْتَجِيب responsive

إِجَابَة response, compliance إِجَابَةً لِ in compliance with

اِسْتِجَابَة granting (of a request) تَجَاوُب harmony مُتَجَاوِب harmonious

116 X **اسْتَفَادَ يَسْتَفِيدُ** *istafāda yastafīdu* to benefit from من, to be informed about هـ\ب **فيد**

ACTIVE Present *yastafīdu* **Past** *istafāda*

نَسْتَفِيدُ		أَسْتَفِيدُ	اسْتَفَدْنَا		اسْتَفَدْتُ
تَسْتَفِيدُونَ	تَسْتَفِيدَانِ	تَسْتَفِيدُ	اسْتَفَدْتُمْ	اسْتَفَدْتُمَا	اسْتَفَدْتَ
تَسْتَفِدْنَ	تَسْتَفِيدَانِ	تَسْتَفِيدِينَ	اسْتَفَدْتُنَّ	اسْتَفَدْتُمَا	اسْتَفَدْتِ
يَسْتَفَادُونَ	يَسْتَفِيدَانِ	يَسْتَفِيدُ	اسْتَفَادُوا	اسْتَفَادَا	اسْتَفَادَ
يَسْتَفِدْنَ	تَسْتَفِيدَانِ	تَسْتَفِيدُ	اسْتَفَدْنَ	اسْتَفَادَتَا	اسْتَفَادَتْ

Jussive *yastafid* **Subjunctive** *yastafīda*

نَسْتَفِدْ		أَسْتَفِدْ	نَسْتَفِيدَ		أَسْتَفِيدَ
تَسْتَفِيدُوا	تَسْتَفِيدَا	تَسْتَفِدْ	تَسْتَفِيدُوا	تَسْتَفِيدَا	تَسْتَفِيدَ
تَسْتَفِدْنَ	تَسْتَفِيدَا	تَسْتَفِيدِي	تَسْتَفِدْنَ	تَسْتَفِيدَا	تَسْتَفِيدِي
يَسْتَفِيدُوا	يَسْتَفِيدَا	يَسْتَفِدْ	يَسْتَفِيدُوا	يَسْتَفِيدَا	يَسْتَفِيدَ
يَسْتَفِدْنَ	تَسْتَفِيدَا	تَسْتَفِدْ	يَسْتَفِدْنَ	تَسْتَفِيدَا	تَسْتَفِيدَ

Vb. Noun اِسْتِفَادَة *istīfāda* **Participle** مُسْتَفِيد *mustafīd*

Imperative اِسْتَفِدْ، اِسْتَفِيدِي؛ اِسْتَفِيدَا؛ اِسْتَفِيدُوا، اِسْتَفِدْنَ
istafid, istafīdī; istafīdā; istafīdū, istafidna

PASSIVE° **Present** يُسْتَفَادُ *yustafādu* **Past** أُسْتُفِيدَ *ustufīda*

Participle مُسْتَفَاد *mustafād*

IV أَفَادَ to benefit ه , to inform of ب ه 101, = X اسْتَفَادَ **116**

فَائِدَة ج فَوَائِد benefit, profit, interest — مُفَاد contents, purport

إِفَادَة usefulness, information, attestation — اِسْتِفَادَة use

مُفِيد useful — غَيْر مُفِيد useless — مُسْتَفِيد beneficiary

تُفِيدُ الأَنْبَاء (بـ) أَنَّ it is reported ('the news tells') that

قَرْض مُنْخَفِض الفَائِدَة low-interest loan — فَائِدَة صَافِيَة net interest

Final-weak

Final-weak verbs are the third sub-class of the weak class. They have a weak letter, و or ي , as final root letter, and two sound root letters. Some roots have alternative final root letters و or ي ; most of these follow the commoner ي pattern.

The final-weak verbs follow the sound patterns shown in §§ 7-11, 15-18, 21-23 and 26 (tenses, participles, verbal noun, imperative) *up to and including the middle root letter without its vowel.*

Past tense, Form I. For this tense we can divide the final-weak verbs into ***aw***, ***ay*** and ***ī*** verbs, according to the vowel following the middle root letter in the 1st and 2nd persons.

Model ***aw*** verb, رجا *raja* (no. **117**), past tense:

animate plural	dual	singular
رجونا *rajawna*	–	رجوت *rajawtu*
رجوتم *rajawtum*	رجوتما *rajawtuma*	رجوت *rajawta*
رجوتنّ *rajawtunna*	رجوتما *rajawtuma*	رجوت *rajawti*
رجوا ***rajaw***	رجوا *rajawā*	رجا ***raja***
رجون *rajawna*	رجتا ***rajatā***	رجت ***rajat***

Model ***ay*** verb, رمى *rama* (no. **118**), past tense:

animate plural	dual	singular
رمينا *ramayna*	–	رميت *ramaytu*
رميتم *ramaytum*	رميتما *ramaytuma*	رميت *ramayta*
رميتنّ *ramaytunna*	رميتما *ramaytuma*	رميت *ramayti*
رموا ***ramaw***	رميا *ramayā*	رمى ***rama***
رمين *ramayna*	رمتا ***ramatā***	رمت ***ramat***

Model ***ī*** verb, نسي *násiya* (no. **119**), past tense:

animate plural	dual	singular
نسينا *nasīna*	–	نسيت *nasītu*
نسيتم *nasītum*	نسيتما *nasītuma*	نسيت *nasīta*
نسيتنّ *nasītunna*	نسيتما *nasītuma*	نسيت *nasīti*
نسوا ***násū***	نسيا *násiyā*	نسي ***násiya***
نسين *nasīna*	نسيتا *násiyatā*	نسيت ***násiyat***

Note:

- In those persons transcribed in **bold** type, the endings shown are a combination of final weak root letter and personal ending. In the other persons, the sound personal endings shown in § 7 are added after the *-aw*, *-ay-*, *-iy-* or *-ī-*.
- The endings *u*, *a* and *ya* shown in small type are dropped in short pronunciation when no pronoun-object suffix follows.

Present tense, Form I. In this tense the general rule is:

verbs with ***aw*** in the past have ***ū/ī*** in the present (رجا يرجو *raja yarjū*):

animate plural	dual	singular
نرجو ***narjū***	–	أرجو ***'arjū***
ترجون ***tarjūna***	ترجوان *tarjuwāni*	ترجو ***tarjū***
ترجونّ *tarjūna*	ترجوان *tarjuwāni*	ترجين ***tarjīna***
يرجون ***yarjūna***	يرجوان *yarjuwāni*	يرجو ***yarjū***
ترجون *tarjūna*	ترجوان *tarjuwāni*	ترجو ***tarjū***

verbs with ***ay*** past have ***ī/ū*** in the present (رمى يرمي *rama yarmī*):

animate plural	dual	singular
نرمي ***narmī***	–	أرمي ***'armī***
ترمون ***tarmūna***	ترميان *tarmiyāni*	ترمي ***tarmī***
ترمينّ *tarmīna*	ترميان *tarmiyāni*	ترمين ***tarmīna***
يرمون ***yarmūna***	يرميان *yarmiyāni*	يرمي ***yarmī***
يرمين *yarmīna*	ترميان *tarmiyāni*	ترمي ***tarmī***

verbs with ***ī*** past have ***a/ay/aw*** present (نسي ينسى *násiya yansa*):

animate plural	dual	singular
ننسى ***nansa***	–	أنسى ***'ansa***
تنسون ***tansawna***	تنسيان *tansayāni*	تنسى ***tansa***
تنسينّ *tansayna*	تنسيان *tansayāni*	تنسين ***tansayna***
ينسون ***yansawna***	ينسيان *yansayāni*	ينسى ***yansa***
ينسين *yansayna*	تنسيان *tansayāni*	تنسى ***tansa***

Note:

- the personal prefixes are as for the sound verbs.
- In those persons transcribed in **bold** type, the endings shown are a combination of final weak root letter and personal ending. In the

other persons, the sound personal endings shown in § 8 are added after the *-w-*, *-ū-*, *-y-* or *-ī-*.

- The *i* terminating the dual endings and shown in small type is dropped in short pronunciation when no pronoun-object suffix follows.
- A few exceptions to this general rule exist, e.g. سعى يسعى *sa'a yas'a* I (no. **120**), which has the ***ay*** pattern in both tenses.

Vowel rule. Whenever a principal part has the vowel *a* after the middle root letter, the whole tense derived from that part (past from the first principal part, present tenses from the second) will have *a* in this position in all persons; otherwise it will not have *a* in this position in any person. The ***aw*** and ***ay*** patterns have *a*; the ***ī/ū*** pattern does not.

Tenses in Forms II to X . The tenses of the increased forms have regular vowelling, and of course the vowel rule (see above) applies:

- Forms II-IV and VII-X, all roots:
  - first principal part ends ى... *-a*, past tense has ***ay*** pattern,
  - second principal part ends ي... *-ī*, present tenses have *ī* pattern.
- Forms V and VI, all roots: both principal parts end ى... *-a*, all tenses have ***ay*** pattern.

Subjunctive. Form the subjunctive from the present tense as follows:

- For those persons ending in و... *-ū* or ي... *-ī*, no change in the short pronunciation; for full pronunciation (e.g. when a suffix follows) change *-ū* to *-uwa* and *-ī* to *-iya*. No change in alphabetical spelling.
- For those persons ending in ى... *-a*, make no change.
- Change personal endings ين... *-īna*/*-ayna* to ي... *-ī*/*ay* (f. s. only), ون... *-ūna*/*-awna* to وا... *-ū*/*-aw*, and the dual ending ان... *-āni* to ا... *-ā*. Leave the f. pl. unchanged.

Jussive. Form the jussive from the subjunctive by changing the endings ى... *-a* to َ... *-a*, و... *-uwa* to ُ... *-u* and ي... *-ī (-iya)* to ِ... *-i*.

Leave the rest unchanged.

Pronoun object suffixes. Certain rules for suffixing a pronoun object, valid for all verbs, are especially important for final-weak verbs:

- Since ى *('alif maqṣūra)* can appear only as last letter of a word, it changes to ا *(-ā)* whenever a pronoun object suffix is added:

  رمى\رماه *rama, ramāhu* he threw, he threw it

- The silent final ا... of the ending وا... *-ū/-aw* is dropped also in writing before a pronoun suffix:

  نسوا\نسوه *nasū, nasūhu* they forgot (it)

- All the 3rd-person object pronoun suffixes except ها... *-ha* change their vowel *-u-* to *-i* after the verb-ending *-i*, *-ī* or *-ay*:

  يرميه. *yarmīhi.* He throws it.

Participles. Construct the participle as for sound verbs, as far as the middle root letter without its vowel. Then proceed as follows.

For the *active participle*, add the following endings (the m.s. has two forms, indefinite and definite; the tables show both):

m.s.	nom. + gen.	indefinite ... *-in* , def. ي... *-ī*	see * below
	acc.	indef. يًا... *-iyan*, def. ي... *-ī/-iya*	
f.s.	(regular)	ية... *-iya*	
m. dual	(regular) nom.	يان... *-iyāni*, acc./gen. يين... *-iyayni*	
f. dual	(regular) nom.	يتان... *-iyatāni*, acc./gen. يتين... *-iyatayni*	
m. pl.	(sound pl.)	nom. ون... *-ūna*, acc./gen. ين... *-īna*	
f. pl.	(sound pl.)	يات... *-iyāt*	

For the *passive participle*:

- Form I: add وّ... *-ūw* for verbs with final-root letter و and يّ... *-īy* for verbs with final-root letter ي .
- Forms II to X; add the following endings:

m.s.	all cases	indef. ًى... *-an*, def. ى... *-a* (see * below)
f.s.	(regular)	اة... *-ā* (*-āt* in a possessive construction)
m. dual	(regular)	nom. ان... *-āni*, acc./gen. ين... *-ayni*
f. dual	(regular)	nom. تان... *-atāni*, acc./gen. تين... *-atayni*

m. pl. (sound pl.) nom. ...ون *-ūna*, acc./gen. ...ين *-īna*
f. pl. (sound pl.) ...يات *-ayāt*

Verbal Noun. Form I verbal noun is irregular. For the increased forms, construct the verbal noun as for sound verbs, as far as the middle root letter without its vowel. Then add the following endings:

- Form II: ...ية *-iya.*
- Form III: ...اء *-ā'* for verbal nouns not beginning ...مـ *mu-*, and ...اة *-ā* (*-āt* in a possessive construction) for verbal nouns beginning ...مـ *mu-*.
- Forms IV, VII, VIII, X: ...اء *-ā'*.
- Forms V, VI: ... *-in*, ...ي *-ī* (as for m. s. active participle) *

* For the participles and verbal nouns, educated spoken Arabic often uses the definite m. s. ending for the indefinite m. s. as well.

Imperative. Imperatives are formed regularly (§ 23) from the jussive. For the imperative forms with a prefixed weak vowel ...ا *u-* or *i-*, it is the *masculine singular* jussive which determines the choice of this vowel, which is always the same for all persons:

(رجا يرجو): أُرجُ *urju* m. s., أُرجي *urjī* f. s. (not [*irjī*])
(رمى يرمي): ارمِ *irmi* m. s., ارموا *irmū* m. pl. (not [*urmū*])

The 'Vowel rule' and the provisions shown under 'Pronoun object suffixes' (see above) apply to the final-weak imperative as elsewhere:

(نسي ينسى): ... انسَ، انسَيْ؛ *insa* m. s., *insay* f. s. (etc.)
انسيهم\انسوهم *insayhim* f. s., *insawhum* m. pl. forget them

Passive. Construct the passive tenses on the sound pattern (§ 26) as far as the middle root letter without its vowel. Then add, for the 3rd persons singular and inanimate plural:

- for the past tense, ...ي *-ī*/*-iya* (m. s.), ...يت *-iyat* (f. s./inan. pl.)
- for the present tense, ...ى *-a* (m. s./f. s./inan. pl.)

Use of the dictionary. When searching for a final-weak verb in a root-based dictionary (§ 16), remember that the final root letter will be either و or ي (or both as alternatives); it will not be ا nor ى *'alif maqṣūra*, which are not root letters.

117 | **I** | رَجَا يَرْجُو *raja yarjū* to expect, hope for هـ, to request من هـ\إلى | **رجو**

ACTIVE	**Present**	*yarjū*		**Past**	*raja*
نَرْجُو		أَرْجُو	رَجَوْنَا		رَجَوْتُ
تَرْجُونَ	تَرْجُوَانِ	تَرْجُو	رَجَوْتُمْ	رَجَوْتُمَا	رَجَوْتَ
تَرْجُونَ	تَرْجُوَانِ	تَرْجِينَ	رَجَوْتُنَّ	رَجَوْتُمَا	رَجَوْتِ
يَرْجُونَ	يَرْجُوَانِ	يَرْجُو	رَجَوْا	رَجَوَا	رَجَا
يَرْجُونَ	تَرْجُوَانِ	تَرْجُو	رَجَوْنَ	رَجَتَا	رَجَتْ
	Jussive	*yarju*	**Subjunctive**		*yarjuwa*
نَرْجُ		أَرْجُ	نَرْجُوَ		أَرْجُوَ
تَرْجُوا	تَرْجُوَا	تَرْجُ	تَرْجُوا	تَرْجُوَا	تَرْجُوَ
تَرْجُونَ	تَرْجُوَا	تَرْجِي	تَرْجُونَ	تَرْجُوَا	تَرْجِي
يَرْجُوا	يَرْجُوَا	يَرْجُ	يَرْجُوا	يَرْجُوَا	يَرْجُوَ
يَرْجُونَ	تَرْجُوَا	تَرْجُ	يَرْجُونَ	تَرْجُوَا	تَرْجُوَ

Verbal Noun رَجَاء *rajā'* **Participle** رَاجٍ\الرَاجِي *rājin/ar-rājī*

Imperative أُرْجُ، أُرْجِي؛ أُرْجُوَا؛ أُرْجُوا، أُرْجُونَ *urj-u, -ī; -uwā; -ū, -ūna*

PASSIVE **Present** يُرْجَى *yurja* **Past** رُجِيَ *rújiya*

Participle مَرْجُوّ *marjūw*

V/X تَرَجَّى\اِسْتَرْجَى to anticipate هـ 124/129

رَجَاء ب\في\ gen. request, hope رَاجٍ\الرَاجِي hopeful

رَجَاة\مَرْجَاة hope, expectation مَرْجُوّ expected, requested, hoped for

الرَجَاء أنْ\المَرْجُوّ أنْ I/We hope that رَجَا فَضْلاً من to ask a favour of

في أَرْجَاء البِلَاد throughout the country

+ definite verbal noun {
الرَجَاء الـ... Please
الرَجَاء عَدَم الـ... Please do not

118 | I | رَمَى يَرْمِي *rama yarmī* to throw, fire هـ\ب | رمي

ACTIVE	**Present**	*yarmī*		**Past**	*rama*
نَرْمِي		أَرْمِي	رَمَيْنَا		رَمَيْتُ
تَرْمُونَ	تَرْمِيَانِ	تَرْمِي	رَمَيْتُمْ	رَمَيْتُمَا	رَمَيْتَ
تَرْمِينَ	تَرْمِيَانِ	تَرْمِينَ	رَمَيْتُنَّ	رَمَيْتُمَا	رَمَيْتِ
يَرْمُونَ	يَرْمِيَانِ	يَرْمِي	رَمَوْا	رَمَيَا	رَمَى
يَرْمِينَ	تَرْمِيَانِ	تَرْمِي	رَمَيْنَ	رَمَتَا	رَمَتْ
	Jussive	*yarmi*		**Subjunctive**	*yarmiya*
نَرْمِ		أَرْمِ	نَرْمِيَ		أَرْمِيَ
تَرْمُوا	تَرْمِيَا	تَرْمِ	تَرْمُوا	تَرْمِيَا	تَرْمِيَ
تَرْمِينَ	تَرْمِيَا	تَرْمِي	تَرْمِينَ	تَرْمِيَا	تَرْمِي
يَرْمُوا	يَرْمِيَا	يَرْمِ	يَرْمُوا	يَرْمِيَا	يَرْمِيَ
يَرْمِينَ	تَرْمِيَا	تَرْمِ	يَرْمِينَ	تَرْمِيَا	تَرْمِيَ

Verbal Noun رَمْي *ramy* **Participle** رامٍ\الرامِي *rāmin/ar-rāmī*

Imperative اِرْمِ، اِرْمِي؛ اِرْمِيَا؛ اِرْمُوا، اِرْمِينَ *irm-i, -ī; -iyā; -ū, -īna*

PASSIVE **Present** يُرْمَى *yurma* **Past** رُمِيَ *rúmiya*

Participle مَرْمِيّ *marmīy*

VI تَرَامَى to extend far 125; = VIII اِرْتَمَى to hurl o.s. at/on في\على 127

رَمْي throwing, firing رَمْيَة throw, shot

رامٍ\الرامِي ج رُمَاة marksman مُتَرَامٍ\المُتَرَامِي extensive

مَرْمًى\المَرْمَى ج مَرَامٍ\المَرَامِي range, aim

119 | I | نَسِيَ يَنْسَى *násiya yansa* to forget ه هـ\أنْ | **نسي**

ACTIVE	**Present**	*yansa*		**Past**	*násiya*
نَنْسَى		أَنْسَى	نَسِينَا		نَسِيتُ
تَنْسَوْنَ	تَنْسَيَانِ	تَنْسَى	نَسِيتُمْ	نَسِيتُمَا	نَسِيتَ
تَنْسَيْنَ	تَنْسَيَانِ	تَنْسَيْنَ	نَسِيتُنَّ	نَسِيتُمَا	نَسِيتِ
يَنْسَوْنَ	يَنْسَيَانِ	يَنْسَى	نَسُوا	نَسِيَا	نَسِيَ
يَنْسَيْنَ	تَنْسَيَانِ	تَنْسَى	نَسِينَ	نَسِيَتَا	نَسِيَتْ

	Jussive	*yansa*		**Subjunctive**	*yansa*
نَنْسَ		أَنْسَ	نَنْسَى		أَنْسَى
تَنْسَوْا	تَنْسَيَا	تَنْسَ	تَنْسَوْا	تَنْسَيَا	تَنْسَى
تَنْسَيْنَ	تَنْسَيَا	تَنْسَيْ	تَنْسَيْنَ	تَنْسَيَا	تَنْسَيْ
يَنْسَوْا	يَنْسَيَا	يَنْسَ	يَنْسَوْا	يَنْسَيَا	يَنْسَى
يَنْسَيْنَ	تَنْسَيَا	تَنْسَ	يَنْسَيْنَ	تَنْسَيَا	تَنْسَى

Verbal Noun نِسْيَان *nisyān* **Participle** نَاسٍ\النَّاسِي *nāsin/an-nāsī*

Impv. اِنْسَ، اِنْسَيْ؛ اِنْسَيَا؛ اِنْسَوْا، اِنْسَيْنَ *ins-a, -ay; -ayā; -aw, -ayna*

PASSIVE **Present** يُنْسَى *yunsa* **Past** نُسِيَ *núsiya*

Participle مَنْسِيّ *mansīy*

IV أَنْسَى to make s.o. forget ه 123;

VI تَنَاسَى to pretend to forget ه، هـ , to neglect هـ 125

نِسْيَان\نَسْي oblivion — نَسِيّ forgetful, oblivious

مَنْسِيّ ج مَنْسِيَات something forgotten — غير مَنْسِيّ not forgotten

نَسِيتُ أَنْ ... I forgot to ...

لن أَنْسَى لُطْفَكَ أَبَداً. I shall never forget your kindness.

ما تَنْسَى لا تَنْسَ هذا. Whatever (else) you forget, do not forget this.

120 | I | **سَعَى يَسْعَى** *sa'a yas'a* to rush, to strive for لِ\إلى, to slander ه, to lead ... to ب إلى | **سعي**

ACTIVE	**Present**	*yas'a*		**Past**	*sa'aytu*
نَسْعَى		أَسْعَى	سَعَيْنَا		سَعَيْتُ
تَسْعَوْنَ	تَسْعَيَانِ	تَسْعَى	سَعَيْتُمْ	سَعَيْتُمَا	سَعَيْتَ
تَسْعَيْنَ	تَسْعَيَانِ	تَسْعَيْنَ	سَعَيْتُنَّ	سَعَيْتُمَا	سَعَيْتِ
يَسْعَوْنَ	يَسْعَيَانِ	يَسْعَى	سَعَوْا	سَعَيَا	سَعَى
يَسْعَيْنَ	تَسْعَيَانِ	تَسْعَى	سَعَيْنَ	سَعَتَا	سَعَتْ

	Jussive	*yas'a*		**Subjunctive**	*yas'a*
نَسْعَ		أَسْعَ	نَسْعَى		أَسْعَى
تَسْعَوْا	تَسْعَيَا	تَسْعَ	تَسْعَوْا	تَسْعَيَا	تَسْعَى
تَسْعَيْنَ	تَسْعَيَا	تَسْعَيْ	تَسْعَيْنَ	تَسْعَيَا	تَسْعَيْ
يَسْعَوْا	يَسْعَيَا	يَسْعَ	يَسْعَوْا	يَسْعَيَا	يَسْعَى
يَسْعَيْنَ	تَسْعَيَا	تَسْعَ	يَسْعَيْنَ	تَسْعَيَا	تَسْعَى

Verbal Noun سَعْي\سِعَايَة *sa'y/si'āya*

Participle سَاعٍ\السَّاعِي *sā'in/as-sā'ī*

Impv. اِسْعَ، اِسْعَيْ؛ اِسْعَيَا؛ اِسْعَوْا، اِسْعَيْنَ *is'-a, -ay; -ayā; -aw, -ayna*

PASSIVE° **Present** يُسْعَى *yus'a* **Past** سُعِيَ *sú'iya*

Participle مَسْعِيّ *mas'īy*

سَعْي course, endeavour سِعَايَة slander

مَسْعًى\المَسْعَى ج مَسَاعٍ\المَسَاعِي endeavour

سَاعٍ\السَّاعِي ج سُعَاة messenger, deliverer, slanderer

121 | **II** | رَبَّى يُرَبِّي *rabba yurabbī* to educate ه, to rear ه هـ | **ربو**

ACTIVE Present *yurabbī*			**Past** *rabba*		
نُرَبِّي		أُرَبِّي	رَبَّيْنَا		رَبَّيْتُ
تُرَبُّونَ	تُرَبِّيَانِ	تُرَبِّي	رَبَّيْتُمْ	رَبَّيْتُمَا	رَبَّيْتَ
تُرَبِّينَ	تُرَبِّيَانِ	تُرَبِّينَ	رَبَّيْتُنَّ	رَبَّيْتُمَا	رَبَّيْتِ
يُرَبُّونَ	يُرَبِّيَانِ	يُرَبِّي	رَبَّوْا	رَبَّيَا	رَبَّى
يُرَبِّينَ	تُرَبِّيَانِ	تُرَبِّي	رَبَّيْنَ	رَبَّتَا	رَبَّتْ

Jussive *yurabbi*			**Subjunctive** *yurábbiya*		
نُرَبِّ		أُرَبِّ	نُرَبِّيَ		أُرَبِّيَ
تُرَبُّوا	تُرَبِّيَا	تُرَبِّ	تُرَبُّوا	تُرَبِّيَا	تُرَبِّيَ
تُرَبِّينَ	تُرَبِّيَا	تُرَبِّي	تُرَبِّينَ	تُرَبِّيَا	تُرَبِّي
يُرَبُّوا	يُرَبِّيَا	يُرَبِّ	يُرَبُّوا	يُرَبِّيَا	يُرَبِّيَ
يُرَبِّينَ	تُرَبِّيَا	تُرَبِّ	يُرَبِّينَ	تُرَبِّيَا	تُرَبِّيَ

Verbal Noun تَرْبِيَة *tárbiya* **Participle** مُرَبٍّ\المُرَبِّي *murabbin/al-murabbī*

Impv. رَبِّ، رَبِّي؛ رَبِّيَا؛ رَبُّوا، رَبِّينَ *rabb-i, -ī; -iyā; -ū, -īna*

PASSIVE **Present** يُرَبَّى *yurabba* **Past** رُبِّيَ *rúbbiya*

Participle مُرَبًّى\المُرَبَّى *murabban/al-murabba*

I رَبَا يَرْبُو (رِبَاء) to increase, to exceed عن\على 117;

III رَابَى to be a moneylender 122; IV أَرْبَى to increase هـ 123;

V تَرَبَّى to be educated/raised 124

تَرْبِيَة education, upbringing تَرْبَوِي pedagogical مُرَبِّيَة governess

مُرَبٍّ\المُرَبِّي educator, breeder مُتَرَبٍّ\المُتَرَبِّي well-bred رِبَاء excess

مُرَبًّى\المُرَبَّى well-bred, jam مُرَابٍ\المُرَابِي moneylender

تَرْبِيَة الحَيَوَانَات stockbreeding تَرْبِيَة الدَجَاج poultry farming

122 III **نَادَى يُنَادِي** *nāda yunādī* to call ه, to call out to ه, to proclaim ه هـ **ندو**

ACTIVE **Present** *yunādī* **Past** *nāda*

نُنَادِي		أُنَادِي	نَادَيْنَا		نَادَيْتُ
تُنَادُونَ	تُنَادِيَانِ	تُنَادِي	نَادَيْتُمْ	نَادَيْتُمَا	نَادَيْتَ
تُنَادِينَ	تُنَادِيَانِ	تُنَادِينَ	نَادَيْتُنَّ	نَادَيْتُمَا	نَادَيْتِ
يُنَادُونَ	يُنَادِيَانِ	يُنَادِي	نَادَوْا	نَادَيَا	نَادَى
يُنَادِينَ	تُنَادِيَانِ	تُنَادِي	نَادَيْنَ	نَادَتَا	نَادَتْ

Jussive *yunādi* **Subjunctive** *yunādiya*

نُنَادِ		أُنَادِ	نُنَادِيَ		أُنَادِيَ
تُنَادُوا	تُنَادِيَا	تُنَادِ	تُنَادُوا	تُنَادِيَا	تُنَادِيَ
تُنَادِينَ	تُنَادِيَا	تُنَادِي	تُنَادِينَ	تُنَادِيَا	تُنَادِي
يُنَادُوا	يُنَادِيَا	يُنَادِ	يُنَادُوا	يُنَادِيَا	يُنَادِيَ
يُنَادِينَ	تُنَادِيَا	تُنَادِ	يُنَادِينَ	تُنَادِيَا	تُنَادِيَ

Verbal Noun مُنَادَاة\نداء *munādā/nidā'*

Participle مُنَادٍ\المُنَادِي *munādin/al-munādī*

Imperative نَادِ ، نَادِي؛ نَادِيَا؛ نَادُوا ، نَادِينَا *nād-i, -ī; -iyā; -ū, -īna*

PASSIVE **Present** يُنَادَى *yunāda* **Past** نُودِيَ *nūdiya*

Participle مُنَادًى\المُنَادَى *munādan/al-munāda*

I (نَدْو) نَدَا يَنْدُو to call ه, to convene ه هـ 117; I (نَدًى\النَدَى) نَدِيَ يَنْدَى to be wet 119; II/IV نَدَّى\أَنْدَى to wet هـ 121/123; V تَنَدَّى to be wetted 124; VI/X تَنَادَى\اسْتَنْدَى to convene 125/129

مُنَادَاة\نداء shout, proclamation

نَادٍ\النَادِي ج أَنْدِيَة club

نَدْوَة council, club

نَدِيّ damp (adj.)

نَدًى\النَدَى ج أَنْدَاء wetness, dew

مُنَادٍ\المُنَادِي caller, announcer

دار النَادِي clubhouse

123 IV **أَعْطَى يُعْطِي** *'a'ṭa yu'ṭī* to give ... to ه ه **عطو**

ACTIVE

Past *'a'ṭa*		
أَعْطَيْتُ		أَعْطَيْنَا
أَعْطَيْتَ	أَعْطَيْتُمَا	أَعْطَيْتُمْ
أَعْطَيْتِ	أَعْطَيْتُمَا	أَعْطَيْتُنَّ
أَعْطَى	أَعْطَيَا	أَعْطَوْا
أَعْطَتْ	أَعْطَتَا	أَعْطَيْنَ

Present *yu'ṭī*		
أُعْطِي		نُعْطِي
تُعْطِي	تُعْطِيَانِ	تُعْطُونَ
تُعْطِينَ	تُعْطِيَانِ	تُعْطِينَ
يُعْطِي	يُعْطِيَانِ	يُعْطُونَ
تُعْطِي	تُعْطِيَانِ	يُعْطِينَ

Subjunctive *yu'ṭiya*		
أُعْطِيَ		نُعْطِيَ
تُعْطِيَ	تُعْطِيَا	تُعْطُوا
تُعْطِي	تُعْطِيَا	تُعْطِينَ
يُعْطِيَ	يُعْطِيَا	يُعْطُوا
تُعْطِيَ	تُعْطِيَا	يُعْطِينَ

Jussive *yu'ṭi*		
أُعْطِ		نُعْطِ
تُعْطِ	تُعْطِيَا	تُعْطُوا
تُعْطِي	تُعْطِيَا	تُعْطِينَ
يُعْطِ	يُعْطِيَا	يُعْطُوا
تُعْطِ	تُعْطِيَا	يُعْطِينَ

Vb. Noun إِعْطَاء *'i'ṭā'* **Participle** مُعْطٍ\الْمُعْطِي *mu'ṭin/al-mu'ṭī*

Imperative أَعْطِ ، أَعْطِي؛ أَعْطِيَا ؛ أَعْطُوا ، أَعْطِينَ *'a'ṭ-i, -ī; -iyā; -ū, -īna*

PASSIVE **Present** يُعْطَى *yu'ṭa* **Past** أُعْطِيَ *'u'ṭiya*

Participle مُعْطًى\الْمُعْطَى *mu'ṭan/al-mu'ṭa*

V/X تَعَطَّى\اِسْتَعْطَى to beg s.o. for charity ه 124/129

عَطَاء ج أَعْطِيَة gift, tender
مُعْطٍ\الْمُعْطِي donor
إِعْطَاء donation
مُقَدِّم عَطَاء tenderer
قدّم عَطَاءً to make an offer
مُعْطَيَات (pl.) data
مُعْطًى\الْمُعْطَى given (also in maths.)
مُعَالَجَة مُعْطَيَات data processing
بَنْك مُعْطَيَات databank
اِسْتِعْطَاء begging
مُسْتَعْطٍ\الْمُسْتَعْطِي beggar
أَعْطَى الكَلِمَةَ to give the floor to, to permit s.o. to speak

124 V **تَلَقَّى يَتَلَقَّى** *talaqqa yatalaqqa* to receive ه هـ **لقي**

ACTIVE	**Present** *yatalaqqa*			**Past**	*talaqqa*
نَتَلَقَّى		أَتَلَقَّى	تَلَقَّيْنَا		تَلَقَّيْتُ
تَتَلَقَّوْنَ	تَتَلَقَّيَانِ	تَتَلَقَّى	تَلَقَّيْتُمْ	تَلَقَّيْتُمَا	تَلَقَّيْتَ
تَتَلَقَّيْنَ	تَتَلَقَّيَانِ	تَتَلَقَّيْنَ	تَلَقَّيْتُنَّ	تَلَقَّيْتُمَا	تَلَقَّيْتِ
يَتَلَقَّوْنَ	يَتَلَقَّيَانِ	يَتَلَقَّى	تَلَقَّوْا	تَلَقَّيَا	تَلَقَّى
يَتَلَقَّيْنَ	تَتَلَقَّيَانِ	تَتَلَقَّى	تَلَقَّيْنَ	تَلَقَّتَا	تَلَقَّتْ

	Jussive *yatalaqqa*		**Subjunctive**		*yatalaqqa*
نَتَلَقَّ		أَتَلَقَّ	نَتَلَقَّى		أَتَلَقَّى
تَتَلَقَّوْا	تَتَلَقَّيَا	تَتَلَقَّ	تَتَلَقَّوْا	تَتَلَقَّيَا	تَتَلَقَّى
تَتَلَقَّيْنَ	تَتَلَقَّيَا	تَتَلَقَّيْ	تَتَلَقَّيْنَ	تَتَلَقَّيَا	تَتَلَقَّيْ
يَتَلَقَّوْا	يَتَلَقَّيَا	يَتَلَقَّ	يَتَلَقَّوْا	يَتَلَقَّيَا	يَتَلَقَّى
يَتَلَقَّيْنَ	تَتَلَقَّيَا	تَتَلَقَّ	يَتَلَقَّيْنَ	تَتَلَقَّيَا	تَتَلَقَّى

Verbal Noun تَلَقٍّ\التَّلَقِّي *talaqqin/at-talaqqī*

Participle مُتَلَقٍّ\المُتَلَقِّي *mutalaqqin/al-mutalaqqī*

Impv. تَلَقَّ، تَلَقَّيْ؛ تَلَقَّيَا؛ تَلَقَّوْا، تَلَقَّيْنَ *talaqq-a, -ay; -ayā; -aw, -ayna*

PASSIVE **Present** يُتَلَقَّى *yutalaqqa* **Past** تُلُقِّيَ *tuluqqiya*

Participle مُتَلَقًّى\المُتَلَقَّى *mutalaqqan/al-mutalaqqa*

I/III لَقِيَ يَلْقَى (لِقَاء)\لاَقَى to encounter ه هـ 119/122; IV أَلْقَى to throw, recite هـ 123; VI تَلاَقَى to come together 125; VIII اِلْتَقَى to meet ب 127

لِقَاء\مُلاَقَاة\لِقَايَة encounter

إِلْقَاء throw, delivery, recital

تَلَقٍّ\التَّلَقِّي receipt, reception

تَلاَقٍ\التَّلاَقِي encounter

مُلْتَقًى\المُلْتَقَى ج مُلْتَقَيَات meeting-place

مُلْقًى\المُلْقَى thrown (away)

أَلْقَى خِطَابًا\مُحَاضَرَةً\بَيَانًا to deliver a speech, make a statement

125 VI تَعَفَى يَتَعَفَى *ta'āfa yata'āfa* to recover in health **عفو**

ACTIVE **Present** *yata'āfa* **Past** *ta'āfa*

نَتعَافَى		أَتعَافَى	تَعافَيْنَا		تَعافَيْتُ
تَتعَافَوْنَ	تَتعَافَيَانِ	تَتعَافَى	تَعافَيْتُمْ	تَعافَيْتُمَا	تَعافَيْتَ
تَتعَافَيْنَ	تَتعَافَيَانِ	تَتعَافَيْنَ	تَعافَيْتُنَّ	تَعافَيْتُمَا	تَعافَيْتِ
يَتعَافَوْنَ	يَتعَافَيَانِ	يَتعَافَى	تَعافَوْا	تَعافَيَا	تَعافَى
يَتعَافَيْنَ	تَتعَافَيَانِ	تَتعَافَى	تَعافَيْنَ	تَعافَتَا	تَعافَتْ

Jussive *yata'āfa* **Subjunctive** *yata'āfa*

نَتعَافَ		أَتعَافَ	نَتعَافَى		أَتعَافَى
تَتعَافَوْا	تَتعَافَيَا	تَتعَافَ	تَتعَافَوْا	تَتعَافَيَا	تَتعَافَى
تَتعَافَيْنَ	تَتعَافَيَا	تَتعَافَيْ	تَتعَافَيْنَ	تَتعَافَيَا	تَتعَافَيْ
يَتعَافَوْا	يَتعَافَيَا	يَتعَافَ	يَتعَافَوْا	يَتعَافَيَا	يَتعَافَى
يَتعَافَيْنَ	تَتعَافَيَا	تَتعَافَ	يَتعَافَيْنَ	تَتعَافَيَا	تَتعَافَى

Verbal Noun تَعَافٍ\التَعَافِي *ta'āfin/at-ta'āfī*

Participle مُتَعَافٍ\المُتَعَافِي *muta'āfin/al-muta'āfī*

Imperative تَعَافَ، تَعَافَيْ؛ تَعَافَيَا؛ تَعَافَوْا ، تَعَافَيْنَ
ta'āf-a, -ay; -ayā; -aw, -ayna

PASSIVE° **Present** يُتَعَافَى *yuta'āfa* **Past** تُعُوفِيَ *tu'ūfiya*

I عَفَا يَعْفُو (عَفْو) to forgive عن, to excuse from ل عن 117; II عَفَّى to eliminate هـ 121; III عَافَى to restore to health ه, to protect from ه من, to exempt from ه هـ من\عن 122; IV أَعْفَى to dismiss ه 123, = III عَافَى 122; X اِسْتَعْفَى to ask pardon of ه 129

عَفْو pardon عَفْواً Pardon./Don't mention it. عَفْوِي spontaneous عَافِيَة good health مُعَافَاة\إِعْفَاء exemption عَافٍ\العَافِي eliminated

126 | VII | **انْقَضَى يَنْقَضِي** *inqáḍa yanqáḍī* to be concluded | **قضي**

ACTIVE

Past *inqáḍa*

انْقَضَيْتُ		انْقَضَيْنَا
انْقَضَيْتَ	انْقَضَيْتُمَا	انْقَضَيْتُمْ
انْقَضَيْتِ	انْقَضَيْتُمَا	انْقَضَيْتُنَّ
انْقَضَى	انْقَضَيَا	انْقَضَوْا
انْقَضَتْ	انْقَضَتَا	انْقَضَيْنَ

Present *yanqáḍī*

أَنْقَضِي		نَنْقَضِي
تَنْقَضِي	تَنْقَضِيَانِ	تَنْقَضُونَ
تَنْقَضِينَ	تَنْقَضِيَانِ	تَنْقَضِينَ
يَنْقَضِي	يَنْقَضِيَانِ	يَنْقَضُونَ
تَنْقَضِي	تَنْقَضِيَانِ	يَنْقَضِينَ

Subjunctive *yanqáḍiya*

أَنْقَضِيَ		نَنْقَضِيَ
تَنْقَضِيَ	تَنْقَضِيَا	تَنْقَضُوا
تَنْقَضِي	تَنْقَضِيَا	تَنْقَضِينَ
يَنْقَضِيَ	يَنْقَضِيَا	يَنْقَضُوا
تَنْقَضِيَ	تَنْقَضِيَا	يَنْقَضِينَ

Jussive *yanqáḍi*

أَنْقَضِ		نَنْقَضِ
تَنْقَضِ	تَنْقَضِيَا	تَنْقَضُوا
تَنْقَضِي	تَنْقَضِيَا	تَنْقَضِينَ
يَنْقَضِ	يَنْقَضِيَا	يَنْقَضُوا
تَنْقَضِ	تَنْقَضِيَا	يَنْقَضِينَ

Vb. Noun انْقِضَاء *inqiḍā'* **Participle** مُنْقَاضٍ\الْمُنْقَضِي *munqáḍin/ al-munqáḍī*

Imperative انْقَضِ، انْقَضِي؛ انْقَضِيَا؛ انْقَضُوا، انْقَضِينَ
inqáḍ-i, -ī; -iyā; -ū, -īna

PASSIVE none

I قَضَى يَقْضِي (قَضَاء) to judge in favour of s.o. against s.o. ل على, to condemn على ب , to accomplish, settle هـ 118; III قَاضَى to sue, prosecute ه 122; V تَقَضَّى 124 = VII انْقَضَى **126**; VI تَقَاضَى to claim from ه\من هـ 125; VIII/X اقْتَضَى\اسْتَقْضَى to claim from ه هـ 127/129

قَضِيَّة ج قَضَايَا (legal) case, cause, issue
انْقِضَاء expiry
قَضًى\القَضَى judgment, sentence
مُقَاضَاة trial, court, hearing
قَضَاء conclusion, accomplishment, court decision, jurisdiction, jury
قَاضٍ\القَاضِي ج قُضَاة judge
قَضَائِي judicial

127 | **VIII** | اِشْتَرَى يَشْتَرِي *ishtára yashtárī* to buy هـ | **شري**

ACTIVE

Present *yashtárī*

أَشْتَرِي		نَشْتَرِي
تَشْتَرِي	تَشْتَرِيَانِ	تَشْتَرُونَ
تَشْتَرِينَ	تَشْتَرِيَانِ	تَشْتَرِينَ
يَشْتَرِي	يَشْتَرِيَانِ	يَشْتَرُونَ
تَشْتَرِي	تَشْتَرِيَانِ	يَشْتَرِينَ

Past *ishtára*

اِشْتَرَيْتُ		اِشْتَرَيْنَا
اِشْتَرَيْتَ	اِشْتَرَيْتُمَا	اِشْتَرَيْتُمْ
اِشْتَرَيْتِ	اِشْتَرَيْتُمَا	اِشْتَرَيْتُنَّ
اِشْتَرَى	اِشْتَرَيَا	اِشْتَرَوْا
اِشْتَرَتْ	اِشْتَرَتَا	اِشْتَرَيْنَ

Jussive *yashtári*

أَشْتَرِ		نَشْتَرِ
تَشْتَرِ	تَشْتَرِيَا	تَشْتَرُوا
تَشْتَرِي	تَشْتَرِيَا	تَشْتَرِينَ
يَشْتَرِ	يَشْتَرِيَا	يَشْتَرُوا
تَشْتَرِ	تَشْتَرِيَا	يَشْتَرِينَ

Subjunctive *yashtáriya*

أَشْتَرِيَ		نَشْتَرِيَ
تَشْتَرِيَ	تَشْتَرِيَا	تَشْتَرُوا
تَشْتَرِي	تَشْتَرِيَا	تَشْتَرِينَ
يَشْتَرِيَ	يَشْتَرِيَا	يَشْتَرُوا
تَشْتَرِيَ	تَشْتَرِيَا	يَشْتَرِينَ

Verbal Noun اِشْتِرَاء *ishtirā'*

Participle مُشْتَرٍ\الْمُشْتَرِي *mushtárin/al-mushtárī*

Imperative اِشْتَرِ، اِشْتَرِي؛ اِشْتَرِيَا؛ اِشْتَرُوا، اِشْتَرِينَ
ishtár-i, -ī; -iyā; -ū, -īna

PASSIVE **Present** يُشْتَرَى *yushtára* **Past** أُشْتُرِيَ *ushtúriya*

Participle مُشْتَرًى\الْمُشْتَرَى *mushtáran/al-mushtára*

I شَرَى يَشْرِي (شِرَاء) to buy, vend هـ 118

مُشْتَرٍ\الْمُشْتَرِي buyer	اِشْتِرَاء\شَرْوَة purchase
شَارٍ\الشَّارِي ج شُرَاة buyer, vendor	شَرًى\الشَّرَى purchase
قُوَّة شِرَائِيَة purchasing power	شِرَاء بِالتَّقْسِيط hire purchase
شَرَى الْمَتَاعِب to ask for trouble	مُشْتَرًى\الْمُشْتَرَى ج مُشْتَرَيَات purchase

128 **VIII** ادَّعَى يَدَّعِي *iddáʻa yaddáʻī* to allege هـ, to accuse of على ب **دعو\دعي**

ACTIVE **Present** *yaddáʻī* **Past** *iddáʻa*

نَدَّعِي		أَدَّعِي	ادَّعَيْنَا		ادَّعَيْتُ
تَدَّعُونَ	تَدَّعِيَانِ	تَدَّعِي	ادَّعَيْتُمْ	ادَّعَيْتُمَا	ادَّعَيْتَ
تَدَّعِينَ	تَدَّعِيَانِ	تَدَّعِينَ	ادَّعَيْتُنَّ	ادَّعَيْتُمَا	ادَّعَيْتِ
يَدَّعُونَ	يَدَّعِيَانِ	يَدَّعِي	ادَّعَوْا	ادَّعَيَا	ادَّعَى
يَدَّعِينَ	تَدَّعِيَانِ	تَدَّعِي	ادَّعَيْنَ	ادَّعَتَا	ادَّعَتْ

Jussive *yaddáʻi* **Subjunctive** *yaddáʻiya*

نَدَّعِ		أَدَّعِ	نَدَّعِيَ		أَدَّعِيَ
تَدَّعُوا	تَدَّعِيَا	تَدَّعِ	تَدَّعُوا	تَدَّعِيَا	تَدَّعِيَ
تَدَّعِينَ	تَدَّعِيَا	تَدَّعِي	تَدَّعِينَ	تَدَّعِيَا	تَدَّعِي
يَدَّعُوا	يَدَّعِيَا	يَدَّعِ	يَدَّعُوا	يَدَّعِيَا	يَدَّعِيَ
يَدَّعِينَ	تَدَّعِيَا	تَدَّعِ	يَدَّعِينَ	تَدَّعِيَا	تَدَّعِيَ

Verbal Noun ادِّعَاء *iddiʻā'*

Participle مُدَّعٍ\المُدَّعِي *muddáʻin/al-muddáʻī*

Impv. ادَّعِ ، ادَّعِي؛ ادَّعِيَا؛ ادَّعُوا ، ادَّعِينَ *iddáʻ-i, -ī; -iyā; -ū, iddaʻīna*

PASSIVE **Present** يُدَّعَى *yuddáʻa* **Past** أُدُّعِيَ *uddúʻiya*

Participle مُدَّعًى\المُدَّعَى *muddáʻan/al-muddáʻa*

I/X دَعَا يَدْعُو (دُعَاء)\اسْتَدْعَى to summon, invite, pray ه, to call for إلى 117/129; III دَاعَى to challenge ه 122

ادِّعَاء allegation, prosecution مُدَّعٍ\المُدَّعِي plaintiff, prosecutor

مُدَّعًى\المُدَّعَى عليه defendant مُسْتَدْعٍ\المُسْتَدْعِي petitioner

دَعْوَة summons, invitation دَعْوَى ج دَعَاوَى allegation, claim, lawsuit

دُعَاء prayer, invocation دِعَاوَة publicity دِعَايَة propaganda

129 X **اِسْتَثْنَى يَسْتَثْنِي** *istathna yastathnī* to except ه هـ, to exclude from ه هـ من **ثني**

ACTIVE Present *yastathnī*

أَسْتَثْنِي		نَسْتَثْنِي
تَسْتَثْنِي	تَسْتَثْنِيَانِ	تَسْتَثْنُونَ
تَسْتَثْنِينَ	تَسْتَثْنِيَانِ	تَسْتَثْنِينَ
يَسْتَثْنِي	يَسْتَثْنِيَانِ	يَسْتَثْنُونَ
تَسْتَثْنِي	تَسْتَثْنِيَانِ	يَسْتَثْنِينَ

Past *istathna*

اِسْتَثْنَيْتُ		اِسْتَثْنَيْنَا
اِسْتَثْنَيْتَ	اِسْتَثْنَيْتُمَا	اِسْتَثْنَيْتُمْ
اِسْتَثْنَيْتِ	اِسْتَثْنَيْتُمَا	اِسْتَثْنَيْتُنَّ
اِسْتَثْنَى	اِسْتَثْنَيَا	اِسْتَثْنَوْا
اِسْتَثْنَتْ	اِسْتَثْنَتَا	اِسْتَثْنَيْنَ

Jussive *yastathni*

أَسْتَثْنِ		نَسْتَثْنِ
تَسْتَثْنِ	تَسْتَثْنِيَا	تَسْتَثْنُوا
تَسْتَثْنِي	تَسْتَثْنِيَا	تَسْتَثْنِينَ
يَسْتَثْنِ	يَسْتَثْنِيَا	يَسْتَثْنُوا
تَسْتَثْنِ	تَسْتَثْنِيَا	يَسْتَثْنِينَ

Subjunctive *yastathniya*

أَسْتَثْنِيَ		نَسْتَثْنِيَ
تَسْتَثْنِيَ	تَسْتَثْنِيَا	تَسْتَثْنُوا
تَسْتَثْنِي	تَسْتَثْنِيَا	تَسْتَثْنِينَ
يَسْتَثْنِيَ	يَسْتَثْنِيَا	يَسْتَثْنُوا
تَسْتَثْنِيَ	تَسْتَثْنِيَا	يَسْتَثْنِينَ

Verbal Noun اِسْتِثْنَاء *istithnā'*

Participle مُسْتَثْنٍ\المُسْتَثْنِي *mustathnin/al-mustathnī*

Imperative اِسْتَثْنِ، اِسْتَثْنِي؛ اِسْتَثْنِيَا؛ اِسْتَثْنُوا، اِسْتَثْنِينَ
istathn-i, -ī; -iyā; -ū, -īna

PASSIVE Present يُسْتَثْنَى *yustathna* **Past** أُسْتُثْنِيَ *ustuthniya*
Participle مُسْتَثْنًى\المُسْتَثْنَى *mustathnan/al-mustathna*

I (ثَنْي) ثَنَى يَثْنِي to fold هـ 118; II ثَنَّى to double, repeat هـ 121;
V تَثَنَّى to be doubled/folded 124; VII اِنْثَنَى to fold 126

اِسْتِثْنَاء exception, exclusion اِسْتِثْنَائِي exceptional ثَنْي folding
اِثْنَتَانِ (f.) اِثْنَانِ، (m.) two ثَانٍ\الثَّانِي second ثَانِيًا secondly
ثَانِيَة ج ثَوَانٍ\الثَّوَانِي a second ثَانَوِي secondary مُثَنًّى\المُثَنَّى double

Doubly Weak

Doubly weak verbs are the fourth sub-class of the weak class. They have two weak letters as root letters. In theory this permits many variations, but in practice the patterns are limited. There are no common doubly weak verbs with initial-root letter ي or with final-root letter و . We also count as doubly weak those verbs which have ي as final root letter and *hamza* as one of the other root letters, or vice-versa.

General rule. In doubly weak verbs each root letter follows in principle the rules dictated by its own class or sub-class, and its position. The provisions relating to assimilated, hollow and final-weak verbs are especially important here. Thus:

أتى يأتي *'ata ya'tī* I to come (no. **130**) consists of

- *hamza* as initial root letter: see page 87,
- a sound middle root letter, see §§ 7, 8, 17, 18, 21-23 and 26,
- a weak final root letter, as in the final-weak verbs (here, ***aw*** group in the past tense, ***ī*** group in the present, see pages 187-191).

There are three important variants to this general rule:

- where the middle root letter is و\ي and the final root letter is ي, the middle و\ي stabilises as a consonant, *w* or *y* respectively:

  نوى ينوي *nawa yanwī* I to intend (no. **138**)

  (sound initial root letter; stabilised weak middle root letter; weak final root letter [here also ***aw*** in the past and ***ī*** in the present]).
- where the final root letter is *hamza*:
  - the active participle of Form I follows the final-weak pattern, ending ...ءٍ\...ئي *-'in/-'ī* in the masculine singular,
  - everywhere else, the ending is that of a final-*hamza* verb (i.e. sound); see §§ 7, 8, 17, 18, 21-23 and 26, and page 87.
- in the root رأي the middle root letter *hamza* is dropped in Form I present tenses and imperative, and in Form IV throughout. See nos. **134** and **145**.

Rare forms. Some Form I imperatives (marked †) are rarely used.

130 I أَتَى يَأْتِي *'ata ya'tī* to come, to bring ب **أتي**

ACTIVE	**Present**	*ya'tī*		**Past**	*'ata*
نَأْتِي		آتِي	أَتَيْنَا		أَتَيْتُ
تَأْتُونَ	تَأْتِيَانِ	تَـأْتِي	أَتَيْتُمْ	أَتَيْتُمَا	أَتَيْتَ
تَأْتِينَ	تَأْتِيَانِ	تَأْتِينَ	أَتَيْتُنَّ	أَتَيْتُمَا	أَتَيْتِ
يَأْتُونَ	يَأْتِيَانِ	يَأْتِي	أَتَوْا	أَتَيَا	أَتَى
يَأْتِينَ	تَأْتِيَانِ	تَأْتِي	أَتَيْنَ	أَتَتَا	أَتَتْ

	Jussive	*ya'ti*		**Subjunctive**	*ya'tiya*
نَأْتِ		آتِ	نَأْتِيَ		آتِيَ
تَأْتُوا	تَأْتِيَا	تَأْتِ	تَأْتُوا	تَأْتِيَا	تَـأْتِيَ
تَأْتِينَ	تَأْتِيَا	تَأْتِي	تَأْتِينَ	تَأْتِيَا	تَأْتِي
يَأْتُوا	يَأْتِيَا	يَأْتِ	يَأْتُوا	يَأْتِيَا	يَأْتِيَ
يَأْتِينَ	تَأْتِيَا	تَأْتِ	يَأْتِينَ	تَأْتِيَا	تَأْتِيَ

Verbal Noun إِتْيَان *'ityān* **Participle** آتٍ\الآتِي *'ātin/al-'ātī*

Impv. †اِيتِ\تِ، اِيتِي\تِي† *īti/ti, ītī/tī* etc.† (one preferred alternative is تَعَالَ، تَعَالَيْ *ta'āl-a, -ay* etc. from تَعَالَى *ta'āla* VI 125 to rise)

PASSIVE° **Present** يُؤْتَى *yu'ta* **Past** أُتِيَ *'útiya*

III آتَى to favour ه , to supply with ب ه **143**;

IV آتَى to bring to ه ه **144**

آتٍ\الآتِي next مُؤَاتٍ\المُؤَاتِي opportune

يُؤَاتِيهِ كُلُّ شَيْءٍ everything goes well for/comes to him

131 I أَبَى يَأْبَى *'aba ya'ba* to decline, deny هـ **أبي**

ACTIVE	**Present**	*ya'ba*		**Past**	*'aba*
نَأْبَى		آبَى	أَبَيْنَا		أَبَيْتُ
تَأْبَوْنَ	تَأْبَيَانِ	تَأْبَى	أَبَيْتُمْ	أَبَيْتُمَا	أَبَيْتَ
تَأْبَيْنَ	تَأْبَيَانِ	تَأْبَيْنَ	أَبَيْتُنَّ	أَبَيْتُمَا	أَبَيْتِ
يَأْبَوْنَ	يَأْبَيَانِ	يَأْبَى	أَبَوْا	أَبَيَا	أَبَى
يَأْبَيْنَ	تَأْبَيَانِ	تَأْبَى	أَبَيْنَ	أَبَتَا	أَبَتْ

	Jussive	*ya'ba*		**Subjunctive**	*ya'ba*
نَأْبَ		آبَ	نَأْبَى		آبَى
تَأْبَوْا	تَأْبَيَا	تَأْبَ	تَأْبَوْا	تَأْبَيَا	تَأْبَى
تَأْبَيْنَ	تَأْبَيَا	تَأْبَيْ	تَأْبَيْنَ	تَأْبَيَا	تَأْبَيْ
يَأْبَوْا	يَأْبَيَا	يَأْبَ	يَأْبَوْا	يَأْبَيَا	يَأْبَى
يَأْبَيْنَ	تَأْبَيَا	تَأْبَ	يَأْبَيْنَ	تَأْبَيَا	تَأْبَى

Vb. Noun إِبَاء\إِبَاءَة *'ibā'(a)* **Participle** آبٍ\الآبِي *'abin/al-'abī*

Impv. ايبَ، ايبَيْ؛ ايبَيَا؛ ايبَوْا، ايبَيْنَ *īb-a, -ay; -ayā; -aw, -ayna*

PASSIVE **Present** يُؤْبَى *yu'ba* **Past** أُبِيَ *'úbiya*

Participle مَأْبِيّ *ma'bīy*

---

131 آبَى = 148 تَأَبَّى V

إِبَاء\إِبَاءَة rejection, disdain

آبٍ\الآبِي ج أُبَاة reluctant

آبِيّ scornful

132 I وَقَى يَقِي *waqa yaqī* to guard ه هـ **وقي**

ACTIVE	**Present**	*yaqī*		**Past**	*waqa*
نَقِي		أَقِي	وَقَيْنَا		وَقَيْتُ
تَقُونَ	تَقِيَانِ	تَقِي	وَقَيْتُمْ	وَقَيْتُمَا	وَقَيْتَ
تَقِينَ	تَقِيَانِ	تَقِينَ	وَقَيْتُنَّ	وَقَيْتُمَا	وَقَيْتِ
يَقُونَ	يَقِيَانِ	يَقِي	وَقَوْا	وَقَيَا	وَقَى
يَقِينَ	تَقِيَانِ	تَقِي	وَقَيْنَ	وَقَتَا	وَقَتْ

	Jussive	*yaqi*		**Subjunctive**	*yáqiya*
نَقِ		أَقِ	نَقِيَ		أَقِيَ
تَقُوا	تَقِيَا	تَقِ	تَقُوا	تَقِيَا	تَقِيَ
تَقِينَ	تَقِيَا	تَقِي	تَقِينَ	تَقِيَا	تَقِي
يَقُوا	يَقِيَا	يَقِ	يَقُوا	يَقِيَا	يَقِيَ
يَقِينَ	تَقِيَا	تَقِ	يَقِينَ	تَقِيَا	تَقِيَ

Verbal Noun وَقْي\وِقَايَة *waqy/wiqāya*

Participle وَاقٍ\الوَاقِي *wāqin/al-wāqī*

Imperative †قِ، قِي *qi, qī* (etc) † no longer used

PASSIVE **Present** يُوقَى *yūqa* **Past** وُقِيَ *wúqiya*

Participle مَوْقِيّ *mawqīy*

V/VIII تَوَقَّى\اتَّقَى to be wary of هـ 148/**152**

وَقْي\وِقَاء protection — وَقِيّ، وَاقٍ\الوَاقِي protective, protector

وِقَايَة precaution, prevention — وِقَائِي preventive

اتَّقَى اللّٰه to fear God — مُتَّقٍ\المُتَّقِي God-fearing

الطِبّ الوِقَائِي preventive medicine — الوِقَايَة المَدَنِيَّة civil defence

133 I وَلِيَ يَلِي *wáliya yalī* to be near/next to ه هـ , to administer هـ\على **ولي**

ACTIVE	**Present**	*yalī*		**Past**	*wáliya*
نَلِي		أَلِي	وَلِينَا		وَلِيتُ
تَلُونَ	تَلِيَانِ	تَلِي	وَلِيتُمْ	وَلِيتُمَا	وَلِيتَ
تَلِينَ	تَلِيَانِ	تَلِينَ	وَلِيتُنَّ	وَلِيتُمَا	وَلِيتِ
يَلُونَ	يَلِيَانِ	يَلِي	وَلُوا	وَلِيَا	وَلِيَ
يَلِينَ	تَلِيَانِ	تَلِي	وَلِينَ	وَلِيَتَا	وَلِيَتْ
	Jussive	*yali*	**Subjunctive**		*yáliya*
نَلِ		أَلِ	نَلِيَ		أَلِيَ
تَلُوا	تَلِيَا	تَلِ	تَلُوا	تَلِيَا	تَلِيَ
تَلِينَ	تَلِيَا	تَلِي	تَلِينَ	تَلِيَا	تَلِي
يَلُوا	يَلِيَا	يَلِ	يَلُوا	يَلِيَا	يَلِيَ
يَلِينَ	تَلِيَا	تَلِ	يَلِينَ	تَلِيَا	تَلِيَ

Vb. Noun وِلاَيَة *wilāya* **Participle** وَالٍ\الوَالِي *wālin/al-wālī*

Imperative لِ، لِي† *li, lī* (etc) † no longer used

PASSIVE **Present** يُولَى *yūla* **Past** وُلِيَ *wúliya*

Participle مَوْلِيّ *mawlīy*

III وَالَى to sponsor ه, to keep doing هـ 142; IV أَوْلَى to entrust to ه هـ **147**; V تَوَلَّى to assume office, to take charge of هـ **148**; VI تَوَالَى to advance **149**; X اِسْتَوْلَى to appropriate على 154

وِلاَيَة rule, province تَوْلِيَة appointment to office اِسْتِيلاَء takeover

وَلِيّ ج أَوْلِيَاء guardian, trustee وَالٍ\الوَالِي ج وُلاَة governor

كَمَا يَلِي as follows تَوَالٍ\التَوَالِي succession مُوَالٍ\المُوَالِي supporter

134 | I | رَأى يَرَى *ra'a yara* to see هـ, to consider ... as هـ هـ | رأي

ACTIVE	**Present**	*yara*		**Past**	*ra'a*
نَرَى		أرَى	رَأَيْنَا		رَأَيْتُ
تَرَوْنَ	تَرَيَانِ	تَرَى	رَأَيْتُمْ	رَأَيْتُمَا	رَأَيْتَ
تَرَيْنَ	تَرَيَانِ	تَرَيْنَ	رَأَيْتُنَّ	رَأَيْتُمَا	رَأَيْتِ
يَرَوْنَ	يَرَيَانِ	يَرَى	رَأَوْا	رَأَيَا	رَأَى
يَرَيْنَ	تَرَيَانِ	تَرَى	رَأَيْنَ	رَأَتَا	رَأَتْ

	Jussive	*yara*		**Subjunctive**	*yara*
نَرَ		أرَ	نَرَى		أرَى
تَرَوْا	تَرَيَا	تَرَ	تَرَوْا	تَرَيَا	تَرَى
تَرَيْنَ	تَرَيَا	تَرَيْ	تَرَيْنَ	تَرَيَا	تَرَيْ
يَرَوْا	يَرَيَا	يَرَ	يَرَوْا	يَرَيَا	يَرَى
يَرَيْنَ	تَرَيَا	تَرَ	يَرَيْنَ	تَرَيَا	تَرَى

Verbal Noun رَأْي *ra'y* **Participle** راءٍ\الرائِي *rā'in/ar-rā'ī*

Impv. †رَ، رَيْ† *ra, ray* etc.† (one preferred alternative is أُنْظُرْ، أُنْظُرِي *unẓur, -ī* etc., from نَظَرَ يَنْظُرُ *naẓara yanẓuru* I 1 to look)

PASSIVE **Present** يُرَى *yura* **Past** رُئِيَ *ru'iya*

Participle مَرْئِيّ *mar'īy*

IV أرَى to show to هـ ه **145**

رَأْي ج آراء opinion	راءٍ\الرائِي observer
مَرْئِيّ visible	رائِيَة viewfinder
الرَأْي العَامّ public opinion	في رَأْيِي in my opinion
... يا تُرَى؟ ..., I wonder?	أتُرَى ... I wonder ...
مِرايَة mirror	أراهُ واجِبِي أنْ ... I think it my duty to ...

135 [I] يَجِيءُ جَاءَ *jā'a yajī'u* to come, to bring, present بِ **[جيء]**

ACTIVE

Past *jā'a*

جِئْتُ		جِئْنَا
جِئْتَ	جِئْتُمَا	جِئْتُمْ
جِئْتِ	جِئْتُمَا	جِئْتُنَّ
جَاءَ	جَاءَا	جَاؤُوا\جَاءُوا
جَاءَتْ	جَاءَتَا	جِئْنَ

Present *yajī'u*

أَجِيءُ		نَجِيءُ
تَجِيءُ	تَجِيئَانِ	تَجِيؤُونَ\تَجِيئُونَ
تَجِيئِينَ	تَجِيئَانِ	تَجِئْنَ
يَجِيءُ	يَجِيئَانِ	يَجِيؤُونَ\يَجِيئُونَ
تَجِيءُ	تَجِيئَانِ	يَجِئْنَ

Subjunctive *yajī'a*

أَجِيءَ		نَجِيءَ
تَجِيءَ	تَجِيئَا	تَجِيؤُوا\تَجِيئُوا
تَجِيئِي	تَجِيئَا	تَجِئْنَ
يَجِيءَ	يَجِيئَا	يَجِيؤُوا\يَجِيئُوا
تَجِيءَ	تَجِيئَا	يَجِئْنَ

Jussive *yaji'*

أَجِئْ		نَجِئْ
تَجِئْ	تَجِيئَا	تَجِيؤُوا\تَجِيئُوا
تَجِيئِي	تَجِيئَا	تَجِئْنَ
يَجِئْ	يَجِيئَا	يَجِيؤُوا\يَجِيئُوا
تَجِئْ	تَجِيئَا	يَجِئْنَ

Verbal Noun مَجِيء *majī'* **Participle** جَاءٍ\الجَائِي *jā'in/al-jā'ī*

Imperative †جِيئِي، جِئْ *ji', jī'ī* etc.† (one preferred alternative is تَعَالَ، تَعَالَيْ *ta'āl-a, -ay* etc. from تَعَالَى *ta'āla* VI 125 to rise)

PASSIVE° **Present** يُجَاءُ *yujā'u* **Past** جِيءَ *jī'a*

Participle مَجِيء *majī'*

جِئَة\مَجِيء coming, arrival — جَاءٍ\الجَائِي coming, next

فِي الأُسْبُوع الجَائِي next week — جِئَة وذَهَاب coming and going

جَاءَ فِي الصَّحِيفَة أَنَّ ... It says/said in the newspaper that ...

جَاؤُوا بِاقْتِرَاح جَدِيد فِيه ... They presented a new proposal in which ...

136 | I | شَاءَ يَشَاءُ *shā'a yashā'u* to wish هـ\أنْ | **شيأ**

ACTIVE

Past *shā'a*			**Present** *yashā'u*		
شِئْتُ		شِئْنَا	أَشَاءُ		نَشَاءُ
شِئْتَ	شِئْتُمَا	شِئْتُمْ	تَشَاءُ	تَشَاءَانِ	تَشَاؤُونَ\تَشَائُونَ
شِئْتِ	شِئْتُمَا	شِئْتُنَّ	تَشَائِينَ	تَشَاءَانِ	تَشَأْنَ
شَاءَ	شَاءَا	شَاؤُوا\شَاءُوا	يَشَاءُ	يَشَاءَانِ	يَشَاؤُونَ\يَشَائُونَ
شَاءَتْ	شَاءَتَا	شِئْنَ	تَشَاءُ	تَشَاءَانِ	يَشَأْنَ

Subjunctive *yashā'a*			**Jussive** *yasha'*		
أَشَاءَ		نَشَاءَ	أَشَأْ		نَشَأْ
تَشَاءَ	تَشَاءَا	تَشَاؤُوا\تَشَائُوا	تَشَأْ	تَشَاءَا	تَشَاؤُوا\تَشَائُوا
تَشَائِي	تَشَاءَا	تَشَأْنَ	تَشَائِي	تَشَاءَا	تَشَأْنَ
يَشَاءَ	يَشَاءَا	يَشَاؤُوا\يَشَائُوا	يَشَأْ	يَشَاءَا	يَشَاؤُوا\يَشَائُوا
تَشَاءَ	تَشَاءَا	يَشَأْنَ	تَشَأْ	تَشَاءَا	يَشَأْنَ

Verbal Noun مَشِيئَة *mashī'a*

Participle شَاءٍ\الشَّائِي *shā'in/ash-shā'ī*

Imperative شَأْ ، شَائِي؛ شَاءَا؛ شَاؤُوا\شَائُوا ، شَأْنَ
sha', shā'ī; shā'ā; shā'ū, sha'na

PASSIVE **Present** يُشَاءُ *yushā'u* **Past** شِيءَ *shī'a*
Participle مَشِيء *mashī'*

مَشِيئَة wish   شَيْئِي objective (adj.)   شَيْء ج أَشْيَاء (some)thing

أَيّ شَيْء anything   لاشَيْئِيَّة nothingness   لا شَيْءَ nothing

لَيْسَ بِشَيْءٍ it does not matter   إِنْ شَاءَ اللّه ('if God wills') I/we hope

ما شَاءَ اللّه ('whatever God wills') Bravo!, God knows ...

137 **I** سَاءَ يَسُوءُ *sāʼa yasūʼu* to hurt, wrong ه **سوء**

ACTIVE	**Present** *yasūʼu*		**Past** *sāʼa*		
نَسُوءُ		أَسُوءُ	سُؤْنَا		سُؤْتُ
تَسُوؤُونَ\تَسُوءُونَ	تَسُوءَانِ	تَسُوءُ	سُؤْتُمْ	سُؤْتُمَا	سُؤْتَ
تَسُؤْنَ	تَسُوءَانِ	تَسُوئِينَ	سُؤْتُنَّ	سُؤْتُمَا	سُؤْتِ
يَسُوؤُونَ\يَسُوءُونَ	يَسُوءَانِ	يَسُوءُ	سَاؤُوا\سَاءُوا	سَاءَا	سَاءَ
يَسُؤْنَ	تَسُوءَانِ	تَسُوءُ	سُؤْنَ	سَاءَتَا	سَاءَتْ

	Jussive *yasuʼ*		**Subjunctive** *yasūʼa*		
نَسُؤْ		أَسُؤْ	نَسُوءَ		أَسُوءَ
تَسُوؤُوا\تَسُوءُوا	تَسُوءَا	تَسُؤْ	تَسُوؤُوا\تَسُوءُوا	تَسُوءَا	تَسُوءَ
تَسُؤْنَ	تَسُوءَا	تَسُوئِي	تَسُؤْنَ	تَسُوءَا	تَسُوئِي
يَسُوؤُوا\يَسُوءُوا	يَسُوءَا	يَسُؤْ	يَسُوؤُوا\يَسُوءُوا	يَسُوءَا	يَسُوءَ
يَسُؤْنَ	تَسُوءَا	تَسُؤْ	يَسُؤْنَ	تَسُوءَا	تَسُوءَ

Verbal Noun سُوء *sūʼ* **Participle** سَاءٍ\السَّائِي *sāʼin/as-sāʼī*

Imperative سُؤْ، سُوئِي؛ سُوءَا؛ سُوؤُوا\سُوءُوا، سُؤْنَ

suʼ, sūʼī; sūʼā; sūʼū, suʼna

PASSIVE **Present** يُسَاءُ *yusāʼu* **Past** سِيءَ *sīʼa*

Participle مَسُوء *masūʼ*

IV أَسَاءَ to harm إلى هـ, to treat badly ه هـ, to misjudge ه 146;

VIII اسْتَاءَ to be offended at من **153**

سُوء ج أَسْوَاء injury, evil   سُوءَة disgrace   اسْتِاءَة offence

اسْتِيَاء indignation   مُسِيء offensive   مُسْتَاء من offended at/by

سَيِّء bad   سُوء الإِدَارَة mismanagement   سُوء المُعَامَلَة ill-treatment

سُوء الحَظّ bad luck   لِسُوء الحَظّ unfortunately   سَيِّء الحَظّ unlucky

138 I — نَوَى يَنْوِي *nawa yanwī* to intend هـ\أنْ — **نوي**

ACTIVE

Past *nawa*

نَوَيْتُ		نَوَيْنَا
نَوَيْتَ	نَوَيْتُمَا	نَوَيْتُمْ
نَوَيْتِ	نَوَيْتُمَا	نَوَيْتُنَّ
نَوَى	نَوَيَا	نَوَوْا
نَوَتْ	نَوَتَا	نَوَيْنَ

Present *yanwī*

أَنْوِي		نَنْوِي
تَنْوِي	تَنْوِيَانِ	تَنْوُونَ
تَنْوِينَ	تَنْوِيَانِ	تَنْوِينَ
يَنْوِي	يَنْوِيَانِ	يَنْوُونَ
تَنْوِي	تَنْوِيَانِ	يَنْوِينَ

Subjunctive *yánwiya*

أَنْوِيَ		نَنْوِيَ
تَنْوِيَ	تَنْوِيَا	تَنْوُوا
تَنْوِي	تَنْوِيَا	تَنْوِينَ
يَنْوِيَ	يَنْوِيَا	يَنْوُوا
تَنْوِيَ	تَنْوِيَا	يَنْوِينَ

Jussive *yanwi*

أَنْوِ		نَنْوِ
تَنْوِ	تَنْوِيَا	تَنْوُوا
تَنْوِي	تَنْوِيَا	تَنْوِينَ
يَنْوِ	يَنْوِيَا	يَنْوُوا
تَنْوِ	تَنْوِيَا	يَنْوِينَ

Verbal Noun نِيَة *niya* **Participle** نَاوٍ\النَاوِي *nāwin/an-nāwī*

Imperative اِنْوِ، اِنْوِي؛ اِنْوِيَا؛ اِنْوُوا، اِنْوِينَ *inw-i, -ī; -iyā; -ū, -īna*

PASSIVE **Present** يُنْوَى *yunwa* **Past** نُوِيَ *núwiya*

Participle مَنْوِيّ *manwīy*

III نَاوَى to be hostile to ه 142; VIII اِنْتَوَى 151 = I نَوَى 138

نَوَاة ج نَوَيَات	core, nucleus	نِيَة	intention
مُنَاوٍ\المُنَاوِي	hostile	نَوَوِي	nuclear
عَقَدَ النِيَة أنْ	to resolve to	على نِيَة أنْ	with the intention to/of
طَاقَة نَوَوِيَّة	nuclear energy	بَحْث نَوَوِي	nuclear research
نَزْع الأَسْلِحَة النَوَوِيَّة	nuclear disarmament	سلاح نَوَوِي	nuclear weapon
سُوء النِيَة	ill will	حُسْن النِيَة	good will

139 | I | سَوِيَ يَسْوَى *sáwiya yaswa* to equal هـ | سوي

ACTIVE

Past *sáwiya*

سَوِيتُ		سَوِينَا
سَوِيتَ	سَوِيتُمَا	سَوِيتُمْ
سَوِيتِ	سَوِيتُمَا	سَوِيتُنَّ
سَوِيَ	سَوِيَا	سَوُوا
سَوِيَتْ	سَوِيَتَا	سَوِينَ

Present *yaswa*

أَسْوَى		نَسْوَى
تَسْوَى	تَسْوَيَانِ	تَسْوَوْنَ
تَسْوَيْنَ	تَسْوَيَانِ	تَسْوَيْنَ
يَسْوَى	يَسْوَيَانِ	يَسْوَوْنَ
تَسْوَى	تَسْوَيَانِ	يَسْوَيْنَ

Subjunctive *yaswa*

أَسْوَى		نَسْوَى
تَسْوَى	تَسْوَيَا	تَسْوَوْا
تَسْوَيْ	تَسْوَيَا	تَسْوَيْنَ
يَسْوَى	يَسْوَيَا	يَسْوَوْا
تَسْوَى	تَسْوَيَا	يَسْوَيْنَ

Jussive *yaswa*

أَسْوَ		نَسْوَ
تَسْوَ	تَسْوَيَا	تَسْوَوْا
تَسْوَيْ	تَسْوَيَا	تَسْوَيْنَ
يَسْوَ	يَسْوَيَا	يَسْوَوْا
تَسْوَ	تَسْوَيَا	يَسْوَيْنَ

Verbal Noun سَوًى\السَوَى *sawan/as-sawa*

Participle سَاوٍ\السَاوِي *sāwin/as-sāwī*

Impv. اِسْوَ، اِسْوَيْ؛ اِسْوَيَا؛ اِسْوَوْا، اِسْوَيْنَ *isw-a, -ay; -ayā; -aw, -ayna*

PASSIVE **Present** يُسْوَى *yuswa* **Past** سُوِيَ *súwiya*

Participle مَسْوِيّ *maswīy*

II سَوَّى to level هـ **141**; III سَاوَى to equal هـ **142**, = I سَوَى **139**; VI تَسَاوَى to be balanced 149; VIII اِسْتَوَى to be(come) level/straight 151

سَوَاء equal(ity) سَوًى\السَوَى equality تَسْوِيَة levelling, settlement

مُسَاوَاة equality مُسَاوٍ\المُسَاوِي equivalent اِسْتِوَاء straightness

اِسْتِوَائِي tropical تَسَاوٍ\التَسَاوِي equality لا سِيَّمَا especially

سَوَى ... أم either ... or مُسْتَوًى\المُسْتَوَى level (noun)

140 | **I** | حَيَّ\حَيِيَ† يَحْيَا *ḥayya yaḥya* to live | **حيّ**

ACTIVE	Present	*yaḥya*		Past	*ḥayya*
نَحْيَا		أَحْيَا	حَيِينَا		حَيِيتُ
تَحْيَوْنَ	تَحْيَانِ	تَحْيَا	حَيِيتُمْ	حَيِيتُمَا	حَيِيتَ
تَحْيَيْنَ	تَحْيَانِ	تَحْيَيْنَ	حَيِيتُنَّ	حَيِيتُمَا	حَيِيتِ
يَحْيَوْنَ	يَحْيَانِ	يَحْيَا	حَيُّوا	حَيَّا\حَيِيَا†	حَيَّ\حَيِيَ†
يَحْيَيْنَ	تَحْيَانِ	تَحْيَا	حَيِينَ	حَيَّتَا\حَيِيَتَا†	حَيَّتْ\حَيِيَتْ†

	Jussive	*yaḥya*		Subjunctive	*yaḥya*
نَحْيَ		أَحْيَ	نَحْيَا		أَحْيَا
تَحْيَوْا	تَحْيَا	تَحْيَ	تَحْيَوْا	تَحْيَا	تَحْيَا
تَحْيَيْنَ	تَحْيَا	تَحْيَيْ	تَحْيَيْنَ	تَحْيَا	تَحْيَيْ
يَحْيَوْا	يَحْيَا	يَحْيَ	يَحْيَوْا	يَحْيَا	يَحْيَا
يَحْيَيْنَ	تَحْيَا	تَحْيَ	يَحْيَيْنَ	تَحْيَا	تَحْيَا

Verbal Noun حَيَاة *ḥayā* **Participle** not used

Impv. اِحْيَ، اِحْيَيْ؛ اِحْيَا؛ اِحْيَوْا، اِحْيَيْنَ *iḥy-a, -ay; -ā; -aw, -ayna*

PASSIVE none

II حَيَّا to greet, keep alive ه 141; IV أَحْيَا to (re)animate ه, to perform 123; X اِسْتَحَى (for اِسْتَحْيَا) to be ashamed of/embarrased by من 129

حَيّ (a)live حَيَاة ج حَيَوَات life

حَيَوِي vital, lively حَيَوَان animal

تَحِيَّة greeeting إِحْيَاء animation, revival

حَيَاء\اِسْتِحْيَاء shame, embarrassment حَيَّة snake

عِلْم الحَيَاة biology عِلْم الحَيَوَان zoology حَدِيقَة حَيَوَانَات zoo

تَحِيَّة طَيِّبَة وبعد Dear Sir (etc.) حَيَّاكَ اللّه God be with ('keep') you

141 II **سَوَّى يُسَوِّي** *sawwa yusawwī* to level هـ **سوي**

ACTIVE

Present *yusawwī*

أُسَوِّي		نُسَوِّي
تُسَوِّي	تُسَوِّيَانِ	تُسَوُّونَ
تُسَوِّينَ	تُسَوِّيَانِ	تُسَوِّينَ
يُسَوِّي	يُسَوِّيَانِ	يُسَوُّونَ
تُسَوِّي	تُسَوِّيَانِ	يُسَوِّينَ

Past *sawwa*

سَوَّيْتُ		سَوَّيْنَا
سَوَّيْتَ	سَوَّيْتُمَا	سَوَّيْتُمْ
سَوَّيْتِ	سَوَّيْتُمَا	سَوَّيْتُنَّ
سَوَّى	سَوَّيَا	سَوَّوْا
سَوَّتْ	سَوَّتَا	سَوَّيْنَ

Jussive *yusawwi*

أُسَوِّ		نُسَوِّ
تُسَوِّ	تُسَوِّيَا	تُسَوُّوا
تُسَوِّي	تُسَوِّيَا	تُسَوِّينَ
يُسَوِّ	يُسَوِّيَا	يُسَوُّوا
تُسَوِّ	تُسَوِّيَا	يُسَوِّينَ

Subjunctive *yusáwwiya*

أُسَوِّيَ		نُسَوِّيَ
تُسَوِّيَ	تُسَوِّيَا	تُسَوُّوا
تُسَوِّي	تُسَوِّيَا	تُسَوِّينَ
يُسَوِّيَ	يُسَوِّيَا	يُسَوُّوا
تُسَوِّيَ	تُسَوِّيَا	يُسَوِّينَ

Verbal Noun تَسْوِيَة *táswiya*

Participle مُسَوٍّ\المُسَوِّي *musawwin/al-musawwī*

Imperative سَوِّ، سَوِّي؛ سَوِّيَا؛ سَوُّوا، سَوِّينَ *saww-i, -ī; -iyā; -ū, -īna*

PASSIVE **Present** يُسَوَّى *yusawwa* **Past** سُوِّيَ *súwwiya*

Participle مُسَوًّى\المُسَوَّى *musawwan/al-musawwa*

See **139**

142 III سَاوَى يُسَاوِي *sāwa yusāwī* to equal هـ **سوي**

ACTIVE

Past *sāwa*

Singular	Dual	Plural
سَاوَيْتُ		سَاوَيْنَا
سَاوَيْتَ	سَاوَيْتُمَا	سَاوَيْتُمْ
سَاوَيْتِ	سَاوَيْتُمَا	سَاوَيْتُنَّ
سَاوَى	سَاوَيَا	سَاوَوْا
سَاوَتْ	سَاوَتَا	سَاوَيْنَ

Present *yusāwī*

Singular	Dual	Plural
أُسَاوِي		نُسَاوِي
تُسَاوِي	تُسَاوِيَانِ	تُسَاوُونَ
تُسَاوِينَ	تُسَاوِيَانِ	تُسَاوِينَ
يُسَاوِي	يُسَاوِيَانِ	يُسَاوُونَ
تُسَاوِي	تُسَاوِيَانِ	يُسَاوِينَ

Subjunctive *yusāwiya*

Singular	Dual	Plural
أُسَاوِيَ		نُسَاوِيَ
تُسَاوِيَ	تُسَاوِيَا	تُسَاوُوا
تُسَاوِي	تُسَاوِيَا	تُسَاوِينَ
يُسَاوِيَ	يُسَاوِيَا	يُسَاوُوا
تُسَاوِيَ	تُسَاوِيَا	يُسَاوِينَ

Jussive *yusāwi*

Singular	Dual	Plural
أُسَاوِ		نُسَاوِ
تُسَاوِ	تُسَاوِيَا	تُسَاوُوا
تُسَاوِي	تُسَاوِيَا	تُسَاوِينَ
يُسَاوِ	يُسَاوِيَا	يُسَاوُوا
تُسَاوِ	تُسَاوِيَا	يُسَاوِينَ

Verbal Noun مُسَاوَاة *musāwā*

Participle مُسَاوٍ\الْمُسَاوِي *musāwin/al-musāwī*

Imperative سَاوِ، سَاوِي؛ سَاوِيَا؛ سَاوُوا، سَاوِينَ *sāw-i, -ī; -iyā; -ū, -īna*

PASSIVE **Present** يُسَاوَى *yusāwa* **Past** سُووِيَ *sūwiya*

Participle مُسَاوًى\الْمُسَاوَى *musāwan/al-musāwa*

See **139**

143 III آتَى يُؤَاتِي *'āta yu'ātī* to favour ه, to supply ... with ه ب

أتي

ACTIVE	**Present**	*yu'ātī*		**Past**	*'āta*
نُؤَاتِي		أُؤَاتِي	آتَيْنَا		آتَيْتُ
تُؤَاتُونَ	تُؤَاتِيَانِ	تُؤَاتِي	آتَيْتُمْ	آتَيْتُمَا	آتَيْتَ
تُؤَاتِينَ	تُؤَاتِيَانِ	تُؤَاتِينَ	آتَيْتُنَّ	آتَيْتُمَا	آتَيْتِ
يُؤَاتُونَ	يُؤَاتِيَانِ	يُؤَاتِي	آتَوْا	آتَيَا	آتَى
يُؤَاتِينَ	تُؤَاتِيَانِ	تُؤَاتِي	آتَيْنَ	آتَتَا	آتَتْ

	Jussive	*yu'āti*	**Subjunctive**		*yu'ātiya*
نُؤَاتِ		أُؤَاتِ	نُؤَاتِيَ		أُؤَاتِيَ
تُؤَاتُوا	تُؤَاتِيَا	تُؤَاتِ	تُؤَاتُوا	تُؤَاتِيَا	تُؤَاتِيَ
تُؤَاتِينَ	تُؤَاتِيَا	تُؤَاتِي	تُؤَاتِينَ	تُؤَاتِيَا	تُؤَاتِي
يُؤَاتُوا	يُؤَاتِيَا	يُؤَاتِ	يُؤَاتُوا	يُؤَاتِيَا	يُؤَاتِيَ
يُؤَاتِينَ	تُؤَاتِيَا	تُؤَاتِ	يُؤَاتِينَ	تُؤَاتِيَا	تُؤَاتِيَ

Verbal Noun مُؤَاتَاة *mu'ātā*

Participle مُؤَاتٍ\المُؤَاتِي *mu'ātin/al-mu'ātī*

Imperative آتِ، آتِي؛ آتِيَا؛ آتُوا، آتِينَ *'āt-i, -ī; -iyā; -ū, -īna*

PASSIVE **Present** يُؤَاتَى *yu'āta* **Past** أُوتِيَ *'ūtiya*

Participle مُؤَاتًى\المُؤَاتَى *mu'ātan/al-mu'āta*

See **130**

144 | **IV** آتَى يُؤْتِي *'āta yu'tī* to bring to ه هـ **أتي**

ACTIVE	**Present**	*yu'tī*		**Past**	*'āta*
نُؤْتِي		أُوتِي	آتَيْنَا		آتَيْتُ
تُؤْتُونَ	تُؤْتِيَانِ	تُؤْتِي	آتَيْتُمْ	آتَيْتُمَا	آتَيْتَ
تُؤْتِينَ	تُؤْتِيَانِ	تُؤْتِينَ	آتَيْتُنَّ	آتَيْتُمَا	آتَيْتِ
يُؤْتُونَ	يُؤْتِيَانِ	يُؤْتِي	آتَوْا	آتَيَا	آتَى
يُؤْتِينَ	تُؤْتِيَانِ	تُؤْتِي	آتَيْنَ	آتَتَا	آتَتْ

	Jussive	*yu'ti*	**Subjunctive**		*yu'tiya*
نُؤْتِ		أُوتِ	نُؤْتِيَ		أُوتِيَ
تُؤْتُوا	تُؤْتِيَا	تُؤْتِ	تُؤْتُوا	تُؤْتِيَا	تُؤْتِيَ
تُؤْتِينَ	تُؤْتِيَا	تُؤْتِي	تُؤْتِينَ	تُؤْتِيَا	تُؤْتِي
يُؤْتُوا	يُؤْتِيَا	يُؤْتِ	يُؤْتُوا	يُؤْتِيَا	يُؤْتِيَ
يُؤْتِينَ	تُؤْتِيَا	تُؤْتِ	يُؤْتِينَ	تُؤْتِيَا	تُؤْتِيَ

Verbal Noun إِيتَاء *'ītā'*

Participle مُؤْتٍ\الْمُؤْتِي *mu'tin/al-mu'tī*

Imperative آتِ، آتِي؛ آتِيَا؛ آتُوا، آتِينَ *'āt-i, -ī; -iyā; -ū, -īna*

PASSIVE **Present** يُؤْتَى *yu'ta* **Past** أُوتِيَ *'ūtiya*

Participle مُوتًى\الْمُؤْتَى *mu'tan/al-mu'ta*

See **130**

145 **IV** أَرَى يُرِي *'ara yurī* to show to ه ه **رأي**

ACTIVE	**Present**	*yurī*		**Past**	*'ara*
نُرِي		أُرِي	أَرَيْنَا		أَرَيْتُ
تُرُونَ	تُرِيَانِ	تُرِي	أَرَيْتُمْ	أَرَيْتُمَا	أَرَيْتَ
تُرِينَ	تُرِيَانِ	تُرِينَ	أَرَيْتُنَّ	أَرَيْتُمَا	أَرَيْتِ
يُرُونَ	يُرِيَانِ	يُرِي	أَرَوْا	أَرَيَا	أَرَى
يُرِينَ	تُرِيَانِ	تُرِي	أَرَيْنَ	أَرَتَا	أَرَتْ

	Jussive	*yuri*	**Subjunctive**		*yúriya*
نُرِ		أُرِ	نُرِيَ		أُرِيَ
تُرُوا	تُرِيَا	تُرِ	تُرُوا	تُرِيَا	تُرِيَ
تُرِينَ	تُرِيَا	تُرِي	تُرِينَ	تُرِيَا	تُرِي
يُرُوا	يُرِيَا	يُرِ	يُرُوا	يُرِيَا	يُرِيَ
يُرِينَ	تُرِيَا	تُرِ	يُرِينَ	تُرِيَا	تُرِيَ

Verbal Noun إِرَاءَة *'irā'a*

Participle مُرٍ\المُرِي *murin/al-murī*

Imperative أَرِ، أَرِي؛ أَرِيَا؛ أَرُوا، أَرِينَ *'ar-i, -ī; -iyā; -ū, -īna*

PASSIVE **Present** يُرَى *yura* **Past** أُرِيَ *'úriya*

Participle مُرًى\المُرَى *muran/al-mura*

See **134**

146 | IV | أَضَاءَ يُضِيءُ *'aḍā'a yuḍī'u* to illuminate هـ, to cast light upon على | ضوء

ACTIVE **Present** *yuḍī'u* **Past** *'aḍā'a*

نُضِيءُ		أُضِيءُ	أَضَأْنَا		أَضَأْتُ
تُضِيؤُونَ\تُضِيئُونَ	تُضِيئَانِ	تُضِيءُ	أَضَأْتُمْ	أَضَأْتُمَا	أَضَأْتَ
تُضِئْنَ	تُضِيئَانِ	تُضِيئِينَ	أَضَأْتُنَّ	أَضَأْتُمَا	أَضَأْتِ
يُضِيؤُونَ\يُضِيئُونَ	يُضِيئَانِ	يُضِيءُ	أَضَاؤُوا\أَضَاءُوا	أَضَاءَا	أَضَاءَ
يُضِئْنَ	تُضِيئَانِ	تُضِيءُ	أَضَأْنَ	أَضَاءَتَا	أَضَاءَتْ

Jussive *yuḍi'* **Subjunctive** *yuḍī'a*

نُضِئْ		أُضِئْ	نُضِيءَ		أُضِيءَ
تُضِيؤُوا\تُضِيئُوا	تُضِيئَا	تُضِئْ	تُضِيؤُوا\تُضِيئُوا	تُضِيئَا	تُضِيءَ
تُضِئْنَ	تُضِيئَا	تُضِيئِي	تُضِئْنَ	تُضِيئَا	تُضِيئِي
يُضِيؤُوا\يُضِيئُوا	يُضِيئَا	يُضِئْ	يُضِيؤُوا\يُضِيئُوا	يُضِيئَا	يُضِيءَ
يُضِئْنَ	تُضِيئَا	تُضِئْ	يُضِئْنَ	تُضِيئَا	تُضِيءَ

Verbal Noun إِضَاءَة *'iḍā'a* **Participle** مُضِيء *muḍī'*

Imperative أَضِئْ، أَضِيئِي؛ أَضِيئَا؛ أَضِيؤُوا\أَضِيئُوا، أَضِئْنَ
'aḍ-i', -ī'ī; -ī'ā; -ī'ū, -i'na

PASSIVE **Present** يُضَاءُ *yuḍā'u* **Past** أُضِيءَ *'uḍī'a*

Participle مُضَاء *muḍā'*

I ضَاءَ يَضُوءُ (ضَوْء) to shine 137, = IV أَضَاءَ **146**;

II ضَوَّأَ to light, illuminate هـ 50; V تَضَوَّأَ to shine 53;

X اسْتَضَاءَ to be lit, to seek enlightenment in ب **155**

ضَوْء ج أَضْوَاء light ضَوْئِي light- (adj.) على ضَوْء in view of
مُضِيء bright ضَوْء الشَّمْس\القَمَر sun-/moonlight ضَوْء النَّهَار daylight
ضِيَاء brightness إِضَاءَة صِنَاعِيَّة artificial lighting سَنَة ضَوْئِيَّة light-year

147 IV أَوْلَى يُولِي *'awla yūlī* to entrust to ه هـ **ولي**

ACTIVE

Past *'awla*

أَوْلَيْتُ		أَوْلَيْنَا
أَوْلَيْتَ	أَوْلَيْتُمَا	أَوْلَيْتُمْ
أَوْلَيْتِ	أَوْلَيْتُمَا	أَوْلَيْتُنَّ
أَوْلَى	أَوْلَيَا	أَوْلَوْا
أَوْلَتْ	أَوْلَتَا	أَوْلَيْنَ

Present *yūlī*

أُولِي		نُولِي
تُولِي	تُولِيَانِ	تُولُونَ
تُولِينَ	تُولِيَانِ	تُولِينَ
يُولِي	يُولِيَانِ	يُولُونَ
تُولِي	تُولِيَانِ	يُولِينَ

Subjunctive *yūliya*

أُولِيَ		نُولِيَ
تُولِيَ	تُولِيَا	تُولُوا
تُولِي	تُولِيَا	تُولِينَ
يُولِيَ	يُولِيَا	يُولُوا
تُولِيَ	تُولِيَا	يُولِينَ

Jussive *yūli*

أُولِ		نُولِ
تُولِ	تُولِيَا	تُولُوا
تُولِي	تُولِيَا	تُولِينَ
يُولِ	يُولِيَا	يُولُوا
تُولِ	تُولِيَا	يُولِينَ

Verbal Noun إِيلاَءَة *'īlā'a*

Participle مُولٍ\المُولِي *mūlin/al-mūlī*

Imperative أَوْلِ، أَوْلِي؛ أَوْلِيَا؛ أَوْلُوا، أَوْلِينَ *'awl-i, -ī; -iyā; -ū, -īna*

PASSIVE **Present** يُولَى *yūla* **Past** أُولِيَ *'ūliya*

Participle مُولًى\المُولَى *mūlan/al-mūla*

See **133**

148 | V | **تَوَلَّى يَتَوَلَّى** *tawalla yatawalla* to assume/hold office, to take charge of هـ | **ولي**

ACTIVE **Present** *yatawalla*

نَتَوَلَّى		أَتَوَلَّى
تَتَوَلَّوْنَ	تَتَوَلَّيَانِ	تَتَوَلَّى
تَتَوَلَّيْنَ	تَتَوَلَّيَانِ	تَتَوَلَّيْنَ
يَتَوَلَّوْنَ	يَتَوَلَّيَانِ	يَتَوَلَّى
يَتَوَلَّيْنَ	تَتَوَلَّيَانِ	تَتَوَلَّى

Past *tawalla*

تَوَلَّيْنَا		تَوَلَّيْتُ
تَوَلَّيْتُمْ	تَوَلَّيْتُمَا	تَوَلَّيْتَ
تَوَلَّيْتُنَّ	تَوَلَّيْتُمَا	تَوَلَّيْتِ
تَوَلَّوْا	تَوَلَّيَا	تَوَلَّى
تَوَلَّيْنَ	تَوَلَّتَا	تَوَلَّتْ

Jussive *yatawalla*

نَتَوَلَّ		أَتَوَلَّ
تَتَوَلَّوْا	تَتَوَلَّيَا	تَتَوَلَّ
تَتَوَلَّيْنَ	تَتَوَلَّيَا	تَتَوَلَّيْ
يَتَوَلَّوْا	يَتَوَلَّيَا	يَتَوَلَّ
يَتَوَلَّيْنَ	تَتَوَلَّيَا	تَتَوَلَّ

Subjunctive *yatawalla*

نَتَوَلَّى		أَتَوَلَّى
تَتَوَلَّوْا	تَتَوَلَّيَا	تَتَوَلَّى
تَتَوَلَّيْنَ	تَتَوَلَّيَا	تَتَوَلَّيْ
يَتَوَلَّوْا	يَتَوَلَّيَا	يَتَوَلَّى
يَتَوَلَّيْنَ	تَتَوَلَّيَا	تَتَوَلَّى

Verbal Noun تَوَلٍّ\التَوَلِّي *tawallin/at-tawallī*

Participle مُتَوَلٍّ\المُتَوَلِّي *mutawallin/al-mutawallī*

Imperative تَوَلَّ، تَوَلَّيْ؛ تَوَلَّيَا؛ تَوَلَّوْا، تَوَلَّيْنَ

tawall-a, -ay; -ayā; -aw, -ayna

PASSIVE **Present** يُتَوَلَّى *yutawalla* **Past** تُوُلِّيَ *tuwulliya*

Participle مُتَوَلًّى\المُتَوَلَّى *mutawallan/al-mutawalla*

See **133**

149 VI تَوَالَى يَتَوَالَى *tawāla yatawāla* to advance **ولي**

ACTIVE **Present** *yatawāla*

نَتَوَالَى		أَتَوَالَى
تَتَوَالَوْنَ	تَتَوَالَيَانِ	تَتَوَالَى
تَتَوَالَيْنَ	تَتَوَالَيَانِ	تَتَوَالَيْنَ
يَتَوَالَوْنَ	يَتَوَالَيَانِ	يَتَوَالَى
يَتَوَالَيْنَ	تَتَوَالَيَانِ	تَتَوَالَى

Past *tawāla*

تَوَالَيْنَا		تَوَالَيْتُ
تَوَالَيْتُمْ	تَوَالَيْتُمَا	تَوَالَيْتَ
تَوَالَيْتُنَّ	تَوَالَيْتُمَا	تَوَالَيْتِ
تَوَالَوْا	تَوَالَيَا	تَوَالَى
تَوَالَيْنَ	تَوَالَتَا	تَوَالَتْ

Jussive *yatawāla*

نَتَوَالَ		أَتَوَالَ
تَتَوَالَوْا	تَتَوَالَيَا	تَتَوَالَ
تَتَوَالَيْنَ	تَتَوَالَيَا	تَتَوَالَيْ
يَتَوَالَوْا	يَتَوَالَيَا	يَتَوَالَ
يَتَوَالَيْنَ	تَتَوَالَيَا	تَتَوَالَ

Subjunctive *yatawāla*

نَتَوَالَى		أَتَوَالَى
تَتَوَالَوْا	تَتَوَالَيَا	تَتَوَالَى
تَتَوَالَيْنَ	تَتَوَالَيَا	تَتَوَالَيْ
يَتَوَالَوْا	يَتَوَالَيَا	يَتَوَالَى
يَتَوَالَيْنَ	تَتَوَالَيَا	تَتَوَالَى

Verbal Noun تَوَالٍ\التَّوَالِي *tawālin/at-tawālī*

Participle مُتَوَالٍ\المُتَوَالِي *mutawālin/al-mutawālī*

Imperative تَوَالَ، تَوَالَيْ؛ تَوَالَيَا؛ تَوَالَوْا، تَوَالَيْنَ

tawāl-a, -ay; -ayā; -aw, -ayna

PASSIVE° **Present** يُتَوَالَى *yutawāla* **Past** تُوُولِيَ *tuwūliya*

Participle مُتَوَالًى\المُتَوَالَى *mutawālan/al-mutawāla*

See **133**

150 VII انْزَوَى يَنْزَوِي *inzáwa yanzáwī* to be isolated **زوي**

ACTIVE **Present** *yanzáwī*

نَنْزَوِي		أَنْزَوِي
تَنْزَوُونَ	تَنْزَوِيَانِ	تَنْزَوِي
تَنْزَوِينَ	تَنْزَوِيَانِ	تَنْزَوِينَ
يَنْزَوُونَ	يَنْزَوِيَانِ	يَنْزَوِي
يَنْزَوِينَ	تَنْزَوِيَانِ	تَنْزَوِي

Past *inzáwa*

انْزَوَيْنَا		انْزَوَيْتُ
انْزَوَيْتُمْ	انْزَوَيْتُمَا	انْزَوَيْتَ
انْزَوَيْتُنَّ	انْزَوَيْتُمَا	انْزَوَيْتِ
انْزَوَوْا	انْزَوَيَا	انْزَوَى
انْزَوَيْنَ	انْزَوَتَا	انْزَوَتْ

Jussive *yanzáwi*

نَنْزَوِ		أَنْزَوِ
تَنْزَوُوا	تَنْزَوِيَا	تَنْزَوِ
تَنْزَوِينَ	تَنْزَوِيَا	تَنْزَوِي
يَنْزَوُوا	يَنْزَوِيَا	يَنْزَوِ
يَنْزَوِيا	تَنْزَوِيَا	تَنْزَوِ

Subjunctive *yanzáwiya*

نَنْزَوِيَ		أَنْزَوِيَ
تَنْزَوُوا	تَنْزَوِيَا	تَنْزَوِيَ
تَنْزَوِينَ	تَنْزَوِيَا	تَنْزَوِي
يَنْزَوُوا	يَنْزَوِيَا	يَنْزَوِيَ
يَنْزَوِيا	تَنْزَوِيَا	تَنْزَوِيَ

Verbal Noun انْزِوَاء *inziwā'*

Participle مُنْزَوٍ\الْمُنْزَوِي *munzáwin/al-munzáwī*

Impv. انْزَوِ، انْزَوِي؛ انْزَوِيَا؛ انْزَوُوا، انْزَوِينَ *inzáw-i, -ī; -iyā; -ū, inzawīna*

PASSIVE none

I (–) زَوَى يَزْوِي to hide, wrinkle هـ 138;

II/V زَوَّى\تَزَوَّى to go into seclusion 141/148

انْزِوَاء seclusion

مُنْزَوٍ\الْمُنْزَوِي secluded

زَاوِيَة ج زَوَايَا corner, angle

زَاوِيَة حَادَّة acute angle

زَاوِيَة مُنْفَرِجَة obtuse angle

زَاوِيَة قَائِمَة right angle

زَوَى ما بين العَيْنَيْن to frown

151 | **VIII** | اِحْتَوَى يَحْتَوِي *iḥtáwa yaḥtáwī* to contain هـ | **حوي**

ACTIVE

Present *yaḥtáwī*

نَحْتَوِي		أَحْتَوِي
تَحْتَوُونَ	تَحْتَوِيَانِ	تَحْتَوِي
تَحْتَوِينَ	تَحْتَوِيَانِ	تَحْتَوِينَ
يَحْتَوُونَ	يَحْتَوِيَانِ	يَحْتَوِي
يَحْتَوِينَ	تَحْتَوِيَانِ	تَحْتَوِي

Past *iḥtáwa*

اِحْتَوَيْنَا		اِحْتَوَيْتُ
اِحْتَوَيْتُمْ	اِحْتَوَيْتُمَا	اِحْتَوَيْتَ
اِحْتَوَيْتُنَّ	اِحْتَوَيْتُمَا	اِحْتَوَيْتِ
اِحْتَوَوْا	اِحْتَوَيَا	اِحْتَوَى
اِحْتَوَيْنَ	اِحْتَوَتَا	اِحْتَوَتْ

Jussive *yaḥtáwi*

نَحْتَوِ		أَحْتَوِ
تَحْتَوُوا	تَحْتَوِيَا	تَحْتَوِ
تَحْتَوِينَ	تَحْتَوِيَا	تَحْتَوِي
يَحْتَوُوا	يَحْتَوِيَا	يَحْتَوِ
يَحْتَوِينَ	تَحْتَوِيَا	تَحْتَوِ

Subjunctive *yaḥtáwiya*

نَحْتَوِيَ		أَحْتَوِيَ
تَحْتَوُوا	تَحْتَوِيَا	تَحْتَوِيَ
تَحْتَوِينَ	تَحْتَوِيَا	تَحْتَوِي
يَحْتَوُوا	يَحْتَوِيَا	يَحْتَوِيَ
يَحْتَوِينَ	تَحْتَوِيَا	تَحْتَوِيَ

Verbal Noun اِحْتِوَاء *iḥtiwā'*

Participle مُحْتَوٍ\المُحْتَوِي *muḥtáwin/al-muḥtáwī*

Imperative اِحْتَوِ، اِحْتَوِي؛ اِحْتَوِيَا؛ اِحْتَوُوا، اِحْتَوِينَ
iḥtáw-i, -ī; -iyā; -ū, iḥtawīna

PASSIVE **Present** يُحْتَوَى *yuḥtáwa* **Past** أُحْتُوِيَ *uḥtúwiya*
Participle مُحْتَوًى\المُحْتَوَى *muḥtáwan/al-muḥtáwa*

I (–) حَوَى يَحْوِي to collect هـ 138, = VIII اِحْتَوَى **151**; V تَحَوَّى to coil 148

مُحْتَوَيَات contents

حَوِيَّة ج حَوَايَا roll, (pl.) intestines

152 | **VIII** | اتَّقَى يَتَّقِي *ittáqa yattáqī* to be wary of هـ | **وقي**

ACTIVE Present *yattáqī*			Past *ittáqa*		
نَتَّقِي		أَتَّقِي	اتَّقَيْنَا		اتَّقَيْتُ
تَتَّقُونَ	تَتَّقِيَانِ	تَتَّقِي	اتَّقَيْتُمْ	اتَّقَيْتُمَا	اتَّقَيْتَ
تَتَّقِينَ	تَتَّقِيَانِ	تَتَّقِينَ	اتَّقَيْتُنَّ	اتَّقَيْتُمَا	اتَّقَيْتِ
يَتَّقُونَ	يَتَّقِيَانِ	يَتَّقِي	اتَّقَوْا	اتَّقَيَا	اتَّقَى
يَتَّقِينَ	تَتَّقِيَانِ	تَتَّقِي	اتَّقَيْنَ	اتَّقَتَا	اتَّقَتْ

Jussive *yattáqi*			Subjunctive *yattáqiya*		
نَتَّقِ		أَتَّقِ	نَتَّقِيَ		أَتَّقِيَ
تَتَّقُوا	تَتَّقِيَا	تَتَّقِ	تَتَّقُوا	تَتَّقِيَا	تَتَّقِيَ
تَتَّقِينَ	تَتَّقِيَا	تَتَّقِي	تَتَّقِينَ	تَتَّقِيَا	تَتَّقِي
يَتَّقُوا	يَتَّقِيَا	يَتَّقِ	يَتَّقُوا	يَتَّقِيَا	يَتَّقِيَ
يَتَّقِينَ	تَتَّقِيَا	تَتَّقِ	يَتَّقِينَ	تَتَّقِيَا	تَتَّقِيَ

Verbal Noun اتِّقَاء *ittiqā'*

Participle مُتَّقٍ\المُتَّقِي *muttáqin/al-muttáqī*

Imperative اتَّقِ، اتَّقِي؛ اتَّقِيَا؛ اتَّقُوا، اتَّقِينَ *ittáq-i, -ī; -iyā; -ū, ittaqīna*

PASSIVE **Present** يُتَّقَى *yuttáqa* **Past** أُتُّقِيَ *uttúqiya*

Participle مُتَّقًى\المُتَّقَى *muttáqan/al-muttáqa*

See **132**

153 VIII

اسْتَاءَ يَسْتَاءُ *istā'a yastā'u*

to be offended at/by مِن

سوء

ACTIVE

Past *istā'a* (sing.)	(dual)	(plural)	Present *yastā'u* (sing.)	(dual)	(plural)
اسْتَأْتُ		اسْتَأْنَا	أَسْتَاءُ		نَسْتَاءُ
اسْتَأْتَ	اسْتَأْتُمَا	اسْتَأْتُمْ	تَسْتَاءُ	تَسْتَاءَانِ	تَسْتَاؤُونَ\تَسْتَاءُونَ
اسْتَأْتِ	اسْتَأْتُمَا	اسْتَأْتُنَّ	تَسْتَائِينَ	تَسْتَاءَانِ	تَسْتَأْنَ
اسْتَاءَ	اسْتَاءَا	اسْتَاؤُوا\اسْتَاءُوا	يَسْتَاءُ	يَسْتَاءَانِ	يَسْتَاؤُونَ\يَسْتَاءُونَ
اسْتَاءَتْ	اسْتَاءَتَا	اسْتَأْنَ	تَسْتَاءُ	تَسْتَاءَانِ	يَسْتَأْنَ

Subjunctive *yastā'a* (sing.)	(dual)	(plural)	Jussive *yastá'* (sing.)	(dual)	(plural)
أَسْتَاءَ		نَسْتَاءَ	أَسْتَأْ		نَسْتَأْ
تَسْتَاءَ	تَسْتَاءَا	تَسْتَاؤُوا\تَسْتَاءُوا	تَسْتَأْ	تَسْتَاءَا	تَسْتَاؤُوا\تَسْتَاءُوا
تَسْتَائِي	تَسْتَاءَا	تَسْتَأْنَ	تَسْتَائِي	تَسْتَاءَا	تَسْتَأْنَ
يَسْتَاءَ	يَسْتَاءَا	يَسْتَاؤُوا\يَسْتَاءُوا	يَسْتَأْ	يَسْتَاءَا	يَسْتَاؤُوا\يَسْتَاءُوا
تَسْتَاءَ	تَسْتَاءَا	يَسْتَأْنَ	تُسْتَأْ	تَسْتَاءَا	يَسْتَأْنَ

Verbal Noun اِسْتِئَاء *'istī'ā'* **Participle** مُسْتَاء *mustā'*

Imperative اِسْتَأْ ، اِسْتَائِي؛ اِسْتَاءَا؛ اِسْتَاؤُوا\اِسْتَاءُوا ، اِسْتَأْنَ

istá', istā'ī; istā'ā; istā'ū, ista'na

PASSIVE° **Present** يُسْتَاءُ *yustā'u* **Past** أُسْتِيءَ *'ustī'a*

Participle مُسْتَاء *mustā'*

See **137**

154 X **اِسْتَوْفَى يَسْتَوْفِي** *istawfa yastawfī* **وفي**

to exhaust, fulfil هـ

ACTIVE

Past *istawfa*

اِسْتَوْفَيْتُ		اِسْتَوْفَيْنَا
اِسْتَوْفَيْتَ	اِسْتَوْفَيْتُمَا	اِسْتَوْفَيْتُمْ
اِسْتَوْفَيْتِ	اِسْتَوْفَيْتُمَا	اِسْتَوْفَيْتُنَّ
اِسْتَوْفَى	اِسْتَوْفَيَا	اِسْتَوْفَوْا
اِسْتَوْفَتْ	اِسْتَوْفَتَا	اِسْتَوْفَيْنَ

Present *yastawfī*

أَسْتَوْفِي		نَسْتَوْفِي
تَسْتَوْفِي	تَسْتَوْفِيَانِ	تَسْتَوْفُونَ
تَسْتَوْفِينَ	تَسْتَوْفِيَانِ	تَسْتَوْفِينَ
يَسْتَوْفِي	يَسْتَوْفِيَانِ	يَسْتَوْفُونَ
تَسْتَوْفِي	تَسْتَوْفِيَانِ	يَسْتَوْفِينَ

Subjunctive *yastawfiya*

أَسْتَوْفِيَ		نَسْتَوْفِيَ
تَسْتَوْفِيَ	تَسْتَوْفِيَا	تَسْتَوْفُوا
تَسْتَوْفِي	تَسْتَوْفِيَا	تَسْتَوْفِينَ
يَسْتَوْفِيَ	يَسْتَوْفِيَا	يَسْتَوْفُوا
تَسْتَوْفِيَ	تَسْتَوْفِيَا	يَسْتَوْفِينَ

Jussive *yastawfi*

أَسْتَوْفِ		نَسْتَوْفِ
تَسْتَوْفِ	تَسْتَوْفِيَا	تَسْتَوْفُوا
تَسْتَوْفِي	تَسْتَوْفِيَا	تَسْتَوْفِينَ
يَسْتَوْفِ	يَسْتَوْفِيَا	يَسْتَوْفُوا
تَسْتَوْفِ	تَسْتَوْفِيَا	يَسْتَوْفِينَ

Verbal Noun اِسْتِيفَاء *istīfā'*

Participle مُسْتَوْفٍ\الْمُسْتَوْفِي *mustawfin/al-mustawfī*

Imperative اِسْتَوْفِ، اِسْتَوْفِي؛ اِسْتَوْفِيَا؛ اِسْتَوْفُوا، اِسْتَوْفِينَ
istawf-i, -ī; -iyā; -ū, -īna

PASSIVE **Present** يُسْتَوْفَى *yustawfa* **Past** أُسْتُوفِيَ *ustūfiya*

Participle مُسْتَوْفًى\الْمُسْتَوْفَى *mustawfan/al-mustawfa*

I وَفَى يَفِي (وَفَاء) to fulfil, compensate fully ب 132; II وَفَّى to treat fully, complete هـ 141; III وَافَى to provide for in full ب ه142; IV أَوْفَى to fulfil هـ\ب, to exceed على 147; V تَوَفَّى to receive in full هـ, *passive* to die 148

اِسْتِيفَاء\وَفَاء\إِفَاء\تَوْفِيَة fulfilment — وَفَاء ج وَفَيَات decease

وَفِيّ ج أَوْفِيَة faithful — وَافٍ\الْوَافِي abundant — وَفَاءً لِ in fulfilment of

155 X **اِسْتَضَاءَ يَسْتَضِيءُ** *istaḍā'a yastaḍī'u* to be lit, to seek enlightenment in بِ **ضوء**

ACTIVE	Present	*yastaḍī'u*		Past	*istaḍā'a*
نَسْتَضِيءُ		أَسْتَضِيءُ	اِسْتَضَأْنَا		اِسْتَضَأْتُ
تَسْتَضِيؤُونَ\ تَسْتَضِيئُونَ	تَسْتَضِيئَانِ	تَسْتَضِيءُ	اِسْتَضَأْتُمْ	اِسْتَضَأْتُمَا	اِسْتَضَأْتَ
تَسْتَضِئْنَ	تَسْتَضِيئَانِ	تَسْتَضِيئِينَ	اِسْتَضَأْتُنَّ	اِسْتَضَأْتُمَا	اِسْتَضَأْتِ
يَسْتَضِيؤُونَ\ يَسْتَضِيئُونَ	يَسْتَضِيئَانِ	يَسْتَضِيءُ	اِسْتَضَاؤُوا\ اِسْتَضَاءُوا	اِسْتَضَاءَا	اِسْتَضَاءَ
يَسْتَضِئْنَ	تَسْتَضِيئَانِ	تَسْتَضِيءُ	اِسْتَضَأْنَ	اِسْتَضَاءَتَا	اِسْتَضَاءَتْ

	Jussive	*yastaḍi'*		Subjunctive	*yastaḍī'a*
نَسْتَضِئْ		أَسْتَضِئْ	نَسْتَضِيءَ		أَسْتَضِيءَ
تَسْتَضِيؤُوا\ تَسْتَضِيئُوا	تَسْتَضِيئَا	تَسْتَضِئْ	تَسْتَضِيؤُوا\ تَسْتَضِيئُوا	تَسْتَضِيئَا	تَسْتَضِيءَ
تَسْتَضِئْنَ	تَسْتَضِيئَا	تَسْتَضِيئِي	تَسْتَضِئْنَ	تَسْتَضِيئَا	تَسْتَضِيئِي
يَسْتَضِيؤُوا\ يَسْتَضِيئُوا	يَسْتَضِيئَا	يَسْتَضِئْ	يَسْتَضِيؤُوا\ يَسْتَضِيئُوا	يَسْتَضِيئَا	يَسْتَضِيءَ
يَسْتَضِئْنَ	تَسْتَضِيئَا	تَسْتَضِئْ	يَسْتَضِئْنَ	تَسْتَضِيئَا	تَسْتَضِيءَ

Verbal Noun اِسْتِضَاءَة *istiḍā'a* **Participle** مُسْتَضِيء *mustaḍī'*

Impv. اِسْتَضِئْ، اِسْتَضِيئِي؛ اِسْتَضِيئَا؛ اِسْتَضِيؤُوا\اِسْتَضِيئُوا، اِسْتَضِئْنَ
istaḍ-i', -ī'ī; -ī'ā; -ī'ū, -i'na

PASSIVE° **Present** يُسْتَضَاءُ *yustaḍā'u* **Past** أُسْتُضِيءَ *ustuḍī'a*
Participle مُسْتَضَاء *mustaḍā'*

See **146**

Part III – Verb List

In this list the particle 'to' is omitted from the English, for brevity.

Many verbs have other meanings, some less common, not shown here.

References and symbols. A **bold** reference number indicates the table in Part II showing the complete verb. A non-bold reference number indicates the table giving a verb of identical pattern. An *italic* reference number indicates the table giving further information about the verb.

For a few less common doubly weak verbs, two tables may be indicated with non-italic figures, one for each of the weak root letters, in the order of their appearance in the root. The table numbers are separated by a comma.

Some verbs, mostly in the sound class, have alternative vowel patterns in Form I. The appropriate table numbers in non-italic figures are shown separated by the sign '/'.

For the abbreviations and symbols used, see the Introduction. The government of the verb is shown only for verbs not appearing in Part II and then only where it differs from the English equivalent or is otherwise not obvious.

Verbal Noun. For verbs of Forms I and IQ not mentioned in Part II, the verbal noun is shown, in parentheses; the sign (-) shows that the verbal noun does not exist or is not used.

ا\أ\آ

ائتلف VIII form a coalition 34, *33*

ائتمّ VIII follow the example of ه 70, *63*

ائتمر VIII deliberate **34**

ائتمن VIII trust 34, *27*

آب I return **91**

أباع IV offer for sale 101, *98*

ابتاع VIII buy 110, *98*

ابتدأ VIII begin **56**

أبّد II perpetuate 28

أبرأ IV absolve 52, *49*

أبطأ IV retard 52, *48*

أبطل IV foil 10

أبعد IV remove 10

أبلغ IV notify ه عن\ب 10

أبى I refuse **131**

ابيضّ IX be/turn white **113**

أتبع IV subordinate s.o. to s.o 10, *15*

اتّبع VIII follow, comply with **15**

اتّجه VIII be directed 82, *76*

اتّحد VIII be united 82

اتّخذ VIII take **35**

اتّسع VIII be expanded/ wide 82, *80*

اتّسم VIII be distinguished/ characterised by ب 82

اتّصل VIII contact 82, *77*

اتّفق VIII agree **82**

اتّقى VIII beware **152**

أتمّ IV complete 65, *60*

أتى I come **130**

آتى III favour, supply with **143**, IV bring **144**

أثار IV excite ه هـ 99

أثّر II influence في\على 28

أثبت IV prove 10

أجاب IV answer 99, *115*

أجاز IV permit ه\ل هـ 99

أجبر IV compel ه على 10

اجتمع VIII have a meeting 14, *3*

اجتهد VIII exert oneself 14

أجر I remunerate 25, *31*

أجّر II hire out 28, *31*

آجر IV hire out **31**

أجرى IV put into effect 123

أجّل II postpone 28

أجلس IV seat 10

أجمع IV agree 10, *3*

أجمل IV sum up هـ 10

أحال IV transform 99, *97*

أحبّ IV love **65**
احتاج VIII need **108**
احتاز VIII possess 108, *106*
احتال VIII deceive 108, *97*
احتجّ VIII plead, justify, object 70, *66*
احترم VIII respect 14
احتفظ VIII preserve 14
احتلّ VIII occupy 70, *69*
احتمل VIII be probable, tolerate 14
احتوى VIII contain **151**
أحدث IV bring about 10
أحضر IV bring 10
أحقّ IV be right 65, *72*
أحلّ IV release, permit, relocate 65, *69*
احمرّ IX be/turn red **22**
أحوج IV need **100**
احولّ IX squint 112, *97*
أحيا IV (re)animate, perform 123, *140*
أخاف IV frighten 99, *92*
أخبر IV inform **10**
اختار VIII (s)elect 110
اختبر VIII do research into 14, *10*
اختصّ VIII be especially qualified/authorised ب 70
اختلّ VIII be(come) defective/deficient 70
اختلط VIII be mixed 14
اختلف VIII differ 14
أخجل IV embarrass 10
أخذ I take 24, *30*
آخذ III blame **30**
أخّر II delay 28, *32*
أخرب IV destroy 10
أخرج IV expel, publish 10
اخضرّ IX be/turn green 22
أخطأ IV be mistaken in في 52
أخلّ IV violate ب 65
أخلص IV be loyal/sincere to ل 10
أخلى IV empty, vacate 123
أدار IV administer, turn هـ 99
أدام IV perpetuate 99
أدّب II educate 28
ادّحر VIII be repelled **16**
ادّخر VIII keep 16 (root ذخر, see § 15)
أدخل IV admit 10, *11*
أدرك IV reach هـ 10
ادّعم VIII be based on على 16

ادّعى VIII summon **128**

أدّى II lead ه هـ
tend towards إلى,
fulfil هـ 28/141

أذاع IV broadcast **101**

أذن I (إذن *'idhn*) permit
ل في 27

آذن IV urge ه،ب,
foreshadow ب 31

أراح IV comfort 99, *114*

أراد IV want هـ\أن 99

ارتاح VIII rest, be content
108, *114*

ارتفع VIII rise 14

ارتقى VIII ascend, climb
هـ 127

ارتمى VIII hurl oneself
127, *118*

أرجع IV turn back
ه إلى 10

أرّخ II date 28

أرخص IV reduce in price
هـ 10

أرسل IV send 10

أرسى IV anchor, moor
هـ 123

أرشد IV guide 10

أرى IV show **145**

ازداد VIII increase **111**

ازدحم VIII throng **17**

ازدوج VIII be in pairs **109**

ازرق IX be/turn blue 22

أزعج IV trouble ه 10

أساء IV harm, treat badly,
misjudge 146, *137*

استاء VIII be offended **153**

استأجر X rent 36, *31*

استأجل X seek to postpone
هـ 36

استأذن X ask permission
من في, take
leave of من 36

استاق VIII herd 108, *90*

استأمن X trust 36, *27*

استأنف X resume **36**

استبدّ X act arbitrarily in
ب 72

استبدل X substitute for
هـ ب 23

استبطأ X find slow 57, *48*

استبعد X single out,
consider unlikely 23

استبقى X retain 129

استتبع X entail 23, *15*

استثبت X verify 23

استثمر X invest 23

استثنى X except **129**

استجاب X grant 114, *115*

استجمع X summarise 23, *3*

استجهل X consider stupid

ه 23

استجوب X interrogate **115**

استحال X be transformed 114, *97*

استحسن X consider good 23

استحضر X send for 23

استحقّ X deserve **72**

استخبر X ask...about 23, *10*

استخدم X employ 23

استخرج X extract 23

استدعى X summon, invite, call 129, *128*

استراح X rest **114**

استرأف X beg mercy **46**

استرجى X anticipate 129, *117*

استردّ X reclaim, retrieve 72, *66*

استزاد X aim for more, demand more 116, *93*

استشار X consult ه 114

استصغر X consider small 23

استصنع X cause to be made 23, *18*

استصوب X approve of هـ 115

استضاء X be lit, seek enlightenment in **155**

استضاف X offer hospitality to ه 116

استطاع X be able هـ\أنْ 114

استطلع X consult 23, *20*

استظلّ X seek the protection of 72, *59*

استظهر X show 23, *12*

استعان X ask for help 114, *104*

استعجل X hurry 23

استعدّ X be prepared ل\أنْ 72

استعرف X perceive 23, *2*

استعطى X beg...for charity 129, *123*

استعظم X be arrogant, consider great 23

استعفى X ask pardon of 129, *125*

استعلم X enquire about 23, *7*

استعمر X colonise 23

استعمل X use 23, *4*

استغرب X find strange 23

استغرق X last هـ 23

استغفر X beg pardon of ... for ه هـ\ل\من 23

استغلّ exploit (wrongly) 72

استغنى X do without عن 129

استفاد X benefit, inform **116**

استفسر X ask for an explanation ه عن 23

استفهم X enquire of ... about ه هـ\عن 23

استقال X resign from من\عن 116

استقام X stand up 114, *99*

استقبل X receive **23**

استقرّ X be(come) stable 72, *62*

استقرأ X investigate **57**

استقصر X consider inadequate 23

استقضى X claim from 129, *126*

استقلّ X consider small, be independent 72

استكبر X consider big, be arrogant 23

استكتب X dictate to 23, *1*

استكثر X find excessive 23, *5*

استكشف X explore 23

استمال X become rich 114, *95*, attract 116, *96*

استمرّ X continue 72, *58*

استملك X appropriate هـ 23

استنبأ X enquire after 57, *53*

استنسب X approve of 23, *9*

استنكر X reject 23

استهلك X consume 23

استودع X store 83

استورد X import **83**

استوصف X consult (medically) 83

استوطن X settle (in a place) 83

استوفى X exhaust, fulfil **154**

استولى X appropriate 154, *133*

استوى VIII be(come) level/straight 151, *139*

استيقظ X awake **89**

استيقن X ascertain 89, *87*

أسر I capture **26**

أسّس II establish 63, *67*

اسمرّ IX be/turn brown 22

اسودّ IX be/turn black **112**

أشار IV refer to إلى 99

اشتدّ VIII be(come) severe 70

اشترع VIII legislate 14

اشترك VIII participate in في 14

اشترى VIII buy **127**

اشتعل VIII catch fire 14

اشتغل VIII work 14

اشتفى VIII be cured 127

أشّر II place on record, grant a visa to

على 28

أشعّ IV radiate (هـ) 65

أشعر IV inform ه هـ\ب 10

أشغل IV keep ... busy ه 10

أصاب IV attain, do well هـ 99

أصبح IV become اً 10

أصدر IV issue هـ 10

أصرّ IV insist on على 65

أصرح IV explain 10

اصطنع VIII manufacture **18**

اصفرّ IX be/turn yellow 22

أصلح IV repair, reform هـ\من 10

أضاء IV illuminate **146**

أضاف IV add هـ 101

أضرّ IV oblige 65, *71*

أضرب IV go on strike 10, *19*

اضطرّ VIII compel **71**

اضطرب VIII clash **19**

أضعف IV weaken ه،هـ 10

اطّبع VIII be printed 20

اطّلع VIII become aware **20**

أطلع IV notify 10, *20*

أطلق IV throw 10

أظلّ IV overshadow 65, *59*

اظّلم VIII suffer wrong **21**

أظلم IV be(come) dark 10, *21*

أظهر IV show 10, *12*

أعاد IV do again هـ 99

أعان IV help 99, *104*

اعتدى VIII act aggressively 127

اعتبر VIII consider, esteem **14**

اعترف VIII acknowledge 14, *2*

اعتقد VIII believe هـ\أن , believe in ب 14

اعتمد VIII rely on على 14

أعجب IV please ه 10

أعجز IV disable ه, make impossible for ه من 10 (NB: vb. noun إعجاز IV not used in this meaning; for 'disability' use عجز *'ajz* I)

أعدّ IV prepare هـ 65

أعطى IV give to **123**

أعفى IV dismiss 123, *125*

أعلم IV notify 10, *7*

أعلن IV announce 10

أعمل IV put to work 10, *4*

اعوجّ IX be(come) bent 112

أغار IV make jealous 101, *103*
أفاد IV benefit, inform 101, *116*
أفاض IV pour, fill, be verbose 101
افترق VIII be(come) separated 14
افتكر VIII think of في 14
أفرد IV isolate 10
أفرز IV isolate, secrete 10
أفطر IV breakfast 10
أفقر IV impoverish 10
أفلس IV be(come) bankrupt 10
أقال IV dismiss 101
أقام IV organise, rectify, raise, reside **99**
أقبل IV approach 10, *23*
اقتبل VIII receive 14, *23*
اقترح VIII propose 14
اقتضى VIII claim from 127, *126*
اقتلع VIII uproot, exterminate هـ 14
أقرّ IV install 65, *62*
أقرض IV lend ه هـ 10
أكأب IV distress **42**
اكتأب VIII be sad about 45, *42*
أكتب IV dictate 10, *1*
اكتتب VIII copy 14, *1*
اكتشف VIII discover 14
اكتفى VIII be content with ب 127
أكثر IV increase 10, *5*
أكّد II confirm **28**
أكرم IV treat with deference 10
أكفأ IV invert 52, *51*
أكل I eat **24**
آكل III dine with 30, *24*
أكّل II feed 28, *24*
أكمل IV complete 10
التأم VIII be mended **45**
التجأ VIII flee 56
التفّ VIII coil 70
التقى VIII meet 127, *124*
التمس VIII request من هـ 14
التهب VIII catch fire, inflame (also medical) 14
التوى VIII be bent 151
ألحق IV annex 10
ألزم IV compel ه هـ 10
ألغى IV cancel 123
ألف I be familiar with 27, *33*
ألّف II compose 28, *33*

ألقى IV throw 123, *124*

أمّ I go to هـ, seek out ه هـ, show the way to ه 58, *63*

أماز IV differentiate 101, *110*

أمال IV incline 101, *96*

امتاز VIII be distinguished **110**

امتحن VIII examine ه 14

امتدّ VIII be extended **70**

أمدّ IV provide 65, *70*

أمر I order 24, *34*

أمرّ IV let pass 65, *58*

أمكن IV enable ه من 10

أمل I hope **25**

أمّل II expect of 28, *25*

أملك IV assign ه هـ 10

أمّم II nationalise **63**

أمن I be safe/reliable **27**

آمن IV believe in 30, *27*

أمّن II insure 28, *27*

انباع VII be sold **107**

انبثق VII gush 13

انبجس VII gush 13

انبسط VII be(come) happy, enjoy من 13

انتبه VIII pay attention to ل\إلى 14

أنتج IV produce 10

انتخب VIII (s)elect 14

انتدب VIII assign ه، ل 14

انتسب VIII belong 14, *9*

انتظر VIII wait for 14

انتقد VIII criticise 14

انتقل VIII be transferred 14

انتهز VIII seize (فرصة *furṣa* an opportunity) 14

انتهك VIII violate 14

انتهى VIII come to an end 127

انتوى VIII intend 151, *138*

انثنى VII fold intr. 126, *129*

انجاب VII be dispelled 106, *115*

أنجز IV accomplish, implement 10

انحاز VII withdraw, join **106**

انحرف VII deviate from عن 13

انحلّ VII be solved **69**

انخفض VII be reduced 13

أنذر IV warn of ه ب 10

أندى IV wet 123, *122*

انزوى VII be isolated **150**

انساق VII be driven 106, *90*

انسحب	VII withdraw (o.s.) 13
أنسى	IV make...forget 123, *119*
أنشأ	IV create, construct **52**
انضرّ	VII be damaged 69, *71*
انضمّ	VII join مع\إلى 69
انطوى	VII be folded/ concealed 150
انظلم	VII suffer wrong 13, *21*
انعقد	VII be tied/held (meeting etc.) 13
أنف	I scorn 27, *36*
انفتح	VII open, be opened 13
انفجر	VII explode 13
انفرد	VII be isolated/ unique 13
انفصل	VII be separated from عن 13
أنفق	IV spend ... on هـ على 10
انقسم	VII be divided 13
انقضى	VII be ended **126**
انقطع	VII be cut off 13
انقلب	VII be overturned **13**
انكتب	VII subscribe 13, *1*
أنكر	IV disown 10
انكسر	VII be broken 13
انكشف	VII be revealed 13
انكفأ	VII be repelled **55**
انهار	VII collapse, crash 106
انهزم	VII be defeated 13
أنهى	IV inform إلى هـ, conclude هـ 123
أهاج	IV excite هـ 101
اهتمّ	VIII care for ب 70
أهّل	II enable ل هـ 28
أهمل	IV neglect هـ 10
أوجب	IV oblige **79**
أوجد	IV bring about, accomplish 79, *73*
أوجز	IV summarise 79
أوسع	IV broaden 79, *80*
أوشك	IV be about to (do) على\أنْ 79
أوصل	IV convey, connect with 79, *77*
أوصى	IV entrust to, (re-) commend to ب ه, bequeath to ل ب 147
أوفى	IV fulfil, exceed 147, *154*
أوقع	IV drop ه هـ 79
أوقف	IV bring to a stop 79

أولى IV entrust to **147**
أيبس IV dry 87, *84*
ايتلف VIII form a coalition 34, *33*
ايتمر VIII deliberate **34**
ايتمن VIII trust 34, *27*
أيّد II support **29**
أيقظ IV waken 87, *88*
أيقن IV be sure **87**

ب

باحث III discuss ... with ه في 9
بادل III exchange ... with ه ه 9
بارك III bless ه\في 9
بؤس I be brave **38**
بئس I be wretched **39**
باض I lay (eggs) 93, *113*
باع I sell 93, *98*
بايع III make a contract with **98**
بحث I (بحث ج بحوث *baḥth buḥūth*) look for ه\عن, discuss ه 3
بخّر II evaporate ه 7
بدأ I begin 47, *56*
بدّأ II give priority 50, *56*
برّأ II absolve 50, *49*
برئ I be free **49**
برد I (-) file (metal) 1
برّد II chill 7
برمج IQ (-) programme 6
برهن IQ (برهنة *barhana*) prove على 6
بسّط II simplify 7
بطّأ II retard 50, *48*
بطؤ I be slow **48**
بطل I (بطل *buṭl*) be(come) useless/obsolete 1
بطّل II foil 7
بعث I (بعث *ba'th*) send ه ه\ب 3
بعد I (بعد *bu'd*) be far 5
بقي I (بقاء *baqā'*) remain أ 119
بكى I (بكاء *bukā'*) cry 118
بلغ I (بلوغ *bulūgh*) reach 1
بلّغ II inform of ه، ه 7
بنى I (بناء *binā'*) build 118
بيّض II whiten, make a fair copy 96, *113*
بيّن II announce 96

ت

تابع III follow up 9, *15*
تأثّر V be influenced 32

تأجّل V be postponed 32
تأخّر V be late **32**
تأسّس V be established **67**
تأسّف V regret على 32
تأصّل V be deeprooted 32
تأكّد V be certain of 32, *28*
تأكّل V be eaten away/eroded 32, *24*
تآكل VI be eaten away/eroded 33, *24*
تألّف V consist of 32, *33*
تآلف VI harmonise with **33**
تآمر VI conspire against 33, *34*
تأمّل V ponder 32, *25*
تأمّم V be nationalised 67, *63*
تأهّل V be(come) qualified 32
تأيّد V be supported 32, *29*
تباحث VI confer with ... about مع في 12
تبادل VI exchange 12
تباطأ VI be slow **54**
تبايع VI conclude a deal 105, *98*
تبخّر V evaporate 11
تبرّأ V clear oneself 53, *49*
تبسّم V smile 11
تبع I follow, comply with 4, *15*
تبيّض V be whitened 103, *113*
تبيّن V be(come) clear 103
تتابع VI occur successively 12, *15*
تثنّى V be double/folded 124, *129*
تجاوب VI harmonise 104, *115*
تجاور VI be adjacent to e.o. 104
تجدّد V be renewed 66
تجزّأ V be(come) separated 53
تجسّس V spy on على 66
تجمّد V freeze (o.s.) 11
تجمّع V congregate 11, *3*
تجمهر IIQ crowd together 8
تجنّس V be naturalised 11
تحاجّ VI dispute with e.o. 68, *64*
تحادث VI converse together 12
تحارب VI wage war against e.o. 12
تحاول VI strive for 104, *97*

تحدّث V talk to ... about 11 إلى\مع في\ب

تحرّك V move 11

تحسّس V touch 66

تحسّن V improve (o.s.) 11

تحقّق V materialise, be convinced 66, *72*

تحوّل V be transferred/ transformed 102, *97*

تحوّى V coil 148, *151*

تحيّز V withdraw from, join 103, *106*

تخابر VI write to e.o. 12, *10*

تخرّج V graduate from في 11

تخصّص V specialise in في 66

تخلّى V withdraw from من\عن 124

تخوّف V fear 102, *92*

تداخل VI intervene, interfere 12, *11*

تدخّل V intervene, interfere **11**

تدرّج V proceed step by step 11

تذكّر V remember 11

ترأّس V be appointed head **43**

تراسل VI exchange letters 12

ترامى VI extend far 125, *118*

تراوح VI fluctuate 104, *114*

تربّى V be educated/ reared 124, *121*

ترجم IQ translate **6**

ترجّى V anticipate هـ 124, *117*

تردّد V hesitate **66**

ترشّح V catch cold, be a candidate for ل 11

ترك I (ترك *tark*) leave ه هـ 1

تركّز V concentrate on في 11

تزاحم VI crowd together 12, *17*

تزاوج VI intermarry, be in pairs 104, *109*

تزايد VI intensify **105**

تزلزل IIQ quake **8**

تزوّج V get married 102, *109*

تزوّى V withdraw 148, *150*

تزيّد V increase, exaggerate 103, *93*

تساءل VI wonder about 44, *37*

تساند VI support e.o 12
تساوق VI form a series 104, *90*
تساوى VI be balanced 149, *139*
تسلسل IIQ be linked together 8
تسلّم V receive 11
تسوّق V deal in the market 102, *90*
تشبّك V be entangled 11
تشرّف V be honoured 11
تصعّب V be(come) difficult 11
تصنّع V feign 11, *18*
تصوّر V imagine, be portrayed **102**
تضادّ VI oppose e.o. **68**
تضارب VI fight e.o. 12, *19*
تضامن VI support e.o. 12
تضخّم V be(come) inflated 11
تضمّن V include 11
تضوّأ V shine 102/53, *146*
تطرّف V be(come) extreme 11
تطلّع V watch 11, *20*
تطوّر V evolve (o.s.) 102
تظاهر VI demonstrate **12**
تظلّل V be overshadowed 66, *59*
تظلّم V complain 11, *21*
تعارف VI get to know e.o. 12, *2*
تعافى VI recover (health) **125**
تعالى VI to rise 125; see also **130** and **135**
تعامل VI do business with e.o. 12, *4*
تعاون VI cooperate **104**
تعجّب V be astonished at من 11
تعدّى V act aggressively toward على 124
تعرّف V become acquainted 11, *2*
تعرقل IIQ be hindered 8
تعطّل V be(come) unemployed 11
تعطّى V beg ... for charity 124, *123*
تعلّق V pertain to ب 11
تعلّم V learn 11, *7*
تعهّد V advocate هـ, undertake ب 11
تعوّد V be(come) accustomed to هـ\على 102

تغاير VI be varied 105, *103*

تغيّر V change **103**

تفاءل VI be optimistic **44**

تفاوض VI negotiate with e.o 104

تفرّد V be unique 11

تفرّق V become separated 11

تفسّر V be explained 11

تفضّل V deign to, be kind enough to ب 11

تفكّك V disintegrate 66

تفلسف IIQ philosophise, claim to be a philosopher 8

تقابل VI face e.o. 12, *23*

تقاتل VI fight e.o.12

تقارب VI approach e.o. 12

تقاضى VI claim from 125, *126*

تقاطع VI part company 12

تقبّل V accept 11, *23*

تقدّم V progress 11

تقرّر V be decided 66, *62*

تقضّى V be concluded 124, *126*

تقلّب V be inverted/ reversed 11, *13*

تقوّى V be strengthened 148

تكاتب VI correspond with e.o. 12, *1*

تكاثر VI band together 12, *5*

تكافأ VI equal e.o. 54, *51*

تكمّل V be completed 11

تكهرب IIQ be electrified/ electrocuted/ charged (electrically) 8

تكوّن V be composed of من 102

تلاقى VI come together 125, *124*

تلفز IQ (-) televise 6

تلفّظ V pronounce ب 11

تلفن IQ (-) telephone 6

تلقّي V receive **124**

تلوّث V be(come) polluted 102

تمّ I end **60**

تمايل VI sway 105, *96*

تمدّن V be(come) civilised 11

تمركز IIQ concentrate on, establish o.s. in في 8

تمسّك V hold on to ب 11

تمكّن V possess, be capable of من 11

تمّم II finish 62, *60*

تمهّد V be clear(ed)/ ready 11

تمهّل V go slowly 11

تموّل V be financed, become rich 102, *95*

تميّز V be distinguished 103, *110*

تميّل V sway 103, *96*

تنادى VI convene 125, *122*

تنازع VI quarrel with e.o. 12

تنازل VI waive عن, cede ل عن 12

تناسب VI (be) relate(d) to e.o. 12, *9*

تناسى VI neglect, pretend to forget 125, *119*

تناوب VI alternate في\على 104

تناول VI reach, take (food/drink) ﻫ 104

تنبّأ V forecast **53**

تندّى V be wetted 124, *122*

تنسّق V be well-ordered 11

تنفّس V breathe 11

تنوّع V be diversified 102

تهنّأ V enjoy 53, *50*

تهوّر V collapse 102

تواجه VI face e.o **81**

توارث VI hold as a bequest 81, *75*

توازن VI counterbalance e.o. 81

تواصل VI be interconnected 81, *77*

تواضع VI humble o.s. 81, *74*

توالى VI follow in succession **149**

توتّر V be(come) tense 80

توجّه V go towards 80, *76*

توسّع V expand **80**

توصّل V gain access 80, *77*

توظّف V be recruited 80

توفّر V abound 80

توفّى V receive in full, *(passive)* die 148, *154*

توقّع V expect 80

توقّف V come to a stop 80

توقّى V be wary of 148, *132*

تولّي V be appointed **148**

تيسر V flourish 88, *85*

تيقّظ V be alert **88**

تيقّن V ascertain 88, *87*

ث

ثبّت II consolidate 7

ثقب I (ثقب *thaqb*) drill, bore 1

ثلّث II triple 7

ثلج I (-) snow 1

ثمّن II assess 7

ثنى I fold 118, *129*

ثنّى II double 121, *129*

ثوّر II agitate 95

ج

جاء I come **135**

جاب I explore 90, *115*

جاوب III answer 97, *115*

جاور III be adjacent to ه هـ 97

جدّد II renew 62

جرّ I (جرّ *jarr*) pull 58

جرّب II attempt هـ\أن , test هـ 7

جرف I (جرف *jarf*) dredge هـ 1

جرى I (جري *jary*) flow 118

جزّأ II separate هـ 50

جزى I (جزاء *jazā'*) compensate for ه ب\علي 118

جسّ I (جسّ *jass*) probe, spy out هـ 58

جسر I (جسور *jusūr*) span 1

جفّ I (جفاف *jafāf*) be(come) dry 60

جفّف II dry هـ 62

جلس I (جلوس *julūs*) sit 2

جمد I (جمد *jamd*) freeze, congeal 1, 5

جمّد II freeze, congeal هـ 7

جمع I collect **3**

جمّع II assemble 7, *3*

جنّس II classify 7

ح

حاجّ III dispute with **64**

حارب III wage war with ه 9

حاز I gain 90, *106*

حافظ III preserve, maintain 9

حاكم III prosecute 9

حال I be changed, prevent 90, *97*

حامى III defend (in law) 122

حاور III converse with ه 97

حاول III try **97**

حبّ I love, like 60, *65*

حبس I (حبس *ḥabs*) arrest

ه, impede هـ 2

حجّ I make the pilgrimage 58, *64*

حجز I (حجز *ḥajz*) reserve 1, 2

حدّ I (حدّ ج حدود *ḥadd ḥudūd*) limit 58

حدث I (حدوث *ḥudūth*) happen 1

حدّد II demarcate, determine 62

حرّر II liberate, edit 62

حرس I (حرس *ḥars*) guard 1

حرّض II incite to ه على 7

حرق I (حرق *ḥarq*) burn 2

حرّك II move هـ 7

حرم I (حرم *ḥirm*) withhold ه\من هـ\من 4

حزم I (حزم *ḥazm*) pack, wrap هـ 2

حسّ I (حسّ *ḥass*) feel 58

حسب I (حساب *ḥisāb*) calculate 1

حسّن II improve هـ 7

حصل I (حصول *ḥuṣūl*) attain على 1

حضر I (حضور *ḥuḍūr*) attend 1

حضّر II prepare هـ 7

حطّ I (حطّ *ḥaṭṭ*) put 58

حظر I (حظر *ḥaẓr*) forbid على هـ 1

حفر I (حفر *ḥafr*) drill 2

حفز I (حفز *ḥafz*) incite ه على\إلى 2

حفظ I (حفظ *ḥifẓ*) preserve 4

حقّ I be true 60, *72*

حقّق II realise, implement, confirm 62, *72*

حكم I (حكم *ḥukm*) pass judgment في\على 1

حكى I (حكاية *ḥikāya*) narrate 118

حلّ I solve 58, *69*

حلّل II analyse, absolve, permit 62, *69*

حمّر II make red, roast, fry 7, *22*

حمل I (حمل *ḥaml*) carry 2

حمّل II charge with (a task) ه هـ , charge (a battery) هـ 7

حمى I (حماية *ḥimāya*) defend 118

حنى I (-) bend intr. 118

حوّل II transfer, transform 95, *97*

حوى I collect 138, *151*
حيّ\حيي I live **140**
حيّا II keep alive, greet 141, *140*

خ

خابر III write to 9, *10*
خاط I (خيط *khayṭ*) sew 93
خاف I fear **92**
خالف III conflict with ه ه 9
خبر I test, experience 1, *10*
خبّر II notify 7, *10*
خبط I (خبط *khabṭ*) strike, knock against ه 2
خجّل II embarrass 7
خرب I (خرب *kharb*) fall into ruin 4
خرّب II destroy 7
خرج I (خروج *khurūj*) go out 1
خرق I (خرق *kharq*) pierce, infringe 1, 2
خزن I (خزن *khazn*) store ه 1
خزّن II store 7
خسر I (خسارة *khasāra*) lose 4
خصّص II specify 7
خصم I (-) deduct, discount ه 2
خطّ I (خطّ ج خطوط *khaṭṭ khuṭūṭ*) draw (a line) 58
خطّط II delineate, plan 62
خفّض II reduce ه 7
خفّف II lighten 62
خلّص II rectify, free from ه من ه من 7
خلط I (خلط *khalṭ*) mix ه 2
خلّى II release 121
خوّف II frighten 95, *92*

د

دار I (دور ج أدوار *dawr 'adwār*) turn (o.s.) 90
دافع III resist ه ه, defend عن 9
داعى III challenge 122, *128*
دان I (دين ج ديون *dayn duyūn*) owe ل ب 93
دبّر II arrange 7
دحر I repel 3, *16*
دخل I enter 1, *11*
دخّل II insert 7, *11*
دخّن II smoke 7
درّب II train 7
درج I (دروج *durūj*) proceed, be

obsolete/extinct 1

درّج II grade, circulate, insert هـ 7

درس I (درس ج دروس *dars durūs*) study 1

درّس II teach 7

دعا I call, pray to 117, *128*

دعم I (دعم *da'm*) support هـ 3

دفع I (دفع *daf'*) push 3

دقّ I (دقّة *diqqa*) hammer, pound هـ 60

دقّق II check هـ 7

دلّ I (دلالة *dalāla*) indicate 58

دوّر II turn هـ 95

ذ

ذاع I spread 93, *101*

ذخر (-) store away 3 see § 15

ذكر I (ذكر *dhikr*) mention 1

ذكّر II remind of ه، ب 7

ذهب I (ذهاب *dhahāb*) go 3

ر

رابى III be a moneylender 122, *121*

راجع III review, revise هـ 9

راح I depart 90, *114*

رأس I head 37, *40*

رأّس II appoint as head **40**

راسل III correspond with ه 9

رؤف I show mercy to 38, *46*

رافق III accompany 9

راقب III oversee هـ ه 9

راهن III bet with ه\عند هـ 9

رأى I see, consider as **134**

ربا I increase, exceed 117, *121*

ربح I (ربح ج أرباح *ribḥ 'arbāḥ*) gain 4

ربط I (ربط *rabṭ*) tie up 1

ربّى II educate **121**

رتّب II arrange in order 7

رتج I (رتج *ratj*) bolt هـ 1

رجّ I (رجّ *rajj*) shake هـ 58

رجا I expect, hope for, request **117**

رجع I (رجوع *rujū'*) come/go back 2

رحّب II welcome ب 7

رخّص II allow ل ب\في 7

ردّ I give back to 58, *66*

ردّد II repel 62, *66*

رسا I (رسو *rasw*) be firm, anchor, moor 117

رسب I (رسوب *rusūb*) sink, fail (examination) 1

رسم I (رسم ج رسوم *rasm rusūm*) draw 1

رشح I (رشح *rashḥ*) sweat, leak 3

رصّد II earmark (funds etc.), balance (account etc.) هـ 7

رضي I (رضًى\الرضَى *riḍan/ar-riḍa*) approve of ب 119

رغب I (رغبة ج رغبات *raghba raghabāt*) want في 4

رفض I (رفض *rafḍ*) refuse, withhold 2, 1

رفع I (رفع *raf'*) raise 3

رقب I (رقابة *raqāba*) supervise هـ 1

رقص I (رقص *raqṣ*) dance 1

رقي I (رقي *raqy*) climb هـ 119

رقّى II promote ه 121

ركب I (ركوب *rukūb*) mount 4

ركّب II assemble هـ 7

ركم I (ركم *rakm*) amass هـ 1

ركن I (ركون *rukūn*) lean on, rely on ه هـ 1

رمّ I (رمّ *ramm*) overhaul 58, 60

رمز I (رمز ج رموز *ramz rumūz*) symbolise إلى 1, 2

رمى I throw **118**

رهن I (رهن *rahn*) pledge (as security), mortgage هـ 3

روّح II revive 95, *114*

روّض II tame 95

روى I (رواية *riwāya*) tell ل هـ 138

روّى II irrigate 141

ريّح II rest 96, *114*

ز

زاحم III jostle 9, *17*

زاد I increase **93**
زار I (زيارة *ziyāra*) visit 90
زال I (زيل *zayl*) stop doing/being π\أ 92
زاوج III pair, join in marriage 97, *109*
زايد III outbid 98, *93*
زحم I jostle 3, *17*
زرع I (زرع *zar'*) cultivate 3
زلزل IQ shake 6, *8*
زلق I (زلق *zalq/zalaq*) slip 1, 4
زلّق II lubricate 7
زوّج II pair 95, *109*
زوّد II supply 95
زوّر II counterfeit هـ 95
زوى I hide, wrinkle 138, *150*
زوّى II go into seclusion 141, *150*
زيّت II lubricate, oil 96
زيّد II increase 96, *93*
زيّن II embellish 96

س

ساء I hurt, wrong **137**
سار I (سير *sayr*) run (of a machine), move 93
سارع III hurry 9
ساعد III help 9
سافر III travel 9
ساق I drive **90**
ساءل III question **41**
سأل I ask (enquire) **37**
سال I (سيل *sayl*) flow, melt 93
ساوق III accompany 97, *90*
ساوى III equal **142**
سبق I (سبق *sabq*) precede هـ ه 1, 2
سجّل II record 7
سحب I (سحب *saḥb*) drag 3
سخّن II heat هـ 7
سدّ I (سدّ *sadd*) plug 58
سدّد II guide ه 62
سرّ I (سرور *surūr*) please 58
سرّح II dismiss ه 7
سرّع II accelerate هـ 7
سرق I (سرقة *saraqa*) steal 2
سعى I strive **120**
سقط I (سقوط *suqūṭ*) fall 1
سقى I (سقي *saqy*) water, irrigate 118
سكت I (سكوت *sukūt*) be silent 1
سكن I (سكون *sukūn*)

live 1

سلب I (سلب *salb*) steal from, rob of ه هـ\من 1

سلّح II arm...with ه هـ 7

سلسل IQ (-) link together with هـ ب 6

سلّم II greet على 7

سمح I (سماح *samāḥ*) permit ل ب\ل\أنْ 3, be generous 5

سمسر IQ (سمسرة *samsara*) act as broker 6

سمع I (سمع *sam'*) hear 4

سمّى II name 121

سنّ I (سنّ *sann*) sharpen هـ 58

سنّن II sharpen هـ 62

سهّل II facilitate 7

سوّد II blacken, draft 95, *112*

سوّق II market 95, *90*

سوِي I equal **139**

سوّى II equalise **141**

سيّر II steer, propel 96

سيطر IQ (سيطرة *sayṭara*) dominate على 6

سيّل II make flow, liquefy, melt هـ 96

ش

شاء I wish **136**

شارك III share with ه هـ\في 9

شاهد III witness 9

شاور III consult ه 97

شبك I (شبك *shabk*) entangle 2

شبّك II entangle 7

شجّع II encourage ه 7

شحّم II grease, lubricate 7

شحن I (شحن *shaḥn*) load with هـ ب 3

شدّ I (شدّة *shidda*) be firm 60, (شدّ *shadd*) strengthen, make firm هـ ه 58

شدّد II strengthen 62

شرب I (شرب *shurb*) drink 4

شرح I (شرح *sharḥ*) explain 3

شرط I (شرط ج شروط *sharṭ shurūṭ*) stipulate 1, 2

شرع I (شروع *shurū'*) begin to π 3

شرّف II honour ه 7

شرى I buy, vend 118, *127*

شعّل II set on fire 7

شغب I (شغب *shaghb*) cause a riot/ dissension 3, 4

شغر I (شغور *shughūr*) be vacant 1

شغل I (شغل ج أشغال *shughl 'ashghāl*) busy ه 3

شغّل II keep ... busy ه, operate هـ (a machine) 7

شفى I (شفاء *shifā'*) heal ه 118

شكّ I (شكّ ج شكوك *shakk shukūk*) doubt في 58

شكا I (شكاية *shikāya*) complain about to ه\من،هـ\من 117

شكر I (شكر *shukr*) thank for ه هـ\ل\على 1

شكّل II constitute 7

شمل I (شمل *shamal*) comprise 4

شهد I (شهود *shuhūd*) witness 4

ص

صاد I (صيد *ṣayd*) hunt 93

صادق III authenticate على 9

صادر III confiscate هـ 9

صار I (مصير *maṣīr*) become π\أ 93

صام I (صوم *ṣawm*) fast 90

صان I (صيانة *ṣiyāna*) maintain 90

صبّ I (صبّ *ṣabb*) pour 58

صحّ I (صحّة *ṣiḥḥa*) be healthy 60

صحّح II attest, correct ه 62

صدر I (صدور *ṣudūr*) emanate from عن\من 1/2

صدّر II export هـ 7

صدّق II believe هـ ه 7

صرّح II explain هـ, announce ب, authorise ل ب 7

صرّف II exchange (money), market, drain (land) هـ 7

صعّب II make difficult 7

صفّى II clarify, filter هـ 121

صلّى II pray 121

صمّم II resolve (to do)

على 62

صنع I contrive 3, *18*

صنّع II industrialise 7, *18*

صنّف II sort هـ 7

صوّت II vote 95

صوّر II depict, photograph 95, *102*

ض

ضاء I shine 137, *146*

ضادّ III oppose 64, *68*

ضارب III fight with 9, *19*

ضاع I (ضيع *ḍay'*) get lost 93

ضبر I (-) file (papers) 1

ضبط I (ضبط *ḍabṭ*) control ه هـ, arrest ه, adjust هـ 1/2

ضحك I (ضحك *ḍaḥk*) laugh at من\ب 4

ضخّ I (ضخّ *ḍakhkh*) pump هـ 58

ضخّم II inflate هـ 7

ضرّ I damage 58, *71*

ضرب I strike, multiply 2, *19*

ضغط I (ضغط *ḍaghṭ*) (com)press 3

ضمّ I (ضمّ *ḍamm*) assemble ه هـ 58

ضمن I (ضمان *ḍamān*) guarantee ل هـ 4

ضوّأ II light, illuminate 95/50, *146*

ضيّع II waste هـ 96

ط

طار I (طيران *ṭayarān*) fly 93

طال I (طول ج أطوال *ṭūl 'aṭwāl*) be(come) long 90

طالع III examine 9, *20*

طبخ I (طبخ *ṭabkh*) cook 1/3

طبع I (طبع *ṭab'*) print 3

طبّق II apply to هـ إلى 7

طرق I (طرق *ṭarq*) reach, hammer, pound هـ 1

طفح I (طفح *ṭafḥ*) overflow 3

طلب I (طلب *ṭalab*) request من هـ 1

طلع I rise, climb, mount 1, *20*

طوّر II develop ه هـ 95

طوّق II encircle, embrace 95

طوّل II lengthen 95

طوى I (طيّ ج أطواء *ṭayy 'aṭwā'*) fold, conceal, contain

ـه 138

ظ

ظلّ I remain **59**

ظلّل II overshadow 62, *59*

ظلم I oppress 2, *21*

ظنّ I (ظنّ ج ظنون *ẓann ẓunūn*) think 58

ظهر I appear 3, *12*

ع

عاد I (عود *'awd*) come back, do again π, *(neg.)* do no longer π, *(neg.)* be no longer أ 90

عادل III equal ـه ه, (counter)balance 9

عارض III resist ـه ه 9

عاز I (عوز *'awaz*) need, lack ـه 90

عاش I (معيشة ج معايش *ma'īsha ma'āyish*) live 93

عافى III restore to health, protect 122, *125*

عالج III treat (medically) ه ـه 9

عام I (عوم *'awm*) float 90

عامل III treat 9, *4*

عاون III help 97, *104*

عبر I cross 1, *14*

عبّر II express 7, *14*

عجز I (عجز *'ajz*) be disabled 2

عجّز II disable ه 7

عجل I (عجلة *'ajala*) be in a hurry 4

عدّ I (عدّ *'add*) count 58

عدا I (عدوان *'udwān*) act aggressively toward على 117

عدّل II adjust ـه 7

عرض I (-) be(come) broad 5, (عرض ج عروض *'arḍ 'urūḍ*) appear, offer, demonstrate ـه 2

عرف I know **2**

عرّف II acquaint with 7, *2*

عرقل IQ (-) hinder 6

عزل I (عزل *'azl*) dismiss 2

عصر I (عصر *'aṣr*) squeeze, wring 2

عطّل II put out of action 7

عفا I forgive 117, *125*

عقد I (عقد *'aqd*) tie, hold (meeting etc.) 2

عقّد II complicate 7

عكس I (عكس *'aks*) reverse, reflect هـ 2

علق I (علق *'alaq*) hang, be caught on ب\في 4

علّق II hang on هـ ب\على 7

علم I know 4, *7*

علّم II teach 7

عمّر II overhaul 7

عمل I do 4

عمّم II generalise هـ 7

عنى I (عني *'any*) mean ه هـ 118

عهد I (عهد *'ahd*) know well ه هـ , entrust to إلى ب 4

عهّد II promise ه على\ب 7

عوّض II compensate for ه عن\من هـ عن\من 95

عوّق II hinder 95

عوّم II launch, float هـ , buoy up 95

عيّن II determine هـ, appoint هـ 96

غ

غاب I (غيب *ghayb*) be absent 93

غادر III leave ه هـ 9

غار I be jealous 93, *103*

غامر III risk 9

غاير III differ from, compete with 98, *103*

غذّى II feed ه هـ 121

غسل I (غسل *ghasl*) wash هـ 2

غضب I (غضب *ghaḍab*) be(come) angry with من\على 4

غلق I (غلق *ghalq*) lock, bolt 2

غمر I (غمارة *ghamāra*) overflow 5, (غمر *ghamr*) flood هـ 1

غنّى II sing to ه هـ 121

غيّر II change 96, *103*

ف

فات I (فوت *fawt*) elude ه أنْ 90

فاض I (فيض *fayḍ*) (over)flow 93

فاق I (فوق *fawq*) surpass 90

فاوض III negotiate with ... about ه\مع هـ\في 97

فتح I (فتح *fatḥ*) open 3

فتّش II inspect 7
فحص I (فحص ج فحوص *faḥṣ fuḥūṣ*) examine 3
فخر I (فخر *fakhr*) be proud of ب 3, (فخر *fakhar*) despise 4
فرّج II show ه على 7
فرد I (فرود *furūd*) be alone/unique 1, 5
فرغ I (فروغ *furūgh*) be empty 1, 4
فرّغ II empty هـ 7
فرق I (فرق *farq*) separate هـ 1
فسّر II explain 7
فشل I (فشل *fashal*) fail 4
فصل I (فصل *faṣl*) separate ه هـ 2
فصّل II set out in detail 7
فضا I (فضاء *faḍā'*) be empty 117
فضّل II favour 7
فعل I (فعل ج أفعال *fi'l 'af'āl*) do 3
فكّ I (فكّ *fakk*) dismantle 58
فكّر II think of في 7
فهرس IQ (فهرسة *fahrasa*) index هـ 6
فهم I (فهم *fahm*) understand 4
فهّم II make ... understand ه هـ 7
فوّض II empower ل\الى 95

ق

قابل III face 9, *23*
قاتل III fight with ه 9
قاد I (قيادة *qiyāda*) lead 90
قارن III compare ه هـ ب؛ بين ... وبين 9
قاس I (قيس *qays*) measure 93
قاضى III prosecute, sue 122, *126*
قال I (قول ج أقوال *qawl 'aqwāl*) say 90
قام I rise, take charge of, undertake 90, *99*
قاوم III resist 97, *99*
قبل I accept 4, *23*
قتل I (قتل *qatl*) kill 1
قدر I (قدرة *qudra*) be able على\أنْ 2
قدّر II estimate, esteem 7
قدم I (قدوم *qudūm*)

precede ه 1,
arrive at هـ 4

قدّم II advance, offer, serve هـ 7

قرّ I settle down 60, *62*

قرأ I read **47**

قرّر II decide, report **62**

قرع I (قرع *qar'*) strike, knock against هـ 3

قرّع II rebuke ه 7

قرن I (قرن *qarn*) connect هـ 2

قسم I (قسم *qasm*) divide هـ 2

قصّ I (قصّ *qaṣṣ*) cut off 58

قصد I (قصد *qaṣd*) intend هـ\أنْ 2

قصر I (قصر *qaṣr*) be(come) small, be inadequate 5

قصّر II fall short of من 7

قضى I judge, condemn, accomplish, settle 118, *126*

قطّر II filter, distil 7

قطع I (قطع *qaṭ'*) cut 3

قعد I (قعود *qu'ūd*) sit 1

قلّ I (قلّة *qilla*) be little, be less than عن 60

قلب I invert, reverse 2, *13*

قلّب II invert, reverse 7, *13*

قلع I (قلع *qal'*) uproot, exterminate هـ 3

قلّل II diminish هـ 62

قنبل IQ (-) bomb 6

قنطر IQ (-) span هـ 6

قوّس II bend (هـ) 95

قوّم II raise, evaluate, adjust 95, *99*

قوي I (قوة *qūwa*) be strong 139

قوّى II strengthen 141

قيّس II measure, calibrate هـ 96

ك

كئب I be sad about 39, *42*

كاتب III correspond with 9, *1*

كاثر III outnumber 9, *5*

كاد I (-) be about to أن, almost to π 92

كافأ III reward **51**

كافح III fight for عن ه ،هـ 9

كال I (كيل *kayl*) weigh, measure هـ 93

كالم III talk to ه 9
كان I (كون *kawn*) be أ 90
كبح I (كبح *kabḥ*) rein in, brake هـ, restrain from ه عن 3
كبس I (كبس *kabs*) pickle, (com)press 2
كتب I write **1**
كتّب II make (s.o.) write 7, *1*
كثر I be numerous **5**, outnumber 1, *5*
كثّر II increase 7, *5*
كثف I (كثافة *kathāfa*) be condensed 5
كثّف II condense هـ 7
كذب I (كذب *kidhb*) tell a lie 2
كرّر II repeat 62
كسر I (كسر *kasr*) break 2
كسّر II shatter هـ 7
كشف I (كشف *kashf*) disclose 2
كفأ I invert, turn away 47, *51*
كفى I (كفاية *kifāya*) suffice ه 118
كلّف II cost ه هـ 7
كمل I (كمال *kamāl*) be complete/perfect 1/3/4/5
كمّل II complete هـ 7
كنس I (كنس *kans*) sweep 1
كنّس II sweep 7
كهرب IQ (-) electrify هـ, electrocute ه 6
كوّن II constitute 95
كيّف II shape 96
كيّل II measure هـ 96

ل

لاحظ III observe هـ\أنّ 9
لاحق III follow ه 9
لاقى III meet 122, *124*
لاءم III suit 41, *45*
لأم I mend 37, *45*
لبس I (لبس *lubs*) wear 4
لحم I (لحم *laḥm*) patch, solder, weld 1
لحّم II solder, weld 7
لعب I (لعب *luʿb*) play with ب, play on على 4
لفّ I (لفّ *laff*) wrap 58
لقي I meet 119, *124*
لمس I (لمس *lams*) touch 1
لمع I (لمع *lamʿ*) shine 3
لوّث II pollute 95
لوّن II colour 95

لوى I (لَيّ *layy*) bend 138
ليس I not to be **94**

م

مات I (موت *mawt*) die 90
مارس III carry out 9
ماز I differentiate 93, *110*
مال I incline 93, *96*
مثل I (مثول *muthūl*) resemble 1
مثّل II represent 7
مدّ I stretch 58, *70*
مدّد II extend 62, *70*
مرّ I pass **58**
مرر II let pass 62, *58*
مرض I (مرض ج أمراض *maraḍ 'amrāḍ*) be ill 4
مرّن II drill, exercise ه 7
مسك I (مسك *mask*) grasp 1, 2
مشى I (مشي *mashy*) walk 118
مصّ I (مصّ *maṣṣ*) absorb 58
مضى I (مضي *muḍīy*) pass 118
مطر I (-) rain 1
ملأ I (ملء *mal'*) fill هـ 47
ملّح II salt 7
ملك I (ملك *milk*) acquire, own 2
منح I (منح *manḥ*) grant ه هـ 3
منع I (منع *man'*) forbid ه هـ\عن\من, prevent ه هـ\عن\من 3
مهّد II level, pave, clear, prepare هـ 7
موّل II finance, enrich **95**
ميّز II distinguish 96, *110*
ميّل II incline **96**

ن

ناب I (نيابة *niyāba*) deputise for عن 90
نادى III call **122**
ناسب III suit **9**
نافس III compete with … in/for ه عن\على 9
نام I (نوم *nawm*) sleep 92
ناوى III be hostile to 142, *138*
نبّأ II inform 50, *53*
نبّه II call attention to ه إلى 7
نجح I (نجاح *najāḥ*) be successful, pass في (examination) 3

نخز I (نخز *nakhz*) puncture 3
ندا I call, convene 117, *122*
ندي I be wet 119, *122*
ندّى II wet 121, *122*
نزل I (نزول *nuzūl*) go/get down 2
نزّل II lower 7
نسب I (cor)relate 1, 2, *9*
نسخ I (نسخ *naskh*) copy, delete 3
نسّق II coordinate هـ 7
نسي I forget **119**
نشأ I arise 47, *52*
نشّأ II bring up 50, *52*
نشر I (نشر *nashr*) publish, saw 1
نشّف II dry هـ 7
نصب I (نصب *naṣb*) erect 1
نضح I (نضح *naḍḥ*) splash, spill هـ, leak 2
نظر I (نظر ج أنظار *naẓar 'anẓār*) see ه, هـ, look at إلى 1; see also **134**
نظّف II clean هـ 7
نظّم II organise 7
نفخ I (نفخ *nafkh*) breathe, inflate هـ, inspire with ه هـ 1
نفّذ II implement 7
نفى I (نفي *nafy*) deny 118
نقّش II paint, engrave 7
نقص I (نقص *naqṣ*) become less 1
نقّص II diminish هـ 7
نقل I (نقل *naql*) transport 1
نمى I (نمي *namy*) grow 118
نوّب II appoint as deputy for ه من 95
نوّع II diversify هـ 95
نوى I intend **138**

هـ

هاجر III emigrate 9
هاجم III attack ه،هـ 9
هار I (هور *hawr*) collapse, demolish هـ 90
هبّ I (هبّ *habb*) blow (of the wind) 58
هدر I (هدر *hadr*) waste هـ, be wasted 2
هرأ I (-) wear out هـ 47

هرب I (هرب *harab*) flee to الى, escape from, evade من 1

هرّب II liberate ه هـ, traffic 7

هزّ I (هزّ *hazz*) shake هـ\ب 58

همّ I (مهمّة *mahamma*) concern 58

هنّأ II congratulate **50**

هنئ I do good to/for 49, *50*

هوّى II ventilate هـ 141

و

واجه III face 78, *76*

وازن III (counter)balance 78

واصل III be connected with 78, *77*

وافق III suit, agree **78**

وافى III provide for in full 142, *154*

والى III sponsor ه هـ 142, *133*

وجب I be necessary 73, *79*

وجد I find **73**

وجه I be distinguished **76**

وجّه II turn towards 77, *76*

ودّ I like, wish **61**

ورث I inherit **75**

ورد I arrive at, appear 73, *83*

ورّد II supply 77, *83*

وزّع II distribute 77

وزن I (وزن *wazn*) weigh هـ 73

وسع I be wide/roomy 75/74, *80*

وسّع II broaden 77, *80*

وسم I (وسم *wasm*) mark هـ 73

وسّم II decorate (with an honour) ه 77

وصل I arrive 73, *77*

وصّل II convey **77**

وضع I put **74**

وظّف II recruit, employ 77

وعد I (وعد ج وعود *wa'd wu'ūd*) promise ه هـ\ب 73

وفر I (وفر *wafr*) abound 73

وفّر II provide هـ 77

وفق I be suitable 75, *78*

وفّق II adjust 77, *78*

وفى I fulfil, compensate fully 132, *154*

Index to Part I

The numbers refer to paragraphs. The sign → refers you to another entry in the Index.

Index to Part II

	25	أمل يأمل	*'amala ya'mulu*	
	26	أسر يأسر	*'asara ya'siru*	
	27	أمن يأمن	*'amina ya'manu*	
II	28	أكّد يؤكّد	*'akkada yu'akkidu*	
	29	أيّد يؤيّد	*'ayyada yu'ayyidu*	
III	30	آخذ يؤاخذ	*'ākhadha yu'ākhidhu*	آ...
IV	31	آجر يؤجر	*'ājara yu'jiru*	آ...
V	32	تأخّر يتأخّر	*ta'akhkhara yata'akhkharu*	
VI	33	تآلف يتآلف	*ta'ālafa yata'ālafu*	
VIII	34	ائتمر يأتمر	*i'támara ya'támiru*	ايـ..†
	35	اتّخذ يتّخذ	*ittákhadha yattákhidhu*	...تّـ..
X	36	استأنف يستأنف	*ista'nafa yasta'nifu*	

Middle hamza

I	37	سأل يسأل	*sa'ala yas'alu*
	38	بؤس يبؤس	*ba'usa yab'usu*
	39	بئس يبأس	*ba'isa yab'asu*
II	40	رأّس يرأّس	*ra''asa yura''isu*
III	41	ساءل يسائل	*sā'ala yusā'ilu*
IV	42	أكأب يكئب	*'ak'aba yuk'ibu*
V	43	ترأّس يترأّس	*tara''asa yatara''asu*
VI	44	تفاءل يتفاءل	*tafā'ala yatafā'alu*
VIII	45	التأم يلتئم	*iltá'ama yaltá'imu*
X	46	استرأف يسترئف	*istar'afa yastar'ifu*

Final hamza

I	47	قرأ يقرأ	*qara'a yaqra'u*
	48	بطؤ يبطؤ	*baṭu'a yabṭu'u*
	49	برئ يبرأ	*bari'a yabra'u*
II	50	هنّأ يهنّئ	*hanna'a yuhanni'u*
III	51	كافأ يكافئ	*kāfa'a yukāfi'u*
IV	52	أنشأ ينشئ	*'ansha'a yunshi'u*

V	53	تنبّأ يتنبّأ	*tanabba’a yatanabba’u*	
VI	54	تباطأ يتباطأ	*tabāṭa’a yatabāṭa’u*	
VII	55	انكفأ ينكفئ	*inkáfa’a yankáfi’u*	
VIII	56	ابتدأ يبتدئ	*ibtáda’a yabtádi’u*	
X	57	استقرأ يستقرئ	*istaqra’a yastaqri’u*	
Doubled				
I	58	مرّ يمرّ	*marra yamurru*	
	59	ظلّ يظلّ	*ẓalla yaẓallu*	
	60	تمّ يتمّ	*tamma yatimmu*	
	61	ودّ يودّ	*wadda yawaddu*	
II	62	قرّر يقرّر	*qarrara yuqarriru*	
	63	أمّم يؤمّم	*’ammama yu’ammimu*	
III	64	حاجّ يحاجّ	*ḥājja yuḥājju*	†حاجج يحاجج
IV	65	أحبّ يحبّ	*’aḥabba yuḥibbu*	
V	66	تردّد يتردّد	*taraddada yataraddadu*	
	67	تأسّس يتأسّس	*ta’assasa yata’assasu*	
VI	68	تضادّ يتضادّ	*taḍādda yataḍāddu*	†تضادد يتضادد
VII	69	انحلّ ينحلّ	*inḥalla yanḥallu*	
VIII	70	امتدّ يمتدّ	*imtadda yamtaddu*	
	71	اضطرّ يضطرّ	*iḍṭarra yaḍṭarru*	...ضط...
X	72	استحقّ يستحقّ	*istaḥaqqa yastaḥiqqu*	
Assimilated				
I	73	وجد يجد	*wajada yajidu*	
	74	وضع يضع	*waḍaʿa yaḍaʿu*	
	75	ورث يرث	*waritha yarithu*	
	76	وجه يوجه	*wajuha yawjuhu*	
II	77	وصّل يوصّل	*waṣṣala yuwaṣṣilu*	
III	78	وافق يوافق	*wāfaqa yuwāfiqu*	
IV	79	أوجب يوجب	*’awjaba yūjibu*	
V	80	توسّع يتوسّع	*tawassaʿa yatawassaʿu*	

VI	81	تواجه يتواجه	*tawājaha yatawājahu*	
VIII	82	اتّفق يتّفق	*ittáfaqa yattáfiqu*	...تّـ...
X	83	استورد يستورد	*istawrada yastawridu*	
I	84	يبس ييبس	*yabisa yaybasu*	
II	85	يسّر ييسّر	*yassara yuyassiru*	
III	86	ياسر يياسر	*yāsara yuyāsiru*	
IV	87	أيقن يوقن	*'ayqana yūqinu*	
V	88	تيقّظ يتيقّظ	*tayaqqaẓa yatayaqqaẓu*	
X	89	استيقظ يسنيقظ	*istayqaẓa yastayqiẓu*	
Hollow				
I	90	ساق يسوق	*sāqa yasūqu*	
	91	آب يؤوب	*'āba ya'ūbu*	
	92	خاف يخاف	*khāfa yakhāfu*	
	93	زاد يزيد	*zāda yazīdu*	
	94	ليس	*laysa*	see § 13
II	95	موّل يموّل	*mawwala yumawwilu*	
	96	ميّل يميّل	*mayyala yumayyilu*	
III	97	حاول يحاول	*ḥāwala yuḥāwilu*	
	98	بايع يبايع	*bāya'a yubāyi'u*	
IV	99	أقام يقيم	*'aqāma yuqīmu*	
	100	أحوج يحوج	*'aḥwaja yuḥwiju*	...حو...
	101	أذاع يذيع	*'adhā'a yudhī'u*	
V	102	تصوّر يتصوّر	*taṣawwara yataṣawwaru*	
	103	تغيّر يتغيّر	*taghayyara yataghayyaru*	
VI	104	تعاون يتعاون	*ta'āwana yata'āwanu*	
	105	تزايد يتزايد	*tazāyada yatazāyadu*	
VII	106	انحاز ينحاز	*inḥāza yanḥāzu*	
	107	انباع ينباع	*inbā'a yanbā'u*	
VIII	108	احتاج يحتاج	*iḥtāja yaḥtāju*	
	109	ازدوج يزدوج	*izdáwaja yazdáwiju*	...زدو...

	110	امتاز يمتاز	*imtāza yamtāzu*	
	111	ازداد يزداد	*izdāda yazdādu*	...زد...
IX	112	اسودّ يسودّ	*iswadda yaswaddu*	
	113	ابيضّ يبيضّ	*ibyaḍḍa yabyaḍḍu*	
X	114	استراح يستريح	*istarāḥa yastarīḥu*	
	115	استجوب يستجوب	*istajwaba yastajwibu*	...جو...
	116	استفاد يستفيد	*istafāda yastafīdu*	

Final-weak

I	117	رجا يرجو	*raja yarjū*	
	118	رمى يرمي	*rama yarmī*	
	119	نسي ينسى	*násiya yansa*	
	120	سعى يسعى	*saʿa yasʿa*	
II	121	ربّى يربّي	*rabba yurabbī*	
III	122	نادى ينادي	*nāda yunādī*	
IV	123	أعطى يعطي	*’aʿṭa yuʿṭī*	
V	124	تلقّى يتلقّى	*talaqqa yatalaqqa*	
VI	125	تعافى يتعافى	*taʿāfa yataʿāfa*	
VII	126	انقضى ينقضي	*inqáḍa yanqáḍī*	
VIII	127	اشترى يشتري	*ishtára yashtárī*	
	128	ادّعى يدّعي	*iddáʿa yaddáʿī*	
X	129	استثنى يستثني	*istathna yastathnī*	

Doubly weak

I	130	أتى يأتي	*’ata ya’tī*	
	131	أبى يأبى	*’aba ya’ba*	
	132	وقى يقي	*waqa yaqī*	
	133	ولي يلي	*wáliya yalī*	
	134	رأى يرى	*ra’a yara*	ء dropped in present
	135	جاء يجيء	*jā’a yajī’u*	
	136	شاء يشاء	*shā’a yashā’u*	
	137	ساء يسوء	*sā’a yasū’u*	

	138	نوى ينوي	*nawa yanwī*	
	139	سوِي يسوى	*sáwiya yaswa*	
	140	حيّ يحيا	*ḥayya yaḥya*	حيي†
II	141	سوّى يسوّي	*sawwa yusawwī*	
III	142	ساوى يساوي	*sāwa yusāwī*	
	143	آتى يؤاتي	*'āta yu'ātī*	آ...
IV	144	آتى يؤتي	*'āta yu'tī*	آ...
	145	أرى يري	*'ara yurī*	root-letter ء dropped
	146	أضاء يضيء	*'aḍā'a yuḍī'u*	
	147	أولى يولي	*'awla yūlī*	
V	148	تولّى يتولّى	*tawalla yatawalla*	
VI	149	توالى يتوالى	*tawāla yatawāla*	
VII	150	انزوى ينزوي	*inzáwa yanzáwī*	
VIII	151	احتوى يحتوي	*iḥtáwa yaḥtáwī*	
	152	اتّقى يتْقي	*ittáqa yattáqī*	...تّـ...
	153	استاء يستاء	*istā'a yastā'u*	
X	154	استوفى يستوفي	*istawfa yastawfī*	
	155	استضاء يستضيء	*istaḍā'a yastaḍī'u*	

Arabic Language Titles from Hippocrene Books

Basic Arabic Workbook

John Mace

One of the foremost writers today of teaching materials for Middle Eastern languages, John Mace, has now produced a key workbook for all learners of Modern Standard Arabic. *Basic Arabic Workbook* is a step-by-step series of exercises and tasks that puts the living standard language into practice, using the most up-to-date vocabulary drawn from everyday situations, mainly the workplace. No previous knowledge is assumed beyond that of the alphabet.

350 pages • 0-7818-1126-0 • $29.95pb

Arabic for Beginners, Revised Edition

Syed Ali

An updated edition of the popular guide, this volume introduces Arabic to those who wish to learn it through the English medium. Lessons clearly and concisely cover the Arabic script, essential grammar points, and an extensive selection of relevant vocabulary. A subsequent section features excerpts in Arabic from the prose and poetry of eminent writers.

231 pages • 0-7818-0841-3 • $13.95pb

Arabic-English/English-Arabic Compact Dictionary

Mahmoud Gaafar & Jane Wightwick

This discreet, transportable dictionary contains 3,700 total entries, and features side-by-side Arabic script and Romanization, as well as an index of regular and irregular verbs. Ideal for travelers, students, and businesspersons.

200 pages • 0-7818-1044-2 • $8.95pb

Arabic-English/English-Arabic Dictionary & Phrasebook

Mahmoud Gaafar & Jane Wightwick

This concise dictionary and phrasebook is perfect for travelers, businesspersons, and foreign aid workers. It includes 4,000 total dictionary entries, a pronunciation guide, an introduction to Arabic grammar, practical cultural information, and a comprehensive listing of essential Arabic phrases, organized by situation for easy reference.

224 pages • 0-7818-0973-8 • $12.95pb

Arabic-English/English-Arabic Practical Dictionary

N. Awde & K. Smith

An essential resource for students of Arabic and English alike, this dictionary contains the most up-to-date vocabulary in handy reference form. With more than 18,000 entries, it is especially useful in navigating the growing terminology of politics, telecommunications, technology, the internet, tourism, business and travel.

439 pages • 0-7818-1045-0 • $22.50pb

Arabic-English/English-Arabic Standard Dictionary

John Wortabet & Harvey Porter

Containing over 30,000 entries, this dictionary is the ideal tool for students of Arabic. It is designed to enable students to read the average Arabic newspaper or book, and features an excellent selection of modern words and expressions. Perfect for translating basic documents and conducting everyday conversations.

900 pages • 0-7818-0383-7 • $27.95pb

Arabic Grammar of the Written Language

G.W. Thatcher

A valuable resource for beginning students of Arabic. It comprises an introduction to the Arabic alphabet, 49 short grammar lessons, Arabic-English and English-Arabic vocabulary lists, a supplement of extracts from modern novels, journals, and correspondence, and indexes in both English and Arabic.

560 pages • 0-87052-101-2 • $22.50pb

Beginner's Iraqi Arabic with 2 Audio CDs

Nawal Nasrallah & Nadia Hassani

This introduction to the Iraqi dialect of the Arabic language is designed for both classroom use and self-study. The 12 lessons combine dialogues with easy-to-follow grammatical explanations, and include vocabulary, cultural information, and exercises that reinforce the material covered. All Arabic words are transliterated into roman script for easy understanding.

360 pages • 0-7818-1098-1 • $29.95pb

Eastern Arabic-English/English-Eastern Arabic Dictionary & Phrasebook

This book provides the traveler to the Eastern Mediterranean with a practical aid for communicating in Arabic. It is based on the spoken language widely understood in Jordan, Lebanon, Palestine/Israel and Syria.

142 pages • 0-7818-0685-2 • $11.95

Emergency Arabic Phrasebook

Mahmoud Gaafar

Small enough to fit in your pocket, and arranged for quick and easy reference, this phrasebook is designed to give you the key words and essential phrases you need in urgent situations.

80 pages • 0-7818-0976-2 • $5.95pb

Hippocrene Children's Illustrated Arabic Dictionary

This dictionary makes learning vocabulary in Arabic at an early age easier and more enjoyable than ever! Intended to be a child's first Arabic dictionary, it features 500 entries, each accompanied by a beautiful full-color illustration.

95 pages • 0-7818-0891-X • $11.95pb

Intermediate Arabic Workbook

John Mace

This sequel to *Basic Arabic Workbook* shares a similar purpose and format with the introductory text. Having already consolidated knowledge of the essential elements and patters of Modern Standard Arabic, the reader of the first book will be well prepared for the material and exercises provided in this second volume.

171 pages • 0-7818-1177-5 • $29.95pb

Mastering Arabic with 2 Audio CDs

Jane Wightwick and Mahmoud Gaafar

This imaginative, comprehensive course in modern, standard Arabic focuses on teaching both the script and the spoken language. Designed for both individual and classroom use and assuming no previous knowledge of the language, it aims to provide the student with a general means for basic communication. The unique combination of step-by-step grammar and practical exercises emphasizes a functional approach to mastering a

new script and acquiring vocabulary. Everyday situations and local customs are explored through dialogues, newspaper extracts, drawings and photos. An exercise key and an English-Arabic glossary are also included. Accompanying CDs are enclosed.
370 pages • 0-7818-1042-6 • $29.95pb

Arabic-English/English-Arabic Modern Military Dictionary

Maher S. Kayyali

Every field of human activity develops its own terms and jargon, and the military field is no exception. This timely and necessary dictionary includes fundamental military terms, contemporary political and technological terms and jargon, military technique terms for the specialist, as well as words in allied subjects such as economics, law, statistics and sociology.
209 pages • 0-7818-0243-1 • $16.95pb

Pocket Guide to Arabic Script

Dr. Fayeq Oweis

This handy booklet offers a complete, easy-to-use reference for the Arabic writing system. Ideal for students, it presents the basics for reading and writing Arabic script, with a summary of word structure and grammar.
92 pages • 0-7818-1104-X • $6.95pb